# PARIS
## inside·out

David Applefield

# PARIS
## inside·out

**The Insider's Guide
for Visitors,
Residents,
Professionals
& Students
on Life in Paris.**

HOUGHTON MIFFLIN COMPANY

Boston   New York

Special thanks go to Sheila O'Leary for
her valuable fact-checking and research.
The author also wishes to acknowledge
Lisa Glazer, Lisa Nesselson, Thierry de Lavau,
Corinne Schnaébelé, Larry Portis, Mike Zwerin,
Betty Abu-Gheida, Cory McCloud, Nathalie Debroise,
Philip Crawford, Corrinne Labalme, Lorie Lichtlen,
Sandra Kwock-Silve, The American University of Paris,
John Calder, and Julia Alvarez-Grosser who have
all made valuable editorial contributions
to this revised edition.

Although every attempt has been made to assure the most up-to-date
and accurate information possible, the nature of information in a
guide book is subject to modification. Thus, the publisher cannot be
held responsible in the case of contents that are no longer valid.

Printed in the United States of America

DOH 10 9 8 7 6 5 4 3 2 1

Cover: photo © Jacques Lebar.

# Contents

# Introduction

Welcome to Paris and to *Paris Inside Out* in its new, updated, and expanded edition!

As a guide book reader, you must have noticed, there is no shortage of literature devoted to Paris. Paris is perhaps the most written about city in the world. In English, I know of at least forty guide books, some very good, many rather useless. So many words to describe a place! So much advice! The reason, in truth, for this glut of verbiage on the City of Lights goes way beyond the statistical and commercial fact that more people visit Paris than any other destination on earth; the real reason, if I can be so bold, is that Paris and its image continues to cast a mythic spell on much of the world. (Admittedly, we all need a geographic place in which to invest our belief in the existence of magic and the possibility of love.) And thus there is always a public ready to read about Paris; for every new way to experience the city there will be another article and another guide book.

Paris is a city you return to over the course of your life, a place in which you take stock of your unfulfilled ambitions, a place you chain to your memory, where bitter-sweet sentimentality runs freely and the pleasure of melancholia returns each time, a city you take a loved one to for a meal, the place you discover your own lips and the sound of your voice, a town to spend your honeymoon in, a memory you name a child after. Paris for the world is a proper noun meaning beauty, art, romance, elegance, design, class, style, literature, history, bohemian self-discovery, love. It's first associations in the mind of the foreign visitor is of fashion, cuisine, perfume, champagne, *mousse au chocolat*, and more recently, the sleekness of new technologies....

Paris plays this imaginary role for many, to such an extent that for a majority, the contemporary reality of the city is an unnecessary and unfortunate distraction, a disappointment. The tourist guidebook that offers up the clichéd image, sprinkles in some history, adds a few key addresses, prices, and closing times, recommends an assortment of hotels and eateries, and provides a color map with *métro* stops, will undoubtedly satisfy the hordes. That is all fine, but that is not what this guidebook is about, and those visitors are not the ones I assume you to be.

Aside from the endless wave of visitors on short holidays, Paris attracts discerning visitors that want to know more and a forever-surprising, self-generating stream of individuals and families who've decided to seize the day and try to incorporate the tedium of predictable, everyday lives back home into the Paris of their dreams. And these people, you in fact, need something more from a guide book.

Thus, the role of a good guide book on Paris, in my way of thinking, isn't to document the history of expatriatism or to lead the reader to the perfect silk scarf—I've noted several excellent ones in the bibliography for that—but rather to sort out the myth of the place from the fact without killing the part of myth that is rooted in fact. Undeniably, Paris really is a beautiful and often enchanting city. In fact, more than a decade after my first arrival I still find myself halted by the splendor of the sight crossing the Pont Alexandre III. Selecting robust artichokes in my local market continues to be a source of delight. And the pleasure of sipping a *kir* while reading the excellent book section of *Le Monde* in a café on a Friday afternoon goes without saying, as does the joy of lounging around a crumb-littered table with a group of friends after a long and satisfying meal with the peels of *clementines* piling up and a discussion about a topical political issue gaining intensity. That's the Paris I like to glorify, but the image is incomplete, and rarely in a guide book will you get the rest of the story, will you be told not only what Paris is like to see, but what it's like to live in, the tiniest details, the cultural nuances, the finest tips that make all the difference. The Paris I try to present to readers is Paris in 3D; it's the *honest person's* guide to Paris and Parisians.

As the author of *Paris Inside Out* I have tried to put myself directly in the position of the reader. Although reading a guidebook can be and to a certain extent should be a pleasurable experience, ultimately you want your questions answered. And you want full information, not half information. If one needs a special permit to work in France it's as important as the hard data to know that the lines will be long or that if you don't make it to the front of the line before 4 p.m. you have to start all over the next day, or that the nasty sounding snicker of the clerk processing your *dossier* (the French love this word; it means file in the *administrations*) is not because you did something wrong, but simply an indication of the impersonal treatment that the public is regularly treated to in France. You need to know that a beer consumed at the zinc bar in a café is half the price of the same beer served at a sidewalk table in the same café. You might want to ask for your baguette *coupée en deux* next time, or know how to deal with the *concierge* in the building you're staying in. It is in this spirit that I have directed my comments. If at times the tone sounds harsh and the criticism barbed it's not cynicism; it's proof of Parisian blood. Parisians love to complain *(se plaindre)* and after a certain amount of years in Paris you'll gain the privilege too.

Parisians also love to seduce *(séduire)* and to please *(plaire)*. In fact, the key to successfully living, studying, working, and playing in Paris is learning the art of both. In French, to seduce and to please does not mean to trick or sleaze, nor does it imply hypocrisy. It is more like the result of successful charm. It is learning how to stay at all costs on the good side of the "other". Once the atmosphere for charm has been broken you can be certain that the experience will be negative. This holds true from buying a cake to getting a job.

One of the advantages of updating an guidebook is the ability to improve it. In this edition I have expanded my comments throughout, amplifying greatly the sections on business, employment, banking, insurance, and commercial life in Paris. I have added entire chapters on French language schools, pop music, computers, children's Paris, and theater, and have embellished the sections on the social scene and art world. Lexicons on famous contemporary French people and common street names have been added.

Otherwise, the book remains faithful to its previous edition and its commitment to up-to-the minute cultural reporting. The information assembled here, both objective and subjective, is based on experience, and experience is the key to knowing a place... *inside out!*

Everything in this book you eventually would have learned anyway. But *Paris Inside Out* should help you save many hours and lots of francs. It will facilitate your integration into French life, and hopefully reduce the frustration of finding yourself alone, dependent, tongue-tied, and handicapped by a totally new setting that you're going to think of at first as "foreign." Remember, everything around you is native; it's you that's foreign—whether you come from New York City, London, Toronto, Dubai, Bombay, Sydney, or Stockholm. Paris is capable of confusing and exhilarating you. Living outside a familiar cultural and social setting always takes adjustment and acclimatization. There will be strange little moments when you crave blueberry pancakes or the Sunday edition of your city's newspaper, and then others, when you simply desire the sound of your own language, when you don't want to have to struggle to be understood. This is all normal. *Paris Inside Out* should be a first step in helping you hurdle early traumas while becoming more Parisian yourself.

Most guidebooks don't approach the feelings inherent in living in a new city; *Paris Inside Out* attempts to provide insight into the interior, as well as material, experience of living and/or studying overseas. Although these pages should be helpful over and over, one can't expect to understand Parisian life and culture intimately by reading a guide book. Learning how a new country and culture functions is a gradual and evolutionary process. It takes time and patience, and a willingness to experience both the exciting and lonely sensation of being isolated and anonymous in a far-off place. There will be a new-found freedom and sense of awareness that accompanies the uncertainty of being away from what you know.

Although the guide tries not to be overly American in its orientation and cultural and linguistic references, it was unavoidable that the book leans a bit that way. You are what you are. While aspiring to address all new residents, the guide had to be created with its largest readership in mind. Every attempt has been made, however, to resist grotesque ethnocentrism and blatant cultural provincialism.

With that said, be reminded that although facts and information are useful and necessary, alone they cannot guarantee you an understanding of French manners, ways of being, attitudes, traditions, tendencies, institutions, and what is commonly called in French, "*la mentalité.*" In giving you the facts, verified and updated for this edition, we've tried as often as possible to comment on the small but significant details that make France culturally distinct. You'll see. Living in another country is a process of losing your innocence all over again. This glorious path, with its share of awkward moments, should create a profusion of pleasurable and thought-provoking experiences. —D.A.

# Orientation

## Basic Facts

Feeling comfortable in a new environment begins with a general sense of orientation. Living in a place requires at least a basic knowledge of a few key facts which function as cultural common denominators. Here are a few of the most basic facts, statistics and bits of background info that will help you situate yourself in France.

**Capital:** Paris
**Form of Government:** Republic
**Official Language:** French
**Regional Languages:** Basque, Breton, Catalan, Corsican (corse), Provençal, Alsatian.
**Surface Area:** 551,965 square km
**Gross National Product:** $8850 US per inhabitant.
**Population:** 56,630,000 (1990)

|  | City | Metropolitan Area |
|---|---|---|
| Paris: | 2,188,918 | 9,060,000 |
| Marseille: | 800,550 | 1,087,276 |
| Strasbourg: | 252,338 | 388,483 |
| Lyon: | 415,487 | 1,214,869 |
| Toulouse: | 358,688 | 608,427 |
| Nice: | 342,391 | 474,459 |
| Bordeaux: | 210,336 | 685,456 |
| Lille: | 363,653 | 950,265 |
| Nantes: | 244,952 | 492,212 |
| Grenoble: | 150,758 | 400,141 |
| Toulon | 167,550 | 437,493 |

**Religions**
Catholic: 5 million (90%); 1 out of 5 French claims to be "practicing."
Muslim: 1.7 million
Protestant: 1 million
Jewish: .7 million

**Ethnic Mix**
(Source: *Ministère de l'Intérieur et de l'aménagement du territoire*)
Official estimation of population legally residing in France as of 31 December 1992. This does not include undeclared and clandestine populations.
Portuguese 700,729
Algerian 585,846
Moroccan 441,000
Italian 268,047
Spanish 246,342
Tunisian 178,217
Turkish 147,558
British 59,790
"Yugoslavian" 58,742
Belgians 57,574
Germans 57,670
Polish 46,193
Cambodian 40,738
Vietnamese 39,059
Senegalese 39,319
Malian 31,886
Americans (USA) 27,053
Cameroonian 15,672
Irish 4,778

**Most Common French Names**
Of the 250 000 family names in France the most common are:

Martin, Bernard, Moreau, Durand, Petit, Dubois, Michel, Marie, Thomas, Richard.

Note that in French your name *(nom)* refers to your last name; otherwise, you will be asked for your *prénom* (first name). When asked to write their name on a form, French students often follow the administrative formality of last name first, e.g. DUPONT, Jean. Last names and city names are almost always written in capital letters *(majuscules)*. Also, in France many people have *noms composés*, attached first names, such as Jean-Marie, Marie-Therèse or Jean-Claude, and numerous people, usually as a result of marriage and mixed cultural backgrounds, have attached last names joined by a hyphen.

**Common References to France and its Institutions in the Press**
*Le Quai d'Orsay:* Ministry of Foreign Affairs
*l'Hexagone:* France
*l'Elysée:* the president's official residence
*Matignon:* the Premier Ministre's residence
*le Quai des Orfèvres:* Police headquarters
*Place Vendôme:* Ministry of Justice
*La demoiselle de fer:* Eiffel Tower

**Common Symbols of the French Republic**
Flag: blue, white, and red as three vertical stripes, created by Lafayette in 1789.

*RF:* these stitched letters stand for *la République française.*

*Liberté, Egalité, Fraternité:* the philosophic slogan of the country.

*La Marseillaise:* the National Anthem

*Marianne:* the muse of the country whose portrait and bust is found in every city hall in France and on many French stamps.

*Le coq:* the cock, symbol of the French people, coming from gallus and signifying the Gauls, the ancestors of modern France.

### French Elections / Terms in Office

In France you have to be 18 years old and a French citizen to vote. Women voted for the first time in France in 1945.

Presidential elections: 7 years
National elections (députés): 5 years
Senate elections (1/3 every 9 years): 9 years
Regional elections: 6 years
Cantonale (county) elections: 6 years
Municipal elections: 6 years
European elections: 5 years

## Conversions

### Weights
1 kilo = 2.2 pounds
demi-kilo = 1 livre = 1.1 pounds

### Lengths
1 centimeter = .394 inches
1 meter = 3.28 feet
1000 meter = 1 kilometer = 0.62 mile (to calculate miles multiply kilometers by .6)

### Measurements
1 litre = 0.265 US gallon
1 gram = .033 ounce

### Temperatures
Converting Fahrenheit to Celsius: Multiply Celsius temperature by 2 and add 32 for approximate conversion.

| *Fahrenheit* | *Celsius* |
|---|---|
| 0 | -17.8 |
| 32 (freezing) | 0 |
| 50 | 10 |
| 68 (room temperature) | 20 |
| 77 | 25 |
| 86 | 30 |
| 98.6 (normal body temp.) | 37 |
| 100.4 | 38 |
| 104 | 40 |

### Conversions for Cooking
1 ounce = 30 grammes
3.5 ounces = 100 grammes
1 lb = 454 grammes
1 tbsp = 15 grammes
1 cup = nearly 1/4 litre
4 1/3 cups = 1 litre
3/4 cup minus 1 tbsp = 100 grammes
1 pint = 0,473 litre
1 quart = 0,946 litre
1 gallon = 3,785 litres

**Dates:** In France, the date 1/3/94 does not mean January 3, 1994, but March 1, 1994.

Clothing Sizes

WOMEN:

| France | 36 | 38 | 40 | 42 | 44 | 46 | 48 |
|--------|----|----|----|----|----|----|----|
| US | 06 | 08 | 10 | 12 | 14 | 16 | 18 |

MEN'S PANTS:

| France | 42 | 44 | 46 | 48 | 50 |
|--------|----|----|----|----|----|
| US | 32 | 34 | 36 | 38 | 40 |

SHOES:

| France | 36 | 37 | 38 | 39 | 40 | 41 | 42 | 43 | 44 |
|--------|----|----|----|-----|----|----|----|------|----|
| US | 5 | 6 | 7 | 7.5 | 8 | 9 | 10 | 10.5 | 11 |

MEN'S SHIRTS:

| France | 37 | 38 | 39 | 40 | 41 | 42 | 43 |
|--------|------|----|------|-------|----|------|----|
| US | 14.5 | 15 | 15.5 | 15.75 | 16 | 16.5 | 17 |

## Survival Tips

**Time of Day:** Is generally expressed by the 24-hour clock. Thus, 8 a.m. = 8h, or 8h00, and 8 p.m. = 20h or 20h00.

**Midnight** = 24h, 24h00, or *minuit,* Noon =12h, 12h00, or *midi.* 12:30 a.m. = 0h30; 5 p.m. = 17h or 17h00.

**Numbers:** Commas are used where Anglo-Saxons use periods, and vice versa. For instance, 1.025,60 in France = 1,025.60 in North America and elsewhere. Similarly, with numbers the decimal point is replaced by a comma, 15,70F or 25,15$.

**Currency:** The French franc (FF) is divided into 100 *centimes.* Coins consist of five, ten, twenty, fifty centimes, and one franc, five franc, and ten franc pieces. In 1991, the old clunky ten franc piece was taken out of circulation and only the new two-tone, smaller piece is used today. In late 1993 a larger, twenty franc coin was put into circulation as well as a colorful new fifty franc note on which French writer Saint-Exupéry appears with his visionary character, Le Petit Prince. This new bill is a step towards a unified look with other EU (European Union) paper currencies, especially the Deutsche Mark, the British Pound, and the Dutch Guilder. (See Money and Banking). Otherwise, bank notes come in twenty, fifty, one hundred, two hundred and five hundred franc denominations.

**Districts:** Called *arrondissements,* the twenty districts that make up Paris, are indicated in postal addresses as the last digits of a postal code. The first two digits are the code for the city. Paris always begins with 75. For example, 75005 = Paris' 5th district, 75020 = Paris' 20th district. See map for a breakdown of Paris by *arrondissement.*

**Electric Current:** France's system is 220 volt, 50 cycles. To use standard American 110 volt, 60 cycle, British 250 volt, 60 cycle, or other appliances you will need a plug adapter and a transformer that is appropriate for the wattage of the appliance. The plug adapter alone is not sufficient and its use will result in fried appliances. Some 220 volt appliances have a combination 50/60 cycle motor that allows them to operate in France without any problems. Many new computers have built in current transformers, but many still do not, so beware. Take no chances. Lamps from the US will work without a transformer with 220 volt bulbs. Clock radios work but the clock part is not always reliable. Plug adapters and transformers, once found nearly exclusively in the basement of the BHV (Bazar de l'Hôtel de Ville) on the rue de Rivoli, may now be found in most department stores and electronics shops, although the BHV does have a special section for adapting foreign telephones, answering machines, fax/computer equipment and other appliances. Note that in France there are two types of light bulbs, *vise* and *bayonnet;* the first screws in and the second hooks into the socket.

**Floor Numbers:** The floor in which you enter a building is not the first floor, but the *rez-de-chaussée* (RdC). In France the street level is not officially an *étage* (floor). Thus, the *premier étage* (first floor) is actually the second level of the building, one floor up from the *rez-de-chaussée.* A majority of pre-war Paris apartment buildings have six floors of apartments, plus a seventh floor of *chambres de bonne* (maids rooms), which now are rented as small studios for smaller rents.

**Paper Size/Format:** In France, standard paper size for typing and photocopying is called A4 or 21 x 29.7 cms. This is slightly larger than the American standard size 8 1/2 x 11 inches. Half of A4 is called A5 and twice the size of A4 is B3.

## Holidays

Holidays in France bring out two typically French traits: the respect for ceremony and ritual and the joy of not having to work. The French custom of taking a long weekend *(faire le pont)*—actually an extended weekend created when a holiday falls on a Thursday or Tuesday—is an occasion for most Parisians to exit to the countryside. The month of May is particularly affected. Beware of heavy traffic on the autoroutes, the *périphérique,* and at the main *portes* (gateways to the city). This is good news for those who stay because the pace of Paris slows down remarkably, leaving the tourist and others to enjoy the reduced traffic and noise. Being aware of holidays helps you stay in touch with the rhythms of French life (see Annual Events). Plan your activities around these dates since many shops, restaurants and museums close on public holidays.

The French are rather conscious of the Christian calendar as far as each day is assigned to a different saint. Best known is *la Sainte-Catherine* on November 25, the day that all 25 year old, single women are presented with funny hats and dances are held in their honor. New Year's Eve is called *la Saint-Sylvestre.*

The French also celebrate April Fools Day *(le premier avril)* with jokes and pranks, namely hanging paper fish on the backs of friends and strangers.

## Vacation Time

French law guarantees everyone who works *(salarié)* five weeks of paid vacation. *Les vacances (congés payés)*, a cherished institution among the French, is a right, not a privilege. People in France live for *les vacances;* the entire year of work is often organized around the sacred period of non-work. *Les vacances* are not a negotiable benefit. If you are legally employed in France, you are entitled to your paid vacation, and if you are employing people in France you are legally obliged to allow for these weeks of paid leave. In general, it's safe to say that the French are willing to trade higher wages for security and benefits, in other words, a higher quality of life. What one plans to do on one's vacation, or what one has just finished doing, is usually the subject of casual conversation for about four months of the year. In fact, vacation plans are often made as early as February for the August break.

Aside from the five week vacation, which most people divide between summer and winter (three to four weeks in summer, one to two in winter), here is a list of holidays and their respective customs. Note that traditionally Paris empties out in August, with July being the second heaviest vacation month, although in recent years, especially among people who are in business, there has begun to be a trend away from the long August break. In any case, avoid traveling on July 1, July 30, August 1 and August 30. Or else be prepared to leave in the pre-dawn hours. The 15th of each summer month are difficult traveling days as well. School vacations *(vacances scolaires)* are nationally coordinated with all schools within each of the three zones of France sharing the same dates. Similarly, train and domestic flight schedules are divided into blue, red, and white days on the calendar with blue days being the cheapest to travel. Check these with a travel agent. The airports, especially Orly, can be absolute mob scenes due to the great French tradition of leaving town at the same time. Taking vacations of up to four weeks at a time is becoming somewhat less practiced although still the norm for many. Although Anglo-Saxons, especially Americans, admire this "luxury", those who are self-employed or have started businesses in France are often frustrated by the difficulty of getting anything done during the holiday period. Eventually you'll learn that it's better to follow the crowd than fight it. Don't try to pull off overly ambitious projects in the month of August. There's no shame or violation of the work ethic to shut down your business, abandon the mail, and forget the phone messages for a month. *Au contraire,* the French believe that a holiday must be long enough to break the stressful patterns of work.

### Public Holidays

*January 1: Jour de l'an* (New Year's Day)* This day is generally devoted to visiting parents and older relatives and exchanging gifts (instead of on Christmas Day). *Concierges* expect to be tipped at this time. Postmen, firemen, street cleaners, etc. solicit their New Year's gifts as early as November, offering dingy and tacky calendars with sappy pictures of flowers and cats in exchange for year-end tokens of appreciation (cash).

*Late March/April : Pâques* (Easter) First Sunday following the full moon of the equinox of spring, at the end of March or early April.

*Monday after Easter: Lundi de Pâques* (Easter Monday)*

**May 1:** *Fête du Travail* (Labor Day)* May 1st was designated an International Labor Day in 1889 and is observed in France as a legal holiday (celebrated everywhere in the world except the US). Labor groups generally parade in different sections of Paris. A custom in France on this day is to present *muguet* (lilies of the valley) to friends and loved ones to bring them happiness and *porte-bonheur* (good luck). Everyone is entitled to pick wild *muguet,* found in the forests surrounding Paris. May 1st is the only day of the year that anyone can sell *muguet* or other flowers without a license. If you find yourself at the Elysées Palace, you might see *Les Forts des Halles* (porters of the Paris market), dressed in the traditional porters outfits, presenting *muguet* to the President of France.

*May 8: Victoire 1945* (V.E. Day)* *Défilés* (parades) take place throughout the city, the largest and most impressive on the Champs-Elysées.

*Sixth Thursday after Easter: Ascension* (Ascension Day)*

*Last Sunday in May: Fête des Mères* (Mother's Day)

*Second Monday after Ascension: Pentecôte* (Pentecost)*

*2 or 3 weeks after Mother's Day: Fête des Pères* (Father's Day)

*July 14: Fête nationale/14 juillet* (Bastille Day)* Celebrations begin on the 13th and include fireworks and street dances. Lively parties take place at most fire houses. Admission is free to performances in all National Theaters on this day. Fireworks over Trocadero.

*August 15: Fête de l'Assomption* (Feast of the Assumption)* Christian holiday commemorating the assumption of the Virgin Mary. Celebrations such as harvest festivals and the blessing of the sea happen on this day.*

*November 1: Toussaint* (All Saints' Day)* Halloween, the North American celebration related to this Christian holiday, is not officially acknowledged in France, although numerous restaurants and shops display pumpkins. A word on buying pumpkins: in Paris pumpkins are often darker in color, flatter, and deeply ridged, making the carving of jack-o-lanterns more difficult. They cost about 10 FF per kilo, a hefty and culturally alienating sum if you're used to having a fat one around for Halloween.

*November 2: Jour des Morts* (All Souls Day)*. It is the custom in France to visit the graves of relatives on the day before the *Jour des Morts* or on the day itself. Flowers (usually chrysanthemums) are placed on the graves. Chrysanthemums were the seasonal flowers before greenhouses existed, and are the traditional flowers used on this day. Thus don't even consider offering chrysanthemums when invited to people's houses for dinner, etc.

*November 11: Fête de l'Armistice* (Veteran's Day)*

*December 25: Noël (Christmas)**
It is the time to eat the holiday foods at the traditional Christmas dinner *(le réveillon): boudin blanc* (white sausage), *foie gras, dinde* (turkey), *saumon fumé, huîtres,* and *bûche de Noël* (yule log-shaped cake).

*December 31: St Sylvestre* (New Year's Eve)
Like everywhere, Parisians eat and drink heartily to bring in the New Year. Massive traffic jams at midnight at Concorde, Odéon, Etoile and the Bastille are to be expected. Kissing a stranger at midnight is tolerated.

*National public holidays are denoted with * (Most schools and businesses are closed).*

## Annual Events

The *Office du Tourisme et des Congrès de Paris* does a monthly brochure called Paris Sélection. which lists the month's manifestations (cultural events), spectacles, conventions, etc., which you can receive for an annual subscription fee of 50F (free if the mailing address is abroad). A *passe musée* (museum pass) is also available from the *Office du Tourisme* which gives you entrance to all the museums and monuments of Paris (including Versailles) and has the considerable advantage of allowing you to bypass the sometimes long waiting lines. It costs 60F for one day, 120F for three days and 170F for five days.

**Office du Tourisme et des Congrès de Paris**
127, av des Champs-Elysées
75008 Paris
Tel: 49.52.53.54. Fax: 49.52.53.00

**Calendar of Events**
*January*
Fashion shows (summer collection).
*February*
Bread and Pastry Exposition.
*March*
Palm Sunday, Prix du Président de la République, at Auteuil race course, Bois de Boulogne.
*April*
April-May: Paris Fair (commercial exhibition) at Parc des Expositions.
April-May: *Foire du Trône* at the Porte Dorée.
Early April-early October: *Son et Lumière* at les Invalides.
*May*
May-September: Illuminated Fountains at Versailles.
Mid-May: Paris Marathon (foot race around Paris).
Mid-May-late June: Versailles Music and Drama Festival.
Late May-early June: French Open Tennis Championships, Roland Garros Courts.
*June*
Early June: Paris Air Show (odd years only), Le Bourget Airport.
Early June-mid-July: Marais Festival (music, drama, exhibitions).
June: a festival of music, drama, and dance at Saint-Denis.
Mid-June: Grand Steeplechase de

Paris at Auteuil race course, Bois de Boulogne.
Mid-June: *Fête du Pont-Neuf* (booths and street performers on the bridge and in the Place Dauphine).
June 21: *Fête de la Musique* — music groups and free open air concerts throughout the city. Tel: 40.36.50.50
June 24: *Feux de la Saint-Jean* (fireworks) at Sacré-Cœur.
End of June: *Grand Prix de Paris,* Longchamp race course, Bois de Boulogne.
*July*
Early July: *Festival de Saint-Denis,* Tel: 48.13.12.10. Classical music festival.
July 14: *Fête nationale* (celebrations throughout the city and military display in the Champs-Elysées).
Mid-July: finish of the *Tour de France* cycle race in the Champs-Elysées.
Throughout July: Fashion shows (winter collection).
*September*
*Fête de l'Humanité,* sponsored by the *Parti communiste* in the northern suburb of La Courneuve.
*Festival de Montmartre*
Late September-early December: *Festival d'Automne,* Tel: 42.96.12.27. Music, drama, ballet, exhibitions.
*October*
First Sunday: *Prix de l'Arc de Triomphe* at Longchamp race course, Bois de Boulogne.
Early October: Montmartre wine festival, Paris Motor Show at the Parc des Expositions (even years only).
Beaujolais Festival: when *"le beaujolais nouveau est arrivé,"* the party

starts at midnight as the first bottle of the new harvest is allowed to be opened. People generally stop whatever they are doing and go for a glass at the nearest café or bar.

*November*
November 11: Armistice Day ceremony at Arc de Triomphe.

*December*
Christmas Eve: midnight celebration at Notre-Dame.

For further details call the *Office du Tourisme de Paris,* Tel: 49.52.53.54.

## Climate

The word for weather, as in "what it's doing out," is *le temps,* not to be confused with "time." Otherwise, the weather report is the *la météo.*

Although the weather in Paris is seldom extremely hot or extremely cold, it is variable since the city lies at the junction of marine and continental climates which have opposite characteristics. Autumn in Paris can be absolutely lovely, mild and somewhat sunny with a tinge of melancholy in the air. The foliage is nice but not always noticeable in the center of the city. Sweaters and light coats are needed. Similarly, the fall and winter can be, and often are, long and gray. The heavy grayness *(grisaille)* often contributes to drawn faces, sadness and depressed moods. In the spring and autumn, temperatures average about 11° Celsius (52°

Fahrenheit) with warm days and cool nights.

During the winter, the average temperature is about 3° Celsius (37° Fahrenheit) and there are rarely more than 20 very cold days a year. The winters are wet, and warm rain gear and an umbrella are indispensable. The winters have tended to be milder and milder over the last few years. There is rarely any snow, other than a few flakes in February and perhaps a strange and short barrage of hail once or twice a year. Nonetheless, winter coats or down jackets can be necessary in that the cold is damp and penetrating and often annoying. Ski jackets aren't usually worn in town, but students can get away with anything.

Spring comes late or winter seems to linger and fuses with summer. The blooming of the nubby, cut-back magnolia and horse chestnut trees along some of the boulevards is a pleasant sight and the leaves give off a sweet but strange fragrance that only seems to be found in Paris. April in Paris is often cold and rainy and the chestnuts do not blossom until the last week of the month. It's a good idea to have an umbrella handy during the months of December through June.

Summers in Paris can be rather hot and uncomfortable. The pollution gets thick and the air heavy. The tourists start arriving on Easter weekend, but the Parisians don't start leaving until July (see Vacations).

Temperatures in the summer average about 18° Celsius (65° Fahrenheit) with some very warm days, especially in July and August.

**A Few Weather Expressions**

*il fait beau:* ..................... it's nice out

*il ne fait pas beau.* ... it's not very nice out

*il fait mauvais:* ...... the weather is bad

*ça caille:* ............... it's freezing (slang)

*il pleut:* ............................ it's raining

*il fait froid:* .......................... it's cold

*il fait chaud:* .......................... it's hot

*il neige:* .......................... it's snowing

*il fait moche:* ...................it's ugly out

**Average Temperatures Range**

| Stations | Altitude (m) | Annual (C°) | January (C°) | July (C°) | Rainfall (mm) | # days rain |
|---|---|---|---|---|---|---|
| Lille | 44 | 9 | 3.1 | 15.9 | 596 | 185 |
| Lyon | 200 | 11.1 | 4.2 | 19.7 | 973 | 186 |
| Strasbourg | 150 | 9.7 | 0.6 | 17.9 | 585 | 184 |
| Brest | 98 | 10.9 | 7.1 | 15.1 | 1,030 | 204 |
| Paris | 75 | 11.6 | 4.9 | 18.6 | 631 | 193 |
| Bordeaux | 47 | 12.4 | 6.6 | 19.6 | 801 | 184 |
| Marseille | 4 | 14.8 | 8.4 | 23.4 | 498 | 79 |
| Nice | 5 | 15.1 | 9.3 | 22.3 | 576 | 59 |
| Ajaccio | 4 | 14.7 | 10.4 | 20.9 | 433 | 185 |

## Dates in French History

(based on the *Economists Guide to Paris*)

**30,000-15,000 B.C.:** Cro-Magnon man, whose cave paintings still exist in the southwest, peoples a France laid bare by the Ice Age.

**600 B.C.:** Greek traders found Massilia, later to be called Marseille.

**59-50 B.C.:** Julius Caesar conquers France.

**AD 987:** Hugh Capet, first of the Capetian monarchs, elected king of France.

**1207-29:** King Philip Augustus brutally suppresses the Cathar (Albigensian) heresy.

**1226-70:** Louis IX (St. Louis), greatest of the Capetian kings, founds Sorbonne (1253) and wages 7th and 8th Crusades.

**1309-77:** The papacy establishes itself in Avignon.

**1337-1453:** The Hundred Years' War (against England).

**1515-47:** Reign of François I; Renaissance flourishes in Europe.

**1562-98:** The Wars of Religion between Catholics and Protestants (Huguenots), ending with the Edict of Nantes under which Protestantism is officially recognized.

**1643-1715:** Reign of Louis XIV, whose revocation of the Edict of Nantes (1685) leads to mass Huguenot exodus.

**1715-74:** Reign of Louis XV (who was heavily influenced by his mistress, Madame de Pompadour).

**1789:** The attack on the Bastille starts the French Revolution, leading to the execution of Louis XVI (1793) and then of the revolutionary leaders themselves, notably Robespierre (1794).

**1799:** Napoleon Bonaparte appointed first consul and then crowned emperor (1804).

**1812:** Napoleon's empire reaches its zenith with the capture of Moscow, but he is then forced into a humiliating retreat from Russia.

**1814-15:** Napoleon is forced to abdicate and is exiled to the island of Elba. He escapes, raises a new army, but is defeated at Waterloo. He dies in exile on St. Helena (1821).

**1814-30:** Bourbon monarchy restored, under Louis XVIII, then Charles X.

**1830:** Revolution in Paris: Charles X replaced by Louis-Philippe.

**1830-48:** Conquest of Algeria.

**1848:** Another Paris revolution. Napoleon's nephew Louis-Napoleon elected president, then becomes emperor (Second Empire, 1852-70).

**1870-71:** The Franco-Prussian War: France is defeated at Sedan, then cedes Alsace and Lorraine to the victors.

**1871:** In Paris, the revolutionary government of "La Commune" is bloodily suppressed.

**1875-87:** French vineyards ravaged by phylloxera epidemic.

**1894-99:** The Dreyfus affair: Jewish officer falsely convicted of treason.

**1909:** Louis Bleriot is first to fly a

non-balloon aircraft across the Channel.

**1914-18:** World War I, leading to Treaty of Versailles (1919) and the return of Alsace and Lorraine to France.

**1936:** "Front Populaire " left-wing government under socialist Léon Blum. The railways, some factories and the Banque de France nationalized.

**1939:** Outbreak of World War II, leading to German invasion and fall of Paris (1940): a collaborationist government is set up at Vichy, in the unoccupied zone, under Marshal Pétain. (See Herbert Lottman's book, *The Fall of Paris.*)

**1944:** Allies liberate France and de Gaulle forms a provisional government. Sweeping nationalization begin.

**1946:** Fourth Republic formed.

**1954:** Fall of Dien Bien Phu leads to French exodus from Indo-China.

**1957:** Treaty of Rome is signed, setting up European Economic Community.

**1958:** de Gaulle returns to power: Fifth Republic is created.

**1962:** France grants independence to Algeria, after a bloody eight-year war.

**1968:** Student uprising and general strike. de Gaulle resigns (1969).

**1974-81:** Presidency of Valéry Giscard d'Estaing.

**1981-86:** Socialist-led government, with François Mitterrand as President. Continued nationalization.

**1986:** Chirac government elected and a period of "cohabitation" begins.

**1988:** Socialists regain power and Mitterrand names Laurent Fabius and later Michel Rocard as premier ministre.

**1991:** Mitterrand replaces Rocard with Edith Cresson as *premier ministre.*

**1992:** Pierre Bérégovoy replaces Cresson following Socialists' loss in regional elections. Major scandal erupts following Aids-contaminated blood transfusions in the 80s given to patients at state-run clinics and hospitals. The government is blamed, and the Socialists pay politically.

**1993:** Plans for implementing European reforms following Maastricht agreement. Bérégovoy is replaced by conservative Edward Balladur, following Socialists loss, thus starting a new period of cohabitation. Bérégovoy, riddled by scandal, commits suicide.

**1994:** EEC renamed the EU, European Union. Restructuring of almost all political parties. Opening of EuroTunnel.

## Geography

**Départements:** The division of France into 95 *départements* is a result of the Revolution and was accomplished in 1790. France is also divided into 22 regions, which are less important for administrative purposes but should not be confused with the *département* names. The present organization of the regions dates from only 1960 and is the result of economical considerations.

**Principal cities and *départements*.** The numbers found after the name represent the postal codes for the *département*. These codes are used in the postal codes, on license plates, and other standardized nation-wide forms. People tend to refer to certain *départements* by their numbers. Paris and its surrounding six *départements* together make up the Ile-de-France.

**ILE-DE-FRANCE**
**Paris** 75
**Seine-et-Marne** 77
**Yvelines** 78

**Essonne** 91
**Hauts-de-Seine** 92
**Seine-Saint-Denis** 93
**Val-de-Marne** 94

Bordeaux (Gironde) 33
Toulouse (Haute-Garonne) 31
Grenoble (Isère) 38
Montpellier (Hérault) 34
Tours (Indre-et-Loire) 37
Lille (Nord) 59
Strasbourg (Bas-Rhin) 67
Dijon (Côte-d'Or) 21
Lyon (Rhône) 69
Aix-en-Provence (Bouches-du-Rhône) 13
Nice (Alpes-Maritimes) 06

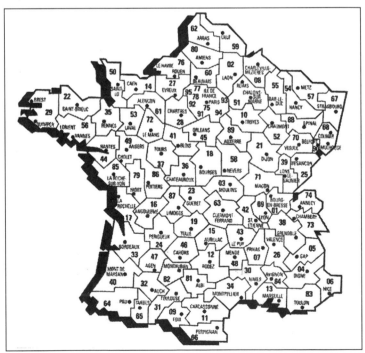

# Getting to Paris Traveling

## Arriving By Air

Traveling to and from Paris is relatively easy from all corners of Europe and the rest of the world. More people visit Paris each year than any other foreign capital in the world. The city is very well served by international airlines and train service. Paris is also a hub for international traffic to Africa, the Middle East, and Asia.

Most likely you'll be getting to Paris by plane. The two main international airports are Charles-de-Gaulle (also known as Roissy because it's located in the northern suburb by that name) and Orly, the older of the two, located twenty kilometers south of Paris. Both are very well served by taxis, public buses, and commuter subway lines called the RER (see Transportation). Those first moments in a foreign airport are always filled with a rush of impres-

sions—you'll immediately notice the aesthetics and details that reflect the local culture and attitudes. The culture's sense of style and aesthetics are present in the design and advertising. The cars and signs are new. A lot of people smoke. Taxis queue. Luggage carts are free. Instantly, you'll notice that the racial and ethnic mix indigenous to France is different than that in London or Amsterdam. The vestiges of France's colonial history are present in the make up of its people.

If you're flying into Paris from North America on a regular scheduled flight, you'll most likely be arriving at Roissy in the early morning. The sounds of Roissy announcements and the strong wafts of expresso coffee are details that you will pleasantly recognize upon each return. After passing through immigrations, nabbing one of the numerous and free baggage carts, and claiming your baggage, you proceed past the customs zone, where you are faced with the choice of whether or not to make a customs declaration. If you're arriving from another EU (European Union) country there will be no customs check because goods, in theory, move freely within the member countries. The two exits are side by side. Most likely, you will have nothing to declare and will be able to pass freely without stopping through the exit marked in green RIEN A DECLARER. Americans are rarely bothered, but should you be carrying many large packages or computers or electronics in their original cartons or else huge and poorly made bundles held together with rope and tape you could be asked to open them and be assessed for duty (see Customs Regulations). If you already hold a French resident card *(carte de séjour)* in addition to your passport, remember, you are subject to French law concerning imports.

A word about arriving with a video camera or laptop computer: occasionally, visitors and residents suspected of bringing in electronics to France are questioned, asked to produce proof of purchase and sometimes assessed for value added tax (TVA). A photocopy of your sales receipt can help avoid this.

If you need to change money right away, proceed to one of the banks located on the arrival level near the exit (for detailed discussion of currency exchange and French banking practices, see Banking).

**From Charles de Gaulle Airport (Roissy)**

If you're not overloaded and are trying to keep down the expenses, the best options for getting into Paris are the public buses which take you to Porte Maillot (Bus 350) in the 16th *arrondissement* (see map) or Nation (Bus 351) in the 12th *arrondissement,* or the well-equipped and comfortable Air France buses which take you to the *aérogare* at les Invalides, the Gare Montparnasse or the Porte Maillot. These can be picked up at the curb outside all terminals and are well-marked. Once in central Paris, it will be cheaper to take a taxi to your place of residence. The Roissybus has continual service between Aéroport Charles de Gaulle (all terminals) and Paris Opéra. For information call: 48.04.18.24. Signs around the Opéra métro station and Auber RER station are clearly marked for the Roissybus.

Another very effective and quick means to get into Paris is the RER commuter train *(Direction St. Rémy-lès-Chevreuse),* which can be easily accessed by a free airport shuttle bus which circles around all terminals. You'll need French francs to buy your ticket in the station. The price of a one way ticket to any of the following Paris stations is 31 FF and includes the shuttle bus from your terminal to the RER station at the airport: the Gare de Nord in the 10th *arrondissement,* Châtelet-Les Halles (the transportation hub for the RER and métro lines in central Paris), St. Michel (Notre Dame-Latin Quarter-Left Bank), Luxembourg Gardens, Port-Royal, Denfert-Rochereau, and Cité Universitaire (international student residences). Note that Charles de Gaulle Airport has two main terminals, *Aérogare 1,* which handles most of the international carriers, and *Aérogare 2,* which primarily serves Air France flights. *Aérogare 2* is divided into 2A, 2B, 2C, and now 2D. So make sure you ask at and from which terminal you arrive and depart.

A recent addition to Terminal One of Charles de Gaulle Airport is *Cocoon,* on the Boutiquaire level, offering 60 "cabins" to sleep, rest, shower or work in during extended visits to this airport. Tel: (1) 48.62.06.16.

### From Orly Airport

To get to and from Orly by train, you want to take the OrlyVal line. You take the RER Line B *(Direction St. Rémy-lès-Chevreuse)* and change at Antony-Orly which corresponds with "le Val d'Orly", serving Orly's main terminals, Orly West (national and some charters) and Orly South (international and many charters) terminals. The OrlyVal's timetable is synchronized with the RER. The Châtelet - Orly connection takes only 30 minutes and the price is 45 FF one way for adults and 22 FF for children. Tickets can be bought in all métro and RER stations. The RER line from Orly serves the Gare d'Austerlitz, St. Michel, Invalides/Orsay, Pont de l'Alma, or the Champ de Mars (Eiffel Tower). The price for any of these Paris stations is: 24 FF. Save your ticket; you'll need it to get out at your desired station (see map for all these options) or to prove you've paid if you are "controlled."

The *Orlybus* serving Orly Airport is also an effective and dependable means of getting to and from Orly. When you exit the arrivals terminal you'll find the Air France bus stops right in front of you. The buses from Orly take you to the RER Denfert-Rochereau RER station or the Air France terminal at les Invalides and cost 21 FF. You can buy your ticket on the bus. For info between 6 a.m. and midnight call: 49.75.15.15.

### Taxi Service

If you are loaded down with luggage or in a great hurry, you'll probably want to take a taxi into Paris, although when the traffic is heavy, the RER is the fastest means to get in and out of town. First, you must wait your turn in the clearly marked Taxi Stand line. This is a strict rule and taxi drivers, who wait in long queues themselves, will almost never break it or risk massive fines. A normal drive into central Paris without heavy traffic should cost between 150-200 FF from Charles-de-Gaulle and 100-150 FF from Orly. From Charles-de-Gaulle, allow 250 FF if you have lots of baggage. If traffic is very heavy, count on an additional

30%. Baggage, pets, skis, bicycles each cost 5 FF extra. You may tip a bit, but don't overdo it. A ten franc tip from the airport is fine. In the city, a few francs is all that is really expected. No need to calculate 15%. Taxis in Paris always operate with set meters (See Taxis).

## Arriving By Train

If you're arriving by train the sensation is very different. If you've never been to Paris before, pulling in under the metal hooded roof of the Gare du Nord, Gare de Lyon, or Gare Saint-Lazare can be exciting. The smell, the pigeons, the cold echo all ruminate with traces of a Europe that hasn't changed in half a century. The Gare Montparnasse has been recently overhauled and modernized so the feel reflects more of the new Europe. When you step down off the train follow the crowds into the *gare.* There are few baggage carts along the long *quais* (platforms), so luggage hauling can be painful. Some porters with large carts can sometimes be hired at the general rate of 5 FF a bag. All Paris train stations have currency exchange points and information stands. Additionally, all stations are served by at least two subway lines. For a list of Paris train stations and the general directions they serve, along with reservation and ticket information, see Public Transport. If you need to make a phone call, you'll

note right away that it is nearly impossible to find a phone that uses coins. You'll need to buy a *télécarte* (see Telephones).

Upon arriving, again you have the choice of RER, *métro,* or taxi. Note that taxi lines at most stations around rush hour (6 p.m.—18h)—French rush hour is about one hour later than its North American equivalent—can be frustratingly long. There are no "share a cab" options unless you strike up a friendly arrangement yourself, which is unlikely, in that Parisians aren't accustomed to becoming familiar too quickly, even if it's practical and cost-efficient.

## Customs and Entry Regulations

Note that the former EEC—European Economic Community—also referred to as the EC, is now (as of 1994) officially called the European Union (EU). No vaccinations are required to enter France from any country. With the new European laws there is now free trade between the twelve European Union countries and no longer any limit on what you can bring from one country to another. Note though that customs control checks have increased along the highways inside France in areas near the borders. From non-European Union countries, if you are 16 years or older, you have the right to bring in 200 cigarettes or 50 cigars or 20 *cigarillos.* As for spirits, the limit is one liter of alcohol over 22° proof and two liters of alcohol under 22° proof. Following the fall of the Eastern bloc, the illegal importation of cut-rate caviar into France, especially from Poland, has been noticed and measures have been implemented to control this. The "legal" importation of abundant and inexpensive eastern bloc fish has led to violent protesting and sabotage by French fishermen who are suffering. New goods or provisions originating outside the EU for personal use are limited to 900 FF per person. There are few restrictions equivalent to the US Agricultural laws concerning foods and plants. You can show up with a bunch of roses, a dozen bagels, or a kilo of corned beef without any problems. Near-extinct birds and reptiles, however, in keeping with the 1990 Washington Convention, as well as exotic meats like monkey and armadillo, as well as ivory in all forms, are forbidden. Particularly controlled are monkeys, pandas, elephants, rhinos, sea turtles, giant salamanders, and most cactus.

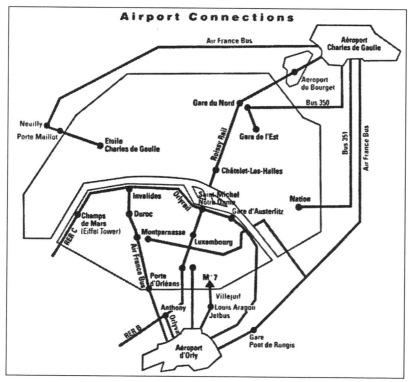

## Air Travel

Leaving Paris or meeting someone's plane, either Charles-de-Gaulle or Orly, make sure you are clear as to which airport and which terminal you're supposed to be at. General airport information and message services can be obtained by calling:

**Aéroport Charles-de-Gaulle: 48.62.22.80**
**Aéroport Orly: 49.75.15.15**
**Minitel: 3615 HORAV**
Minitel service is also available for flight information/departure and arrival times by dialing on your telephone: 3615, and HORAV on your Minitel unit (See Minitel under Communications).

## MAJOR AIRLINES SERVING PARIS

**Aer Lingus**
47, av de l'Opéra
75002 Paris
Tel: 47.42.12.50

**Air Outre-Mer (AOM)**
Strategic Orly
13-15, rue du Pont des Halles
94526 Rungis Cedex
Tel: 49.79.12.34

**Air Canada**
31, rue Falguière
75015 Paris
Tel: 42.18.19.20
Fax: 43.21.30.80

**Air France**
119, av des Champs-Elysées
75008 Paris
Tel: 44.08.24.24 / 44.08.22.22
Fax 42.99.24.09
Minitel: 3615 AF or 36.16AF

**Air Inter**
17, rue de Provigny
94230 Cachan
Tel: 45.46.90.90
Minitel: 3615 AIR INTER

**American Airlines**
109, rue Fbg St. Honoré
75008 Paris
Tel: 42.89.05.22 / Fax: 42.99.99.95
Minitel: 3615 AMERICAN AIRLINES

**British Airways**
12, rue Castiglione
75001 Paris
Tel: 47.78.14.14
Fax (à Lyon): (16) 72.33.14.26
Minitel: 3615 BA

**Canadian Airlines**
24, av Hoche
75008 Paris
Tel: 48.53.07.07
Fax: 49.53.04.81
Minitel: 3615 CANADIAN

**Continental Airlines**
92, av des Champs-Elysées
75008 Paris
Tel: 42.99.09.09
Fax: 42.25.31.89
Minitel: 3615 CONTINENTAL

**Delta Airlines**
Immeuble Lavoisier
6, pl des Vosges
92052 Paris Cedex 74
Tel: 47.68.92.92
Fax: 47.68.52.82

**Northwest Airlines**
16, rue Chaveau Lagarde
75008 Paris
Tel: 42.66.90.00
Fax: 42.66.94.66

**Qantas Airways Limited**
7, rue Scribe
75009 Paris
Tel: 44.94.52.00
Fax: 42.66.90.03
Minitel: 3615 QANTAS

**Trans World Airlines
(TWA)**
6, rue Christophe-Colomb
75008 Paris
Tel: 49.19.20.00
Fax: 49.19.20.09
Minitel: 3615 TWA

**United Airlines**
40, rue Jean-Jaurès
93170 Bagnolet
Tel: 49.72.14.14
Fax: 48.98.88.70
Minitel: 3615 UNITED

**US Air**
23bis, rue d'Anjou
92100 Boulogne
Tel: 49.10.29.00
Toll Free No: 05.00.30.00

**OTHERS**

**Aeroflot**
Admin: 42.25.31.92
Res: 42.25.43.81

**Aerolineas Argentinas**
Res: 42.56.31.16

**Air Afrique**
Admin: 44.21.32.00
Res: 44.21.32.32

**Air Algérie**
Tel: 42.60.30.62

**Air Gabon**
Tel: 43.59.20.63

**Air India**
Admin: 42.66.90.60
Res: 42.66.13.72

**Air Lanka**
Admin: 42.96.90.22
Res: 42.97.43.44

**Air Madagascar**
Tel: 43.79.74.74

**Air Malta**
Tel: 44.86.08.40

**Austrian Airlines**
Admin: 48.66.3743
Res: 42.66.34.66

**Aéromexico**
Tel: 47.42.40.50

**Cameroon Airlines**
Tel: 47.42.78.17

**Cathay Pacific Airways**
Admin: 40.68.61.00
Res: 40.68.98.99

**China Airlines**
Tel: 42.25.63.60

**Egypt Air**
Tel: 44.94.85.00

**El Al**
Admin: 44.55.00.00
Res: 40.20.90.90

**Finnair**
Tel: 47.42.33.33

**Gulf Air**
Admin: 47.23.48.48
Res: 49.52.41.00

**Icelandair**
Tel: 44.51.60.51

**Japan Airlines**
Admin: 44.35.55.25
Res: 44.35.55.00

**Kenya Airways**
Tel: 47.42.33.11

**L.O.T. Polish Airlines**
Tel: 47.42.05.60

**Lufthansa**
Admin: 40.17.12.00
Res: 42.65.37.35

**Malaysia Airlines**
Admin: 47.42.20.28
Res: 47.42.26.00

**Mexicana Airlines**
Tel: 30.61.08.35

**Middle-East Airlines**
**Air Liban**
Admin: 42.66.93.57
Res: 42.66.93.93

**Olympic Airways**
Admin: 47.42.87.99
Res: 42.65.92.42

**Pakistan International Airlines**
Tel: 45.62.92.41

**Philippines Airlines**
Admin: 42.96.01.52
Res: 42.96.01.40

**Royal Nepal Airlines**
Tel: 40.46.95.21

**Sabena World Airways**
Admin: 44.94.19.00
Res: 44.94.19.19

**Saudi Arabian Airlines**
Tel: 53.57.50.50

**Scandinavian Airlines (SAS)**
Admin: 42.66.93.53
Res: 47.42.06.14

**Singapore Airlines**
Admin: 45.53.52.44
Res: 45.53.90.90

**Swissair**
Admin: 40.78.10.00
Res: 45.81.11.01

**Syrian Arab Airlines**
Tel: 47.42.11.06

**TAAG (Angola Airlines)**
Tel: 42.96.82.99

**TAP (Portugal)**
Admin: 44.86.89.50
Res; 44.86.89.89

**Thai Airways**
Admin: 44.20.70.15
Res: 44.20.70.80

**Tunis Air**
Admin: 42.12.31.00
Res: 42.12.31.31

**Varig**
Admin: 47.23.35.44
Res; 47.20.03.33

---

## Train Travel

The French rail system, the SNCF, is, on the whole, extremely extensive and efficient. You may have heard of the TGV, *train à grande vitesse,* or high speed train that has cut the traveling time in half between Paris and, for example, Marseille, 900 kilometers away, to four hours and forty minutes instead of eight. The TGV currently serves the Paris, Lyon, Marseille line to the south,

Geneva and Lausanne in the east in three and a half hours, and the newer ultra high-speed Bordeaux Atlantic line to the southwest (three hours to Bordeaux), and northern line which reaches Lille in one hour and is to connect with the EuroTunnel to Great Britain (TGV Eurostar Paris-London/Brussels-London service). In 1996, the Paris-Brussels-Amsterdam TGV line is to open, connecting to Cologne a year later.

The TGV requires reservations, which can be made in most travel agencies, all train stations, and at home with the Minitel (see Communications). Seat reservations for regular trains are also recommended during busy periods. Automatic ticket and reservations machines are located in all train stations and are called *billetterie automatique.* They take VISA and MasterCard cards as form of payment.

Paris has six main rail stations, all of them on *métro* lines. All offer a wide range of services: bars and restaurants, refreshment stands, newsstands and information booths (sporadically staffed).

**SNCF Train Information**
Information and Reservations:
45.82.50.50
Ile-de-France (regional lines):
45.65.60.00
Minitel:  36 15 SNCF
Open daily from 8h-20h

**Paris Train Stations
and the Directions They Serve**
*Gare du Nord:* Serves the north, including the Channel ports, where trains connect with ferries and hover crafts from Britain; also services Belgium, Holland and the Scandinavian countries.
*Gare de l'Est:* Serves the east, Nancy and Strasbourg, and Germany and eastern Europe, including ex-Yugoslavia and Moscow. (The former Paris-Frankfurt train now continues to Leipzig.)
*Gare d'Austerlitz:* Serves the southwest; Bordeaux, Toulouse, and Spain and Portugal via Orléans, Tours, Poitiers and Angoulême.
*Gare St. Lazare:* Serves Normandy and boat trains to/from Dieppe.
*Gare Montparnasse:* Serves western France, especially Bretagne.
*Gare de Lyon:* Serves southwestern France, Switzerland, Italy and Greece.

When leaving Paris by train, make sure you know from which station your train leaves. Before boarding your train make sure you punch *(composter)* your ticket and reservation stub in one of the automatic cancellation machines located at the head of each platform. Failure to do so may result in a stiff fine—train travel within France is essentially based on the honor system. In most cases a conductor will check your tickets anyway. You can purchase tickets onboard, but you pay a supplement. Tickets in Europe are valid for two months from the date stamped on the ticket.

The SNCF also publishes a variety of reduced train fares which they have organized into categories. The fares have names and the cheaper days and times to travel are assigned colors which are at times confusing; inquire thoroughly to make sure you get the best deal available. Discounts depend on destinations, dates, and times. Here are the color coded days, cheapest to most expensive.
*Jour bleu:* Saturday noon through Sunday 15h.
*Jour blanc:* Friday noon through Saturday noon, and Sunday 15h through Monday noon. Plus holidays.
*Jour rouge:* Principal days of departure.

**Principal Discounts:**
*Carrissimo* and *Joker:* youth fares, 12-25 years old, up to 50%.
*Carte Kiwi* and *Joker:* When traveling with children (even one child) discounts can go to 60%.
*Carte Vermeil* and *Joker:* Senior citizens discounts for the over 60 bracket. Under 4 years old is free, but child does not get a seat.
Animals pay half fare of a 2nd class ticket or 28 FF if the animal is under 6 kilos and is carried in a bag measuring not more than 45 x 30 x 25cms.
If you want to travel with your car or motorcycle on the train, the SNCF has a complete list of destinations applicable to this service. Motorail is a European network of special trains,

generally overnight, carrying passengers with vehicles on journeys up to 900 miles. In Paris, reservations can be made by calling 45.65.60.60. Otherwise, inquire at:

*Gare Austerlitz* (Tolbiac): 45.82.73.62.
*Gare de Lyon* (Bercy): 40.19.60.11.
*Gare Montparnasse* (Vaugirard): 40.48.14.72.

Avis Car Rental offers an instant rental service at 200 French train stations called AVIS TRAIN & AUTO. This is very convenient but not always the most economical. Tel: 46.10.60.60.

## Student Travel

Traveling to and from Paris is relatively easy from all corners of Europe and the rest of the world. If you are coming from the United States or Canada there are a number of reduced-rate travel possibilities available to students. Reduced rates are also possible for those under 30. The Council on International Educational Exchange (CIEE) issues international student and youth cards which allow substantial discounts on flights. Otherwise, you should consult your travel agent for the most recent rates on scheduled airlines serving Paris. The CIEE and its affiliate Council Travel specialize in student travel and are able to answer most travel and foreign-work related questions. Here is a list of their French and overseas offices.

**Council on International Educational Exchange (CIEE)**
Centre Franco-Américain Odéon
1, Pl. de l'Odéon
75006 Paris
Tel: 40.75.95.10 or 44.41.74.74
Fax: 43.26.97.45

**The Council on International Educational Exchange**
205 E. 42nd Street
New York, NY 10017
Tel: (212) 661-1450
Fax: (212) 972-3231

**Other CIEE Locations in the US**

CALIFORNIA
• *Berkeley*
2488 Channing Way
Berkeley, CA 94704
Tel: (415) 848-8604
• *La Jolla*
UCSD Price Center
9500 Gilman Drive
La Jolla, CA 92093
Tel: (619) 452-0630
• *Long Beach*
1818 Palo Verde Avenue
Suite E
Long Beach, CA 90815
Tel: (213) 598-3338 (714) 527-7950
• *Los Angeles*
1093 Broxton Ave
Los Angeles, CA 90024
Tel: (213) 208-3551
• *San Diego*
953 Garnet Avenue
San Diego, CA 92109
Tel: (619) 270-6401

• *San Francisco*
312 Sutter Street
Suite 407
San Francisco, CA 94108
Tel: (415) 421-3473
919 Irving Street
Suite 102
San Francisco, CA 94122
Tel: (415) 566-6222
• *Sherman Oaks*
14515 Ventura Blvd.
Suite 250
Sherman Oaks, CA 91403
Tel: (818) 905-5777

**CONNECTICUT**
Yale Co-op E., 77 Broadway
New Haven, CT 06520
Tel: (203) 562-5335

**DISTRICT OF COLUMBIA**
3300 M Street, NW
Washington, D.C. 20007
Tel: (202) 337-6464

**FLORIDA**
1 Datran Center
Suite 320
9100 S Dadeland Blvd.,
Miami, FL 33156
Tel: (305) 670-9261

**GEORGIA**
1561 North Dacatur Road
Atlanta, GA 30307
Tel: (404) 577-9997

**ILLINOIS**
• *Chicago*
1153 N. Dearbom Street

(2nd floor)
Chicago, IL 60610
Tel: (312) 951-0585
• *Evanston*
1634 Orrington Avenue
Evanston, IL 60201
Tel: (312) 475-5070

**INDIANA**
409 East 4th Street
Bloomington, IN 47408
Tel: (812) 330-1600

**LOUISIANA**
• *New Orleans*
Danna Student Center
6363 St. Charles Avenue
New Orleans, LA 70118
Tel: (504) 866-1767

**MASSACHUSETTS**
• *Amherst*
79 South Pleasant Street
(2nd floor rear)
Amherst, MA 01002
Tel: (413) 256-1261
•*Boston*
729 Boylston Street
Suite 201
Boston, MA 02116
Tel: (617) 266-1926
• *Cambridge*
1384 Massachusetts Ave
Suite 206
Harvard Square
Cambridge, MA 02138
Tel: (617) 497-1497
Stratton Student Center
M.I.T., W20-024
84 Massachusetts Ave

Cambridge, MA 02139
Tel: (617) 225-2555

**MICHIGAN**
1220 S. University Avenue
Room 208
Ann Arbor, MI 48104
Tel: (313) 998-0200

**MINNESOTA**
1501 University Ave, SE
Room 300
Minneapolis, MN 55414
Tel: (612) 379-2323

**NEW YORK**
235 East 42nd Street
New York, NY 10017
Tel: (212) 661-1450
148 West 4th Street
New York, NY 10011
Tel: (212) 254-2525

**NORTH CAROLINA**
137 East Franklin Street
Suite 106
Chapel Hill, NC 27514
Tel: (919) 942-2334

**OHIO**
8 East 13th Avenue
Columbus, OH 43201
Tel: (614) 294-8696

**OREGON**
715 S.W. Morrison
Suite 600
Portland, OR 97205
Tel: (503) 228-1900

**PENNSYLVANIA**
3606A Chestnut Street
Philidelphia, PA 19104
Tel: (215) 382-0343
118 Meyran Avenue
Pittsburgh, PA 15213

**RHODE ISLAND**
171 Angell Street
Suite 212
Providence RI 02906
Tel: (402) 331-5810

**TEXAS**
• *Austin*
2000 Guadalupe Street
Austin, TX 78705
Tel: (512) 472-4931
• *Dallas*
6923 Snider Plaza
Suite B
Dallas, TX 75205
Tel: (214) 350-6166

**UTAH**
1310 East 200 South
Salt Lake City, UT 84112
Tel: (801) 582-5840

**WASHINGTON**
1314 NE 43rd St
Suite 210
Seattle, WA 98105
Tel: (206) 632-2448

**WISCONSIN**
2615 N. Hackett Ave
Milwaukee, WI 53211
Tel: (414) 332-4740

**Other Locations in France**
* *Aix en Provence*
12 rue Victor-Leydet
13100 Aix-en-Provence
Tel: (16) 42.38.94.00
* *Lyon*
36 quai Gailleton
69002 Lyon
Tel: (16) 78.37.09.56
* *Montpellier*
20 rue de l'Université
34000 Montpellier
Tel: (16) 67.60.41.26
* *Nice*
37bis rue d'Angleterre
06000 Nice
Tel: (16) 93.82.23.33
* *Paris*
22, rue des Pyramides
(*Métro*: Pyramides)
75001 Paris
Tel: 44.55.55.44
16, rue de Vaugirard
(Métro: Odéon, Luxembourg)
75006 Paris
Tel: 46.34.02.90


**Other Locations in the World**
**BRITAIN**
28A Poland Street
London W1V 308
Tel: (071) 437-7767
**GERMANY**
18, Graf Adolph Strasse
4000 Dusseldorf 1
Tel: (211) 32 90 88
Adalbertstr. 32
8000 München 40
Tel: (089) 395 022

**JAPAN**
Sanno Grand Building
Room 102
2-14-2 Nagata-cho
Chiyoda-ku
Tokoyo 100
Tel: 581-7581
**SINGAPOUR**
110D Killiney Road
Tai Wah Building
Singapore 00123
Tel: (65) 7337-421

If you are a student, a number of university programs are accustomed to making special travel arrangements for their in-coming students from New York City and other cities in the United States at special group rates. Inquire with the program that concerns you.

If you are coming from other parts of the world, you should consult local airline offices for information on youth and student reductions. Many national airlines offer reduced rates. Students may be required to show a certificate of student status completed by the registrar of their university: make inquiries well in advance of your departure date. University registrar's offices will usually certify the student status of any new student on the form provided by the airline, but it is your responsibility to send the form to the university in a timely fashion. Student air fare certificates are not transferable to other persons.

The national student associations of

most European countries participate in an international network of student flights under the aegis of the Student Air Travel Association. Connections between Paris and cities in Europe, Africa, the Far East and Australia do currently exist. The fares on SATA flights are normally 40% below commercial fares. More information is available from the national student association of your country of residence. These same offices can supply information on special student train and ship fares. For example, the Deutsche Bundesbahn offers a reduction to students traveling from Germany to Paris. The reduction applies only to the portion of the trip made in Germany. Applications, which must be certified by the University Registrar, are available in any German train station.

Remember, persons under 26 are eligible for discounts of up to 50% on train travel in Europe. These special tickets—often called BIGE—can be purchased at the following agencies:

**Frantour**
Gare St. Lazare
75008 Paris
Tel: 43.87.61.89
Fax: 43.87. 33.87
**Tours 33**
85, bd St. Michel
75005 Paris
Tel: 43.29.69.50
Fax: 43.25.29.85

**Usit Voyages**
12, rue Vivienne
75002 Paris
Tel: 42.96.15.88
Fax: 30.75.30.11

The most advantageous and inexpensive way to travel extensively in Europe is with the INTER RAIL card. This offers students (under age 26) unlimited train travel in second class during one month from the date of the first part of the journey for the fixed sum of 2390 FF. The Inter Rail Card is valid for all of western Europe, Greece, Hungary, Romania, and Morocco. It gives a 50% reduction in the country of purchase.

Other reductions are possible at certain times of the year for destinations more than 1000 kilometers from Paris. Information can be obtained from:

**SNCF**
127, av des Champs-Elysées
75008 Paris
Tel: 47.23.54.02
Minitel:  36 15 SNCF

For train information on other national railroads for other countries:
**U.K.**
Les Chemins de Fer Britanniques
57, rue St Roch
75001 Paris
Tel: 44.51.06.10
Fax: 42.66.40.43

**GERMANY**
Chemin de Fer Fédéral Allemand
13, rue d'Alsace
75010 Paris
Tel: 46.07.13.40
Fax: 40.37.26.64

**SPAIN**
Chemins de Fer Espagnols
3, av Marceau
75016 Paris
Tel: 42.09.62.04
Fax: 47.20.88.33

**AMTRAK RAILWAYS**
c/o Wingate
19 bis, rue du Mont-Thabor
75001 Paris
Tel: 44.77.30.00

**CANADIAN NATIONAL RAILWAY**
1, rue Scribe
75009 Paris
Tel: 47.42.76.50
Fax: 47.42.24.39

**VENISE SIMPLON ORIENT EXPRESS**
75, av des Champs Elysées
75008 Paris
Tel: 45.62.00.69
Fax: 49.53.07.75

A few notes on long distance train travel. Aside from the ultra-modern TGV, the SNCF uses primarily two models of train cars. The older ones are divided into compartments of six moderately uncomfortable seats, while the newer ones are merely organized into rows of comfortably reclining seats. Trains are always divided into Second Class and First Class, Smoking and Non-Smoking. Most trains offer snacks and drinks and many are equipped with dining cars. Having your dinner on a train, elegantly seated at a table with linen tablecloth and real silverware can be a lot of fun, but you will spend close to 150 FF per person for the meal. Otherwise, bring along your own provisions, especially a bottle of water.

The least expensive sleeping arrangement on a night train is the *couchette* or six-bunk compartment. Depending who you get in your compartment, you may be able to sleep well or not at all. Be warned: theft does exist in trains, even on first class. Though rare, the most remarkable thefts happen on trains going to or coming from Southern France and Italy, where entire cars have been gassed and robbed! We can offer no advice for these Mediterranean journeys, unless you wish to take a gas mask with you. The overnight trains to Amsterdam, Copenhagen, Frankfurt, Venice, Athens, Rome, Madrid, etc. can make for highly memorable experiences.

Each bunk comes with a blanket, pillow, and sleeping-bag shaped sheet which comes sealed in a plastic wrapper to insure hygiene. When crossing international borders at night, the train conductor will keep your passport until morning to be able to show to the border police. Customs inspectors have been reduced between EU countries but controls and some drug checking does exist.

In recent years, cut-rate travel agencies who often advertise in *The Paris Free Voice, Paris City Magazine,* and *Fusac,* have been able to offer real bargain air fares from Paris to other European cities, profiting by the Paris stop-over portion of longer journeys. The Cathay Pacific flight from Hong Kong to London stops over in Paris and tickets can be had on the London continuation for 400 FF. The Qantas flight to Sydney similarly takes you to Frankfurt for the same, as does the Pakistan International flight to Karachi and the Philippine Airline flight to Manila.

**Student Excursions**

The following student organizations have planned domestic and international excursions at reasonable rates. Write or call for their programs and schedules. Traveling with French students can be an excellent way to meet new friends, improve your French and see new parts of the world.

*Bureau des Voyages de Jeunesse*
20, rue Jean-Jacques Rousseau
75001 Paris
Tel: 42.33.55.00
Fax: 42.33.40.53
(Spain, Greece, Tunisia, Turkey, Egypt, Sicily, West Indies)

*Centre de Coopération Culturelle et Sociale*
7, rue Notre-Dame-des-Victoires
75002 Paris
Tel: 42.61.53.84
Fax: 42.60.24.74
(England, Germany, Hungary, USA)

*Centre Touristique des Etudiants et de la Jeunesse*
20, rue des Carmes
75005 Paris
Tel: 43.25.00.76
Fax: 43.54.48.98
(charter flights)

*Fédération Unie des Auberges de la Jeunesse*
27, rue Pajol
75018 Paris
Tel: 44.89.87.27
(issues student hostel cards for all of Europe)

*Office du Tourisme Universitaire (OTU)*
39, av Bernanos
75005 Paris
Tel: 44.41.38.50
(cheap charters, good bulletin board. International Student Card required)

*Usit Voyages*
12, rue Vivienne
75002 Paris
Tel: 42.96.15.88
Fax: 30.75.30.11
(international travel and student IDs—English speaking staff)

*Voyageurs aux Etats-Unis*
5, place André Malraux
75001 Paris
Tel: 42.86.17.20

*Alek's Travel*
Fax: (19) (1) (305) 462-8691
(to pay for your ticket to the states in dollars—fax only)

## Bus/Coach Travel

There are some very cheap bus excursions from Paris to London, Amsterdam, and other European cities. In the days prior to the Islamic Revolution in Iran, there were weekly buses originating in London and passing through Paris on their way across Europe to Istanbul, Tehran, Kabul, and finally India. For $30 a rugged individual could get from Paris to Bombay. The route changed in the Seventies, passing through Pakistan instead of Afghanistan on its way to India. There are still bus excursions, but few foreigners risk going through Iran anymore. Bus information can be obtained from:

*Eurolines (buses)*
Av. du Général-de-Gaulle
93000 Bagnolet
Tel: 49.72.51.51
Fax: 49.72.51.61

*Nouvelles Frontiers (bus trips)*
90, bd Montparnasse
75014 Paris
Tel: 43.35.40.91

*Fédération Nationale des Transports Routiers*
6, rue Paul-Valéry
75016 Paris
Tel: 45.53.92.88
Fax: 45.53.11.39

## Crossing the Channel (*La Manche*)

Crossing the channel by land can be accomplished in numerous ways. The train to London, of course, takes you to the train ferry, which connects to the British Rail connection in Folkston for one price. There are numerous ferry companies offering crossing service for passengers and cars. Check for promotional offers, ports and schedules.

With the much promoted opening of the EuroTunnel in May 1994 travel between the United Kingdom and France becomes more interesting. The EuroTunnel promises to be the fastest way across the channel with a car but also, to begin with, at least, the most expensive. Depending on time of day and number of passengers, the cost ranges from 1200 to 1800 FF each way. For starters, cars are grouped on a special shuttle train car called Le Shuttle that is pulled through the tunnel in some thirty minutes. The price of ferries currently runs about 30% cheaper with rumors having it that prices will fall to dissuade travelers from taking the tunnel. A host of tunnel-related industries are erupting including hotels, rest stops, restaurants and licensed products, as well as maps, guides, and books on the mutil-million dollar, project of the decade. On site address: BP 69, 62231 Coquelles, Tel: (16) 21.00.60.00.

*EuroTunnel*
19, rue des Mathurins
75009 Paris
Tel: 44.94.88.80 (information
and reservations).
Minitel: 3615 Le Shuttle
**Boats/Ferries**
*Brittany Ferries*
Tel: 0898.333.421
Hoverspeed(hydrofoil to U.K.)
135, rue Lafayette
75010 PARIS
Tel: 42.85.44.55

*Sealink Ferries*
21, rue Louis le Grand
75002 Paris
Tel: 47.42.86.87/47.42.00.26

*P. & O. Lines*
9, place de la Madeleine
75008 Paris
Tel: 42.66.40.17

*Irish Ferries*
8, rue Auber
75009 Paris
Tel: 42.66.90.90

## Hitchhiking

It's rare to see people *faire du stop* (hitchhike) in Paris itself, but you may see hitchhikers (with signs), called *auto-stoppeurs,* at the entrance ramps to the beltway around Paris called the *périphérique,* especially at the Porte d'Orléans and Porte d'Italie, where the *autoroute du Sud* feeds in. Hitchhiking is illegal on the *autoroute* ramps themselves. This is essentially the only route to Lyon, Orléans, and the rest of central France (Midi) and the south of France. Hitchhiking is not ill-advised but it tends to be slow in that Europeans are rather cautious and slightly distrustful about letting strangers into their cars, or houses for that matter.

A much better solution exists in most European countries: an organized hitchhiking agency that dispatches riders with drivers for a small fee. For 70 FF *Allô-Stop* will find you a seat in a car leaving for most destinations at around the same time you want to leave. Participation in the expenses for gas and tolls depends on the driver but tends to be standard. Weekend bus trips one-way to Amsterdam for 245 FF (225 FF for those under 26) and London for 360 FF (300 FF for those under 26) are also organized by *Allô-Stop.* Round trip price for Amsterdam and London are respectively 400 FF/360 FF (under 26) and 530 FF/480 FF (under 26).

*Allô-Stop*
84, Passage Brady
75010 Paris
Tel: 42.46.00.66

## Distances From Paris

| | | | |
|---|---|---|---|
| Amsterdam: | 504 km | Madrid: | 1316 km |
| Athens: | 2918 km | Marseilles: | 776 km |
| Berlin: | 1054 km | Mexico City: | 9194 km |
| Boston: | 5531 km | Milan: | 826 km |
| Brussels: | 308 km | Miami: | 7361 km |
| Budapest: | 1257 km | Montreal: | 5525 km |
| Cairo: | 3210 km | Moscow: | 2851 km |
| Chicago: | 6664 km | Munich: | 832 km |
| Dublin: | 854 km | New York: | 5837 km |
| Edinburgh: | 867 km | Oslo: | 1337 km |
| Florence: | 878 km | Prague: | 1035 km |
| Frankfurt: | 465 km | Rio de Janeiro: | 9166 km |
| Geneva: | 402 km | Rome: | 1388 km |
| Helsinki: | 1894 km | San Francisco: | 8971 km |
| Hong Kong: | 9982 km | Stockholm: | 1549 km |
| Istanbul: | 2243 km | Tel Aviv: | 3289 km |
| Koweit: | 4403 km | Tokyo: | 9998 km |
| Lisbon: | 1817 km | Toronto: | 6015 km |
| London: | 414 km | Venice: | 838 km |
| Los Angeles: | 9107 km | Vienna: | 1227 km |
| Lyon: | 460 km | Warsaw: | 1044 km |
| | | Washington, D.C: | 6164 km |

## *Promenades* and Excursions

Within an hour of Paris and easily accessible by train there are wonderful side trips to take: Versailles, Fontainebleau, Giverny (seasonal), Chartres, Chantilly, Compiègne. The *Michelin Green Guide* for Paris and its environs is your best bet for full explanations. In Paris, the sights and monuments that eventually must be visited include: the Tour Eiffel, l'Arc de Triomphe, le Sacré Coeur, Notre-Dame, the *cimetières* Montparnasse and Père-Lachaise, la Bastille, la pyramide du Louvre, les Invalides, la Grande Arche de La Défense, la Villette, les Tuileries, l'Institut du Monde Arabe, les Halles, etc. There are organised bus tours, but cheaper and more fun are the public bus circuits recommended in *Pauper's Paris*. Also, take the public boat on the Seine which makes four stops in Paris. The *Bateaux-Mouches* and a host of other Seine boats, despite the hoards of tourists, can be a lovely way to spend a sunny afternoon or enchanting evening. The barge rides up the St. Martin canal between the Bastille and the Villette Boat Basin is a pleasant way of seeing another side of Paris.

**Bateaux-Mouches**
Pont de l'Alma *(Rive droite)*
75008 PARIS
Tel: 42.25.96.10
**Batobus**
Seine Commuter Boat
Pont de Solférino
75007 Paris
Tel: 45.56.06.35
If you're looking for a more unusual outing, try a barge trip or better yet a hot air balloon ride over Burgundy, private *châteaux* visits, ballooning bed and breakfast weekends, and special TGV ballooning packages are available from an American-run outfit:
**France Montgolfières**
76, rue Balard
75015 Paris
Tel: 40.60.11.23
Fax: 45.58.60.73

A wonderful little day trip in the summer is an outing to Joinville where the *guinguettes* are moored on the banks of the Marne, the wine flows freely and the tango dancers move to the melodies of accordian music. Eat *moules* and *frites* and imagine you're in a Renoir painting.

**Chez Gégène**
162, quai Polangis
94340 Joinville le Pont
Tel: 48.83.29.43
Paris is a great place to live and work, but you'll appreciate it more if you leave it once in a while. Paris is a particularly endearing place to return to.

But in order to return, you have to leave first, and fortunately, Paris is an excellent point of departure for international as well as domestic travel. The French travel considerably and spend sizeable portions of their savings on travel. As residents or students in Paris you'll undoubtedly want to capitalize on the fine opportunities to visit the diverse regions of France, as well as other European countries. For travel information of all sorts concerning Paris and its environs consult:

**Tourist Office of Paris**
127, av des Champs-Elysées
75008 Paris. Tel: 49.52.53.54.

**Branch offices:**
Gare du Nord: 45.26.94.82
Gare de l'Est: 46.07.17.73
Gare de Lyon: 43.43.33.24
Gare d'Austerlitz: 45.84.91.70
Gare Montparnasse: 43.22.19.19
Tour Eiffel: 45.51.22.15

## Visiting provinces
Other regions have their own information centers and travel offices in Paris. Regional information on rentals, hotels, sports facilities, *gites* (inexpensive, rural farmhouse and vacation rentals), festivals, etc. can be obtained at the following addresses:

**ALPES-DAUPHINE**
2, place André Malraux
75001 Paris
Tel: 49.53.00.50

**ALSACE**
39, av des Champs-Elysées
75008 Paris
Tel 42.56.15.9

**BRETAGNE**
17, rue de l'Arrivée
75015 Paris
Tel: 45.38.73.15

**FRANCHE-COMTÉ**
2, bd de la Madeleine
75009 Paris
Tel: 42.66.26.2

**GERS ET ARMAGNAC**
16, bd Haussmann
75009 Paris
Tel: 47.70.32.63

**HAUTES-ALPES**
4, av de l'Opéra
75002 Paris
Tel: 42.96.05.08

**LIMOUSIN**
30, rue Caumartin
75009 Paris
Tel: 40.07.04.67

**LOT-ET-GARONNE**
15-17, passage Choiseul
75002 Paris
Tel: 42.97.51.43

**LOZERE**
4, rue Hautefeuille
75006 Paris
Tel: 43.54.26.64

**NORD PAS-DE-CALAIS**
18, bd Haussmann
75009 Paris
Tel: 47.70.59.62

**PÉRIGORD**
30, rue Louis-Legrand
75002 Paris
Tel: 47.42.09.15

**POITOU-CHARENTES**
68, rue du Cherche-Midi
75006 Paris
Tel: 42.22.83.74

**PYRÉNÉES**
46, rue Berger
75001 Paris
Tel: 42.33.73.82

**SAVOIE**
31, av de l'Opéra
75001 Paris
Tel: 42.61.74.73

**TARN**
34, av de Villiers
75017 Paris
Tel: 47.63.06.26

## Going further

Additionally, Paris is well connected to numerous locations around the Mediterranean as well as points in Africa.

Reasonably priced charter flights are readily available to Corsica, Greece, Canary Islands, Spain, Turkey, Tunisia, Sicily, and others. Lastly, there has been a veritable proliferation of travel agencies specializing in cut fair tickets to North America, Australia, and Asia. Here is a partial list of travel agencies that offer inexpensive trips, charters, and flights to North American and European destinations.

Access Voyages
6, rue Pierre Lescot
75001 Paris
Tel: 42.21.46.94
Fax: 45.08.83.35

**Amérique Conseil**
10, rue St. Claude
75013 Paris
Tel: 40.27.81.17
Fax: 40.27.96.88
**Any Way**
46, rue des Lombards
75001 Paris
Tel: 40.28.00.74
**Australie Tours**
129, rue Lauriston
75016 Paris
Tel: 45.53.58.39
Fax: 47.55.95.93
**Blue Marble Travel**
(organizes bicycle trips)
2, rue Dussoubs
75002 Paris
Tel: 42.36.02.34
Fax: 42.21.14.77
**Cash & Go**
54 rue Taitbout
75009 Paris
Tel: 44.53.49.49.
Fax: 42.82.94.24
**Carrefour des Etats-Unis**
5 place André Malraux
75001 Paris
Tel: 42.60.32.51. Fax: 42.60.35.44
Minitel: 36.15 CDV
**Club Mediterranée**
Place de la Bourse
75002 Paris
Tel: 42.61.85.00. Fax: 40.20.91.44
**Forum Voyage, USA**
140, rue du Fbg St. Honoré
75008 Paris
Tel: 42.89.07.07
Fax: 42.89.26.04
Minitel: 36.14 FV

**Go Voyages**
22, rue de l'Arcade
75008 Paris
Tel: 45.66.18.18
Fax: 42.66.10.96
Minitel: 36.15 Go Voyages
**Maison des Amériques**
4, rue Chapon
75003 Paris
Tel: 42.77.50.50
**Nouvelles Frontières**
87, bd de Grenelle
75015 Paris
Tel: 42.73.10.64
Fax: 43.06.72.20
Minitel: 36.15 NF
**Usit Voyages**
12, rue Vivienne
75002 Paris
Tel: 42.96.15.88
Fax: 47.03.39.14
**Voyageur du Canada**
5, place André Malraux
75001 Paris
Tel: 40.15.06.60
Fax: 42.60.35.44
**World Class Air**
90, rue de Richelieu
75002 Paris
Tel: 42.96.20.55
Fax: 40.15.91.65

## Tourist Offices

Here is a list of official European tourist offices in Paris which provide travel information and documentation:

AUSTRIA
47, av de l'Opéra
75002 Paris
Tel: 47.42.78.57
Fax: 42.66.30.96
Minitel: 36.15 AUTRI
**BELGIUM**
21, bd des Capucines
75002 Paris
Tel: 47.42.41.18
Fax: 47.42.71.83
Minitel: 36.15 BELGIQUE
**BULGARIA**
45, av l'Opéra
75002 Paris
Tel: 42.61.69.58
**FINLAND**
13, rue Auber
75009 Paris
Tel: 42.66.40.13
Fax: 47.42.87.22
Minitel: 36.15 FINLAND
**GERMANY**
9, bd Madeleine
75001 Paris
Tel: 40.20.01.88
Fax: 40.20.17.00
Minitel: 3615 ALLEMAGNE TOUR
**GREAT BRITAIN**
19, rue Mathurins
75009 Paris

Tel: 44.51.56.20
Minitel: 36.15 BRITISH
**GREECE**
3, av de l'Opéra
75001 Paris
Tel: 42.60.65.75
Fax: 42.60.10.28
Minitel: 36.15 GRECE
**INDIA**
8, bd de la Madeleine
75009 Paris
Tel: 42.65.83.86
Fax: 47.42.19.74
**IRELAND**
33, rue Miromesnil
75008 Paris
Tel: 47.42.03.36
Fax: 47.42.01.64
Minitel: 36.15 IRLANDE
**ISRAEL**
14, rue de la Paix
75009 Paris
Tel: 42.61.01.97
Fax: 49.27.09.46
Minitel: 36.15 ISRAEL
**ITALY**
23, rue de la Paix
75002 Paris
Tel: 45.66.66.68
Fax: 42.66.03.96
**JAPAN**
4, rue Sainte Anne
75001 Paris
Tel: 42.96.07.94
**MONACO**
9, rue de la Paix
75002 Paris
Tel: 42.96.12.23
Fax: 42.61.31.52
Minitel: 36.15 MC INFO

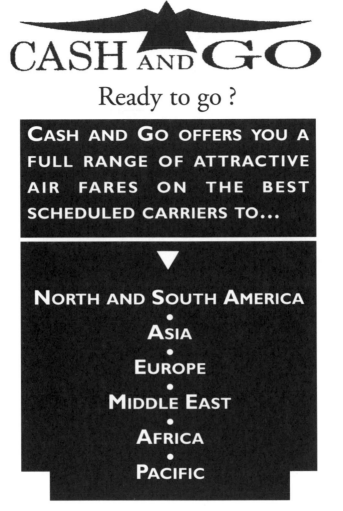

# CASH AND GO

Ready to go ?

CASH AND GO OFFERS YOU A FULL RANGE OF ATTRACTIVE AIR FARES ON THE BEST SCHEDULED CARRIERS TO...

▼

NORTH AND SOUTH AMERICA
•
ASIA
•
EUROPE
•
MIDDLE EAST
•
AFRICA
•
PACIFIC

## Service is our Business

Cash and Go
Tel: 44.53.49.49
Fax: 42.82.94.24
Minitel: 3615 CASHGO
or stop by at: 54, rue Taitbout 75009 Paris

**MOROCCO**
161, rue St. Honoré
75001 Paris
Tel: 42.60.63.50
Fax: 40.15.97.34
**NETHERLANDS**
31-33 av des Champs-Elysées
75008 Paris
Tel: 42.25.41.25
Fax: 42.25.78.85
Minitel: 36.15 HOLLANDE
**NORWAY**
88 av Charles de Gaulle
92200 Neuilly-sur-Seine
Tel: 46.41.48.00
Minitel: 36.15 OTNOR
**POLAND**
49 av de l'Opéra
75002 Paris
Tel: 47.42.07.42
Fax: 49.24.94.36
Minitel: 36.15 POLOGNE
**PORTUGAL**
7 rue Scribe
75009 Paris
Tel: 47.42.55.57
Fax: 42.66.06.89
Minitel: 36.15 LE PORTUGAL
**ROMANIA**
38, av l'Opera
75002 Paris
Tel: 47.42.75.46
**RUSSIA**
7 bd des Capucines
75002 Paris
Tel: 47.42.47.40
Fax: 47.42.87.28
**SOUTH AFRICA**
61, rue La Boétie
75008 Paris

Tel: 45.61.01.97
Fax: 45.61.01.96
**SPAIN**
43ter, av Pierre I$^{er}$ de la Serbie
75008 Paris
Tel: 47.23.65.61
Fax: 47.23.56.38
Minitel: 36.15 ESPAGNE
**SWEDEN**
11, rue Payenne
75003 Paris
Tel: 42.72.58.77
Fax: 42.72.58.49
Minitel: 36.15 OTSUE
**SWITZERLAND**
11bis, rue Scribe
75009 Paris
Tel: 47.42.45.45
Fax: 47.42.43.88
Minitel: 36.15 SUISSE
**TUNISIA**
32, av de l'Opéra
75002 Paris
Tel: 47.42.72.67
Fax: 47.42.52.68
Minitel: 36.15 TUNISINFO
**TURKEY**
102, av des Champs Elysées
75008 Paris
Tel: 45.62.78.68
**USA**
Tel: 42.60.57.15

# Legal & Administrative Matters

## General Comments

Let's start off with a positive and friendly word. Everything you've heard about French bureaucracy is true. And the French will admit that their administration is *lourde* (heavy). To complicate matters, the laws are changing as public sentiment shifts and the economy worsens. The overall situation is not getting easier for foreigners to live and work in France. Laws concerning the legal status of individuals in mixed (French-non-French) marriages, multi-national kids, political refugees, etc. are in a state of flux. Under normal circumstances seeking legal status in France can already be taxing. If you are naive and inexperienced and are planning to stay for a while, you'll be heading for an epiphany. You'll sense the weight of the State as you get sent around feeling like a complete idiot, tracking

down a succession of illogical documents for something called your *dossier*, a multi-headed animal that you never quite seem to be able to complete. The French have a love affair with papers, stamps, signatures, and procedures. And procedures are always being changed and modified and modernized, sometimes to your advantage, but often adding only new confusion. The French carry with them at all times their *carte d'identité*, which is proof of their identity. When one French student learned that Americans didn't have national identity cards, he gasped, "How does anyone know who you really are?" The French not only have national identity cards, they often require for administrative matters a *fiche d'état civil*, which is an official document proving your identity and status, as in affirming your birth, your parents' names, your marital status, etc. It has a 90 day validity, after which a new one can be created by visiting or writing to the city hall in the town or *arrondissement* of your birth. In France, your birth certificate remains at the *mairie*, which issues a temporary *extrait de naissance* as proof of your birth. Americans do not have the equivalent, but the US consulate will issue a convincing facsimile of the *état civil* to US citizens.

## Entering France

### Entering France as a Short-Term Visitor

Entering France from North America, Western Europe, and Japan is an easy procedure. EU citizens don't even need a passport, just their national identity card. North Americans and non-EU western Europeans need their passports but no longer a tourist visa to enter the country as a visitor. The US signed a reciprocal deal in 1989 commemorating the French bi-centennial, and thus lifting pre-obtained tourist visas for French citizens visiting the US, although EU Europeans still must sign an application upon arrival in the US affirming their political correctness and innocence of all major offenses, international drug smuggling, crimes against humanity, and other egregious offenses. Fair enough. For France, you just show up with a valid passport and all is dandy for a *séjour* (stay) of less than 90 *workless* days. Read on.

### Entering France as a Student, an Extended Visitor, or Resident

France's international reputation represented by those three great words: *Liberté, Egalité, Fraternité* tell only a part of the story. Anyone who has lived in France for at least a year will be able to confirm the same thing: as already stated, French bureaucracy can be enough to provoke fits of rage. You have to learn to flow with the tide, to figure out the inner logic and, when applicable, use it to the ends that you're after. Don't panic. Everything administrative in France takes time, and most things, you will learn, are *en cours* (in process), which can be one of your greatest tools of defense. There are, nonetheless, a number of practical pointers that can ease you through the administrative labyrinth.

The fact that you're not just visiting France, you're no longer a passing visitor, means your legal and administrative status in France takes on new proportions. If you have long-term intentions, you must face the reality of your choices. If you're self-sufficient and don't need to administratively establish your legal presence in France, you may choose to opt for the easy anonymity of tourist status, which means you circulate freely with only your passport. You cannot legally live or work in France. And in fact many foreigners who want to stay in France for more than three months, but do not want to start the administrative process in motion for regularizing their long-term status, simply take the train to Brussels or Geneva or London at the end of each three-month period to have their passports stamped and thus re-initiate another three-month period. This is feasible but somewhat impractical and of course not a real solution for those who think they might want to stay longer or hope to study or work legally in France. And, local border authorities have in the last few years been on alert for people trying to use this technicality to subvert the law. However, if you don't need to work and you're sure you're only staying 6-12 months, this may be your best option. Tax experts will tell you that if you opt for this round-about subterfuge, you may be legally responsible for filing a French tax return even if you didn't officially work in France. Tax implications come with physical presence in the country. This may be so, but for many individuals, this is too close a reading of the law.

If you do hope to make Paris your home, and you intend to work in France, and thus participate fully in French society, read on carefully. Your sojourn into the dark post-Kafkaesque caverns of French administration are about to begin.

All foreigners residing in France for more than three months must have either a long-term visa (*visa de long séjour*) allowing them to do so, or a *carte de séjour.* (Until the age of 18 minors may reside in France without a *carte de séjour* but they must still enter the country legally.) If you haven't heard of the infamous *carte de séjour* (extended visitors card) required of all foreign residents, be prepared for initiation. EU citizens, fortunately, have a relatively easy time obtaining their cards. For the rest of you, your greatest asset is your innocence, for if you knew what was in store when you started the haul towards legality—*regularisation*—you might not do it.

If you are not an EU citizen and you want to live, study, and or work in France, the first step is to obtain a *visa de long séjour* (one year) or a student visa from a French consulate in your home country. In that regulations, procedures, and requirements change frequently, begin the process to legally reside in France with inquiries at the French consulate nearest you. Do this before coming to France in that in many cases, procedures and visas must be obtained in your home country first, and you will be told to return home to set the process in motion. To start, here is a list of French consulates around the world. If your country or city is not present here you can obtain a complete list *(Représentation diplomatique et consulaire)* by writing to the *Ministère des affaires étrangères* information center on 34, rue La Pérouse, 75116 Paris. Tel: 40.66.60.79.

## French Consulates

**AUSTRALIA**
492 St. Kilda Road
Melbourne Vic. 3004
Tel: (61.3) 820.09.21

St. Martins Tower (20th floor)
31 Market Street
Sydney N.S.W. 2000
Tel: (61.2) 261.57.79

**AUSTRIA**
Wimpplingerst - 24/26
A-1040 Wien
Tel: (43-222) 535.62.09

**BAHRAIN**
Diplomatic Area 319
Road 1901
P.O. Box 26134
Manama
Tel: (973) 29.17.34

**BELGIUM**
4, Avenue des Arts
1040 Brussels
Tel: (32.2) 220.01.11

**CANADA**
1, Place Ville Marie
Bur. 2601
Montreal, Quebec H3B 4S3
Tel: (1.514)878.43.81

130 Bloor Street West, Suite 400
Toronto, Ontario M5S 1N5
Tel: (1.416)925.80.41

**DENMARK**
Ny östergade 3 II
1101 Copenhagen K
Tel: (45.33) 35.50.90

**FINLAND**
Itaïnen Puistotie 13
00140 Helsinki 14
Tel: (358.0) 17.15.21

**GERMANY**
**Embassy**
Kappellenweg 1 A.
5300 Bonn 2
Tel: (49.228) 36.20.31 or 36.20.36

Cecilienallee 10
40474 Düsseldorf 30
Tel: (49.221) 49.90.77/78

Ludolfstrasse 13
6000 Frankfurt-am-Main
Tel: (49.69) 79.50.960

Pöseldorferweg 32
2000 Hamburg 13
Tel: (49.40) 41.41.060

Springerstrasse 6
C. 7022 Leipzig
Tel: (49.341)515.16

Kaiserstrasse 39
BP 1927
6500 Mayence
Tel: (49.6131) 67.46.03

Möhlstrasse 5
81675 München 80
Tel: (49.89) 47.50.16/17

Johannisstrasse 2
66111 Sarrebruck
Tel: (49.681) 306.26

Richard Wagnerstrasse 53
70184 Stuttgart 1
Tel: (49.711) 23.55.66

**GREECE**
5-7, av Vassileos Constantinou
Athens 10674
Tel: (30.1) 729.01.51

**NETHERLANDS**
Vijzelgracht 2, P.O. Box 20018
1017 HA Amsterdam
Tel: (31.20) 624.83.46

**ISRAEL**
Immeuble "Migdalor"
1-3, rue Ben Yehouda
63801 Tel-Aviv
Tel: (972.3) 510.14.15

**ITALY**
Via Giulia 251
00186 Roma
Tel: (39.6) 656.52.41

1, Piazza Ognissanti
50123 Firenze
Tel: (39.6) 654.21.52

Corso Venezia, 42
20121 Milano
Tel: (39.2) 79.43.41/42/43

**JAPAN**
11-44,4 Chome, Minami Azabu
Minato-ku

Tokyo, 106
Tel: (81.3)54.20.88.00

**KUWEIT**
Villa 24, rue 13 Bloc 1
Quartier Mansouriah, PO Box 1037
13011 Safat—Kuwait City
Tel: (965) 257.10.61

**MEXICO**
Alexandre Dumas 16
11560 Mexico D.F.
Tel: (52.5)250.42.22

**MONACO**
Immeuble Monte-Carlo Sun
74, Bd d'Italie
P.O. Box 365
Monte Carlo 98006 Monaco cedex
Tel: (16) 93.50.51.67

**MOROCCO**
Rue du Prince Moulay Abdallah
B.A. 15810 Casablanca Principal
Tel: (212.2) 227.14.18 & 27.99.81

49, Avenue Allal Ben Abdallah
P.O. Box 139, Rabat
Tel: (212.7) 76.38.24

**NEW ZEALAND**
1 Willeston Street
PO Box 1695
Wellington
Tel: (64.4)72.02.00

**NORWAY**
Drammensweien, 69
0271 Oslo 2
Tel: (47.2) 44.18.20

**PORTUGAL**
123, Calçada Marquês de Abrantes
Lisboa 1200
Tel: (351.1) 60.51.31

**RUSSIA**
15, quai Moika
St. Petersbourg
Tel: (7.812)312.11.30

**SAUDI ARABIA**
Immeuble Adham Commercial
Center
Route de la Medine, BP 145
Jeddah 21411
Tel: (966.2) 651.00.82

**SOUTH AFRICA**
Carlton Centre, 35the floor
Commissioner Street
PO Box 11278
Johannesburg 2000
Tel: (27.11)331.34.60

1003 Main Tower Standard Bank
Center
8001 Cape Town
Tel: (27.21)21.56.17

**SPAIN**
Paseo de la Castellana N°79
Edificio U.A.P.
Madrid 28046
Tel: (34.1) 597.32.67

28, rue Madrid
11, Paseo de Gracia
08007 Barcelona
Tel: (34.3) 317.81.50

**SWEDEN**
Narvavagen 28
115-23 Stockholm
Tel: (46.8) 663.06.85

**SWITZERLAND**
11, rue Imbert-Galloix
P.O. Box 1200 Geneva
Tel: (41.22) 311.34.41

Muhlebachstrasse 7
P.O. Box A 112
CH 8008 Zurich
Tel: (41.1) 251.85.44

**TURKEY**
8, Istiklâl Caddesi (Taksim)
Istanbul
Tel: (90.212) 43.18.52

**UNITED KINGDOM**
58 Cromwell Road
London SW7 2DQ
Tel: (44.71)838.20.00

11 Randolph Crescent
Edinbourgh EH3 7TT
Tel: (44.33)225.79.54

**UNITED STATES**
*Embassy —Washington, DC*
4101 Reservoir Road NW
Washington, DC 20007
(202) 944-6195

*Atlanta*
Marquis Two Tower
285 Peachtree, Center Avenue
Suite 2800. Atlanta, GA  30303
Tel: (404) 522-4226/4423

*Boston*
3 Commonwealth Avenue
Boston, MA 02116
(617) 266-1680

*Chicago*
737 No. Michigan Avenue
Olympic Center, Suite 2020
Chicago, IL 60611
(312) 787-5359/60/61 and 5385

*Honolulu*
2 Waterfront Plaza, Suite 300
500 Ala Moana Boulevard
Honolulu, HI 96813
(808) 599-4458/59/60

*Houston*
2727 Allen Parkway
Suite 976
Houston, TX 77019
(713) 528-2181

*New Orleans*
Lykes Building
300 Poydras Street
Suite 2105
New Orleans, LA 70130
(504) 523-5772/73

*Los Angeles*
The Oppenheimer Tower
10990 Wilshire Blvd., Suite 300
Los Angeles, CA 90024
(310) 479-4426

*Miami*
One Biscayne Tower, Suite 1710
33rd Floor
2 South Biscayne Blvd

Miami, FL 33131
(305) 372-9798/99

*New York*
934 Fifth Avenue
New York, NY 10021
(212) 606-3688

*San Francisco*
540 Bush Street
San Francisco, CA 94108
(415) 397-4330

*San Juan*
Mercantil Plaza Blvd. Suite 720
Avenida Ponce de Leon
Stop 27-1/2, Hato Rey
San Juan, PR 00918
(809) 753-1700/01

## Visas

**Student Visa Procedures**
A student falls into a slightly different category than a foreigner coming to work or reside in France. Non-EU (European Union) students can be in France on either short or long term basis, and the visa they solicit reflects the length of their stay. Students who are nationals of one of the EU countries (with the exception of Spain and Portugal) do not require student visas, but must still follow French requirements to obtain the temporary resident permit or *carte de séjour*. Nationals from Andorra and Switzerland fall under the requirements for EU nationals. Spanish and

Portuguese students must first solicit a student visa in their home countries and then obtain the *carte de séjour*. If you hold non-EU passports but you have parents or grandparents who were born in an EU country, you might qualify for a passport from that country. Cases of this are known concerning Ireland, Italy, France and Portugal. Then your legal presence in France is virtually assured.

EU students as well as Andorran, Austrian, Finnish, Icelandic, Norwegian, Swedish, and Swiss nationals do not need a visa in their passports, but ALL students except French nationals need a *carte de séjour*.

Most students who are planning to pursue university-level studies in France are required to obtain a student visa *(not* a tourist visa) **before leaving their country of residence.** Visas are a strict requirement of French law and may be issued to you only in your country of residence. The French police refuse to "normalize" students who enter France without visas. Once you have arrived in Paris, your university may assist you in completing the necessary formalities which allow you to reside legally in France, although with immigration laws tightening up even sympathetic university administrators may not be able to help. **It is not possible to obtain a visa after arriving in France.**

**What Type of Visa is Necessary?**
Since Sept. 1989, non-EU students intending to study in France for six months have been issued a six month or 180 day student visa which enables them to stay in France without having to complete *carte de séjour* procedures. The visa is the temporary residence permit. However, it must say this *("le titulaire de ce visa est dispensé de solliciter une autorisation de séjour,"* or *"le présent visa vaut autorisation de séjour").* If these words are not found somewhere on the visa, you have to follow the *carte de séjour* routine like everybody else. The type of visa you request depends on two factors: your nationality and the amount of time you plan to spend at a university in France.

•If you will be attending a university program for just one semester, a "*visa d'étudiant pour six mois avec plusieurs entrées*" should be requested. This releases you from "*carte de séjour*" or temporary residence permit formalities as the visa is, in itself, your temporary permit. PLEASE NOTE THAT THIS VISA IS NOT GRANTED TO ALL NATIONALITIES. CONSULT YOUR LOCAL FRENCH CONSULATE FOR FURTHER INFORMATION.

•If you are applying for at least one year, a *"visa de long séjour pour études"* should be requested.

**How is the Application Made?**
The French consulate nearest you will require the following:
•A certificate of admission from the university in Paris that has accepted

you. Most consulates will not issue a visa without a certificate of admission or some proof of official contact. The visa is valid if you matriculate as a full-time student.

•A financial guarantee as specified by your consulate. In most countries, this will be a letter from your parents or your bank, signed in the presence of a public notary. It will certify that you will have an income of at least 1,800 FF per month for the duration of your stay in France. This figure is subject to change.

•A statement proving that your health insurance covers you in France. This is also required to apply for a residence permit and to register at the university you've selected (See Health).

•Authorization by a parent or guardian if you are under 18 years of age.

•Several photographs as specified by the consulate.

•Your valid passport (should not expire before the visa does).

In order to avoid unnecessary delays, it is recommended that you write or telephone the consulate, requesting exact details concerning the documents required. Since different procedures are in effect for students seeking admission to French universities, if you're attending an American program you must clearly request visa information for study in France *outside the French university system.* Since the time required to issue a visa will vary from consulate to consulate and from country to country, you are urged to apply for your student visa as far in advance of your departure date as possible.

### Extended Visitor or Resident Visa Procedures

As already stated, request precise procedures at your local French consulate. If you want to come to France but do not intend to work, but plan to write, research, work on translations, paint, play music, etc. the procedures are not very different than those for requesting a student *visa de long séjour,* except you will have to prove that you have sufficient funds available for the year on deposit. If you are applying with the intention of working—either for yourself or for a company—you'll need to satisfy other criteria. If you have been offered a job at a high rank, your company will have to show why the company needs you and not a French national and prove that you are being hired at a minimum salary of about 22000 FF per month.

### The *Carte de Séjour*

Once in France, you must proceed to obtain the *carte de séjour.* Caution: French administration is famous for its own sense of logic, the long lines, the eternal delays, the mammoth frustrations, the dragon-breathing clerk. It is always useful to request a complete list of all necessary documents before making your *demande* (request) for the *carte de séjour*. This will minimize the amount of trips to the *préfecture*, the time spent in lines, the frustrations, etc. Sometimes it's hard getting your questions answered. Often to obtain one document on your list you have to provide six additional items, some of which you have already provided on the previous lists. Welcome to administrative cyberspace! Don't try to resist or change their way of thinking. In the end, remember, you're the one who will have changed. Your sensibility to procedures and form will be forever heightened. State employees handling these requests can be impatient, short-tempered, and seemingly spiteful. They are as stuck in the system as you. Remember to be as organized and efficient and as polite and pleasant as possible, even when you really want to scream and punch. You might not get very far by charming the clerk, but you certainly will slow down the procedure if you create an adversary relationship. Nothing at all administrative can be done over the phone so don't even give it a thought. And don't ask for the clerk's name or to see the supervisor. French employees never give out their names, will rarely call over a supervisor, and will only be vexed by your attempt to overpower them. Don't get huffy; just learn how to manœuvre, and be determined to persevere to the end.

So be prepared. Aside from your battery of papers, documents, certifi-cates, photocopies, letters, receipts, statements, etc. always be equipped on your person with stamped envelopes, pictures of yourself, bank statements, electric and gas bills (EDF-GDF—the only reliable and widely accepted proof of address in France), a stack of one, two, five, and ten franc coins for photocopies, instant photos, envelopes, etc. (Make sure you keep copies of *all* bills and receipts.) And remember, in France it's the written document that matters. Everything must have an official stamp *(tampon)* on it so the more *tampons* the better your documents will be received. The written document carries more weight in France than the spoken word. This comes from a tradition of distrust. European history is filled with deception and corruption and back-stabbing. Only the legal, stamped, and approved document in conformity with law and regulation has the weight of authority. This cannot be overstated as a cultural underpinning for French administrative life.

And, don't forget, as well prepared as you think you are for your administrative procedures you will have to come back at least once or twice. "*C'est comme ça*," and it's like that for everyone. In some cases, your employer or university may have established regular inside contacts, *pistons*, as they're called in French, with the local authorities and will proceed to procure your papers for you. The system or practice of having a *piston* is inherent in the centralized bureaucracy. Don't get moralistic about this; if you have a good contact and are really in need of help call your *piston*, but don't waste a favor on a small and banal matter. In other cases, you'll be on your own. And you'll complain. But that's okay; the French complain all the time; it's built into the national charm. Soon, but not right away, you'll have the right to complain yourself.

Some contend that living legally in France is not as difficult as most foreigners tend to think. The key is learning the ropes fast. Problems only arise when people decide to remain in France after having entered as a visitor or tourist. The French are taking illegal immigration with increasing seriousness, although most cases of severe legal action being taken usually have been directed toward North Africans, black Africans, and Asians. The Bangladeshi *métro* vendors of nougat-coated peanuts are often rounded up. North Americans and Europeans are usually dealt with more leniently. But nonetheless French employees of the State, *fonctionnaires* (Federal employees—a term you will hear a lot), don't appreciate broken laws and the public at large has grown less tolerant of illegal foreigners in France; they key is being legal, or "*en règle*".

### Cartes de séjour
### for non-EU nationals

The French authorities issue two types of *cartes* to foreigners, depending on their status: a *carte de séjour temporaire* and a *carte de résident.*
*Cartes de séjours* are issued to individuals of 18 years of age and above. Parents of children below the age of 18 should obtain a *visa de long séjour* for their children before coming to France.

Most foreigners coming to France for more than three months are issued a *carte de séjour temporaire*. This card is valid for up to one year, and it may be renewed. There is no fee for the initial *carte*. Spouses of French citizens and parents of French-born children, however, are automatically entitled to the ten-year card, although the process may take a year or longer to complete.

### Carte de séjour for EU Citizens

EU nationals have the right to seek or take up residence and employment in France and to establish themselves in business and are not required to possess a work permit. On entry, if you are seeking employment, you have three months to obtain the *carte de séjour* (residence permit). A contract of employment is a prerequisite, and the residence permit is valid for the duration of the work contract if less than a year. Otherwise, the *carte* is valid for five years and is renewable automatically. Apply for your *carte de séjour* at the

(CRE) *Centre de réception des étrangers* or *Préfecture de police* in your *arrondissement* listed below. Note that general telephone inquiries in theory can be made at: 53.71.51.68. Spouses who are not nationals of EU citizens must apply for a visa (when applicable) at his or her nearest French consulate before traveling to France.

Once you've arrived in Paris, you'll have to report to one of the following centers.

If you live in the 1st, 2nd, 3rd, 4th, 5th, 6th, 7th, 13th, 14th and 15th *arrondissements* report to:
**Centre de réception des étrangers du 14ᵉ**
114-116, av du Maine
75014 Paris
*Métro* Montparnasse or Gaîté

If you live in the 11th, 12th, and 20th *arrondissements:*
**Centre de réception des étrangers du 12ᵉ**
163, rue de Charenton
75012 Paris
*Métro* Reuilly Diderot

If you live in the 8th, 9th, 10th, 16th and 17th *arrondissements:*
**Centre de réception des étrangers du 17ᵉ**
19-21, rue Truffaut
75017 Paris
*Métro* Clichy or La Fourche

**Students Applying for the *Carte de Séjour***

Students entering certain programs in Paris, like The American University of Paris, benefit from a group procedure which makes obtaining a *carte de séjour* a simpler routine. This is obviously the easiest for you. The only thing demanded of the student is that he or she: a) comply with the basic physical examination required by the French Government for the first card (not required for EU nationals) and b) pick up the card on the required date.

If you're a returning student living in Paris you may submit requests for renewals at the same office in your university.

Legally enrolling at a university in France entails showing proof that the student has entered France legally and has completed, or is in the process of completing, *carte de séjour* formalities. So, don't take these instructions too lightly. Listed below are the basic documents required by the *Préfecture de police* when soliciting a *carte de séjour.* This list is in no way definitive as *préfecture* requirements can undergo modifications and can vary from *département* to *département.*

Those arriving in France with the appropriate long-stay visa and planning to live in Paris should, within eight days of arrival, present themselves with their visa-stamped passport at the appropriate center (*centres d'accueil des étrangers*) listed here, open from 8:45 a.m. to 4:30 p.m. daily except Saturdays, Sundays and French holidays.

All non-EU students residing in Paris must report to:
**Centre de réception des étrangers du 19ᵉ**
218, rue d'Aubervilliers (first floor)
75019 Paris
*Métro*: Crimée

EU students residing in Paris should report to:
**Centre de réception des étudiants**
13, rue Miollis
75015 Paris
*Métro*: Cambronne or La Motte Picquet

For the suburbs, you'll have to report to the *Préfecture* or *Sous-Préfecture de police* in the *départment* in which you live.

At the center, the visitor takes the initial step of filling out a questionnaire and providing proof of a local address. The applicant will immediately be given a convocation to the *Préfecture de Police* for a date fixed two to twelve weeks later, depending on the number of pending applications. The convocation will cite the date, time and location of the office at which the applicant should appear. You're on your way.

**Location of the *Préfecture de Police***
The main *Préfecture de Police* for Paris is centrally located at:

*Services des Etrangers*
1, rue de Lutèce (Place Louis Lépine)
75195 PARIS RP (4e)—*Métro* Cité
Tel: 42.77.11.00 or 42.60.33.22 or 43.29.12.44 Ext. 4873
Hours: Monday through Thursday: 8:35 a.m.—5:00 p.m.
Friday: 8:45 a.m.—4:30 p.m.

Those of you living outside Paris should inquire at your local police station or at the *Mairie* (town hall) about procedures for obtaining a *carte de séjour*. As stated, in some *départements*, the *Préfectures* have delegated the authority to process such applications to local officials. In others, the individual may have to apply at the *Direction de la règlementation* of the *Préfecture* or the nearest *Sous-Préfecture*.

At certain times of the year, September and October, for example, lines can be four to five hours long. Arriving early, curiously enough, is not always the best strategy, because everyone else will have had the same idea. Some prefer going later in the afternoon (the *carte de séjour* service closes at 16h). There is no best bet. Bring a good book and a picnic, however, because even with the best strategies, lines are inevitable. All others go to their local *Préfecture* (each *arrondissement* has its own).

**Required Documents for Non-EU *Carte de Séjour* Applicants**
To apply for a *carte de séjour*, the following basic documents must be

submitted (others may be required in individual cases). Remember that laws, rules, regulations, and worse of all, interpretations of all of these are subject to change and modification at any time. Roll with the punches.

•Valid passport with the long-stay visa (with photocopy of passport title page and French visa page); for students, the *carte de séjour* will be a label stuck into the passport.
•Three recent and identical black and white or color passport-type photographs (3.5 cm x 4.5 cm);
•Proof of financial resources (applicable in all cases); the most acceptable proof of financial resources is a statement from the applicant's French bank showing account number and amount, or a letter from the French bank certifying that the applicant's account is regularly credited with a specified amount from an external source. In subsequent years, you should keep receipts of bank transactions or bank statements from your French bank to prove that you have been receiving funds regularly from abroad to support yourself.
•Medical Insurance/Medical Certificate issued by a doctor approved by the French consulate; full translation of a foreign medical insurance; or results of medical visit from the OMI (*Office des migrations internationales*). This you will get once you have done the exam at the date requested by the *Préfecture*. It is taken with you when you go to pick up your card, and thus it is extremely important that you do not miss this. If you have your own medical insurance you must be able to prove that all medical expenses, hospitalization and repatriation are included. Not only does the document have to be in French, it must be translated by an officially recognized translator or the Official Translation Office at 90, Bd. Sébastopol at *Métro* Réaumur-Sébastopol. No appointment is necessary and there is no fee for this service. The OMI exam costs 320 FF. Note that the medical exam you had for the visa requirement does not count in the *carte de séjour* requirement.
•Proof of domicile in France (i.e.: electric and gas bill—EDF/GDF—in your name or your rent contract, or a letter from the person who is housing you, a copy of their electric and gas bill and a copy of their *carte d'identité française* or *carte de séjour*;
•For students: pre-registration form (*certificat de scolarité*) or letter of admission to a school; the *Préfecture de Police* will require evidence that the student is a full-time student. Before issuing a student's *carte de séjour temporaire*, for example, the *Préfecture* expects to see a pre-registration form that clearly indicates the schedule of classes and the number of hours of study. The *Préfecture* reports that 20 hours is the minimum weekly requirement for French-language studies; prefectoral authorities are, therefore, not likely

to automatically waive the 20-hour requirement, especially if the student has already been in France for some time. Students who attend only evening classes or who are enrolled as auditors only ("*auditeurs libres*") do not qualify for student status.

•For students: proof of adequate health insurance coverage in France with specific mention of medical repatriation. This should be in French, and clearly state the exact coverage for which the student is insured.

•For an *au pair*: contract approved by French Ministry of Labor, 80, rue de la Croix Nivert, 75015 PARIS, and pre-registration form or letter of admission to a school.

•For a worker: contract with an employer;

•One self-addressed and stamped envelope (2,80 FF stamp).

•Some *Préfectures* require birth certificates, while others request originals as well as copies of all documents listed above.

### Required Documents at the *Préfecture* for EU *Carte de Séjour* Applicants

The *carte de séjour* for an EU national gives the right to work for the period indicated on the card. It is also the official residence permit and it should be carried at all times.

•Passport and three photocopies of passport

•Four passport-size photographs

•Two letters from employer called *contrat d'engagement* stating the duration of contract, qualifications, working hours.

•Proof of residence, or *attestation de domicile* (EDF-GDF bills in your name) or a bill in the owner' name and a letter from him or her attesting to your living at the said address and a photocopy of his or her *carte d'identité* or *carte de séjour*.

•*Fiche d'état civil* (obtained at your embassy upon presentation of your original, long-form birth certificate).

•One self-addressed and stamped envelope (2,80 FF stamp).

### The *récépissé* (Receipt)

If it is not possible to issue the *carte de séjour* immediately, (you can be sure it won't be), the applicant will be given a temporary authorization "*récépissé de demande de carte de séjour*" which is evidence that an application has been made for a residence permit. The applicant should carry it until he/she receives his/her *carte de séjour*. This could take several months. Keep a photocopy in a safe place; it's your only proof. Yes, it's depressing; you provide all these great looking original documents and all you get is a ratty stamped form that has been photocopied so many times that the type is blurry and crooked. Treasure it like gold and photocopy it again. The card itself, as of 1994 in more than 40 *départements*, is computerized and plasticized with several layers of laminated watermark paper and covered with a high-security imprint to prevent falsification. This new card will enable the police to track one's identity instantly and to limit the clandestine use of fake and stolen documents, which in the words of Interior Minister Charles Pasqua concerns principally 13 sensitive nations.

You must have the appropriate long-stay visa *(visa de long séjour* or *visa de plus de trois mois)* in his/her passport on arrival in France in order to be able to apply for a *carte de séjour.* The visa must be obtained from the French consulate having jurisdiction over the non-French citizen's place of residence in their country. US citizens may consult the US Embassy's information sheet: "Visa Requirements for France"). Applications for long-term validity French visas cannot be made by individuals in third countries, e.g., England or Belgium, unless the individual is a local resident of that country for one or more years.

It is not possible to come to France without a long-term visa and then apply within France for a residence permit. The French authorities will require such persons to return to their country of residence to apply for the appropriate visa.

It should be noted that the US Embassy is *not* in a position to intervene on behalf of American citizens who, knowingly or unknowingly, enter France without any visa or

without the appropriate visa, or who change their plans after their arrival in France. Such Americans will have to comply with the French Government visa requirement before they can apply for a *carte de séjour.*

If the holder of a residence permit moves, he/she must inform the police *commissariat* having jurisdiction over his/her new place of residence in France. This is especially important if the resident is in the process of renewing his/her *carte de séjour* as the *Préfecture de Police* will not approve the application unless the change of address has been recorded by the local police in the appropriate space on the card.

### Renewal of the *Carte de Séjour*

In the years that follow your first *carte de séjour,* you no longer need to solicit a new visa. The card must never expire in order to avoid having to repeat all the above steps. Renewals are simple, but you should be aware that in the case of students you have to justify your student status of the past year. You have to take the same documents listed above with the exception of the medical results. In addition, students need a *certificat d'assiduité* (letter from school or university you attended stating that you attended classes and passed your exams) and a copy and the original of the *carte de séjour.*

Renewal of the *carte de séjour* costs 224 FF (160 FF for students) payable by *timbre fiscal* (government tax stamp) that can be purchased at a Tax Office or, easier, in any *tabac* (tobacco shop). Sometimes they're out of stock, so you'll have to hunt down another. For renewal as a student, in addition to the documents listed under "Required Documents at the *Préfecture*," you will have to produce proof of the amounts of money received from your home country during the previous year.

To renew a *carte de séjour*, the holder again contacts one of the five police centers to obtain an appointment at the *Préfecture de Police*. This initial step should be taken one month before the expiration date of a *carte de séjour temporaire* (two months for *carte de résident*). If the *Préfecture* is satisfied with the explanation given by the applicant, the renewal of the *carte de séjour temporaire* is granted upon payment of the fiscal stamp.

For renewal of a *carte de séjour 'salarié'* and *'visiteur,'* the bearer must have proof that he/she has declared and paid (if appropriate) taxes *(les impôts)*. The documents must either be originals or copies certified by the tax authorities.

### Carte de résident

The *carte de résident*, created in 1984, permits its holders to live and work in France. It is valid for 10 years and is automatically renewable, and it replaces a former system of *carte de séjour* and *carte de travail*, both of which were valid for periods of one, three or ten years. According to the *Office national d'immigration*, you can request the ten-year *carte de résident* if you have a *carte de séjour temporaire* and have been present in France for at least three years. Additionally, you need to prove that you have regular and sufficient revenue to support yourself and your dependents. This proof takes the form of a work contract or promise of contract. Foreign students are considered to be a valuable asset to their country of origin and for this reason the French government tends to discourage the awarding of the ten-year card to students who want to remain in France after their studies. Spouses of French citizens and parents of French-born children have traditionally been able to obtain the ten-year card automatically. This is not easily the case any more as more jurisdiction has been placed in the hands of municipal mayors's offices. And in some cases, the process to naturalize a child may taken a year or two. Children of non-French parents who have been legally living and working in France for five or more years are entitled to request French nationality. The process is long in that the dossier passes through the judicial system and is finally approved or denied by your local *Tribunal d'instance*. With the tightening of immigration laws under Minister of the Interior Charles Pasqua, obtaining naturalization papers is increasingly difficult, but it's worth trying in that numerous Americans, for example, have finally obtained their ten-year cards only after having a child in France who has become French.

There are other legal means of residing and working in France for both short and long-term periods. Aside from the short-term possibilities, it is advised that you consult a lawyer. For all administrative questions, a new *Préfecture* Hotline telephone service with recorded messages covering everything from visa requirements to car registration has been installed. The service is exclusively in French, and although it may answer some of your questions, it does not really respond to the needs of anglophone residents. Try it if you like: *Préfecture*: Tel: 36.67.22.22. It costs 1,46 FF per minute.

## Getting Married in France

To get married in France, inquire both at your own consulate and at the *Mairie* in the *arrondissement* in which you live. At the very best, it will take a minimum of three weeks to satisfy the administrative work. If you or your partner are not *en règle* (legal) you may have difficulty marrying in France.

## Recording Births in France

The office of *Etat civil* in the hospital or clinic in which the child is born will handle the paperwork for declaring the birth of the child to the local *mairie*. You have two days, following the birth of the child to go to the *mairie* yourself and sign the *extrait d'act de naissance*, or official birth certificate. You will be given copies which you will need for the *Securité sociale*, local *crèche* and school, etc. Americans will also need this when requesting a birth certificate from the US consular services. You should also request several *fiches d'état civil* at the Mairie at the same time, in that these are very useful for all sorts of administrative tasks, like passport requests. When recording the child's name on the forms in the hospital, indicate precisely how you want the name composed. If the parents are not married, but the child is recognized by the father, the child automatically takes the father's last name. French law since the mid-80s allows the child to take the name of both parents, but many administrators and clerks refuse to apply the law. Insist if you want the child to have both names. The US consular office recognizes the child's name according to what is written on the French *extrait de naissance*. European countries differ greatly as to nationality laws and the naming of children. American law grants US citizenship to children born outside the US as long as at least one parent is a US citizen and can prove that he or she was physically present in the US for five years before the age of 18.

# Cultural Awareness

## Overview

Figuring out how French society works and how its people interact will undoubtedly take a fair amount of time. Think about your understanding of the society you live in—all those cumulative years spent learning to participate in a system with its multitude of layers of unspoken rules, codes and underlying assumptions. With an open mind you will broaden your knowledge of both French society and your own; you'll get sharper at knowing what people are saying when they're not talking. Also, don't forget that contemporary culture is like living tissue; it lives, dies, and changes, like slang. There is no way you can be up on the latest inside variations and cultural references, however, here are a few basic observations designed to help you get oriented to the physical and psychic environment. In that all things

are political in France, notes on the political arena come first.

## The Political Arena

*American political scientist and labor activist, Larry Portis, who teaches at The American University of Paris, has contributed the following comments on French politics, the unions, and the press.*

Ever since the French Revolution of 1789 France has been a place where political opinions are expressed so openly and frequently that they seem to be more a sport or amusement than anything else. Certainly the French differ from Americans, who are said to consider political debate in bad taste outside of electoral contests. French families relish gathering for Sunday dinner and shouting about their political differences. Voltaire had one of his characters in *Candide* say that "wherever you go in

France, you will find that their three chief occupations are making love, backbiting, and talking nonsense." This unflattering portrait could be attributed to a somewhat jaundiced view of what is often taken to be the superficiality of the French (and especially the Parisians), but the political intensity characterizing French culture results from the peculiar evolution of the society and governmental institutions.

It is generally known that the terms "Right" and "Left" in relation to politics stem from the seating arrangements of the first National Assembly created during the French Revolution. What is less understood is that a tradition of radical confrontation and extra governmental means of political expression is not only rooted in social relations and political practice, but remains entirely respectable to much of the population. If the state bureaucracy is considered a monolithic and virtually impregnable entity, the French do not worship their institutions, laws and constitution(s). After all, over the past two centuries they have had five republics, two imperial dictatorships, and several other experiments in constitution-building. The present regime is the Fifth Republic, founded in 1958 during the colonial war in Algeria that threatened to provoke civil war in France. Many believed then that only a strong executive power could end the rapid changes of government that plagued the par-

liamentary system of the Fourth Republic, and the new constitution was virtually tailor-made for ex-general Charles de Gaulle. Like rules in general, the French do not believe their political institutions to be divinely inspired. Consider the remark of Mr. Charles Pasqua, right-wing Minister of the Interior, responding in 1993 to news that the high court had ruled his new law regulating immigration and naturalization to be not in conformity with the Constitution. "Very well," he said, "the Constitution is defective." His comment is representative of the spirit in which the French regard politics in general. In spite of the decline of some of the anti-establishment political parties and movements (especially the Communist Party), it is not difficult for the French to entertain at least the possibility of a significant restructuring of laws and institutions.

In recent years developments in French politics have revealed both how swiftly change can come and how some very basic attitudes tend to remain constant. When François Mitterrand, leader of the Socialist Party, won the presidential election in 1981 and immediately called for legislative elections that his party handily won, few were surprised or outraged that he launched an extensive program nationalizing banks and major corporations, raising the minimum wage, and legislating progressive reform of labor laws. By 1983, he and his party reversed themselves entirely, calling for incentives to private enterprise. When, in 1986, the right-wing parties won the legislative elections and Mr. Mitterrand was obliged to appoint a conservative prime minister, the new government promptly began privatizing state corporations and even part of the public television network. Such radical changes in public policy and institutional development were seemingly taken into stride by the French people, until, that is, one constituency felt threatened. An attempt to call into question the liberal system of universal entrance into universities quickly provoked one of the mass entrances of the French people into the arena that have punctuated French history. In a series of demonstrations, French students and their supporters filled the streets and forced the government to retract their plan. At one point, there was a million demonstrators in the streets in Paris alone. More recently, in January 1994, popular reaction against a plan to increase public financing of private, primarily Catholic schools brought another million people into the streets (many of whom must have been the same ones). This readiness of the French people, whether of the right or the left, to take "direct action" means that French political life retains a special kind of volatility, the kind that produced the revolutions of 1789, 1830, 1848, 1871 and more recent developments such as those connected with June 1936 and the student riots of May 1968. The repercussions of the latter explosion are still reverberating profoundly in the changed attitudes and habits of the country. Since 1968, most of the French are less formal, more open, more conscious of living in an interdependent world where French culture is no longer the standard by which all others should be judged. For these reasons May 1968 remains a powerful point of reference. The most prominent *soixante-huitards* (sixty-eighters), the student leaders of that time, continue to be models of political action, even if they have gone in different directions. Alain Geismar has joined the power structure, Daniel Cohn-Bendit is active in the German Greens, and Jean-Pierre Duteuil continues to follow the anti-establishment, alternative politics of 1968.

But French political life also revolves around the personalities of its most prominent representatives and leaders. Mr. Mitterrand remains France's most important politician, in spite of being obliged to "cohabit" with a prime minister from the right wing coalition which won the legislative elections in 1993. Called "the Florentine," Mitterrand, some way, has a well-earned reputation for machiavellianism that has turned into a negative quality as more and more is learned about how members of the socialist governments feathered their own nests and filled party treasuries at public expense. The suicide of ex prime minister Pierre Bérégovoy (under investigation for accepting interest-free *loans*) immediately after the socialist defeat in the legislative elections of Spring 1993, and the judicial investigation of Socialist Party secretary Henri Emmanuelli (for irregular fund raising practices) did not help an already declining reputation. Indeed, if mining and sinking the Greenpeace ship, Rainbow Warrior, in 1983 was not enough, the ghastly story of how the government and health officials mis-handled the use of unsterilized blood, ignoring the risk of infection (hundreds of patients have already died of AIDS as a result) has crippled the political careers of some, especially former prime minister Laurent Fabius. In anticipation of the presidential election of Spring 1995, the socialists are something at a loss, as their only viable candidates appear to be former prime minister Michel Rocard (an old rival and antagonist of Mitterrand) and Jacques Delors, president of the Commission of the European Union, whose political credit has suffered in accordance with disillusionment about the possible consequences of European political union that he has championed.

As the Communist Party appears to be in the terminal stage of its long and largely self-inflicted decline, the political left in France is drifting at sea, vainly searching for a new identity. Fortunately, for them, the political right is scarcely more healthy. Like the left, it is split into different parties and factions. The two major parties are the RPR (Rally for the Republic) led by Jacques Chirac, mayor of Paris and perpetual candidate for the presidency, and the UDF (French Democratic Union), led by Valéry Giscard d'Estaing, a former president who is still doggedly on the comeback trail (although visibly tiring). The hopes of both of these heavy contenders are compromised by the record of Edouard Balladur, prime minister since Spring 1993, who has been remarkably successful in public opinion polls in spite of (or perhaps because of) undertaking no ambitious programs and forthrightly admitting that he has no solutions to outstanding problems (such as unemployment and declining competitiveness in agriculture and industry). A wild card in this game is Jean-Marie Le Pen, leader of the extreme right National Front, who *does* claim to have a solution to all economic and social woes: ship immigrant workers back to where they came from.

Underlying all political reality in France at the present time is one central fact: economic contraction. Ordinary working people have suffered from declining real income and rising unemployment for a good decade. France is known for its powerful labor movement, and it could be expected that these conditions have elicited the kind of militant aggressiveness that contributed to the events of 1968. It is true that labor unions remain major players on the political scene. The most powerful is the CGT (General Federation of Labor). Created in 1895, it has gone through some important changes of orientation over the past century, but has always retained its character of working-class militancy. Although linked informally to the Communist Party since the Second World War, the decline of that party and the dissolution of the USSR has rendered any such attachment irrelevant. An off-shoot of the CGT, formed in 1947, is the CGT-FO, most often called *Force Ouvrière* (Workers' Power) or simply FO. More oriented towards cooperation with employers and governments, the direction of FO still reflects the cold-war ideological preoccupation which attended its birth. The fact that its split from the CGT was facilitated by money secretly provided by the US Central Intelligence Agency has never helped its reputation, and now that the appeal to anti-communist sentiments seems baseless, FO's claim to be "apolitical" is even less convincing. Another major union is the CFDT (French Democratic Labor Federation), formed in 1964. The rising star of French unions in the aftermath of 1968, advocating autonomy from political parties and workers' self-management at the work place, its slavishness to the Socialist Party after the latter's electoral victory in 1981 has alienated masses of its members. In 1988 the CFDT even purged itself of its most militant (and critical) adherents. On the whole, French labor unions are declining in members and in their effectiveness. The de-industrialization of the economy, cumbersome union bureaucracies and political entanglements have reduced their effectiveness and appeal. But this does not mean that the time of strikes, demonstrations and other types of working-class "direct action" is over. For the past several years the most dramatic actions have been carried out by "coordinations" of employees who suspiciously avoid any type of union control over the organization of strikes and negotiations. The expertise and contacts of the unions are used, but their tendency to make secret deals with management and government has disqualified them in the eyes of the always critical French. The upshot is that continued and even intensified strike activity can be expected, something that the French tolerate as a normal course of events (although governments, especially on the right, would like to outlaw much of it, as it has been done in the US and in England). Strikes, demonstrations and marches are an integral part of life in France and any extended stay would be incomplete without attending a good-sized *manifestation.*

You may find it to be an inspiring experience. But don't forget to keep a very respectful distance between yourself and the riot police, the (in)famous CRS (Companies for Republican Security).

### The Politics of the French Press

The newspapers in France generally reflect different political tendencies. The most well-known and respected newspaper remains *Le Monde.* With little advertising content, no photos and straightforward, serious reporting and editorials, it is such an institution that students often carry it simply to enhance their image. Once moderately but critically leftist, its orientation is now centrist, close to that of the Socialist Party. Another major newspaper that has changed its perspective significantly is *Libération.* At one time, in the first years after May 1968, banning advertising from its pages, it expressed the idealism and alternative politics of the young rebels. It was, in fact, the first such paper in the world to be published daily. But since 1981 it has striven for respectability, and has succeeded in becoming a profit-making enterprise with easy access to the corridors of power. More flamboyant in format and journalistic style than *Le Monde, Libération* is also critically socialist in orientation. The major newspapers of the political right are *Le Figaro* (mornings) and *France Soir* (evenings). Both owned by publishing baron Robert Hersant, they go for the conservatively sensational and represent the traditional, bourgeois France that foreigners come for and (often) learn to detest. *Le Figaro* is thought to have the best want ads. A more politically bland, *USA Today* type of newspaper is *Le Parisien.*

In a class by itself is the hallowed *Canard Enchaîné.* A self-styled political satire paper of opinion and commentary created in 1915 which hits the news stands Wednesday mornings, its biting humor is studded with exceedingly clever puns that will baffle the uninitiated or foreign reader (or the reader without extensive knowledge of French slang). But it is no joke. It is read by everyone who wants to know what is happening behind the scenes, especially by French politicians. The only French newspaper that specializes in investigative journalism, it has informants in the highest reaches of government and industry. Sued countless times, financially dependent on its sale (no advertising), the *Canard Enchaîné* is a vestige of the French Enlightenment. It is a beacon of principled idealism in a politically murky environment. A positive, new addition to the French press scene is *Courrier International,* a weekly composite of articles, commentary, and cartoons from the world press, translated into French.

## The French Language

### The Spoken Word

Speaking the language is absolutely essential and clearly one of the most significant prerequisites for participating in the life of the society that surrounds you. And in France this is particularly true. So much of French culture and so many French attitudes are present in the language—the verbal and facial gestures, the syntax, the vocabulary, the role of dialogue. You may find it difficult at first, especially when you realize that what you say and what you mean may not be the same thing. You may feel a sense of loss in that expressing yourself in another language means losing the comfort of the personality through which you have learned to define yourself. But making the effort will pay off in ways that are incalculably enriching—learning French will open your eyes to a different way of thinking and living in the world, and enable you to share the concerns and feelings of the French.

The French in general like to talk, and the language in all its richness gains much of its melodic quality from the long and circular phrases needed to express what could be said in a word or two in English or German. This love of words and dialogue, though, is reserved for specific places and contexts...the café, the dinner table, the *table ronde*, the conference. You might notice that people don't talk very loudly in sub-

ways, buses, streets or public places. This comes from the French distinction between public and private life. Personal life is private and is handled discretely. The French will not openly talk about or be overheard discussing family matters, emotions, or money. With this silent backdrop it's not surprising that tourists seem remarkably loud and obnoxious.

On the other hand, the French can be highly vocal and overt when in the public mode—partaking in a *débat* (debate), *manifestation* (demonstration), or *grève* (strike), for example—and these are regular institutions in Parisian life. French intellectual life, which often carries over into the popular culture, tends to be characterized by obsessive analysis and verbal gymnastics. This is a phenomenon that applies mostly to political and social issues as opposed to personal or emotional ones. Very often, films shown on television are preceded and followed by a panel discussion or debate. Such was even the case with the popular Spielberg film, *ET*. Learning to speak French doesn't mean that you'll be an effective communicator right away. So much of communicating in France is learning the social coding that accompanies the language (See *Working in France* section). Whereas Anglo-Saxon culture emphasizes information, Francophone culture places much importance on form. In a way, form is everything in France; the way you speak, the way you write, the way you dress, all impact the effect you'll have on French people.

You might also note that the expressions and vocal sounds that French people make when reacting to situations are different than those you are accustomed to. The French often begin their response with a quick jerk or tilt of the head. More often a reply begins with the curious duck-like sound made by pushing a bit of air through pursed lips. This is the French equivalent of hunched shoulders. The French also utter things like, "*berk !*" for mild disgust, "*tant pis*" for what-the-heck, and a quick breathy version of "*oui*" for "yeah" or "sure" (*"Ouais"*).

## The Written Word

To repeat, attention to form is primordial. When it comes to written French there are no short cuts; you must abide by the set forms for addressing someone or some problem, even in the most banal circumstances. Salutations and forms of *politesse* (politeness) may strike you as long-winded and even hypocritical but their absence may very well be read as an insult. The best bet here is to memorize one of the following and use it to close all your letters of official or administrative nature. Otherwise, purchase a small and inexpensive book called *La correspondance pratique* by Jean-Yves Dournon (Livre de Poche) which, although a bit dated, provides models for all necessary forms of correspondence. If you violate these rules, be prepared to be judged poorly. At best you'll get away with it because you're not French and you don't know better. One of the most revealing bits of ironic, written politeness is the line used to open formal letters announcing equally positive and dreadful news: *"Monsieur/Madame, j'ai l'honneur de vous annoncer que... "* and then it can go on to say that you've just been rejected from the university program you applied to or have been assessed an additional 10000 FF in back taxes, etc. Another such example is the French use of the verb *inviter* in official and formal letters. You could be invited to present yourself to the police to be arrested for arson as easily as you could be invited to an official function in your honor. Otherwise, when someone invites you in French, it implies that the person doing the inviting will pay. If you invite someone, he or she is your guest and thus you pay. *C'est normal !* (Note that in written French there is always a space before the punctuation at the end of a sentence, which is a typographical mistake in English. Additionally, the French use commas to join sentences, which in English of course is the fatal and forbidden comma splice.)

## Forms of *Politesse*

**Some Standard *formules de politesse* for Letter Writing**

For formal letters addressed to someone you don't know well, here are three polite but neutral ways to close, roughly equivalent to the English sincerely yours, yours very truly, or yours truly. Remember that *Monsieur* can be changed to *Madame*. When you're not sure, it's best to write *Madame, Monsieur*, instead of the more traditional *Messieurs*, which is now not highly appreciated by women.

—*Je vous prie de recevoir, Monsieur, l'assurance de mes sentiments distingués.*

—*Veuillez croire, Monsieur, en l'expression de mes sentiments les meilleurs.*

In writing to a "superior" (i.e. cover letters to possible employers, etc.):

—*Veuillez agréer, Monsieur, l'expression de ma respectueuse considération.*

For friends and parents:

—*N'oublie pas d'embrasser Jeanine pour moi.*

—*Meilleurs/Affectueux souvenirs.*

—*Amicalement.*

—*Bien cordialement à vous/toi.*

—*Grosses bises !*

—*Salut !*

**Note:** the French have a high regard for the handwritten letter. In France you are judged by your handwriting (See Graphology in Working in France). Telephone skills tend to be less than proficient, spotty at best, but the way the hand constructs words on a page in even the individual with the most basic level of education is taken seriously. And the skills are surprisingly high. The handwriting you may find difficult to decipher at first, but this is no fault of the writer (See Handwriting). Even the *clochard* (beggar), now replaced by the more accurate and politically correct SDF (*sans domicile fixe)* or down and out street person in the subway station or along the street often takes the trouble to write out his or her story in chalk on the sidewalk or on a piece of cardboard. "I am 56 years old, unemployed, recently released from the hospital. Can't you help me?" Or the more direct and classic: *"J'ai faim. S.V.P."* When applying for a job or responding to a classified ad, it is always appropriate to reply with a handwritten letter, neatly formulated, beginning with your name and address, the city you're writing from and the date.

All documents and contracts require that you close with *"Lu et approuvé"* in your handwriting, followed by the date and your signature.

Handwriting is often analyzed professionally as an indicator of character and stability. Often the most inoffensive and slightest error will provoke the average French person to start all over. Don't send messy letters.

The letter plays an important role in France for a number of historic reasons. Whereas Americans often prefer the quickness and effectiveness of a telephone call, the French opt for the *courrier* (correspondence) especially in business, financial, and official matters. A letter creates a *trace* or proof of the exchange and everything done in France must be backed up by a signed piece of paper, as you will soon learn (if you haven't already). In areas where there could be legal or financial repercussions, get in the habit of sending *lettres recommandées avec accusé de réception* (registered letters with notice of receipt). This is the only real proof in France that a letter was sent and received. The French are menaces about this. The French are *méfiant* (distrustful) of the spoken word,

banking everything on the signed contract, whereas the English sense of honor relies deeply on the spoken word and the handshake; the Gentleman's Agreement. So don't be overly casual when leaving a note for even the gas company, let alone your banker or the owner of the apartment you are renting. And, yes, penmanship counts a lot.

The typewriter kind of got skipped over in the history of French communications. The French jumped from the handwritten page and carbon paper to the computer. Many young people in Paris own personal computers, whereas the typewriter has been a far rarer item in the French household. Not surprisingly, most French students cannot type and those who study at North American universities or business schools complain bitterly when required to type academic papers. French university professors never require that papers be typed.

Sample of how letters and numbers are formed in French.

## *"ça va"*

Even if it was only French 100 or some light-weight course in rudimentary *français* at night or summer school, chances have it that you probably know at least that one great French catch-all: *"Comment allez-vous ?"* or its familiar counterpart *"Comment ça va ?* (How goes it?) simplified as *ça va ?* (It goes?). But, did anyone tell you that you can't just prance down the *pâté de maisons* (block) and sputter to complete strangers, *ça va?* You just can't ask any random person how he or she is doing, the way you'd toss into the air a friendly or mechanical "Hi!" "Howdy!" "What's up?" "What's happening?" or "How ya doin?" Make eye contact and ask a passerby how he or she is doing and in most cases the person will look behind him to see if you're addressing someone else, ignore you totally, or stop in his tracks with a perplexed glaze on his face, lower lip pursed, and inquire: *On se connaît ?* Have we met? Do we know each other?

The textbooks back home often forget in their first lessons on "Greetings" to discuss language as a function of culture. And face it, understanding a culture foreign to your own is precisely what's needed to assure a rewarding and meaningful *séjour* (stay) in your new, albeit temporary, country. The more you absorb about the social relations and interactions of the French and the cultural underpinnings of French

society the more you will not only enjoy being part of Parisian life but begin to comprehend better your own culture and language. The world doesn't grow, but your conception of it does. So, if you're ignored on Day One or you let yourself be influenced by the derogatory comments of cursory travelers who lambaste the French for alleged rudeness, arrogance, or chilliness, you're missing the much larger point and only widening cultural barriers.

A good rule of thumb is to suspend all judgments for at least a month! Admittedly, there is a certain formality and pace of interchange deeply engrained in French culture (as witnessed in both verbal and written expression) that is at first going to separate the friendly and direct North American from his new environs. This is par for the course. It shouldn't be distressing; it's interesting! As North American or non-French students or newly-arrived residents in Paris, an openness to your surroundings in a French—not North American—context will be your passport to an enriching and pleasurable time.

The two of the main exchanges with the familiar *ça va* reveal several important attitudes.

—*Ça va ?* the question, literally meaning How goes it?, is often answered with itself, *Ça va!* meaning "It goes." This makes for easy language learning, but what in fact does it mean? Everything lies in the intonation of the response. *Ça va* could reflect a great enthusiasm for life, a pang of desperate depression, or a plain moment of daily mediocrity. The nuances abound. So learn to listen for them and use them yourself. These are rich words.

—*Ça va ?* or the formal *Comment allez-vous ?* are often answered directly with the question *Et vous ?* (And you?)

The first few times you get involved in this interchange you are liable to get annoyed. Don't ignore me, that's not an answer, you'll want to complain. The repetition of the answer for the question simply demonstrates the French love of form. It's the asking of the question that counts, not the answer. There is nothing I can do if you aren't doing well; the best I can do is to ask you how you're doing. Soon, you'll see that this little tidbit of dialog is really very adorable and convenient.

## Franglais

A note on *franglais*. A 1994 law was passed limiting the use of English in the French language. In the 80s, there was much to do about finding French equivalent nouns for English (mostly American and Japanese) technology that invaded the international marketplace. A prime example was *le baladeur* for the Walkman. The French care deeply about their language and linguistic influence in the world. Former Culture Minister Jack Lang often invited leading world intellectuals to Paris to discuss in French the state of international culture. Current Minister Jacques Toubon, whose ministry now includes the word *francophonie* in its title, is battling to preserve the language with legislation. Nonetheless, the following words are commonly heard in everyday French life. And there are lots more.

(Remember to pronounce these as if they were French words.)

### Commonly Used English in French— *"Franglais"*

| | |
|---|---|
| best | jogging |
| best seller | label |
| brain storming | listing |
| cash | loft |
| check up | mailing |
| chewing gum | marketing |
| copyright | okay |
| design | package |
| designer | pickpocket |
| ferry | sandwich |
| gadget | shopping |
| interview | stand by |

## Greetings

### Les bises

When greeting someone you know, the French shake hands and/or give a quick succession of impersonal kisses on alternating cheeks called *les bises*. There are lots of nuances here that only experience can sort out, but here are a few. Some people give two kisses, some three, and others four. If there are six people in the room and you give four *bises* each, that calls for a lot of kissing. Remember this is just a form of saying *bonjour*. What's interesting to note here is that the French are used to and comfortable with close personal contact. They are not bothered by human proximity or touching. They don't require the same distance Anglo-Saxons insist upon when talking. So get used to *les bises*. Even French people have cute little moments when two people are unsure if it'll be two, three, or four *bises*. Two is the most common, four is more classical; three is for those who want to be a bit different without abandoning tradition. People from the south of France and the younger generation tend to kiss more. *Les bises* are usually for men and women or women and women, but good male friends *font les bises* also. Start on the left cheek and don't really kiss, just touch cheeks and steer your lips inwards.

Handshakes are required particularly when men greet each other equally for the first time or the zillionth time. When you arrive at work, you shake your co-workers' hand and say *bonjour*. It may seem highly repetitious, but it's a very pleasant way for people to acknowledge each other. Similarly, the handshake and *les bises* are repeated when leaving. Every time you enter and exit a room you greet everyone. Failure to say hello and good-bye is perceived as rude.

## Salutations

What French people say to each other when they leave depends on how they leave and when they expect to see the other person next. Here is a brief list of possibilities and what they mean.

*à tout à l'heure:* this common phrase is a gem in that it can refer to a moment in time slightly in the future, usually in an hour or two or later in the day, but it can also refer to a moment in the near past.

*salut:* this is a very familiar and friendly way of saying hello or good-bye, said between good friends or people whom you can tell instantly are not stuck up on old forms of protocol.

*au revoir:* your standard good-bye. Never wrong.

*à tout de suite:* this means that you'll see the person in a matter of seconds or minutes, as in I'll call you right back. It implies relative immediacy. While talking about time, it should be noted that a French person telling another person to wait a moment might say, Wait, I won't be but *cinq minutes*. French people take this to be an acceptably short reference to the time they must wait even though the wait may not really be as long as five minutes; Anglo-Saxons indicating a short wait tend to exaggerate in the opposite direction, I won't be a minute, or Can you hold for five seconds? Five minutes sounds too long.

*ciao:* This international phrase of dated Italian chicdom is still widely used everywhere. The French say *ciao* to people they know well and rather well.

*à plus tard:* See you later. This simply means that you plan to see the other person again that day or night.

*à demain:* See you tomorrow.

*à la prochaine:* This means that you have no real plans, but you want to be positive and friendly, and thus say Till the next time we see each other.

*bonsoir:* Good evening is said when you greet someone or say good-bye. Polite from late afternoon on.

*bonne soirée:* A friendlier version used when leaving someone in the late afternoon or early evening, wishing him or her a good continuation of the evening and night.

*bonne nuit:* This is said before going to sleep. Good night.

*bonne continuation:* This particularly French expression imparts your wish that the other person carries on whatever he or she is presently doing with continued pleasure and success.

*bon courage:* This is a salutation indicating that you are supportive of the task the other person has in front of him or her, be it something specific or just the act of continuing life.

*bonne chance:* A rather dramatic form of leaving someone while communicating your wishes for his or her general or specific success.

*bonne journée:* A generalized, drippy but good-hearted equivalent of Have a nice day.

*bon après-midi:* A more time-specific way of saying have a nice day.

*bonne fin d'après-midi:* This one is applicable when most of the afternoon is already over and you want to wish someone well for the part of the afternoon that's left.

*dors bien:* Sleep well. A cozy good night for kids, loved ones, and close friends.

*beaux rêves:* Sweet dreams.

*adieu:* Classic good-bye for good. Not used very often anymore, except for emphasis, when you're really leaving and not coming back or wish the other person takes flight.

## Going Out/Dating/Dining...

The French almost always organize their social lives around a meal. This is true also for a lot of professional and commercial activities. So usually count on a long and languorous dinner if you get asked out by a French person. If you're doing the asking, you should probably count on a meal too, although your guest might be interested in or impressed by a meal indigenous to your culture. And remember a meal means a meal. You must be conscious of the form of the French meal. In other words, a first dish (even if it's a simple salad or a plate of healthy radishes with salt and bread and butter —yes, common), a main course, bread, cheese, salad, dessert, and coffee. Younger people are less rigid but still most expect the meal to take this form. Often the cheese course gets skipped but you should be prepared to offer one. And not just a block of Swiss or a wheel of Camembert; a nice selection of ripe cheeses is always appreciated, even by less traditional and younger folks. Also offer to change dishes from course to course even though more familiar guests are likely to accept the salad on the same plate. It's good to know these things.

It's very common to meet someone at a café at 20h or 20h30, have an *apéritif* (a *kir* or a glass of wine) and then proceed to dinner somewhere. A *kir royal* is delicious, but it's made with champagne and it'll put you back at least 30 FF). Learn by heart the names of a few cafés that you like and that are convenient, so you'll be able to suggest a meeting point. This writer uses the Café Beaubourg next to the Pompidou Center, the Café Danton at *Métro* Odéon, and Café de l'Industrie near the Bastille. Find your own.

Remember that usually, even among young people, the person who does the inviting also pays for the dinner. For the French this is highly normal. Going "Dutch" is foreign. Often the guest will offer to pay the next time. *Je t'invite la prochaine fois*. You will almost never see French people dividing up a bill at the table. Sometimes they'll fight over who will pay, each wanting to pay, but the idea of determining who ordered what and the "did you have wine?" kind of thing is alien, and even distasteful. So be forewarned. Money still has a vulgar connotation.

If you're invited to someone's house in the evening, it's almost always going to be for dinner, unless it has been clearly stated otherwise. It's always appropriate to bring something, usually a good bottle of wine—never a *vin de table* (table wine) or inexpensive unknown wine (see Wine). A well-wrapped bouquet of flowers, not the plain ones sold in the *métro*, is always appreciated. But don't show up empty-handed. As the economy weakens and people are more conscious of their budgets, more and more groups of friends are adopting the collective dinner or pot luck concept, but if you're not sure of the folks don't suggest such a thing to start. Dress slightly better than you think is appropriate. The French, even young people and students, tend to dress well when going out socially. Only in the last five years or so have people dared go out in the streets in sweatpants and sweatshirts, even for food shopping, etc.

## Sexuality

It's always very difficult and dangerous to generalize about how people think and act. In the area of sex this is particularly so, but a few comments might be useful. First, Parisians like to talk about sex. They love to verbalize fantasies, exhibitionist yearnings, private desires, etc. Sex is in the air. Sex is even in the Renault car commercials on TV. The popularity of sex as a subject doesn't necessarily translate into the act. It would be absurd to say, and hard to verify, that the French make love more than any other people, although they like to think they do. In fact, they're more driven by the pleasure of the act of seduction than by the results. As one French professor at The American University commented "the French are caught in the nostalgia of the *coup de foudre*" (the crush). The film *La Discrète* captures perfectly the French obsession to seduce and dominate the other for no other purpose than to possess the soul of the other, to dominate verbally. The supreme art is the *affrontement verbal*. If you find yourself impatient with the relationships in contemporary French films, maybe this explains it.

Young French women, although not prudish, can often be highly sentimental. Women are more jealous of other women than in Anglo-Saxon culture. There are less, close female friendships, less of a notion of "the girls" going out together. (Careful not to use the word female, *femelle* in French; it refers exclusively to animals. Use *femme* as a noun and *féminin* as the adjective.) The French woman, protects with jealousy her "couple." The men, although not extremely macho, tend to embrace a fair amount of Latin attitudes. The French concept of flirting—with the intention of "picking up" someone, is called *draguer* (to drag). This is actual-ly closer to "chatting up" than "picking up." It has a million variations and nuances and can be either flattering or annoying. Paris is the northern edge of the Latin spirit. Male attitudes in general aren't as obviously macho as in Spain or Italy, but there are still attitudes here that might seem sexist to you. (73% of French married men, a recent survey found, have mistresses or extra-marital affairs, whereas 38% of married women have extra-marital lovers. What proportion of the 73% are seeing the 38% has never been established.)

On the whole, it is fair to say, in any case, that the French are less inhibited or up-tight and have less hang-ups about sex, nudity and human functions than Anglo-Saxons, for instance. Some French men, though, have pre-conceived notions about North American women, especially Californians, in terms of accessibility, "openness," "wildness." These can be reinforced unknowingly by the fact that North Americans do tend to be more publicly expressive and open; however, in terms of attitudes, they are still more puritanical than the French. On the whole, you will see a general lack of puritanical attitudes. The French are quite comfortable with nudity and all that concerns the human body. The same ad in a London subway station with a clothed woman would show her topless in Paris. Topless advertising is not considered sexist by either women or men. *C'est beau* or *c'est normal*.

Toplessness isn't even really considered nudity. In some boutiques, you may see women try on blouses without stepping into a changing room or change from their swimsuit into street clothes on the beach. It is hard to watch French television for more than ten minutes without spotting a pair or two of bare breasts. No French shampoo commercial would be complete without at least a passing shot of a lovely women lathering up in the shower and then conclude with a *beau mec* later enjoying her luscious hair. Aesthetics and sensuality, the textual surface of things, appeal to the French mentality.

Porno doesn't come with the sick or dangerous edge that characterizes hard core porn in American cities, and the French are on the whole not too judgmental about its existence. There are no Tipper Gore's trying to clean up the streets and airwaves in Paris. And the line between eroticism and pornography isn't so clear in France, with no one in particular interested in sharpening the line of distinction. If anything, women, instead of battling against a male-dominated industry that has traditionally objectified women, have responded with their own programming. Several *magazines de cul* (skin mags) for women have appeared, including *Bagatelle*. And TV sex star, Amanda Lear, hosts on prime time (22h30) on TF1 the show *Méfiez-Vous des Blondes*, in which between

highly erotic strip tease dances, she interviews stars on their sexual fantasies. The subject is purely sex.

The French don't judge public officials by their private lives, and view sex scandals (like the one which ruined Gary Hart's political career) as silly and typically American in their puritan values. The talk of Bill Clinton's extra-marital relations only elevates the average French person's regard for him.

**Safe Sex**

The movement for safe sex in France didn't get much further at first than the sensuous television ads for the use of condoms. The French approach was not to scare the public with AIDS (SIDA) but to convey the positive message that sex with condoms is beautiful and exciting, and thus an advantage. The ads themselves are pretty exciting. For Valentines Day, Yves St. Laurent launched a designer condom, associating condoms with lovers. The AIDS situation in France is much like in any western country today, although perhaps young French people remain a bit more cavalier than elsewhere. Free public health centers provide confidential *dépistages* (AIDS tests) and accurate information (see Health). Generally, there are less stigmas regarding health, sexuality, and illness in France than in Anglo-Saxon culture, but on the whole the situation isn't all that different. In 1993 and 1994 a new public health campaign to encourage young people to use condoms was put in place with the introduction of state subsidized condoms available at all pharmacies for 1 *franc* each, a scheme called *tarif jeunes* or "youth price." The *métros* and TV were smattered with pictures of condoms and one franc coins. Condom sales have increased dramatically and the pharmacy at Charles de Gaulle airport has limited sales to two per person to discourage travelers from hoarding at the low prices.

Note that the *tarif jeunes* model is your basic condom distributed with clear, no-nonsense instructions. More affluent or demanding users prefer other brands which run from 30F-60F for twelve. The French consumer report magazine, *50 Millions de Consommateurs*, recently ran a survey of all condoms on the French market with the Japanese made Manix gaining top kudos. Even six year-old school kids know what condoms are, that they prevent unwanted babies, and prevent the spreading of AIDS. And there is absolutely no stigma at all in France in going for a free AIDS test, and no impact whatsoever on your health insurance premiums as there is in the States.

The gay and lesbian communities in Paris, although more open and public now than ten years ago, are still somewhat discreet. On the rue Vieille-du-Temple in the Marais a number of busy, gay night spots and bookstores can be found. The gay community has a Paris magazine called *Gai Pied Hebdo*, 45 rue Sedaine, 75011 PARIS, Tel: 43.57.52.05 (which also has an *SOS Ecoute Gaie* phone line, Tel: 48.06.19.11). There are also several Minitel services catering to the gay community. *Fréquence Gaie* (FG) on 98.2 FM is a 24-hour gay radio station, the only one in Europe, and it hosts the only rave pre-party show featuring guest mixers live in the studio. The Tuileries gardens at night have become known as the *grand lieu de pick-up* for their *rencontre éclair* or flash meetings, whereby homosexual men can find quick and anonymous sex lasting five to fifteen minutes. The same is true along the quay of the Seine at night as well as in the Square Henri IV. Gay prostitution has found a home along the rue St. Anne and around Trocadéro. The highly acclaimed French film *Nuit Fauves* by Cyril Collard (who died of AIDS shortly after the film's success), heightened the gay-AIDS (SIDA) sensibility in France.

The rue Saint Denis and parts of Pigalle have traditionally been the main turf for heterosexual prostitution in Paris. One recalls Henry Miller, *n'est ce pas*? There has always been a romanticizing element to French prostitution, dating back to the naturalism of Zola. There's almost a tradition of prostitutes that carries on, although the scene has clearly lost much of those associations, and the streets have become more dangerous with the increased presence of drugs and AIDS. Women, still stand out by their doors openly and, for the most part, unharassed day and night. Around 16h it's interesting to observe the undisturbed mixture of prostitutes coming out to work and school kids returning from school. This is indicative of a larger tolerance. Occasionally, there will be police round-ups and the prostitutes are each fined 2000 FF, which is about the equivalent of one night's work. Other areas of dense prostitution have traditionally included the Bois de Boulogne, where prostitutes and dazzling Brazilian transvestites line the roadways peddling their wares to passing motorists, as well as all the major boulevards near the *portes de Paris*. Due to the AIDS situation, the Bois has now been shut down to vehicular traffic at night. Prostitution is not considered an illegal activity but soliciting business in an aggressive manner is, so you won't see pimps doing this for the girls. The area around *Métros* Blanche and Clichy are also filled with prostitutes and pornography, with the rue Fontaine being noted for its transvestites. The *portes de Paris* around the edges of the city and the *Axes Rouges* or major arteries leading into town are usually spotted at night with women for hire. Cars stop to negotiate the deal and the women often get in and drive away although will systemati-

cally refuse cars with more passengers than the driver.

As for other possibilities, in the spirit of great tolerance, or kinky perversion, depending on how you view it, couple swapping occurs at the Place Dauphine, and a number of *boîtes échangistes* (swapping clubs) can be found in the first *arrondissement*. Le Triangle specializes in triples as its name suggests and the entry charge is around 150 FF. One spectator reports that there are alcoves for semi-discrete meetings and a boxing ring in the center. Another is called Adam's Club. Additionally, all sorts of sexual-oriented programming is found on the Minitel, but as one social observer remarked, "there is a deficiency in sexual communication in France today; the screen has replaced the body."

All this adds up to a culture attitudinally very different from perhaps what you're used to.

## Drinking

The legal drinking age is 16 years of age. But there is essentially no enforcement of this law. You'll rarely get "carded" or turned away in a café, bar or liquor store. You can buy whiskey along with your daily groceries in supermarkets, local shops, and even gas stations. As a positive consequence, public drunkenness by rowdy youths is not very prevalent. When people go out to a concert or club, they don't usually end up drunk as is true in an English, American, or Australian context; they listen to the music or talk. The need to "let loose" or partake in anti-social behavior is not as prevalent in France, mostly in that the culture is socially less repressed in general. It has been estimated that the average French person over 20 years old consumes an average of 53 grams (1.87 ounces) of pure alcohol per day, making him a participant in an impressive percentage: the French remain the world's heaviest consumers of alcohol per capita after the Luxembourgeois. Wine is still served with both lunch and dinner in many families, but the meal is no longer considered incomplete without it (see Wine). Alcoholism in France is responsible for 17,000 deaths a year, caused more by cheap red wine than hard alcohol, and it is a phenomenon which is vastly more common in rural and slum areas.

## Smoking

A very large portion of French society smokes cigarettes. Anti-smoking consciousness is changing but very slowly. In 1992 a bill limiting smoking in public places was passed which polarized French society to some extent: the smokers vs. the non-smokers. All cafés and restaurants must provide clearly marked sections or areas for non-smokers. Most cafés have complied by assigning the worst areas and back tables for this purpose. Some cafés have simply placed signs in the window announcing that theirs is a smokers café, thereby discouraging the rare non-smoker from ever entering. Smoking, like drinking, eating or having sex, is integral to the French belief in the eminence of pleasure, *plaisir;* the act of pleasing and being pleased is essential to the French soul, and for many this still includes smoking.

Cigarettes can only be purchased in a *tabac.* They are not available in drug stores, gas stations or department stores. Some cafés sell cigarettes as a service to their customers. They will cost about 20 FF a pack in the cafés, 12-14 francs in the *tabacs.*

If you are a non-smoker, as many of you undoubtedly are, be prepared for a lot of smoke and an overall indifference to the rights of non-smokers. If the smoke has a pungent, unfamiliar odor this is because in France hard-core smokers often consume the classic, blue packed and filterless Gauloises or Gitanes, made of *blonde,* untoasted tobacco. Also, a number of people roll their own cigarettes. It's cheaper.

Smoking is now forbidden in the *métro* too, although this has yet to be fully enforced. Due to the outlawing of cigarette advertising in French publications, television, and cinemas, tobacco companies have launched huge and somewhat perverse campaigns to keep their names at the fore of smokers' lips. Camel has a travel agency. Marlboro offers its own line of clothes. Lucky Strikes, the naughtiest of the lot, plays on the reverse attractiveness of the banned, using the interdiction *le tabac nuit à la santé* (tobacco consumption is harmful to your health) as a marketing lure.

## Drugs

Drug possession is a serious offense in France, and laws are particularly harsh on foreigners. Drug use isn't nearly as much of a social problem, though, as it is in the United States, England, Germany, or Holland. Nor has it resulted in as desperate and wide spread urban violence as is true of elsewhere. Nonetheless, the area around *Métro* Stalingrad has become the most drug exposed area in Paris with the recent arrival of crack. Crack dealers and users are concentrated in that district as are undercover police agents. A majority of crack and hard drug users and addicts are *antillais* and African and the correlation between drugs, crime, and illegal immigration is an unfortunate one in that the police, special police (RG), and the Ministry of the Interior (currently run by right winger, Charles Pasqua) use drug control as a prime pretext for cracking down on foreigners.

Heroin use is relatively limited with some 30,000 addicts estimated in Paris. Although French drug laws are nowhere as lenient as in Holland, there was, until recently, a cinema in Paris where it was understood that marijuana smokers would not be bothered. And late at night in the *métro* as well as in certain bars and clubs a whiff or two of the popular hash and tobacco mixture may come your way. But *attention!* If you want to remain in France without problems, think twice before breaking the law. It is strictly ill-advised to buy drugs from anyone on the street. Crossing international borders with drugs is of course particularly unwise, especially traveling from any island of southern latitude or returning from Amsterdam, where charter buses are often searched with the aid of police dogs.

Even at parties, smoking hash—marijuana is nearly impossible to find—can be met with disapproval. Cocaine use is not nearly as widespread as in North America and is the drug of snobbery and trendiness, often found in the fast lane parties of journalists, models, advertising execs, etc. It's the "baba cool" sign of superficial "in"ness.

In general, French youths seem to feel less pressured to spend time, energy and money on socially rebellious activities and habits.

## Parties

Even among young people, parties are rarely given without a specific occasion to celebrate. A party can be called *une fête, une soirée* or *une boum*. To party can be referred to as *faire la bringue*. A *fête* is usually a celebration like a birthday or graduation. A *soirée* is a civilized evening party with not necessarily a lot of people. *Une boum* tends to be larger and louder, and usually reserved for the high school crowd. Every city, however, has its limits for noise and rowdiness: for weeknights, Parisian law requires that all noise stop after 22h (1h for weekends), but once or twice a year, weekend festivities are allowed to go all night—as long as you inform the local police station and the neighbors as far in advance as possible. On weekdays, the police will come banging on the door if you exceed the 22h code. A surefire strategy to avoid problems with the neighbors is to start the party in the early afternoon, and have it wind down of course before 22h. Not very practical, admittedly. In any case, be very sensitive about loud noises, blasting stereos, etc. in public places in Paris; rowdy partying is not part of the French version of decadence and hedonism. They have their own which you'll have to discover on your own. Even be careful the way you shut doors, talk in the stairwells of apartment buildings, and walk on parquet floors. These will lead to complaints. Don't get off to a bad start with neighbors; it's hard to win back good relations.

As is true all over, some sectors of Paris society have recently experien-

ced a return to the adolescent habits and aesthetics of the formerly privileged class. *Rallies* or debutante *piplette* coming-out parties of the BCBG crowd *(bon chic bon genre)* or Yuppies are being organized by parents in the bourgeois 16th *arrondissement.*

## *Chez* Jim Haynes

Of the Americans in Paris few are as colorful, free-spirited, and community-minded as Jim Haynes, teacher, publisher of Handshake Editions, spiritual guru of limitless love and spiritual networking. In the Sixties, with friend Germaine Greer, Jim founded *Suck Magazine*, a sexual revolution paper. Every Sunday night in his atelier more than 50 friends, visitors, and new guests take part in (for a nominal fee) a wonderful blue-plate dinner with unlimited wine and beer. Proceeds go to buy food shipments for people in oppressed places. Jim's 14 volume address book tells all, as does his autobiography, *Thanks for Coming* (Faber & Faber). Reservations for Sunday are made by phone on Saturday afternoon. Jim Haynes Atelier A2, 83, rue de la Tombe-Issoire 75014 Paris. Tel: 43.27.17.67.

## Common Abbreviations

Note that these are spoken and readily understood in daily Parisian conversation. Also note that for some odd reason the French adore making-up abbreviations.

| Abbv. | French | Explanation |
|---|---|---|
| A/R | *aller-retour* | round trip |
| BD | *bande dessinée* | comic strip books |
| BHV | *Bazar de l'Hôtel de Ville* | major department store |
| BN | *Bibliothèque Nationale* | national library |
| BNP | *Banque Nationale de Paris* | large bank chain |
| BP | *boîte postale* | post office box |
| CB | *carte bleue* | bank payment card associated with VISA |
| CNRS | *Centre national de la recherche scientifique* | national institute for research |
| CP | *cours préparatoire* | kindergarten |
| CCP | *compte chèque postal* | checking account offered by the post office |
| CV | *curriculum vitae* | resumé |
| DEA | *Diplôme d'études approfondies* | first diploma in doctoral program |
| EDF | *Electricité de France* | electric company |
| FISC | *la fiscalité (les impôts)* | tax collectors |
| FN | *Front National* | extreme right political party |
| GDF | *Gaz de France* | gas company |
| HLM | *Habitation à loyer modéré* | subsidized housing |
| HT | *Hors taxe* | before sales tax |
| PC | *petite ceinture* | ring road around Paris inside of the *Périphérique* |
| PD | *pédéraste* | pejorative term for homosexual |
| PDG | *président-directeur général* | equivalent to CEO |
| PQ | *papier cul* | toilet paper |
| PTT | *Poste Téléphone Télégraph* | former name of post office |
| PV | *procès verbal* | parking ticket or fine |
| RATP | *Régie autonome des transports parisiens* | subway authority |
| RC | *rez-de-chaussée* | ground floor |
| RER | *Reseau express régional* | commuter train system |
| RF | *République française* | the French republic |
| SDF | *Sans domicile fixe* | the homeless |
| SECU | *Sécurité Sociale* | Social Secuity system |
| SMIC | *salaire minimum interprofessionnel de croissance* | minimum wage |
| SNCF | *Société nationale des chemins de fer français* | the national train system |
| TGV | *train à grande vitesse* | ultra fast train |
| TP | *trésor public* | national treasury |
| TTC | *toutes taxes comprises* | sales tax included |
| TVA | *taxe sur valeur ajoutée* | value added tax/sales tax |
| UV | *unité de valeur* | course credit |

## Common Street Names

### 50 of the Most Common Street Names & Who These People Were

(From the *Dictionnaire des noms de rues*, by Bernard Stéphane, Editions Mengès, 1986.)

Note that in Paris, streets are often named after writers and artists and other cultural and military figures. Additionally, the selection of street names reveals a lot about the municipal government of the town, with left wing towns, for example, honoring leaders from the socialist world, such as Lenin and Marx and national socialist heroes. Even the selection of great names from the French Revolution reveals the political slant of the local government. Salvador Allende and Nelson Mandela are favorite names in the most politically progressive towns with communist governments, such as Bobigny, Montreuil, and Malakoff.

**Albert Camus**, Algerian-born French writer, died in 1960, best known for *The Stranger* (1942) and *The Plague* (1947). Won the Nobel Prize in 1957.

**Alexandre Dumas** (1803-1870), French writer and playwright, author of *The Three Musketeers, La Dame de Montsoreau* and *La Dame aux Camélias*.

**André Malraux** (1901-1976), writer and statesman born and died in Paris. Best known for his work *Man's Fate*. "The only domain where the divine is visible is in art," he said.

**François Arago** (1786-1853), Noted thinker and scientist, mathematician and astronomer, minister of war in 1848, contributed to the abolition of slavery in the colonies.

**Austerlitz**, Austrian town made famous for Napoleon's 1905 victory over the Austro-Russians in what was known as the Battle of the Three Emperors.

**Barbès** (1807-1870), politician who attempted to form an insurrection in 1839. Condemned to death, saved at the request of Victor Hugo, he was sentenced to life imprisonment, pardoned by Napoleon III.

**Balzac** (1799-1850) Failed as a printer and publisher, he turned to literature where he made his name for such works as *La Cousine Bette, Le Père Goriot,* and *Vautrin*.

**Beaumarchais** (1732-1799) Writer, explorer, and libertine, best known for *The Barber of Seville* and *The Marriage of Figaro*.

**Bonaparte** (1769-1821), Napoleon Bonaparte, born in Corsica. Celebrated military leader, defeated the English in Egypt and successfully executed a *coup d'état* of the 18th Brumaire (1799). Defeated at Waterloo in 1815. Drafted the legendary Civil Code known as the Napoleonic Code.

**Champs-Elysées**, in mythology, these fields were a part of heaven where heroes and virtuous men meet after their death. One of the most famous streets in the world, the Champs-Elysées took its name after the Revolution.

**Danton** (1759-1794), The king's lawyer, Danton played a key role in the fall of royalty in France. Known for his line "To defeat the enemies, we need audacity..." Robespierre had him arrested and put to death in 1794.

**Descartes** (1596-1650), philosopher, who

believed intuition and deduction were the only methodologies proper to philosophy.

**Diderot** (1713-1784), philosopher, mathematician and writer. Worked extensively with Alembert on the famous *L'Encyclopedia* of the 18th century.

**Drouot** (1774-1847), well-known military figure in Napoleon's day, nicknamed *"Le sage* (wise one) *de la grande armée."*

**Ernest Renan** (1823-1892), having started out as a seminarian, Renan went on to write and philosophize. Principle works include *"La vie de Jésus,"* and *"Ma Soeur Henriette."*

**Etienne Marcel** (1310-1358), provost of the shopkeepers in Paris from 1355, Etienne Marcel was to become an important popular leader of Paris after the English victory at Poitiers in 1356 but soon displayed an unfortunate liking for dictatorship which finally led to his bloody assassination.

**Charles de Gaulle** (1890-1970), a General and statesman, retreated to London in 1940 to take charge of the Free French Army and participated in the invasion of France in 1944. After the war, he became prime minister of France and returned to power in 1958 when France was in danger of invasion by the French *colons,* and by his authority quelled the rebellion and brought the Algerian War to an end. Elected president in 1959. He reconstituted the French presidency as the top executive position and in 1968 successfully put down the rising of students and trade unions which brought the country to a halt in May and June.

**Félix Faure** (1841-1899), became president of the French Republic after holding various other ministerial offices. Contributed to good Franco-Russian relations.

**Gabriel Péri** (1902-1941), journalist and communist deputy who was shot by the Germans during the war.

**Gambetta,** (1838-1882) Barrister, made a closing speech in court against the Empire which won him widespread fame. Went on to become a radical deputy. It was he who called for the deposition of the emperor on 4 September 1870. After the fall of Paris, he was elected and was leader of the radicals, founding the newspaper, "La République Française."

**Gay-Lussac** (1778-1850), physicist and chemist who went up 6636 meters in a balloon to collect air so he could to analyze it. Discoverer of boron and flouboric acid.

**Général Leclerc** (1902-1947), sided with General de Gaulle at the outbreak of war and among other distinctions was the first to enter Paris after the invasion at Normandy, at the head of his famous 11th division.

**Gustave Eiffel** (1832-1923), engineer born in Dijon Built several important viaducts around France and in 1885 designed the inner structure of the Statue of Liberty in New York harbor, but of course is best known for the tower which is named after him, built in 1889 for the World Exhibition of that year, 300 meters high, 9000 tons weight.

**Gustave Flaubert** (1821-1880), born in Rouen, abandoned a medical career to devote himself to literature and in so doing left an indelible mark on French letters though he was not a proliferous writer. Among his works, *Madame Bovary, L'Education sentimentale, Salammbô.*

**Guy de Maupassant** (1850-1893), French short-story writer (300 during his life) and novelist, a disciple of Flaubert, portrayed a wide range of society and embraced themes of war, mystery, hallucination and horror, written in a simple direct narrative style. Best known novels are *Une Vie* and *Pierre et Jean.*

**Haussmann** (1809-1891), prefect of Paris between 1853 and 1870 he was responsible for the building of the *grands boulevards* which changed the face of Paris. Often criticized for having destroyed old sections of Paris (the Marais being the only part of the city untouched) but his avenues also seen as farsighted and futurist for his day.

**Henri Barbusse** (1873-1935), writer who became famous for one novel *Le Feu* (1916) about life in the trenches during the First World War. Barbusse was one of the spiritual fathers of the left in the post-war generation.

**Hoche** (1768-1797), a general of whom Napoleon said "*C'est un véritable homme de guerre.*" Leader of the Sambre and Meuse army, he agreed to plot against the royalists in 1797 but found he didn't have the support of his officers and found himself alone. Died shortly after. Hoche is one of the symbolic figures of the French Revolution.

**Jean Bart** (1650-1702), famous pirate before the king invited him to become captain of a ship and later a frigate in the Royal Marine. Managed to get a cargo of ammunitions through treacherous Channel waters during the battle of Augsbourg in 1688. Escaped from prison in England but returned there to avenge himself in a famous attack in which he sank 100 merchant ships, landed in England and burned down 200 houses before coming back to France laden with loot.

**Jean-Jacques Rousseau** (1712-1778), philosopher and writer born in Geneva, died at Ermenonville. His *Discourse on the Arts and Sciences* won him fame and he went on to write *The Social Contract* which was an influential text on the American Declaration of Independence and the French Revolution. Believing in the original goodness of human nature he considered that the rise of property and human pride had corrupted the 'noble savage.'

**Jean Jaurès** (1859-1914), founder of the French Socialist Party in 1901 and the newspaper *L'Humanité,* Jaurès was a politician, professor and talented orator.

**Jean Moulin** (1899-1943), born in Béziers, he was the founder of the National Council for the Resistance and was its first president. Betrayed, he was arrested and tortured by the Germans and died as he was being transferred to Germany. He was re-buried in the Panthéon in 1965.

**Jeanne d'Arc** (1412-1431), while shepherding her sheep, Jeanne d'Arc heard voices urging her to deliver France from the English invasion. She got permission to lead a small band of men and deflected the English attack at Orléans. Finally she was captured and burned at the stake at Rouen at the hands of the English represented in France by the Archbishop of Beauvais.

**Jules Ferry** (1832-1893), statesman noted for his contribution to the French education system; he made primary education free, obligatory and secular. Also involved in colonial affairs and was responsible for the conquest of Tunisia.

**Léon Blum** (1872-1950), writer and politician. In 1936, as leader of the socialist party, he led two *Front Populaire* governments (1936-37 and 1938). He was deported to Germany in 1943. At the end of the war in 1946, he again became Prime Minister of a socialist government. Instigated important social measures.

**Marcel Proust** (1871-1922), French novelist, essayist and critic. Severe asthma precluded any regular profession. He defined the artist's task as the releasing of creative energies of past experience from the unconscious, an aesthetic which found its most developed literary expression in his novel *A la recherche du temps perdu* which occupied him from 1907 until his death.

**Maréchal Gallieni** (1849-1916), he was the commanding officer of Paris when the First World War broke out and was credited with the victory at Marne. Subsequently became Minister for War but died before the war ended.

**Michelet** (1798-1874), writer and historian and teacher at the *Ecole normale supérieur*, who became director of the national history archives in 1831. His master work is *Histoire de France*.

**Molière** (1622-1673), is the name assumed by Jean-Baptiste Poauelin, French comic dramatist. Began his career as groom upholsterer to the king, but soon became an actor and founded a dramatic company for which he composed comedies and farces. He introduced the ridicule of French society, with its various types of folly, oddity, pedantry, or vice, as the subject of French comedy. Among his most famous plays are *Tartuffe, Don Juan, Le Misanthrope*, and *Le Bourgeois Gentilhomme*.

**Pasteur** (1822-1895), chemist and bacteriologist. Laid the basis for a new approach to chemical structures and composition. Became a French hero for his "germ theory." Discovered that through sterilization or "pasteurization" that products such as milk could be preserved. From this he developed an interest in diseases. His last triumph was to make a successful vaccine against rabies.

**Paul Bert** (1823-1886), physiologist and politician. Remembered for his studies on atmospheric pressure and his analysis of the gases contained in the blood.

**Rabelais** (1494-1553), French humanist, satirist and physician who became successively a monk, priest, bishop's secretary, and Bachelor of Medicine. He acquired a widespread reputation for his erudition and is remembered for his five great books which are linked together by a narrative thread, providing a vivid panorama of contemporary society: *Pantagruel, Gargantua, Tiers Livre, Quart Livre*, and *Cinquième Livre*. His work gained wide popularity and remains a unique expression of Renaissance energy and plenitude.

**Racine** (1639-1699), dramatist, one of the great figures of the French classical period. His tragedies derive from various sources; from Greek and Roman literature and from Roman and Turkish history. Among them are *Phèdre, Iphigénie* and *Bérénice*.

**Richelieu** (1585-1642), cardinal and statesman. Chief minister of Louis XIII from 1624 until his death in 1642, Richelieu completely dominated French government, establishing a strong central government at home, and pursuing an aggressive foreign policy, particularly against Spain, which made France indisputably the strongest nation in Europe.

**Tolbiac,** name of an old German town near Cologne, today called Zülpich, site of a decisive victory over the Germans in 496 which also marked the beginnings of Christianity in France.

**Victor Hugo** (1802-1885), great French poet of the 19th century, novelist and dramatist, the central figure of the Romantic movement in France. *Notre Dame de Paris* and *Les Misérables* are among his best known novels.

**Voltaire** (1694-1778), writer, author of plays, poetry, and histories, not so much a philosopher as a publicizer of the philosophical ideas of others. Fought against religious intolerance and was imprisoned more than once and exiled to England for some years as a result of his pungent political satires. Author of *Candide*.

## Animals & Society

The French are highly indulgent with animals, children and senior citizens. However, they clearly have a love affair with dogs. Paris alone counts 500 000 dogs, or 4760 dogs per square kilometer, which by far outnumbers the number of children.

The colloquial French equivalent of "pooch" is *toutou,* and *minou* for "kitty." The most popular dog name in France is Rex. Supermarkets all sell fresh cuts of meats and animal organs, like spleens (*rate*), especially

for your pets. French dog owners are less obsessed with the macho image of "all-meat" for their hounds; they feed their dogs well balanced meals which include lots of vegetables. On the other hand, your average citizen is likely to offer your over-weight beagle a few sugar cubes at the zinc bar of your local café. *Vive les contradictions!*

Dogs are allowed in restaurants and most public places, although they must be leashed in parks and "bagged" in the *métro* and on trains. For an assortment of dog bags, go to Samaritaine. As long as you are not leasing a furnished apartment for a short period of time, there is no problem renting apartments if you have pets. No extra fees. There are animal *auberges* for vacation time, and numerous chic dog salons, where the poodles recline on mock Louis XIV fauteuils. There are several taxi services for pets, as well as pet ambulances.

On the rue Maître Albert, in the 5th *arrondissement*, there is an animal *dispensaire* for inexpensive veterinary services. Otherwise, call: *SOS Vétérinaires,* Tel: 47.55.47.00 This recording gives the telephone numbers for Paris and the suburbs where emergency veterinary care can be obtained. The French SPA shelters homeless pets, many of which are abandoned along the *autoroutes* during vacation times. Beware—some are not healthy and not vaccinated.

Société Protectrice des Animaux
(SPA)
39, Bd. Berthier
75017 Paris
Tel: 43.33.94.37

It is relatively easy to bring dogs and cats into France. Although a valid health certificate, showing a recent rabies vaccination, is required, chances are you won't even have to show it at the airport when you arrive, but you may have you show it when you leave the country. But it's ill-advised to arrive without one. Technically, animals without proper certification can be deported or destroyed! If you're planning to pass through or visit the U.K. with a pet, be advised that a strict, six-month quarantine is enforced for animals, vaccinated or not! This can be a terribly cruel and costly surprise, so inquire first if you have any doubts. Pets can travel on international airlines, in approved kennel cages, for the price of a piece of extra baggage. (The only airline, by the way, that charges nothing for kennels is Air France.) On regularly scheduled flights, animals travel in the hold of the plane in temperature-controlled and well-lit storage areas. Be wary of charters.

There are some regulations though that should be carefully noted. Dogs under the age of three months old and cats under six weeks are prohibited from international travel. You cannot bring more than three ani-

mals at one time, only one of which can be a puppy or a kitten. Rabies vaccination certificates must state that the vaccine had been administered more than 30 days and less than one year prior to the date of departure. Birds are limited to two psittacidaes and ten birds of small species with health certificates issued within five days of departure. All other animals require special import permits from the Ministry of Agriculture. Fortunately, the bottom line is that living and traveling in France with pets generally poses few problems, and can even be an easy and agreeable way to make acquaintances quickly.

### *Caca* on the Streets

It should be pointed out that the infamous problem of *un*curbed dogs, which had given Paris a bad name for many years, has been somewhat rectified. Although the law states that you have to curb your dog, directing him to do his *besoins* (needs) in the *caniveau* (gutter) off the curb—and there are even cute graphic reminders painted onto certain sidewalks—you used to have to hop-skip-and-jump to avoid landing in a rude pile. The city has recently launched a clever and graphically-pleasing poster campaign designed by famed-illustrator Sempé to remind dog owners of their civic responsibilities. Now, in the nicer neighborhoods at least, the city cleans up with the use of a technician with a green designer suit on a converted motorcycle equipped with a high-powered vacuum cleaner. Much of the eye-sore has been aspirated away. As of October 1991, there is a new law that allows you to be fined on the spot for not curbing your dog.

While on the subject, Paris has other ways of keeping itself clean. You may wonder why water gushes out of sewers and runs through the gutters so often—even when it's not been raining. Paris street cleaners, mostly Africans in green municipal jump suits, open valves of clean, but undrinkable water and direct the flow up- or down-street, by positioning soggy bolts of tied-up cloth. Then they sweep with their green plastic-branched brooms, loose papers, *mégots* (cigarette butts), trash and unclaimed dog-doo into the moving stream, which drains into the city sewers and eventually into the Seine system for recycling. You can visit the impressive sewers, *les égouts de Paris*, daily at Pont de l'Alma in the 7ᵉ. Every address in Paris has an equivalent one underground. This complex, unlit network was extensively used by Resistance fighters during the Nazi Occupation. For humans, Paris streets are equipped with automatic, self-disinfecting pay toilets. For two-francs, you gain access to a futuristic compartment whose cleanliness and comfort is guaranteed.

## Safety & Security

Safety is always relative to what you're used to. Although Paris is a big city and a degree of prudence and common sense should always be applied, it is fair to say that Paris streets, day or night, are relatively safe. In fact, there's little sense in even comparing the safety of Paris to that of any city in the United States although the city has taken on a harder tone over the last few years. There are fewer dangerous weapons and drugs on Paris streets, and not many desperate and crazed individuals despite increased numbers of homeless people and drug users. Nonetheless, one should always be careful and prudent. Incidents do occur. There are cases of muggings, theft and attack. A bigger problem is learning how to remain street-wise while leaving home that defensiveness and massive phobia that you were most likely, and for sound reason, brought up to maintain at all costs. For all practical purposes, you should not be frightened to take the *métro*. In the last few years there has been a slight increase of cases of theft and harassment in certain *métro* stations, especially late at night. Châtelet and Les Halles should be avoided late at night. Stalingrad can be pretty uninviting as can Strasbourg St. Denis and République late at night. And, it's true that certain quartiers can be a bit intimidating or less reassuring. Women may feel the harassment of being followed or catcalled by bothersome men. As unpleasant as this may be, these encounters are in most cases harmless. Many working immigrant men, often from North Africa, are in Paris without their wives or girlfriends and the presence of single women on the streets reminds them of their desires. Just ignore such advances and carry on. Of course, it's never a bad idea, especially when going out at night into areas you're not familiar with, to have a friend or friends along. If you feel harassed or simply bothered by someone in the street or in a café or club it's best to ignore them at first. If they persist, a clever retort works better than an insult. Try one of these: *"J'attends mon mari," "J'attends ma femme,"* or, *"Est-ce que je vous ai donné la permission de me parler?"* Make sure you have these mastered before you attempt them, however. Common sense is the key. You need to be careful like in all big cities, but not frightened. *Au contraire,* Paris is a city that has a relatively late social life and vibrant street/café life and needs to be negotiated by foot.

Paris is dense; the space between people is often less than in cities in other countries. The social coding between individuals is different. The body language is as distinct as the verbal language. For example, some women have complained that French men in clubs or discotheques become aggressive if they don't get their way after their graciously offered drinks

have been accepted. As a rule, you should remember that Americans are more open, verbal and casual than the French in initial social contacts. This difference can lead to misunderstandings which, although not usually unsafe, can be uncomfortable. Some discos attract individuals who want to pick up foreigners.

Areas of town that are known to be a bit less comforting to foreign students, especially women, include the area between Place Clichy and Barbès-Rochechouart, which delineates the Pigalle district. This area is filled with a lot of porno shops and single men. Being one of the poorer areas of Paris, there are a lot of immigrants, mostly Algerian, Moroccan and African. Although crime is higher here than in the chic parts of central Paris, these ethnic groups usually get an unfair reputation. There is nothing to be frightened about, but it's always good to have an idea about where you're going, and to dress more conservatively in those areas.

Street people, formerly called *clochards*, are for the most part harmless, despite their frequent drunkenness, desperate look and sometimes angry-sounding comments. Some of the side streets near the Gare Montparnasse and the desolate back streets of the 14th *arrondissement* were known to be frequented by drug dealers. Now the drug zones are Stalingrad and the Gare de Lyon and more recently the eastern part of the Pont de Sèvres/Mairie de Montreuil line has experienced some drug problems, especially *Métro* Oberkampf. The drug situation in Paris is a fraction of what it is in North American and other European cities, but is growing steadily worse. Far more dangerous than anywhere in Paris are some of the stark concrete HLM complexes in the northern suburbs. There would be little reason for you to head out that way. Again try to avoid the larger *métro* stations such as Châtelet/Les Halles late at night, as they can be a refuge for late-night partyers of the slightly dubious type and generally a hang-out for unsavory characters. The same goes for the area around Les Halles/Beaubourg—the rue St. Denis, a notorious sex shop/prostitution street, is not far away. But, in any case, compared to any city in the US, Paris' worst is manageable.

## Crime Statistics

In 1985 there were some 22,358 homicides in North America, which translates to 8.3 per 100,000 citizens. France has 2,413 annual homicides, or 4.0 per 100,000 citizens. In the greater Paris area, 306 homicides were committed in 1985, that is, less than five per 100,000 and almost one fifth the rate of Washington, D.C. Officially, there were 100,000 homeless people and 19,000 *clochards* (street people) in France. No one is certain how many fold this has increased, but the increases of the homeless is substantial.

Crime that does exist is primarily directed at property and cars. House or apartment theft is called *cambriolage*. A great many apartment-dwellers and home owners have steel-enforced doors called *portes blindées*, with five locking points which enables purchase of better theft insurance. You won't see grilled-over windows like you do in New York or nineteen locks per door, but you will see these heavy doors and peek holes. In many apartment buildings, there is a *concierge* who adds to the safety. Most break-ins happen in France during the month of August when a large percentage of Parisians leave for holidays. Be somewhat dubious about individuals who knock on your door offering services and wanting to check the inside of your apartment. This is an old trick for determining which apartments are worth hitting. Thieves have an entire hieroglyphic language of codes which they leave for each other in chalk by the door or outside the apartment building.

## Pickpockets

Like in any big city, incidents occur. There is some pickpocketing in the flea markets, in the *métro*, on buses, and in tourist areas like the Champs-Elysées and St. Michel. If you're careful with your possessions you will have no problems. Be especially careful in the Barbès métro station and on certain bus routes, where pickpockets are known to work in groups. One person drops something, and while you politely bend over to pick it up, another one empties your pocket or bag. Having your papers replaced at the *préfecture* is a real hassle. Be careful. Muggings are not very common, but they happen. Ironically, they seem to occur more frequently at night in the quiet, wealthy and residential parts of the 16th or 17th *arrondissements* rather than the seedier, densely populated areas near Pigalle.

In the warm months there can be bands of immigrant children, often Romanian, falsely labeled *gitans* or gypsies, that hang out between Place de la Concorde and the Louvre. Their M.O. is to swarm around a confused tourist and pick him or her clean like the sharks and the great fish in Hemingway's *Old Man and the Sea*. This has not been as acute as in the past, however, be careful with your wallet, passport, camera and jewelry, especially in crowds during the summer. You could be targeted on the street, *métro* or bus. To minimize problems, try to always look as if you know where you're going, even if you don't. Professional thieves can quickly spot foreign tourists who look like fair game. Otherwise, don't think twice about this. But keep your passport and money well concealed, never in your back pocket

or backpack, which can be cut and easily emptied. It's not a bad ideas to keep back up photocopies of all your documents in that the replacement of papers is the most difficult and time consuming in case of loss or theft. Some people prefer carrying photocopies and leaving the originals at home.

If someone from the street offers you a better exchange rate than the bank, refuse. Magicians either earn money pulling rabbits out of hats or switching the rolls of money they give to you. After the transaction, you will examine your impressive roll of money only to find two one hundred franc notes wrapped around a bulk of white paper. And legally, you are helpless, since you are as much to blame for accepting the illicit transaction.

**Lost or Stolen Property**

If you have lost anything of importance or had it stolen, there are two things to do immediately following the discovery: go to the nearest police station and fill out a report *(déclaration de vol)*, which you will need to make an insurance claim. You may want to check the city's lost and found *(Objets Trouvés)* at 36, rue des Morillons, 75015 Paris, Tel: 45.31.14.80 between 9h00 and 17h00 in that papers are often turned in (for lost credit cards or traveler's checks, see Banking). Secondly, pay a visit to your country's embassy and they will provide you with additional helpful instructions including a means to replace your passport.

## Police, Law & Authority

By law, every person in France has a legal status and an identity card. North Americans often see the question of "papers" as a psychological hurdle. The United States and Canada do not have National Identity Cards, like most countries in the world. Any policeman has the right to demand that you prove your identity at any time. No real reason or provocation is required. So, it's advisable to carry your passport or *carte de séjour* with you at all times. If you're stopped (*contrôlé*) and you don't have identification or valid papers, say you're a tourist. Don't speak French; smile and be submissive. Show the *agent* (officer, *le flic* or *poulet* in slang) that you respect his power, and in most cases you'll get a banal warning and be sent on your way with a polite salute. But you might have to provide identification within 24 hours or even be accompanied to the local police station. There is a lot of intimidation here. It's better to steer away from any unnecessary encounters with the police.

The relationship that citizens have to authority is different in all countries. In France, the police control the public; in the North American scheme of things one tends to feel that the police works for the public. In France, the police are employees either of the Ministry of the Interior or the Ministry of Defense, thus functionaries of the State, the federal government. The police represents the State. In the US, aside from the FBI or state troopers, the police work for the municipality; they attempt to enforce the law but they are not the law itself. A large psychological difference.

There are several types of police in France. Basically, the *agent de police*, the local officer, is an employee of the Ministry of Interior. The *gendarmes*, the ones you see on the highways out of town and in the small towns, are connected to the Ministry of Defense. The police who ride around in gray-green armored vans and carry Plexiglas shields are the CRS *(Compagnies Républicaines de Sécurité)*, the National Security Police. They are called in to enforce order and maintain security in situations of demonstrations, strikes, riots, protests or upheaval. France experiences numerous national strikes and scores of organized *manifestations (manifs)* (demonstrations) each year. Be prepared to be inconvenienced. *En masse*, these guys are scary looking. In general, you'll find the police to be polite, formal and mildly helpful. Not more. As already stated, you can be asked for seemingly no reason to *"présentez vos papiers"*—either your passport or your *carte de séjour*. This is a routine called *un contrôle*. You'll see systematic control points in the streets for drivers. From time to time, especially at moments particularly vulnerable to terrorism, you'll see a lot of armed police in the *métro* stations as well. The RATP has recently hired supplementary private security police to answer the rise of crime in the *métro*. Although you may not be used to this, and may even be repulsed by the idea, don't be overly alarmed. Very recently there have been highly visible cases of arrested illegal immigrants, usually black Africans, handcuffed, being escorted to deportation planes at the airport.

Remember, in keeping with the Napoleonic Code, the burden of the proof is upon the accused. For instance, in the case of legal accusations, you can be detained twenty-four hours before you have the right to make a phone call. Yet this concept is just as applicable in numerous sectors of French life; everyday interactions with individuals and administrators are mostly laced with an initial *méfiance* (mistrust). When dealing, for example, with the French tax authorities, even if you are certain that there has been an error, you're obliged to pay first. Justice will follow in due course; the system may be slow, but it is assumed to be right.

### A Word on Terrorism

Many visitors have been highly concerned since the late 80s with the risks and fears of terrorist activities in Europe. Admittedly, there was an atmosphere of uncertainty and distrust in Paris during the Gulf War. The streets, cafés, and stations were empty and mistrustful looks were cast at perfectly innocent Arab or Arab-looking individuals in Paris. Prior to that, there was a short period in Paris in 1985 and early 1986 when an atmosphere of suspicion and terror permeated the air, following the bombings of a shopping complex on the Champs-Elysées and the popular working-class department store Tati, near Montparnasse, in which innocent people were killed and maimed. Other than that, many still remember the terrorist attack on Goldenberg's Restaurant on the predominantly Jewish rue des Rosiers. Ironically, two Jews, two Moslems, and two Christians were killed in the blast and the event ultimately served to create a new feeling of inter-religion solidarity in the community. Aside from these selected incidents, the actual risk of being subjected to any danger of this sort is highly remote and should not—at least for the moment—figure in your thinking about life in Paris.

### Documentation

Information Available to the English-Speaking Community

The Office of American Services at the US Consulate (2, rue St. Florentin 75001 Paris, Tel: 42.96.12.02, Fax: 42.61.61.40) provides free of charge the following pamphlets:

• Principal American and Franco-American organizations in Paris
• Notorial Services
• Registration of births and obtainment of birth records for US citizens born abroad
• Citizenship provisions of the Immigration and Nationality Act of 14 November, 1986
• Photograph requirements for passport applicants
• Religious Institutions in Paris
• Private Detective Agencies in Paris
• List of Doctors and Dentists in Paris
• Insurance companies and agents
• OCS Emergency Trust Fund
• Schools
• Stenographer (court reporters)
• Warning about pickpockets
• Taking evidence in France—civil and commercial matters
• List of sworn translators and interpreters in Paris area
• Visa requirements for France
• French sales tax (TVA) Refund Procedure
• Tax accountants and consultants in Paris
• Shipping companies

• Residence permits *(cartes de séjour)*
• Marriage formalities for Americans in France
• Lost or stolen property
• French consulates in the United States
• Student part-time employment in France
• Employment in France
• Divorce
• Banking and foreign exchange facilities
• *Au pair* employment in France
• Obtaining a birth record
• Motor vehicle operations in France
• List of attorneys in Paris area

The British Community Committee, (c/o Mme. Beryl Jones
17, villa Chaptal
92300 Levallois-Perret
Tel: 47.58.81.42)
provides the following documentation upon request:

• *Digest of British and Franco-British Clubs, Societies and Institutions* (free), and a
• *Quarterly of British Community Social Events* (100 FF)

# THE WAY THINGS WORK

# Transports

## The *Métro* and RER

The Paris *Métro* (RATP) has been in existence since the turn of the century and gained its name from its first line, the *Métropolitain*. It truly plays an essential role in the life of the city and is filled with its own character, energy, and mythology. The system has 13 lines that reach 322 stations, the newest being *La Défense* beyond *Pont de Neuilly*, and the final destination, opposite *Château de Vincennes,* on the Number 1 line. A 14th line called *Météor,* which will be rubber-wheeled and electronically driven, is currently being built which will run between Gennevilliers and southern Paris and link 18 stations, seven in central Paris. Some 5.5 million commuters use the system each day. You can get nearly everywhere in a relatively short period of time for a reasonable price in relative safety and security on the Paris *Métro*. Don't be afraid of it. At times it gets a bit overcrowded, odoriferous, noisy, and confused, but on the whole the Paris underground subway system is among the best in the world. It'll be one of your greatest resources.

Whether you live in Paris or intend to commute by train from the Paris suburbs, you should purchase a monthly pass, *une carte orange,* which allows unlimited travel within five specific zones. This is one of Paris' greatest bargains. Avoid purchasing your *carte* on the first day of the month in that the lines can be brutal. Cards go on sale during the last week of each month, so think ahead. French employers often pay half of the *carte orange* price per month as an employee benefit. The five circular zones are organized in concentric circles with Paris-proper consisting of zones 1 and 2. The other three zones extend far into the suburbs. A single ride (a powder-blue magnetized ticket) costs 5,50 FF and this flat fee allows you to go anywhere wihin the system. NOTE: all *métro* and RER ticket prices are expected to increase by about 5% in the summer of 1994. If not buying the *carte orange* or the weekly equivalent, *coupon jaune* (49 FF), buy a *carnet* (pack of ten individual tickets) for 34,40 FF. This is a substantial saving over the purchase of individual tickets at 5,50 FF. The same card is also valid on Paris buses and *le métro* and on the Regional Express trains (R.E.R.). The *carte orange* currently costs 208 FF for two zones; three zones costs 247 FF, four zones for 342 FF, and five zones 516 FF. This is a real bargain. Your first time, you need a photograph of yourself, easily obtained from the instant photo booths located in many stations, and the orange card with plastic sleeve that you get at any *métro* station ticket window. A yearly *carte orange* ticket *(la carte intégrale)* is also available. You are supposed to carry the magnetized ticket in a little slot in the sleeve and inscribe the number of the card onto the ticket. Failure to

do either can cause you a fine upon verification. The same is true for the lack of a picture. The card is strictly for the use of the person whose name and picture appear on the card. Periodically, controllers stake out *métro* stations and selected cars, usually at the beginning of the month, when some decide to rough it by not renewing their *carte orange* for the month.

One *métro* phenomenon you're likely to observe is gate-hopping. A fair amount of people duck under or jump over the turnstiles either to avoid payment or because they are too lazy to get out their *carte orange.* RATP officials have reduced some of this by installing quick-moving stop gates that make cheating harder. Often people sneak in for free behind someone who has paid. So, if someone pushes in behind you or asks to pass through the turnstile with you, don't be alarmed. If by some odd chance you get caught without a ticket, speak your mother tongue, play dumb and innocent, and when asked for your name and address, remember, you're from Oshkosh. If you *are* fined, though, you may be asked to pay from 85 FF to 230 FF on the spot for jumping over, sliding under, or riding without a valid ticket. If you cannot pay or refuse to pay immediately, the controller will write you a ticket (PV, *procès verbal),* for which there is of course a supplementary fine. You are supposed to send in the payment. A commonly controlled station is Franklin D. Roosevelt on the *Champs-Elysées* where controllers hide behind the *guichet* (ticket booth) waiting for cheaters. Controllers have recently had the color of their uniforms changed from military blue to khaki brown, a move designed to render their public image less agressive. Plain clothes controllers are now in service as well. According to Public Relations director Patrick Pigault, the RATP is getting tougher on cheaters. So, pay for your fare; it's a good deal and the embarrassment and hassle of being caught without a ticket isn't worth it.

Be aware of the *"dernier métro"* phenomenon. For a city the size and complexity of Paris, it is surprising that the *métro* doesn't remain open all night. The métro runs till about 0h50, and you must keep this in mind if you want to get home the easiest and cheapest way. Be careful about catching the *métro* on one line but missing your transfer. If you miss the last *métro* you'll have to either find a taxi, walk, "stay over" or, when completely desperate, sleep in a *métro* station (which is funky but not recommended, though tolerated) until the first train at 5h45. The disco scene revolves around the first *métro* concept. Otherwise, you can tempt fate with the funky and sometimes punky, late-night bus service *Noctambus* (see Buses). Although the *métro* is safe, use precaution when riding the *métro* alone late at night.

Also watch out for pickpockets during rush hour when people are squeezed in. Monsieur Pigault especially warns riders to take care in the Barbès station, heading towards Pigalle, which is notorious for sly pickpockets who work in gangs. The scam is that one person "accidentally" drops his or her bag and while a polite tourist bends over to pick it up, a second person in the gang removes wallets, watches, cameras, and the like. So, don't bend over at Barbès.

If you ever do feel insecure or unsafe on the *métro*, climb in the car right behind the driver. There is a window into his cabin and you can watch the ride through the front windshield while being in the safest spot on the train.

**How to Use the *Métro***

The *métro* is easy to use, once you've mastered the symbols employed to indicate exits, transfers, and train directions. First of all, *métro* lines are named after their end points, i.e. the Orléans/Clignancourt line is called *Direction Porte de Clignancourt;* and the same line traveling in the opposite direction is called *Direction Porte d'Orléans*. Naturally, it serves all the stations in between. Signs indicating *direction* are white. For transferring from one line to another, orange signs on the *quai* (platform) marked *correspondance* indicate the path to other *quais* and other *directions*.

You can usually switch to a *métro* heading the opposite direction for free, though in some smaller stations there are separate turnstiles. Blue signs marked *sortie* point you in the direction of the exit, and often you'll have a choice of exits, all emerging onto different streets or different sides of the street. When meeting friends at a *métro* station, make sure to specify which exit and whether you will meet underground or above ground. In every big station, you will find a *plan du quartier* (neighborhood map) on the platform, but all *métro* stops have maps at the ticket office exit. When with a group, if one of you gets left behind, a good policy is to get off at the next stop and wait for your friend to arrive. Then continue. Here is a list of *métro* lines and their respective *directions*:

| | |
|---|---|
| **Line 1** | Château de Vincennes/La Défense |
| **Line 2** | Nation/Porte Dauphine |
| **Line 3** | Gallieni/Pont de Levallois-Bécon |
| **Line 3 bis** | Porte des Lilas/Gambetta |
| **Line 4** | Porte de Clignancourt/Porte d'Orléans |
| **Line 5** | Bobigny-Pablo Picasso/Place d'Italie |
| **Line 6** | Nation/Charles de Gaulle-Etoile |
| **Line 7** | La Courneuve-Mairie d'Ivry/Villejuif/Louis Aragon |
| **Line 7 bis** | Pré-St. Gervais |
| **Line 8** | Créteil Préfecture/Balard |
| **Line 9** | Mairie de Montreuil/Pont de Sèvres |
| **Line 10** | Gare d'Austerlitz/Boulogne-Pont de St. Cloud-Porte d'Auteuil |
| **Line 11** | Mairie des Lilas/Châtelet |
| **Line 12** | Porte de la Chapelle/Mairie d'Issy |
| **Line 13** | Gabriel Péri-Asnières-St. Denis Basilique/Châtillon-Montrouge |

**The RER (*Réseau express régional*)**

The RER system (also run by the RATP) is the high speed city-suburb network that in a short amount of time can zoom you across the city, out to Versailles or St. Germain-en-Laye, and even Euro Disneyland. The aesthetics are very different, the stations are vast tunnels with deep platforms, and the trains are fast and silent. Note that the *métro*s approach each platform from your left while the RER trains approach from your right. There are four lines (A, B, C, D) and each one, with the exception of line D, forks into numerous directions. Of course the RER and *métro* lines connect at various points and though the RER is not designed to be used for very short distances, it makes longer distance traveling across the city or from city to suburb incredibly easy and efficient. Key junctions (*correspondences*) stations are Châtelet/Les Halles, Nation, Etoile, and Auber. Don't confuse Charles de Gaulle / Etoile, where the Arc de Triomphe is located with Charles de Gaulle / Roissy, the site of the airport. On the platform there are lit panels indicating the precise direction and list of stations the next train will be serving. All trains stop at all Paris stations. Be careful at Nation and Etoile that you haven't mounted a train on the correct line but the wrong branch. Otherwise, you'll have to circle back and pay another fare. Note that you can go to the Château de Vincennes *métro* stop with the same one *métro* ticket but

to get off the RER at Vincennes you need an additional fare. Controllers often stake out the Vincennes RER station catching hoards of violators in their net. Also note that on those lit panels the name of the train and the time of arrival is posted. The trains have funny four-letter names which are written in lights on the front of the first car. And some trains are longer than others. The stopping point for both *Train Long* and *Train Court* is indicated by fixed signs suspended over the platforms at the points where the *tête* and *queue* of the train will stop. This is important in that you could be waiting for a train on the correct platform but 100 meters behind or in front of the train.

There is normally one First Class carriage on the RER trains which, in order to avail of, you must pay a premium on your ticket. There is absolutely no advantage.

| | |
|---|---|
| **RER A1** St. Germain en Laye | **RER A3** Boissy St. Léger |
| **RER A2** Cergy | **RER A4** Marne La Vallée |
| **RER B2** Robinson | **RER B3** Roissy-Charles-de-Gaulle |
| **RER B4** St. Rémy-lès-Chevreuse | **RER B5** Mitry-Claye |
| **RER C1** Montigny-Beauchamp | **RER C2** Chemind'Antony |
| **RER C3** Argenteuil | **RER C4** Dourdan |
| **RER C5** Versailles RG | **RER C6** St. Martin d'Etampes |
| **RER C7** St. Quentin-en-Yvelines | |
| **RER D1** Ory-la-Ville | **RER D2** Châtelet-Les Halles |

## Buses

The sign of a real Parisian is the mastery of the bus system. The Parisian Bus System is excellent, although its efficiency suffers from the generally congested traffic situation. The bus does have the advantage of allowing you to see more of the city than traveling underground by *métro*. And there are still some lines with buses that have open, trolley-like back sections. Aside from the pollution, these are fun. *Paris par arrondissements* (street map book sold at kiosks and *papeteries*) has maps of individual bus routes, otherwise stops are indicated on maps inside the *métro*, at bus stops, and in large black letters on the side of each bus. Buses use the same tickets as the *métro*, which are cancelled or punched (*oblitérés*) in the machine located at the front of the bus. Don't cancel your *carte orange* ! Just flash it by the driver. The driver also sells individual tickets which must be punched upon boarding and are only good on the bus. If you do not have a *carte orange*, traveling long distances on the bus is more expensive, because you must buy a new ticket for every *section* through which you travel. There are about six or seven *sections* for a bus going from one side of Paris to the other, of which you can see clearly indicated on the maps at bus stops and inside the bus. When standing at a bus stop, signal the driver if you want to be picked up. Inside the bus, there are red stop request buttons located on the aisle posts. Several lines have now new vehicles which you can enter via the middle doors without showing your card to the driver.

Most buses, whose numbers are indicated at stops by black numbers on a white circle, run every day of the year from about 5h30-0h30. Buses whose emblem is a white number on a black circle generally run only from about 6h00-20h30 Monday through Saturday except holidays.

When the number on the front of the bus has a slash through it, the bus runs through only half of the route. This short range service usually happens only at rush hours and on certain routes. If you're a late nighter, familiarize yourself with the Noctambuses which leave the Châtelet-Hôtel de Ville area (avenue Victoria) every hour from 1h30-5h30 for 15 FF and traverse Paris in every direction. The mob scene to get on these can be intimidating, but the service is safe and reliable. Here's a complete list of night buses, all marked with the sign of a black owl in a yellow circle:

**A:** Pont de Neuilly
**B:** Levallois Mairie
**C:** Clichy Mairie
**D:** Saint Ouen Mairie
**E:** Pantin Eglise
**F:** Les Lilas Mairie
**G:** Montreuil Mairie
**H:** Vincennes Château
**J:** Porte d'Orléans
**R:** Rungis Marée

The *Balabus* is a specially routed bus that for a simple fare takes you past the most important sites of Paris. This is a very good way to see Paris and to orient yourself to the city by yourself or with friends for next to nothing. The route begins and ends at the Gare de Lyon and the Grande Arche, every Sunday afternoon from mid-April till late September. Even long-time residents of the city should cash in on this prime opportunity to relax and take in a visual reminder that you live in one of the most beautiful cities in the world.

For more information stop in at the information stand in the concourse of the Châtelet/RER station or else at RATP headquarters:

**RATP Info**
53ter, quai des Grands Augustins
75006 PARIS
Tel: 40.46.41.41
Fax: 40.46.40.37
Minitel: 3615 RATP

---

## Taxis

In general, Paris taxis are readily available and reasonably priced. However, finding a taxi in Paris is different from finding one in, for example, New York. Paris taxi drivers frequently do not feel obliged to stop for you if they don't have a passenger. When you do get them to stop, if your destination doesn't appeal to the driver, he will tell you so and drive off. Although relatively orderly, taxi stands can be competitive scenes—stand your ground. When ordering a taxi between 18h-21h, don't be surprised to find 20 or 30 FF already on the meter. French taxis, when ordered, start counting from the moment they set out to fetch you. It's always a better idea to find the number of the taxi stand closest to where you live, work, or usually need taxis. The system of lit bulbs on the roof of taxis indicates if the taxi is in service, is already carrying a fare, or is free. Hailing a cab mid-block is practically unheard of. When the taxi crosses the *périphérique* into the suburbs, the driver, presses a button on the meter, changing it over to Fare C, a higher rate. The *périphérique* itself though is considered Paris and the meter should indicate so. The lit display on the back ledge of taxis indicates how many hours and minutes that particular driver has been on duty that day. Taxis drivers are legally limited to a 10 hour day and are heavily fined if they exceed this and are controlled by the police.

## Taxi Stands By *Arrondissement*:

| | |
|---|---|
| (1°) Pl. André Malraux | 42.60.61.40 |
| (1°) Pl. Châtelet | 42.33.20.99 |
| (1°) Métro Concorde | 42.61.67.60 |
| (2°) Pl. Opéra | 47.42.75.75 |
| (3°) Métro Rambuteau | 42.72.00.00 |
| (4°) Métro Saint Paul | 48.87.49.39 |
| (5°) Pl. Monge | 45.87.15.95 |
| (5°) Pl. Rostand/rue Soufflot | 46.33.00.00 |
| (5°) Pl. St. Michel | 43.29.63.66 |
| (5°) Pl. Maubert | 46.34.10.32 |
| (6°) Pl. 18 juin 1940 | 42.22.13.13 |
| (6°) Métro St. Germain des Prés | 42.22.00.00 |
| (6°) Observatoire | 43.54.74.37 |
| (7°) Tour Eiffel | 45.55.85.41 |
| (7°) Pl. du Palais Bourbon | 47.05.03.14 |
| (7°) Métro Latour-Maubourg | 45.55.78.42 |
| (7°) Pl. de l'Ecole Militaire | 47.05.00.00 |
| (7°) Métro Solférino | 45.55.00.00 |
| (7°) Pl. Léon-Paul-Fargue | 45.67.00.00 |
| (7°) Métro rue du Bac | 42.22.49.64 |
| (8°) Pl. Rio de Janeiro | 45.62.00.00 |
| (8°) Pl. St Augustin | 47.42.54.73 |
| (8°) Rond-Point des Champs-Elysées | 42.56.29.00 |
| (8°) Pl. des Ternes | 47.63.00.00 |
| (9°) Square de Montholon | 48.78.00.00 |
| (9°) Métro Richelieu-Drouet | 42.46.00.00 |
| (10°) Métro Goncourt | 42.03.00.00 |
| (11°) Métro Ménilmontant | 43.55.64.00 |
| (11°) Pl. de la Nation | 43.73.29.58 |
| (11°) Pl. Léon-Blum | 43.79.00.00 |
| (11°) Métro Père-Lachaise | 48.05.92.12 |
| (12°) Pl. Félix-Eboué | 43.43.00.00 |
| (13°) Métro Glacière | 45.80.00.00 |
| (13°) Pte d'Italie | 45.86.00.44 |
| (13°) Pl. Pinel | 45.86.00.00 |
| (13°) Carrefour Patay-Tolbiac | 45.83.00.00 |
| (14°) 1, av Reille | 45.89.05.71 |
| (14°) Métro Alésia | 45.45.00.00 |

(14°) Pte d'Orléans................................................45.40.52.05
(14°) Pte de Vanves...............................................45.39.87.33
(14°) Métro Plaisance............................................45.41.66.00
(14°) Pl. Denfert-Rochereau...................................45.35.00.00
(15°) Pont Mirabeau .............................................45.77.48.00
(15°) Métro Bir Hakeim..........................................45.79.17.17
(15°) Métro La Motte-Picquet ................................45.66.00.00
(15°) Pl de Breteuil...............................................45.66.70.17
(15°) Mairie annexe du 15° ....................................48.42.00.00
(15°) Métro Convention .........................................42.50.00.00
(15°) Pl. Charles-Michels .......................................45.78.20.00
(15°) Pte de Versailles............................................48.28.00.00
(16°) Pl. Clément-Ader ..........................................45.24.56.17
(16°) Métro Muette................................................42.88.00.00
(16°) Pl. Jean-Lorrain ...........................................45.27.00.00
(16°) av Victor-Hugo-Etoile...................................45.01.85.24
(16°) Métro Porte Dauphine ...................................45.53.00.00
(16°) Pl. de Barcelone............................................45.27.11.11
(16°) Gare Henri-Martin.........................................45.04.00.00
(16°) Pl. de la Porte d'Auteuil.................................46.51.14.61
(16°) Pl. du Trocadéro ...........................................47.27.00.00
(16°) Métro  Passy ................................................45.20.00.00
(16°) Pte Molitor..................................................46.51.19.19
(16°) Métro Jasmin ...............................................45.25.13.13
(17°) Pl. Aimé-Maillard.........................................46.22.40.70
(17°) Pl. du Maréchal-Juin .....................................42.27.00.00
(17°) Pte de Clichy................................................46.27.90.06
(17°) Métro Villiers...............................................46.22.00.00
(17°) Pte de St-Ouen.............................................42.63.00.00
(17°) Pl. de la République de l'Equateur ...................47.66.80.50
(17°) Pl. Charles-de-Gaulle....................................43.80.01.99
(17°) Pte d'Asnières..............................................43.80.00.00
(18°) Pl. du Tertre................................................42.59.00.00
(18°) Métro Guy Moquet........................................42.28.00.00
(19°) Eglise de Belleville ........................................42.08.42.66
(19°) Porte de Pantin ............................................42.41.00.62
(20°) Métro Porte de Montreuil ..............................43.70.00.00
(20°) Métro Pyrénées ............................................43.49.10.00
(93)  Montreuil (Croix de Chavaux) ........................42.87.00.00
**Here is a space for you to add your own** .................................

## Cars/Driving

Newcomers to Paris most likely will neither need a car nor want one, but still there are a number of things you might want to know regarding cars, driving and parking in France. Young people in France are in no way as obsessed with cars as are their contemporaries in many other countries, certainly in the US. Driving in France is not seen as a symbol of freedom, status and virility although you're certain to encounter a fair amount of nervous drivers with a passion for tailgating, passing on the right, and cheating on left turns. On the other hand, cars are often marketed in France as objects of luxury, style, design, pleasure, seduction, desire and grace and less as practical vehicles for families and their pets. Some French students have cars—traditionally the 1968 style, weak but brave and charming 2CV (*deux chevaux*)—but this is certainly no longer the rule. The attitudes you may witness among drivers should tip you off to a lot of things. Although the French are fast and aggressive, relatively few acts of real meanness or violence occur in traffic. The largest difference between French and American urban drivers is a question of morality or principle. If you're waiting on a long line to make a left turn, undoubtedly some feisty guy in a Renault 25 will barrel past you in the on-coming lane, zoom to the front of the line and steal the light. In the US, the UK or Germany this would cause instant anger because it's a violation and it's unfair. In France, drivers might show discontent too but not out of moral outrage; they'd envy him or at least not fault him for making the most of an opportunity. Opportunism, in general, isn't seen negatively. Other drivers would be angry because he pulled ahead and they were left in the dust, not because he demonstrated a lack of respect for society and its rules. At the risk of over-generalizing, when the French can profit for their own gain and get away with it, they tend to do it. Higher principles are reserved for higher matters than daily traffic.

Parisian drivers are filled with facial and hand gestures. They speed up at lights and breeze past slow cars or j-walkers, but they will never (rarely) hit you. And pedestrians usually stroll across streets with an indifferent gaze. The *priorité à droite* (yield right-of-way) is often seen as a peculiarity among North Americans, where the opposite is the rule. Essentially, just remember that anyone coming from your right in almost all situations has the right-of-way. Sometimes a car will pull out onto a busy road from a dinky side street. You must yield unless there is a sign that tells you otherwise. Often drivers take unfair advantage of this rule of the road and swing far to the right and loop around to make left turns or merge into another road. The *priorité à droite* seems well-engrained in the Parisian mind-set in that people tend to follow this even when walking. For British drivers and pedestrians, the right-hand system will just take a bit of getting used to. As will the lack of outward, public politeness.

In France, the law requires that seat belts be worn by all passengers. Failure to do so can result in a 230 FF fine for the driver and 500 FF for the passenger (1992 figures). Although this law is a good safety measure, it sometimes can be employed as a pretext for the police to stop cars at random to check identity papers. The law also states that you must carry your *permis de conduire* (driver's license), *carte grise* and *certificat d'assurance* at all times. Failure to present these can mean stiff fines, up to 900 FF. *Brûler un feu rouge* (running a red light) is a serious offense that will cost you a minimum of 2000 FF and perhaps an afternoon in court. Crossing a solid white line is also seen as a major fault. U-turns are illegal. You can be stopped, remember, for no reason at all other than a check of your identity. Hide your indignation or be prepared for some sort of fine for an infraction of some sort. Driving without a license can result in a fine of 10000 FF as of the 1994 stricter laws concerning *la route*.

## Driver's Licenses

EU nationals with valid driver's licenses from their respective countries have no problems receiving French driver's *permis*. Apply at your local *préfecture* or *mairie*. The following information is for US citizens driving in France, and was provided by the Paris *Préfecture de Police* via the Office of American Services at the US Consulate. Addition information can be obtained by calling: 42.96.02.02, *poste* 2667 or 2203. French regulations distinguish between persons in France on short tour-ist or business trips (less than 90 days) and those who are here as long-term residents.

If you are a temporary visitor to France, you may drive with a valid US (state) or international driver's license. If a US permit is used, the French government recommends, but does not require, that it be accompanied by an officially recognized French translation (by a *traducteur assermenté*).

If you are a resident of France (holder of a *carte de séjour* or *carte de résidence*), you may drive in France with a valid US (not international) license for a one-year recognition period, beginning on the date of validity of the first *carte de séjour*. The license must be accompanied by a translation made by a sworn translator *(traducteur expert-juré)*.

Persons with valid driver's licenses from the states of Illinois, South Carolina, Michigan, Kentucky, and New Hampshire may directly exchange their state driver's licenses for French permits. These states offer a reciprocal privilege of exchange for persons holding French permits. Legislation is pending to make this possible for other states as well. Note that for driver's licenses from those five states must have been issued prior to the holder's first entry into France as a resident. If you have a license from one of these states you must apply for your French *permis de conduire* at least three months before the expiration of the one-year recognition period. Beyond this delay, the exchange will not be possible. To apply, go to the *Préfecture de Police,* ground floor, at 7 bd. du Palais, 75004 Paris between 8h30 and 17h00, Monday through Friday.

Applicants with licenses from all states must take the written *(code de la route)* and driving portions of the French licensing examination. All applicants must furnish the following documents:

• completed application form
• US driver's license with sworn translation in French
• *carte de séjour* with photocopy of both sides;
• two passport size photographs;
• Proof of current address;
• 150 FF in cash or check.

In France, almost everyone applies for a license through an *école de conduite* (Driving School), private companies that practically have a monopoly on the market. Almost no one succeeds in getting a license as a *candidat libre* (independent applicant). You can try, but, due to new laws *préfectures* insist that you show up at the road test with a duo-control car, which needs to be rented from a driving school. Thus with the required 20 hours of classroom and road time, getting your license is time-consuming and costly (from 3000-6000 FF). For the first year though, your national or state driver's license, along with an International Driver's License, will suffice. This license can be obtained at AAA offices throughout the US for $15. or by contacting AAA at 1000 AAA Drive, Heathrow, FL 32746-5063. It's not possible to obtain one in France.

For more precise information on driving in France and driving lessons contact the legendary but costly English-speaking:

Fehrenbach Driving School, 53 bd Henri Sellier, 92150 Suresnes, Tel: 45.06.31.17.

For a list of driving schools with English language teachers, call or write the Office of American Services at the US Consulate.

**Replacing Expired, Lost and Stolen Drivers' Licenses**

Foreign embassies are not authorized to replace expired, lost or stolen drivers' licenses. If you have lost your driver's license or had it stolen in France, immediately report it to the *commissariat* of police having jurisdiction over the area where the loss of the theft occurred. The *commissariat* will issue a *récépissé de déclaration de perte ou de vol de pièces d'identité*

(Acknowledgement of Declaration of Loss or Theft of Identity Documents). This *récépissé* will generally cover the lack of a driver's license for a few weeks while a replacement is being obtained. The *récépissé* is good for this purpose only in France. In the case of US residents, if the US citizen's home state requires a sworn affidavit or a notarized application for a replacement license, the Embassy's Office of American Services can notarize the application from 9:00 a.m. to 12:30 p.m. Monday through Friday, French and US holidays excepted.

## Purchasing a Car

When purchasing a car, you need to bring the *carte grise*, the French car registration papers of the seller (on which he has written VENDU and signed and dated it), to the *préfecture* in your *arrondissement* or *département*. You also need to obtain, at the *préfecture* or *mairie* of the *arrondissement* where the car has been previously registered, a *lettre de nongage*, which means that there are no *liens* (encumbrances) or outstanding debts on the car. For cars over five years old, the law requires that all such vehicles must undergo a technical inspection (*contrôle technique*) and receive a *certificat d'inspection*, which can be obtained for 290 FF from certified service stations by no later than five years to the day from the date the vehicle first appeared in circulation. *Plaques d'immatriculation* (license plates) must be changed by the new buyer within 48 hours after the new *carte grise* has been issued. New plates are stamped out at many service stations for about 150 FF while you wait.

### Annual Registration Sticker (*vignette*)

*Vignettes* can be purchased in the month of November in any *tabac* in the *département* in which the car is registered, upon presentation of the *carte grise*, and are renewed annually. Affix it on the inside lower right-hand corner of the *parebrise* (windshield) by December 1 or you risk a fine. The tax varies depending on the size, age and horsepower of the car. Count on 300-400 FF.

## Auto Insurance

Anne Deshayes of Advantage Insurance has contributed much of the following information for *Paris Inside Out* readers needing to know about car insurance in France.

An unlimited third party liability insurance policy is compulsory for all automobiles entering France. Whether the owner accompanies the automobile or not, the vehicle must be insured. As proof of insurance, the owner must present an international motor insurance card (green if the policy is purchased in France) showing that the vehicle is insured in France. A temporary policy is available from the vehicle insurance department of the French Customs office *(la douane)* at the point of entry (border-crossing or seaport). These policies have a validity of eight, fifteen, or thirty days. For those who wish longer-term or additional insurance, the your embassy has a list of English-speaking companies.

Often you'll be told that if you can prove that you've been insured for two years you can benefit from a French insurer's *bonus* (discount). This is wrong. Even if you've been insured for one year, you should qualify for a discount. You absolutely must find proof of previous insurance elsewhere. Try to have your former insurance agent at home send you a letter affirming your insurance record. The further back you can go the better. The motor vehicle department of the state in which you lived can also issue a "no collision accident letter" which may suffice when the insurance agency cannot be reached. In France, ask for a *relevé d'informations*. Each year of insurance with no claim entitles you to an additional 5% bonus. This bonus is extremely important if you'd like to save on insurance premiums. For salaried employees, the best rates for cars bought in France may be obtained from the MACIF and MAAF, two large insurance cooperatives, but don't expect snappy service, and don't plan on communicating by telephone. The rates may be low, but the frills are missing. In the case of stolen cars, you may be obliged to wait 60 days or more before settling your claim, and the cost of a car rental in the interim is not included.

If you are considering the purchase of a car in France the following list should be of interest. These vehicles are very difficult and very expensive to insure because of their statistical chances of being stolen and/or of provoking accidents.

Ford Escort Cabriolet
Honda Accord Berline
Opel Corsa Berline
Opel Kadett 2000
Peugeot 205
Peugeot 405 MI
Renault Super 5
Renault Clio Baccara
Renault 19-16S
Renault 21 Baccara
Renault 25 Turbo
Renault Cherokee
Seat Ibiza
Volkswagen Travelling
Volkswagen Golf

**Documentation of Motor Vehicles**
Foreign-registered automobiles entering France by road or ferry are not normally documented by the French Customs at the point of entry. Vehicles shipped to France are treated differently. The shipping company is issued a *déclaration d'admission* by French Customs at the seaport

and this is delivered to the owner with the car.

The French Customs Office decides if foreign license plates can be used in France or if French plates *(plaques d'immatriculation)* are required. In general, cars imported for less than three months can keep their foreign plates; those brought in for more than three months need French plates. After having cleared their vehicles through a French port of entry, foreigners who plan to reside temporarily or permanently in France should consult the local Customs Office to establish the status of their vehicles In Paris, the address is:

**Bureau de Paris-Douane**
**Tourisme:** 11, rue Leon Jouhaux
75010 Paris
Tel: 40.40.60.35.

In addition to license plates, imported automobiles should have a nationality sticker *(plaque de nationalité)* mounted near the rear license plate. These stickers (usually an adhesive plastic disk) can be purchased at most auto accessory stores. The sticker or disk for France obviously is the letter F.

Once an imported vehicle has been processed through the French Customs Office in Paris (or elsewhere, if applicable) the most practical way to document the vehicle or, if necessary, to register it (obtain a *certificat d'immatriculation*, often referred to as *carte grise*) and get license plates is to apply to:

**Automobile Club de l'Ile de France**
14, avenue de la Grande Armée
75017 Paris
Tel: 43.80.68.58.

The Automobile Club has offices or representatives in most cities and larger towns in France, but motorists outside of Paris should contact the regional offices in major cities to document their vehicles.

For information on sales and transfers of ownership, consult the embassy of your home country; they have printed material available upon request.

If you want to bring a car to France from the United States or from another country, you'll need to apply for a French registration card (*carte grise*) for the car. This *carte grise* is required for an insurance company in France to be able to insure a vehicle against theft. Some agents will take your money for a full risk policy, but no company will ever pay you if a car that has no *carte grise* is stolen. So, if the car is worth insuring against theft, you must go through the steps. First of all, be prepared to suffer. At the end of all the administrative rigmarole and fees, it's not certain that it was worth bringing the car into the country. But, if you want to proceed, here's how to do it. If you enter France from an EU country, which is always the case, you no longer need to clear customs at the border. Proceed to your home city. First step is the *centre des impôts*, where you need a tax clearance form. On cars more than five years old there is no TVA or duty to pay. Newer cars are subject to a tax. Then you must go to your local *préfecture de police, Service des Mines*, and ask for a "*dossier de demande d'immatriculation*". You will be asked to fill out numerous forms and will be required to provide the previous registration, the car title, the Form 846A, your identification card or passport, a *timbre fiscal* for 200 FF, and an *attestation de conformité*. The circus continues. To obtain this *attestation* which affirms that the make and model of your car complies with French conformity laws, you must find a dealer or importer of that make of car and have him verify your car's conformity. There may be a fee for this ranging from several hundred francs to several thousand, depending on the make and, above all, if the car needs changes to meet French conformity. Assuming your car easily meets conformity, you will receive a letter from the DRIRE requesting you to produce the car and all the paperwork at a control center in Gonesse, a dreary urban suburb north of Paris. Be prepared to wait. They might then ask you to return to the dealer and change a number of small or not so small items on your car. This can continue to happen several times, until they are satisfied. Finally, you will receive a letter from the Ministry informing you that you are entitled to a French *carte grise*, which then will be issued within the next six to 24 months! The *carte grise* comes with an annual fee as well depending on the size of the engine. Wouldn't it have been better to have bought a car locally?

**Practical Advise Against Auto Theft**
300,000 cars are stolen in Paris each year. Don't tempt thieves.

-Don't leave anything in the car, particularly valuable objects and papers.

-Never leave your *carte grise* in the car. If you do, it makes it very easy for the thief to resell the car.

-Use the steering lock.

-Remove the radio/cassette if possible.

-Engrave the windows with the license plate number of your car. This makes the resale more difficult.

-Install an alarm

For more specific information ask for Advantage's prepared Auto Policy Pack.

**Advantage Insurance**
Anne Deshayes
57, rue du Fbg. Montmartre
75009 Paris
Tel: 53.20.03.33/Fax: 44.63.00.97.

## Car Rentals

To rent a car in France you must be at least 21 years old and hold a valid drivers license (at least one year old). A major credit card facilitates matters.

**Avis Location de Voitures S.A.**
5, rue Bixio
75007 Paris
Tel: 46.10.60.60 (Res. & Info)

**Budget**
4, av Franklin Roosevelt
75008 Paris
Tel: 42.25.79.89
**Europcar (National)**
5, av Italie
75013 Paris
Tel: 43.31.58.99
**Hertz France S.A.**
Tel: 47.88.51.51 (Res. & Info)
Minitel: 3515 HERTZ
**EuroRent**
27, bd. Diderot
75012 Paris
Tel: 43.42.90.90 (Res. & Info)
Toll Free: 05.33.22.10

## Parking

Parking in Paris can be a nightmare. There are just too many cars in Paris for the amount of space. Throughout most of central Paris, on-street paid-parking is the rule. Instead of parking meters, Paris had adopted a system whereby you purchase a paper ticket from a parking meter machine on the block where you've parked, indicating until what time you have paid. This, you leave on your dashboard. The flock of women in blue coats (in the past pejoratively called *aubergines*) you'll see parading up and down the avenue writing tickets can rarely be charmed. Now they're called *pervenches* (periwinkles) in that they've changed the color of their coats. The basic parking ticket is 75 FF, which skyrockets to 220 FF if unpaid after

three months. Parking in an illegal spot is an automatic 230 FF, which becomes 500 FF if unpaid, later to jump to 1100 FF, etc.
At the same time, the style of Paris parking is somewhat chaotic, as you'll habitually see cars pulled up on sidewalks, over curbs, and into other seemingly illegal spaces. This is especially true at night in the Latin Quarter and around Montparnasse where cars park along the center of the Boulevard du Montparnasse. Parisian drivers, who often leave parked cars in neutral *(point mort)*, also have the odd habit of pushing cars forward or backward with their bumpers to make room for their vehicle. One Japanese student observed this and gasped, "In Japan that'd be considered an accident."
If you get towed, call the police in the neighborhood in which you've parked for the address of the tow yard *(fourrière)*. Be prepared to pay in cash or by French check. Some take *carte bleue*.
Curiously, there is a tradition in France that all parking fines are waived by the new administration after each Presidential election, so if elections are coming up within a year, you might want to hold out on paying, otherwise, better pay promptly to avoid the accumulation of penalties. Parking tickets are, of course, paid by purchasing the *timbre fiscal* again in the *tabac*, sticking half on the return portion of the ticket and retaining the other for

your records. When you receive a note in the mail and a bill for the penalty on unpaid tickets you can no longer *régler* (pay) with a *timbre fiscal*; you must send a check to or visit the *Trésor public*. Payment schedules can be negotiated. With the increase of greater European cooperation, tickets given to other EU cars are forwarded for collection in those respective countries.

If you want to utilize the reduced parking rate for local residents indicated on parking meters, go to the *mairie* of your *arrondissement* with documentation that you reside there and they will issue you a resident permit in a little plastic pouch which you adhere to the right hand corner of your windshield. There is a place to put your meter receipts next to your residence permit. There is soon to be parking meter subscription cards usable like the *télécartes*.

## Traffic Patterns

Traffic in and around Paris is often heavily congested. The *périphérique* (the ring road that encircles the city) is particularly affected especially in the mornings and late afternoons. Paris rush hours tend to be nearly constant. The areas around the Porte d'Orléans, Porte d'Italie, Porte de Bagnolet, Porte de la Chapelle, and Porte Maillot can be particularly clogged up. Traffic jams are called *bouchons*, and backed up traffic is

called *un embouteillage*. Friday afternoons are hard getting out of Paris and Sunday evenings are miserable getting back.

France, being so centralized, the French are pre-programmed, and schedules are set so that everyone travels at the same time and usually in the same directions. The school vacation periods for the entire country are divided into three zones and sets of dates. In the winter, the *départ* for the *sports d'hiver* (winter sports) resorts (*stations*) in the Alps and Pyrenees cause major and predictable bottle necks. The same phenomenon occurs at the Easter break and of course in the summer. For traffic info, weather conditions, and recommended alternative routes consult 36.15 *Bison Futé* on the Minitel.

### Motorcycles *(Motos)*
Paris hosts a proliferation of motorcycles, scooters, *mobylettes* and other motorized two-wheelers. Most of Paris' internal message and delivery services *(coursiers)* move this way.

For those considering scooters and mopeds, a special driver's license is not needed, although helmets are required. These vehicles run on a special gas/oil mixture called Gasoil.

### Bicycles
Riding your bike in Paris can be a hazardous but exhilarating experience, existential even, in that the narrow bike lanes that are painted onto some streets between the bus/taxis

lane on the right and the car lane to the left, is nothing more than an ignored concept in the minds of Paris drivers. Helmets, although required, are practically never worn, and are highly recommended. Although sports cyclists are respected in France, and the Tour de France holds an important place in the average French person's view of the world, Parisian drivers are not the most respectful to recreational bicycle riders. The traffic circles at the Bastille, Nation, Etoile, and Concorde require Indiana Jones' sense of daring. Otherwise, getting around Paris on bike, especially in the Spring and Summer, is lovely and practical.

The SNCF rents bikes in most train stations around France for a very modest fee, and is also equipped to take on your bike on most trains. One particularly nice bike trip from Paris in the summer is to follow the Marne river along its banks. For bike rentals and repairs there is the **Maison du Vélo**, at 11, rue Fénelon, 75010 Paris, Tel: 42.81.24.72. To buy and sell new and second-hand bikes, you can try **Bicloune**, 7 rue Froment, 75011 Paris, Tel: 48.05.47.75. Some people go up to Amsterdam to buy excellent and sturdy used bikes and bring them back by train.

**Auto Parts/Used Parts**

If you do have a car and feel like doing some mechanics or body work yourself, you might have need for a junk yard. In French, the word you want is *la casse*, and you can find a strange stretch of urban sprawl specializing in used and wrecked automobiles along the N7 *(Nationale 7)* heading south from the Porte d'Italie in the towns of Vitry and Villejuif. Here, on both sides of the road you'll find ugly heaps of cars of all makes and years, gutted, stripped, and available for your perusal for just that missing seat belt or wing window or smashed fender or carburetor. Bring your own tools and always bargain down the prices. Here, you'll see a part of Paris that they don't show you in the travel brochures, and for just this reason, you might want to take a weird stroll through the land of stripped chassis.

As for taking your vehicle in for work at a dealer or garage, you might need some vocabulary specific for the task. Be vary of little added gems on your bill like *petites fournitures*, which sounds like joints and washers and stuff like that, but is really just an invented way to add 3% to your bill. The garages all try to do this and get away with it all the time.

**Lexicon**

| | |
|---|---|
| *batterie* | battery |
| *boîte de vitesses* | gear box |
| *capot* | hood or bonnet |
| *carburant* | gasoline |
| *carrosserie* | chassis |
| *ceinture* | seatbelt |
| *coffre* | trunk or boot |
| *embrayage* | clutch |
| *essuie-glaces* | windshield wipers |
| *freins* | brakes |
| *klaxon* | horn |
| *pare-brise* | windshield |
| *pneus* | tires |
| *point mort* | neutral |
| *siège* | seat |
| *volant* | steering wheel |

# Telecommunications

France's sophistication in communications is impressive. On the whole, you will see that the telecommunications field is one of the most dynamic areas of French industry. The Post Office *(La Poste),* formerly the PTT (*Postes Téléphones, Télégraphes*) has been separated administratively from the dynamic and expanding France-Telecom, the nationalized telephone company, in an effort to increase efficiency. There is discussion about privatising France Telecom the way other industrial giants in the public sector have gone in 1992 and 1993. France has worked hard to bridge new technology and *la vie quotidienne* (daily life). France-Telecom, has brought the latest technological developments into the home with the Minitel, an on-line computer and screen accessed through the telephone system which is at once a visual telephone book, reservation network, and research library, as well as a home shopping tool, a direct means of written communication with other users, computer and video link-up, and more. Use of the Minitel as a fax, printer, modem, etc. already exists. Minitels can be obtained free from the local telephone office in your *arrondissement* (See Minitel).

## The Public Telephone Booth (*Cabine téléphonique*) and *Télécarte*

Over the last several years almost all public coin-operated phone booths have been replaced with a new type that accepts only micro-chipped cards, called the *Télécarte,* which can be bought in post offices and *tabacs* (certain cafés which have a licence to sell cigarettes, etc.) in units of 50 or 120 for 40 FF and 96 FF respectively. Buy one right away; they're very practical! Plus, it's getting virtually impossible to find a public phone that takes coins (local calls require a one franc coin). If you find yourself caught out, try a café or bar; many of them still have coin-operated phones.

All Paris and the close suburbs have numbers beginning with 4 and now a few with 5 (the more distant suburbs begin with 3 or 6). Calls from Paris to other parts of France require the prefix 16. Calls from provinces to Paris require the prefix 16 and 1. International calls must be preceded with 19. In any case, wait for a second dial tone and then dial your number. On the last remaining coin phones, you'll get a round blinking sign or beep on the phone when your money is about the run out. Shove in more coins—one, two, or five franc pieces are accepted. Otherwise, with your *télécarte* you can call anywhere in the world as long as you still have units left on the card. You can change cards in the middle of a call.

In the Sixties and Seventies, broken phones were occasionally discovered which allowed free unlimited international calls to go through undetected. When the word got around, lines would form with foreign students at all hours of the night to call families and friends around the world at no charge. These wonderful little finds have all but disappeared with the new telephone card. The advantage of the card is that there is no money to deal with. Each unit as of Spring 1994 costs 73 *centimes* and units are deducted electronically from the micro-chip

*(puce)* of the card automatically at a rate which depends on where and when you're calling. Telecom's rates have radically been reduced over the last two years, reversing a former situation whereby the French rates were prohibitively higher than those offered by US companies. Now, using a card or calling from home, one minute to the United States or Canada costs 6,69 FF TTC at peak hours, and only 4,98 FF TTC per minute during the reduced periods. One minute to England costs 3,65 FF TTC at prime time, and only 3,04 FF TTC per minute during the reduced periods.

If you get cut off or have disturbing interference on the line, don't count on asking the operator for credit. It's not an option.

To use *télécarte* phones, pick up the receiver, slide in the card, arrow facing forward, close the *volet* (sliding mechanism), wait for a dial tone, and make your call. After hanging up wait about five seconds; the *volet* will open and a beep will sound, reminding you not to forget your card. Note that these cards have become collectors items in France much like baseball cards in America. The card with the Van Gogh portrait had been very popular as were the cards commemorating the 1992 winter Olympics in Albertville. Hundreds of private companies have paid France Telecom to advertise on the face of these cards. Collectors and traders, a vast number, curiously, African and West Indian, hang around the cluster of *cabines*

| Quick Reference Telephone Rates (France Telecom) | | |
|---|---|---|
| **USA** One minute to the US and Canada | 6,69 FF | High rate |
| One minute to the US and Canada | 4,98 FF | Low rate* |
| *Everyday from 2 a.m. till noon. | | |
| **UK** One minute to the UK | 3,65 FF | High rate |
| One minute to the UK | 3,04 FF | Low rate* |
| *Mon.-Fri. from midnight to 8 a.m. and from 9:30 p.m. till midnight. Sat. from midnight to 8 a.m. and from 2 p.m. till midnight. Sundays and holidays from midnight till midnight. | | |

*téléphoniques* in the concourse at the Châtelet/Les Halles *Métro*/RER station dealing these cards. France Telecom offers a voice mail service called *Mémophone* at no charge. You simply create your own voice mail number and access code and anyone you give them to can leave or pick up messages. Ask for details at your local France Telecom agency.

 **France Telecom**

## National & International Telephone Dialing Codes

**Calling the French provinces from Paris:** dial 16, wait for the tone, dial the number.

**Calling between the provinces:** Dial the number; no 16 needed.

**Calling the Paris area from the provinces:** Dial 16, wait for the tone, dial 1, and then the number.

**Making an international call from anywhere in France:** Dial 19, wait for the tone, dial the country code, the city code and the number.

The American telephone giants along with an outcrop of smaller and ambitious outfits have been investing heavily for what AT&T calls its "expatriate accounts." You can compare and choose.

**AT&T Dial Direct Service:** To call the US collect or to use an AT&T calling card, dial 19 then 0011 to get an AT&T operator.

The MCI Direct dial code from France is: (19) 0019 then wait for operator.

The Sprint code is: (19) 0087 then wait for operator.

Collect calls can be made with any of these three services. France Telecom offers its own *Carte France Telecom* (formerly *Carte Pastel*) for direct dialing France from overseas or nationally. In the case of loss or theft of this card, call (*numéro vert*) Toll-Free 05.10.20.40 (in France); or (33) (1)42.46.36.36 (if you are outside France).

A few of the newer, smaller, and potentially more economical services advertise regularly in Paris. By far, the most intriguing is Telegroup Global Access, the first Call Back service in France, set up by American George Apple. Its VIP American-style service is free and there is no minimum usage requirement with high savings to the US, Japan and elsewhere.
Telegroup Global Access
Tel: 30.61.43.22

### Cordless and Portables

A note on cordless phones. Brands not accredited by France Telecom tend to have less secure frequency protection systems. Numerous cases in 1993 were reported of pirated calls and large unexpected phone bills especially to Turkey, Pakistan and The Philippines caused by people breaking into unprotected frquency bands on portable telephones and dialing away at the subscriber's expense. France Telecom has not reimbursed users who had non-approved cordless phones and claims no responsibility despite a class action suit brought against Telecom by angry citizens with inflated bills.
Also note that models of portables

bought in the US and the U.K. will not work in France. New worldwide portable cellular systems are expected in the future, but for the time being the best bet in France is the *Itineris* system for pan-European service, marketed ubiquitously as GSM, the rage of 1994.

### International Country Codes

After dialing 19 and reaching the international dial tone, the following country codes give you access to the country desired. Consult the Quick Reference Chart for country and city codes most often dialed.

| | |
|---|---|
| Afghanistan: | 93 |
| Albania: | 355 |
| Algeria: | 213 |
| American Virgin Islands: | 1809 |
| Angola: | 244 |
| Antilles néerlandaises: | 599 |
| Argentina: | 54 |
| Ascension: | 247 |
| Australia: | 61 |
| Austria: | 43 |
| Azores: | 351 |
| Bahamas: | 1809 |
| Bahrain: | 973 |
| Bangladesh: | 880 |
| Belgium: | 32 |
| Belize: | 501 |
| Benin: | 229 |
| Bermuda: | 1809 |
| Bolivia: | 591 |
| Botswana: | 267 |
| Brazil: | 55 |
| British Virgin Islands: | 1809 |
| Brunei: | 673 |
| Bulgaria: | 359 |
| Burkina Faso: | 226 |

Burundi: ...................................257
Cameroon: ..............................237
Canada: ......................................1
Cap Vert: .................................238
Cayman Islands: .....................1809
Central African Republic: ..........236
Chad: ......................................235
Chile: ........................................56
China: ........................................86
Cyprus: ....................................357
Colombia: ..................................57
Comores: ..................................269
Congo: .....................................242
Cook: .......................................682
Costa Rica: ...............................506
Croatia....................................385
Cuba: ........................................53
Czech Republic: .........................42
Denmark: ...................................45
Djibouti: ..................................253
Dominican Republic: ..............1809
Egypt: ........................................20
El Salvador: ..............................503
Ecuador: ..................................593
Ethiopia: ..................................251
Falkland Islands: .......................500
Faroe Islands: ...........................298
Fiji: .........................................679
Finland: ...................................358
French Polynesia .......................689
Gabon: .....................................241
Gambia: ...................................220
Germany:....................................49
Ghana: .....................................233
Gibraltar: .................................350
Greece: ......................................30
Grenada: ................................1809
Greenland: ...............................299
Guadeloupe: .............................590
Guam*:.........................19.33.671
Guatemala: ...............................502
Guinea: ....................................224
Guinea Bissau: ..........................245
Guinea Equatorial: ....................240

Guyana: ...................................592
Guyane: ...................................594
Haiti: .......................................509
Honduras: ................................504
Hong Kong: ..............................852
Hungary: ....................................36
India: .........................................91
Indonesia: ..................................62
Iraq: ........................................964
Iran: ..........................................98
Ireland: ....................................353
Iceland: ....................................354
Israel: ......................................972
Italy: .........................................39
Ivory Coast: .............................225
Jamaica: .................................1809
Japan: ........................................81
Jordan: .....................................962
Kenya: .....................................254
Korea (South): ............................82
Korea (North): ..........................850
Kuwait: ....................................965
Laos: ........................................856
Lesotho: ...................................266
Lebanon: ..................................961
Liberia: ....................................231
Libya: .......................................218
Liechtenstein: .............................41
Luxembourg: ............................352
Macao: .....................................853
Madagascar: .............................261
Madeira: ...................................351
Malaysia: ....................................60
Malawi: ....................................265
Maldives: ..................................960
Mali: ........................................223
Malta: ......................................356
Martinique: ..............................596
Mauritius Island: ......................230
Mauritanie: ..............................222
Mayotte ...................................269
Mexico: ......................................52
Monaco**: ..................................93
Mongolia*:....................19.33.976

\* Via operator only.
\*\* French province, 16 instead of 19.

Montserrat: ....................1809
Morocco: .........................212
Mozambique: ....................258
Namibia: ..........................264
Nauru Islands: .................674
Nepal: ..............................977
Netherlands: .....................31
New Caledonia .................687
New Zealand: ....................64
Nicaragua: ........................505
Nieue Islands*: .......19.33.683
Niger: ................................227
Nigeria: .............................234
Norfolk Island: ................6723
Norway: ..............................47
Oman: ................................968
Uganda: .............................256
Pakistan: .............................92
Panama: .............................507
Papua/New Guinea: ...........675
Paraguay: ...........................595
Peru: ...................................51
Phillipines: ...........................63
Poland: ................................48
Portugal: .............................351
Puerto Rico: .....................1809
Qatar: .................................974
Réunion: .............................269
Romania: .............................40
Russia: ...................................7
Rwanda: ..............................250
Samoa US: ..........................684
Samoa Western: ..................685
Sao Tome e Principe: ..........239
San Marino: ..........................39
St Pierre et Miquelon: ..........508
St Vincent: ........................1809
St Kitts: .............................1809
St Helene: ...........................290
St Lucia: ............................1809
Saudi Arabia: ......................966
Senegal: ..............................221
Seychelles: ...........................248
Sierra Leone*: ..........19.33.232

Singapore: .............................65
Slovenia: ..............................386
Somalia: ...............................252
Solomon Islands: ..................677
South Africa: ..........................27
Spain: .....................................34
Sri Lanka: ...............................94
Sudan*: .....................19.33.249
Surinam: ...............................597
Sweden: ..................................46
Swaziland: .............................268
Switzerland: .............................41
Syria: .....................................963
Taiwan: ..................................886
Tanzania: ...............................255
Thailand: .................................66
Togo: .....................................228
Tonga: ...................................676
Trinidad and Tobago: ..........1809
Tunisia: ..................................216
Turks and Caicos Islands: ....1809
Turkey: ....................................90
United Arab Emirates: ...........971
United Kingdom: ......................44
Uruguay: ................................598
U.S.A.: ......................................1
Vanauatu: ..............................678
Vatican City: ............................39
Venezuela: ...............................58
Vietnam: ..................................84
Wallis et Futuna: ...................681
Yemen (Republic): .................967
Yemen (Dem. Pop. Rep.)*: ....19.33.969
Yougoslavia: ..........................381
Zaire: .....................................243
Zambia: ..................................260
Zimbabwe: .............................263

**Quick Reference List
for World Cities**
Amsterdam: ...................(19) 31.20
Athens: ...........................(19) 30.1
Auckland: ......................(19) 64. 9
Beijing: ...........................(19) 86.1

Berlin: ....................................(19) 49.30
Bombay: .................................(19) 91.22
Boston: ...................................(19) 1. 617
Brussels: ................................(19) 32.2
Budapest: ...............................(19) 36.1
Cairo: .....................................(19) 20.2
Casablanca: ...........................(19) 212.2
Chicago: .................................(19) 1.312
Copenhagen: ..........................(19) 45
Dublin: ...................................(19) 353.1
Edinbourg: .............................(19) 44.31
Frankfurt: ...............................(19) 49.69
Hamburg: ................................(19) 49.40
Helsinki: .................................(19) 358.0
Istanbul: ...............(19) 90.212 or 216
Jerusalem: ..............................(19) 972.2
Johannesburg: ........................(19) 27.11
Kyoto: ....................................(19) 81.75
Lisbon: ...................................(19) 351.1
London: .................(19) 44.71 or 44.81
Los Angeles: ..........................(19) 1.213
Luxembourg: ..........................(19) 352
Madrid: ..................................(19) 34.1
Manchester: ...........................(19) 44.61

Melbourne: .............................(19) 61.3
Mexico City: ..........................(19) 52.5
Miami: ...................................(19) 1.305
Milan: ....................................(19) 39.2
Montreal: ...............................(19) 1.514
Moscow: .................................(19) 7.095
Munich: ..................................(19) 49.89
New York: ..............................(19) 1.212
Oslo: ......................................(19) 47.2
Prague: ...................................(19) 42.2
Rio de Janeiro: .......................(19) 55.21
Rome: .....................................(19) 39.6
San Francisco: ........................(19) 1.415
Shanghai: ...............................(19) 86.21
St. Petersberg: ........................(19) 7.812
Sydney: ...................................(19) 61.2
Tel Aviv: ................................(19) 972.3
Tokyo: ..................(19) 81.3 or 1.905
Toronto: .................................(19) 1.416
Tunis: .....................................(19) 216.1
Vancouver: .............................(19) 1.604
Warsaw: ..................(19) 48.2 or 48.22
Washington, D.C.: ...............(19) 1.202

## Getting Information

Directory Enquiries is acquired by **dialing 12** on your telephone, and it costs 3.50 FF.

By Minitel, the same service is had by **dialing 11**. There is no cost for the first three minutes.

For international directory assistance, **dial 19**, wait for the tone, **dial 33-12** and the country code.

To get US directory information at no cost, call one of the American telephone companies followed by the area code 555 1212.

To lodge complaints and report technical problems **dial 13**.

For all commercial and billing questions **dial 14**.

Medical Emergencies: **dial 15**.

Police: **dial 17**

Fire Department (*pompier*): **dial 18**.

---

### Telephone Skills in French

Those first few calls can be traumatic. It's especially difficult to integrate your French into dialogue when you cannot see the other person and can't rely on gestures. Here are a few simple telephone dialogue patterns for the uninitiated:
How to ask for someone:
—*Bonjour, est-ce que je peux parler avec...?* (Hello, can I speak with...?)
—*Bonjour, puis-je parler avec..?* (Hello, may I speak with...?)
—*Bonjour, est-ce que Monsieur (Made-moiselle, Madame) ... est là?* (Hello, is...there?)
Answering the telephone:
—*Allo* (Hello.)
—*Ne quittez pas.* (Don't hang up, or, hang on.)
—*Il/Elle n'est pas là.* (He/she is not here.)
—*Vous vous êtes trompé de numéro.* (You have the wrong number.)
—*Qui est à l'appareil?* (Who's calling?)
—*Est-ce que je peux laisser un message?* (Can I leave a message?)
—*C'est* (your name) *à l'appareil.* (It's ...calling.)
—*Comment ça s'écrit?* (How is that spelled?)
—*Je suis désolé(e).* (I'm sorry.)
—*Répétez, s'il vous plaît.* (Please repeat that.)
—*Lentement, s'il vous plaît.* (Slowly, please.)

---

## Minitel

The Minitel is a small, on-line computer with multi-services that can be connected to any French telephone line and can be accessed internationally via modem hook-up. The basic telephone directory service which has virtually replaced the telephone book in France is available free of charge to anyone possessing a telephone. Although the basic service, the information directory, obtained by simply dialing 11, is free for the first two minutes, other services such as banking, shopping, research, ticket reserva-

tions, dating services, porno, etc. accessed by dialing 36.14, 36.15, 36.16, and 36.17 prefixes on the phone, followed by different *serveur* codes on the Minitel unit, are charged by the minute directly to your semi-monthly telephone bill. Prices vary for different services, ranging from 37 *centimes* a minute to over 3 FF, with some highly specialized services costing much more. Rates are listed at the beginning of the connection. So be careful with this fascinating, seductive, and vastly useful tool, and toy.
The Minitel 2, a new generation of Minitel, is now in place with some 8000 services. The Minicom 3612

service permits you to conduct constant on-line correspondence with any other Minitel. Additionally, Minitel 12 is available, the state of the arts Minitel unit which affords users all sorts of telecommunications services and can be connected to modem, computer, printer, video.... The Agoris 55 is a personal fax machine that sits on the Minitel and prints from the Minitel.

Throughout Paris you will see a strange host of billboards advertising Minitel services. These begin with the access numbers plus a usually catchy code, the most embarrassing one for Anglo-Saxons being 36.15 CUM, a service for singles to meet, talk, play, seduce, sometimes marry. The 2000-plus porn-oriented services, better known as *messageries roses,* have generated some controversy; the State has tried to limit "unhealthy" use of the Minitel while it reaps the huge financial benefits of electronic quasi-porn. Minitel services have erupted over the last few years. Additionally, telephone numbers with 36 are often special-rate services, games, contests, and pay-for-information lines. Many television shows have 36 services for viewers. Rates can be as steep as 9 francs per minute, but the idea is moving the industry swiftly towards interactive television.

## User's Instructions

To use the Minitel, turn on the unit, dial the code number on your tele-

phone, wait for the Fax-like tone, type in the rest of the code on the Minitel, and then press *Connexion fin* on the Minitel keyboard. Now, you're on-line. The rest should be self-evident. To break the connection and stop the billing clock, but not erase the information on the screen, touch *Connexion fin.*

Though France Telecom doesn't have a satisfactory guide for the Minitel, periodically you will find Minitel guides at newspaper kiosques. Though often saturated with tacky and tasteless ads, they can provide a helpful listing. *Libération* publishes a mini-directory from time to time as well. You can consult the guide to services when connected to the Minitel, but that costs. Here is a sampling of some of the more useful services and their access codes. The price of each service per minute is displayed on your monitor as you sign-on. The list grows daily.

## Minitel List

**3615 AF** Air France information.

**3615 AIRTEL** National and international airline schedules and airfares.

**3615 AMNESTY** A good way to join Amnesty—this connection lists their accomplishments, the when and where of their protest marches, who their contacts are, plus educational games and even the possibility to aid prisoners.

**3615 ASTRO** This service lets you know your sign, or your *Chinese* sign, your horoscope of the day, or of the year.

**3614 BBC** British and international news broadcast in English by the BBC.

**3615 BHV** Information, bargains, services, and job offers of the Bazar de l'Hôtel de Ville.

**3615 CORUS** Information on 150 mountain resorts.

**3615 DICO** The first dictionaries available by Minitel: orthography, synonyms, conjugations.

**3614 ED** Administrative and emergency phone numbers and addresses.

**3614 EMS** Chronopost—fast mail service.

**3615 EPARGNER** This service is essentially the same as the first two, though slightly less expensive, making it practical for frequent use.

**3614 EVAZUR** Tourist guide to the Cote d'Azur and the Midi. Useful addresses: hotels, restaurants, camping sites, discos.

**3617 FAX** In order to send a message by fax, you type in the fax number and the correspondent, then the message for a fee, *via* Minitel, will arrive by fax.

**3615 FLORITEL** Send some flowers—to anywhere in France. Prices range from 100 FF to 1500 FF, plus 30 FF delivery charges.

**3615 FNAC** A listing of all existing CD's (no listing of which are available and no way to order them).

**3611 FUAJ** Specify FUAJ under *Nom* and Paris under *Ville* and you will find information on all youth hostels in France.

**3615 GAULT** Listing of 2500 selected Paris restaurants with Henri Gault's opinions on the best ones.

**3615 HORAV** Airport guide: parking, services, hotels. Flight departure and arrival times.

**3615 INVESTIR** The stock market —live.

**3615 ITOUR** National directory of tourist bureaus by region, department and town.

**3615 JDF** The stock market with advice on how to invest your money.

**3615 LIBE** American and international news in English direct from USA TODAY.

**3615 LOCAT** Looking for an apartment? Find one through classifieds and agencies on the Minitel.

**3615 METEO** Weather forecast. Average time to connect: five minutes.

**3615 MICHELIN** To establish a detailed itinerary, to know the prices of tolls, hotels, restaurants on the road: this service can answer all these questions. Takes about ten minutes.

**3614 NATURISM**
Information on *naturisme* and naturist holiday centers (nudist colonies).

**3615 PARISCOPE** This allows you to reserve your seat at a movie theater.

**3615 PAT** Tourist and medical information on French thermal resorts, oceanotherapy, regeneration.

**3615 RANDO** Guide of walking trips in France. List of maps and guides.

**3615 RATP** Helpful in determining the best means of transport (*métro*, bus) to use and how long it will take you. About four minutes is average.

**3615 ROQUE** If you are a chess fanatic, then this service will interest you. Not only can you play chess with the computer, but with many other players at the same time.

**3616 SEALINK** Times and prices for ferries to England and Ireland.

**3615 SNCF** While indicating the station of arrival and departure, and the chosen date of your journey, this service offers all the possibilities of travel. For instance, you can reserve your ticket and pick it up later at either an SNCF window or a travel agency, on the condition of having kept the reference number that the Minitel provides. The catch? This service is always blocked up during rush hour, but the average time to reserve two tickets from Paris to Marseille is about six minutes.

**3615 T7J** Not only does this give a listing of all the TV programs but also a large list of wines for sale.

**3615 TMK** Allows you to order your groceries via Minitel, and delivered to your door the same day—for a 60 FF charge if your purchase is less than 1200 FF—or the next day for 45 FF. If your purchase is over 2000 FF, delivery charges are free. Order before 10h if you want it delivered the same day, and after 10h to choose the day you want it delivered. Pay by credit card or check, but make sure to order the catalogue, or you will spend most of your costly time browsing the selection on the Minitel.

**3615 UPI** International news in English.

**3617 USACCESS** News in English; yellow pages for New York and Boston

**3617 VAE** This new service, *ventes aux enchères*, is a complete listing of merchanize being sold off at auction following the bankruptcies and liquidations of companies.

**3617 VOCALE** If the person you're calling is absent, then type your message on the Minitel and it will be delivered by a synthesized voice at the time of your choice. You can also send a song, if you wish.

**3615 VOYAGEL** Formalities, addresses and practical information (hours and days of banking, shopping, etc.) to enable foreign tourists to have trouble-free holidays.

**3615 WELCOME** An English language minitel service from *Paris City Magazine* essential for remaining in touch with community news, gaining instant access to services, announcements, advertisments, astrology, games...

**3619 PC FLOWERS** A 24-hour on-line flower ordering service. Also plants and even balloons. Next day delivery to North America.

## New France-Telecom Services

In keeping with the times, France Telecom has continued to introduce a host of new services and products. France Telecom has also invested heavily in up to the minute telephone units, fax and answering machines, and portable telephones. You can request for nominal fees these features by visiting your Telecom office, dialing 3614 on your Minitel, or calling 14 on your telephone (*agence commerciale*). You should also note that the way the French telephone company has undergone a face-lift and has changed its corporate image in France and around the world as an international leader in the telecommunications industry. The logo was modernized in 1993. Here are some services and products:

• *Facturation détaillée* (itemized bill). Otherwise you'll just receive a bill for the total. Bills come every two months and you have ten days to pay or risk a 10% fine.

• *Signal d'appel* (call waiting). By touching the key on your phone marked R and then 2 you can put one call on hold while you take an incoming call.

• *Conversation à trois* (conference call). Dial R then 3 to call two numbers at once.

• *Transfert d'appel* (call transferring). By using the * and # keys you can program your phone to transfer your incoming calls automatically to another number at your command.

• *Bi-Bop* is a portable phone that works in the vicinity of some 40000 red, white and blue striped markers in public places and Paris streets. Very handy and very hip Parisian.

• *Itineris* is France Telecom's mobile phone service or GSM (Global System for Mobile Communication), which functions with a small card with a built-in chip which is replaced monthly on a subscription basis for around 250 F per month for the service.

The portable phone units are manufactured by several firms, notably the Swedish Erikson, Motorola, Canon and others. The service, marketed under the trade name of Cellway, is rapidly expanding its area of use. Currently valid in France and most other European countries, *Itineris* does not work outside of Europe, and there is no immediate plans for a wholly international mobile telephone. Marketed by numerous companies, including Hutchison, Telecom GSM, the portable telephone, has suddenly erupted in the French market.

• *Mémophone* (Voice Mail). Dial 3672 for an explanation on how to set up this useful voice mail service.

• *Numeris*. This is one of France Telecom's most sophisticated telecommunications technologies. *Numeris* is designed primarily for commercial concerns to transfer data bases, high fidelity sound, and video imaging from computer to computer through the telephone system. The implications of this technology are vast in that any phone line with this service and hardware can function as a computer terminal, video or film set, or recording studio.

## Post Office (La Poste)

Although the French postal service has been rated tenth among the twelve European Union countries, you will probably be both impressed and frustrated by your experiences concerning the mail. The latest PR slogan for La Poste is "*Pas de problème*." First, you will have to get used to longer lines than you're probably accustomed to. The French post office handles so many functions that sending a simple letter sometimes gets caught in the shuffle of all the rest. *La Poste* handles long distance telephone calls, telegrams, an express mail system called Chronopost, the entire array of letter and package possibilities, plus numerous financial and banking functions such as savings accounts, money markets, cables or wire transfers of funds, payment of telephone bills, distribution of major mail house catalogues, retirement plans, checking accounts, tax consulting, investment plans, housing funds, mortgages and more. *La Poste* is in direct competition with commercial banks. Of eight windows *(guichets)* open in an average post office, sometimes only two or three will be equipped for sending letters or packages—marked *Envoi de lettres et paquets* or *Toutes opérations* — but it is becoming more frequent to have other windows open for more services. If you plan to ask a lot of questions across that awful pane of plexiglass, don't expect to be treated like a human. You must sound apologetic if you are asking for something unusual like the price of a postcard to Mexico or an extra form for customs. Clearly mark your letters *par avion* if that's how you want them sent. Mark letters *lettres.* For small packages and heavy letters, always request *service économique.* You'll save money and not lose time. Don't expect to borrow tape, paper, string, etc. If you are displeased, don't yell, just ask for the *inspecteur.* you may or may not get to speak to him or her, but it's your only chance at satisfaction, short of writing to the Ministry for La Poste. Don't show up three minutes before closing time. Chances are you won't be allowed in.

**Paris central Post Office**
(open 24 hours a day/7 days a week)
52, rue du Louvre
75001 Paris
Tel: 40.28.20.00

## Postal Products and Services

*lettres:* All letters should be marked *LETTRE* to insure that they go first class. Your basic letter in France currently costs 2,80 FF. It's the same price for letters to all of the European Union countries. *Aérogrammes* are 4,20 FF for the whole world. The basic 10 gram air mail letter to North America and the Middle East is 3,50 FF. The price for post cards is the same. The French often send post cards in envelopes, a habit that seems bizarre to North Americans. In any case, they usually put the same postage as a letter, in that it then goes as fast as a letter. In that postal rates change periodically, it's a good idea, upon arrival, to request from your local post office a rate sheet.

*une lettre recommandée* (registered letter): the French use this rather expensive means (28 FF) not so much for security as to have proof that a particular letter, document, bill or administrative measure was executed. Post offices tend to be cheap with the forms so you often have to wait to get to the front of the line to fill in your registered letter form. When picking up a registered letter or package (and don't delay too long to collect it—it's not unusual for La Poste to be temporarily unable to find things), you must bring (in person) your *avis* (notice) plus valid identification that has a picture. If you want someone else to fetch it for you, you must file a form ahead of time or send that person with their identification card plus yours. The post office will only hold a registered letter (or package) for 15 days, so be careful when leaving town on holiday to have someone pick up your important mail with a *procuration* (signed proxy). Otherwise, you will find that registered letters and packages have been returned to the send-

er, and in most cases, the post office will not be able to tell you who the sender was. Very annoying.

*avec accusé de réception* (return receipt requested): this can be added to the registered letter if you want proof that your letter was in fact received on a certain date. Note: there is no such thing as insuring your letters or parcels, however, items sent *recommandé*—if lost, stolen, or damaged—can be reimbursed up to 750 FF. But you will never meet anyone who has ever collected.

*service économique,* formerly, *pli non urgent* (PNU) (Third class mail): This is cheaper but can be considerably slower, especially for items mailed near the end of the week in that PNU items do not travel on weekends. The *tarif economique* is designated by its new green sticker. Advisable for Air Mail packages overseas and for sending books.

*Colissimo*: Packages require more work to send in France than in many other countries. First of all, they need to be packaged in a special wrap, so you are better off just buying the ready-made boxes at the post office. Also, first class letters and packages are limited to two kilos (4.4 pounds). Books and packages are limited to five kilos (11 pounds). For heavier items, you are obliged to take your wares to a special window at the main post office of any *arrondissement* or the Central Post Office at 52, rue du Louvre in the first *arrondissement*. This post office, it should be noted, is the only 24 hour/7 days a week postal facility in Paris. This is useful when you have applications and other materials that need to be postmarked by a particular date. Enquire about special postal *sacs* for sending books and *classe économique* for cheaper air mail service. A new *colissimo* service for packages up to ten kilos has been introduced.

**Chronopost International:** Chronopost is the French Post Office's Express Mail service. Letters sent to North America by Chronopost arrive in 48 hours, guaranteed. Packages can also be sent by Chronopost up to 30 kilos. A letter will cost you about 200 FF. Minitel provides information on everything you ever wanted to know about Chronopost—3614 EMS. Items sent via US International Express Mail arrive via Chrono-

post, and can be delivered to a post office box, whereas Federal Express or DHL parcels cannot. Service valid for 190 countries.

*Poste restante:* If you find yourself in France without a reliable address, remember that you can always receive mail by having it sent to the post office of your choice marked with your name and *poste restante*. Other options include the American Express Office (*Métro*: Opéra) or Western Union. Attention: *poste restante* costs 1,40 FF for a newspaper, 2,80 FF for other objects.

**Distingo:** For domestic French mail, this pre-stamped over-sized envelop is designed for express mail up to 250 grams and costs 20 FF for small format and 25 FF for large format.

**Posteclair:** The post office offers this fax service. 32 FF a page for Paris-London. It's expensive but at least you have a way to fax something.

---

### Terminology

| | |
|---|---|
| *cedex* | PO box address |
| *la/le destinataire* | addressee |
| *l'aérogramme* | aérogram |
| *par avion* or *poste aérienne* | air mail |
| *le carnet de timbres* | book of stamps (10) |
| *le changement d'adresse* | change of address |
| *le timbre philatélique* | commemorative or collector stamp |

| | |
|---|---|
| *le guichet* | counteror window |
| *la déclaration de douane* | customs declaration |
| *la distribution* | delivery |
| *la réexpédition* | forwarding |
| *la poste restante* | general delivery |
| *la réclamation* | inquiry |
| *l'assuré* | insured |
| *le facteur* | letter carrier |
| *le courrier* | mail |
| *la boîte aux lettres* | mail box |
| *le paquet* or *le colis* | package |
| *le bureau de poste* | post office |
| *la boîte postale (B.P.)* | post office box |
| *le mandat* | money order |
| *l'imprimé* | printed matter |
| *le récépissé* | receipt |
| *recommandé* | registered |
| *l'avis de réception* | return receipt |
| *l'expéditeur* | sender |
| *la dimension* | size |
| *par express* | special delivery |
| *la carte postale pré-affranchie* | stamped post card |
| *le poids* | weight |
| *emballage* | mailing box |

# Wish they were here?

## Call home.

No matter how exciting the places you visit on your travels, chances are you're still going to miss relatives and friends back home. So dial some smiles with the AT&T access number below. An AT&T Operator (or simple English-language voice prompts) will help connect you to the States quickly and easily. Between 80 other countries, too. With convenient billing either on your AT&T Card or U.S. Local Telephone Company calling card, or by calling collect.*

So don't miss a thing while you're here. Catch up back home with AT&T.

**To apply, call us toll-free at 05-48-51-11. To use it, just dial 19-0011 from France.**

# Media

## Television

French television has progressively loosened up and expanded over the last five years. Some would argue that the quality has diminished. The arrival of cable too has changed the face of what's seen on the tube in France. For example, CNN, Sky, BBC, Eurovision, MTV and other networks are now available. Not so long ago there was no programming before noon so that kids wouldn't be fixed to TV sets. And there were few programs after midnight. France has changed.

There are five French television stations and one subscriber station currently available to Parisian viewers. The channels are: TF1 which is privately owned, France 2 (formerly Antenne 2) which is state owned and shares much of its programming with France 3 (formerly FR 3) which is also state owned but more region-ally oriented than France 2. The subscriber station, Canal Plus, is on channel 4 and can only be viewed with a decoder which comes with the subscription. Canal Plus is particularly useful for those interested in catching Monday Night Football, World Boxing matches and NBA playoffs. The films are often worthwhile but more than often B-class. There are certain programs on Canal Plus during the day which are transmitted *en clair* (unscrambled). One of these *en clair* moments includes a 7h or 8h (depending on the season) transmission of Dan Rather's CBS Nighly News from the previous evening. Dan is of course speaking English, but subtitles have been added for French viewers. It can be fun to watch your shifting perceptions of American life and media as you live overseas and begin to see the world from a wider, more international perspective.

*La Cinq*, channel 5, a highly commercial station, went belly-up a few years back, and, fortunately, has been replaced with a station providing by far the best quality cultural programming in Europe, *Arte*. *Arte* is a joint venture between France and Germany and includes funding and imput from a host of sources. The documentaries—mostly in French and/or German—are sometimes in English or Russian or something else—and are excellent. Although not watched by too many folks, *Arte* offers the viewer an idea of how television can be used with creative intelligence. M6, on channel 6 and harder to *capter* (receive/tune in), has recently attempted to beef-up its image and programming.

French television programming has lost some of its didactic edge, and has taken on some of the worst aspects of American television, such as the taste for violence, and thus American cops in Los Angeles and Miami are rather well known in France. The French viewing public has become increasingly consumer-motivated. Wheel of Fortune is a favorite. French game shows are derivitive of American television of the 70s, although far more sexist in their blatant objectification of women, not inconsistent with French culture in general. There is really no French equivalent of political awareness! On subjects that do not have a bearing on French government, French television documentary news can be

excellent; cultural reporting is extensive, and panel discussions and interviews are frequent and lively. Subjects are afforded time and people are allowed to speak at length. On the other hand, don't count on any of the channels to bring you tenacious, investigative reporting on politically hot issues. There is little editorial criticism of the government. The newness of investigative journalism in France stems from a general public tolerance for not knowing, unlike the American fundamental belief that the public has the right to know everything instantly, and the competitiveness of private stations renders news more of a product in the US than in France. In defence of French television, it is refreshing to have the Prime Minister or Defence Minister, or even President Mitterrand, as the guest on the nightly news, live. French politicians are more candid and less packaged, and less reduced to "sound-bites." Here are a few more notes on the various stations:

TF1 has been privately owned for only a handful of years. The programming is solid but a bit conservative. The news reporting seems a bit less riveted to the government line. Some good films.

**France 2** is more liberal and more progressive in its programming. It programs many special events, interviews and cultural happenings.

There is an excellent film series on Friday nights in V.O. *(version originale)*—often in English.

**France 3** sharing much of its programming with France 2, adds a lot of regional transmissions, news, documentaries, and does some excellent environmental programming. France 3 has certainly come up substantially in the last few years. The morning news program, *Continentale*, with its impressive polyglot host, Englishman Alexander Taylor, is first rate.

Alex introduces that morning's news segment from television stations all over Europe and often beyond. The Ile-de-France show features a new spot, *Télé Bobine*, in which anyone can go to Aquaboulevard, enter a photo booth, and be filmed ad lib. The best are aired. France 3 also has a fine film series in VO on Sunday nights.

**Canal Plus** shows a lot of films, many of which are second rate. It also provides a fair amount of American sports coverage otherwise unavailable in France.

**Arte** High quality programming. Excellent documentaries with a tendency to focus on 20th century German history. Free in France, but available only by cable subscription in Germany. Again, if you're fed up with American TV, this will refresh you.

**M6** has a lot of entertainment, show biz and video clips. Some good programming here, despite a former lack of promotion and general low visibility.

There's a seventh channel filled with wonderfully enriching cultural programming, but is only available on cable, although at several times during the week its programs are seen on France 3.

Cable has reached almost all of Paris by 1994. There are two cable companies exclusively for France. Each town decided whether, first, it would accept cable installations and, secondly, to which company the contract would be awarded. Generally, cable costs each user around 150 FF a month plus one time *"frais de dossier"* of 500 FF, the great French catch-all fee to gauge the public. You can argue it but they'll think you're nuts and won't budge. Some people have opted for the satellite dish *(antenne parabolique)* instead. To receive cable contact: Paris TV Cable at 44.25.80.00 or Canal Cable at 40.16.98.98.

## Video/TV

If you buy a television or VCR video player in France don't forget that you can only receive French channels. A US or British video player usually will not work with a French set, which is in the PAL standard. Britain and the rest of Europe use SECAM, while North America and Japan use NTSC. Multisystem video players and recorders (*magnétoscopes*) are sparse and expensive although the prices are coming down. The FNAC carries both a multisystem video and TV. Some North Americans opt for two VCRs and two TV sets. Note many multisystems can only play NTSC videos recorded in SP (standard play).

French law requires a special annual users tax *(la redevance)* for TV and video owners. Electronics stores were obliged to report all sales to the government, so quick-witted and *laisser-faire* consumers paid in cash and gave fictitious addresses; although the tax rate has come down some, you will still probably find yourself with around 600 FF to pay each year. Prerecorded video films are readily available but expensive, with some in English. An old standby has been Reels-on-Wheels, which, both sells and rents English and American films (on PAL only), and delivers and picks up, too. New video services in Paris are springing up all the time. Check the local papers. The FNAC's service stores, found in almost every neighborhood, now offer a service that converts and copies videos from and into all standards.

## Radio

French radio bands were strictly controlled in the seventies. The airwaves were certainly not free. Numerous unofficial pirate stations were hidden around the city. Most radio emissions now come from one centralized building complex in the sixteenth *arrondissement* called the *Maison de la Radio*. When Mitterrand came into power, radio in France was decontrolled. Scores of little radio stations sprang up at once. Many represented ethnic groups, alternative attitudes, or regions. The result was a glut on the airwaves; it became difficult to pick up clear signals except for the huge and powerful commercial radio stations RTL, Radio Luxembourg, Radio Monte Carlo, NRJ and a few others. So, new rules were clamped on. Things have leveled out now but the airwaves are packed tight. Radio programming can be quite original in France, and if you are used to turning the dial to hear a different style of music, you may be pleasantly surprised to hear a Chopin Nocturne followed by Led Zeppelin followed by John Coltrane. It seems that to the French, either quality transgresses the bounds of style or the art of the smooth "seguy" is still to be learned.

The irreverent expat DJ from New Jersey, Bart Platenga, whose former show *Wreck This Mess* had been heard on the feisty Radio Libertaire, writes: "Paris radio is more open and unpredictable in general than American or British radio. Just spin the dial & one gets an amazing variety of sound. But Paris radio is formating fast. Their station id's are VERY inventive, often better than the music they play. While in America there is lots of talk about nothing, in Paris there is too much talk about significance. The French like to talk ABOUT music. That's why you'll hear five minutes of music & then fifteen minutes of discussion about it. Perhaps that's why jazz is popular."

Alternative rock producer and *libertaire* DJ, Thierry de Lavau, has updated Bart's comments. If you're unused to the crowded French airwaves, a list of major FM stations in Paris can be a handy guide.

**Paris' Major FM Radio Stations**
* State-owned radio
• national FM radio

## 87.8
### *FRANCE INTER
Tel: 45.24.70.00
French variety & cultural chandelier chats (a 3 minute Leon Redbone song commands a 15 minute panel discussion). Unadventurous forays into culture Muzak from this state-run station. Worth tuning in for "*Là-bas si j'y suis*," an original program in the early afternoon. Also Zoom, 10h - 11h. Evenings (after 20h) given over to French songs and later on "Anglo-Saxon" music.

## 88.2
### EFM INTERGÉNÉRATION
### ICI ET MAINTENANT
Tel: 49.59.45.45
Tel: 40.58.10.34
EFM Intergénération: all kinds of music, rock, jazz, etc...
Ici & Maintenant: Decent stuff, depending on the show. Unique dedication to listener call-ins. Best: *Spiral Insana* (experimental, cut-up), Tues. 17h-18h30. Otherwise, afternoons host call-ins.

## 88.6
### FRANCE MÉDITERRANÉE —
### RADIO SOLEIL
Tel: 44.62.00.44
Tel: 43.48.43.43
FRANCE MÉDITERRANÉE: from 6h to 15h, modern Arabic songs and music, also French and Mediterranean music (Top Méd.), news from Arab countries in French and in Arabic, also BBC news in French. There is cinema and theater discussion (on Mondays and Fridays at 10h30), and time is given to horsey talk (the races etc.).

## 89
### *RFI
### (Radio France Internationale)
Tel: 42.30.22.22
Pretty good world news, World Music (*Musiques du Monde*), interviews with musicians, writers and other leading or emerging lights from all over the world: "*La radio mondiale.*"

## 89.4
### RADIO LIBERTAIRE
Tel: 42.62.90.51
Anarchist federation's *Voice Without Master*. Eclectic embrace of world's disinherited and disaffected. Some of Paris' best blues, jazz and alternative info.

## 90.0
### KISS
Wallpaper muzak demographically aimed at the spineless upward-bound consumers who dance to Pink Floyd and Madonna with no discernable change in step.

## 90.4
### FIP PARIS
Tel: 42.20.12.34
Commercial-free sublime simmer of soothing woogie music from Barbieri to Mingus, Lester Young to Neil. Mellifluous DJ's, casual traffic (26 updates daily), weather, news interruptions.

## 91.3
### •CHÉRIE FM
Tel: 42.48.50.50
Sirupy French and international tunes, light stuff - *"l'amur tujurs l'amur"*.

## 90.9
### CANAL
Leans heavy on plod-plod ballady pop. Best: *Intérieurs Nuits* (live personal column with secret, sexy and perverse announcements), Fri. 23h–1h.

## 91.7 / 92.1
### *FRANCE MUSIQUE
Tel: 42.30.18.18
Though this state-run station is mainly devoted to classical (Friday night concert at 20h30 and on Sunday mornings at 11h), it wanders into jazz, ethnic and experimental sounds. Monday to Fridays at 18h (also 23h on Fridays) two programmes devoted to jazz.

## 92.1
### RADIO CVS
Tel: 42.79.92.47
Ding-a-ling songs that make you want to stuff Malobars in your ears.

## 92.6
### TROPIC FM
Tel: 48.97.91.00
Truly one of the cream. Joyous equatorial notes that are eclectic and human. Great creole-juju-mambo-salsa-zulu-ethno-pop-reggae bubbling stew. Ads aimed at the West Indian populace of Paris and its 'burbs - jewels, clubs, restaurants, etc.

## 93.1
### RADIO ALIGRE —RADIO PAYS
Tel: 43.43.59.59
Tel: 48.59.22.12
**Radio Aligre:** multicultural radio, early morning literary programmes at 8h45 "Espace Livre", acid jazz around 17h, "rock for show" on Thursdays. **Radio Pays:** pluricultural, into cultural minorities: *Bretons, Basques, Alsaciens, Provençaux,* etc.

**93.5 / 93.9**
*FRANCE CULTURE
Tel: 42.30.19.19
France Culture (perhaps the only station in the world exclusively concerned with culture) broadcasts serious cultural topics 24-hours-a-day uninterrupted by advertising. Heated debates, (everyone talks at once *bien sûr*), programmes on history, music, literature, also special documentaries.

**94**
RADIO FRANCE MAGREB
Arabic music with an edge.

**94.4**
FUTUR GENERATION
The pop future as seen from the cyber-souls of *E.T.* fans.

**94.8**
RADIO SHALOM
Tel: 40.73.83.00
Vegas comes to Tel Aviv.

**95.2**
RADIO TOUR EIFFEL
Tel: 42.36.24.00
Some good, cool jazz that is unfortunately hindered by incessant interruptions.

**95.6**
RADIO COURTOISIE
This station is national-Catholic and interview-heavy (and we mean heavy). Shares frequency with Radio Asie.

**96**
•SKYROCK
Tel: 42.36.96.96
This giant describes itself as "chewing gum for the ears." Chain-talking DJ's vaccinated with phonographic needles whack off crappy, headless recordings.

**96.4**
BFM
Tel: 41.25.19.00
Cocktail of continuously flowing financial and economic info and classical music.

**97.4**
PACIFIC FM
Describes itself as *"la radio évasion"* (escapism radio). Intriguing mishmash of junk and gems from all over the world: from gut-wrenching segues of airhead nostalgia (John Denver) to real Delta blues.

**98.2**
RADIO BEUR
Arab pop & ethno-music with integrity. Best: Raîkoum (Raî), Monday 16h30-18h.

**98.2**
RADIO F.G. 98,2
Tel: 42.45.86.86
Music *essentiellement* house, infos by themes: night-clubbing (18h15), fashions, theater, homosexuality, etc.

## 98.6
### ALFA
Tel: 46.71.98.60
Is schmaltzy sentimentality just a universal affliction? French with a Portuguese accent. Radio *bilingue français-portugais*, info on Portugal.

## 99
### RADIO LATINA
Tel: 44.06.99.00
Solid and adventurous jazz daily like Cecil Taylor compositions actually allowed to stretch and explore. Latin culture (Spain, Portugal, Italy, France) is the speciality. International news, tourism and food talk.

## 99.5
### RADIO FRANCE MAGHREB
Tel: 42.70.22.22
Radio France Maghreb: traditional & modern Arabic music, clairvoyancy.

## 99.6
### REUSSIR FM
Why succeed when you can fail so effortlessly. Station of "professional info & business communication." Obviously looking for its niche among the career-oriented. Shares frequency with Jazzland.

## 99.9
### O'FM
Tel: 47 28 92 92
Light music, French and international, games, more clairvoyance, "culture and politics": the TF1 of FM.

## 100.3
### •NRJ
Tel: 42.48.42.48
The giant which boasts 5 million listeners. A fair selection of pop, house and rock. Hits, hits and more hits.

## 101.1
### RADIO CLASSIQUE
Tel: 46.92.15.15
Commercial-free, 24-hour-a-day classical music. One exception is the financial news, Mon.–Fri. 7h–8h30. Classical, nothing but classical.

## 101.5
### RADIO NOVA
Tel: 43.46.88.80
Everything from urban-warfare rap, love-funk and acid garage-jazz to zulu. Easiest station to pop on anytime. Whizzes you around the five continents, north to south, east to west. Great promo spots in English.

## 101.9
### •FUN RADIO
Tel: 47.47.11.72
Noisy like your worst pinball nightmare on speed. Pop without pulp. Bump without bang. Note "Lovin' Fun" the most listened to programme on FM, at 18h45.

## 102.3
### OUI FM
Tel: 48.04.70.25
Overrated computer-generated rock format that's white as nose candy. A bit of self-serious rock NOOZ.

## 102.7
### •RADIO MONTMARTRE
Tel: 42.23.32.33
French popular songs, complete with accordion, cocked béret, baguette and indispensible string of onions.

## 103.1
### •RMC
Tel: 40.69.88.00
Traditional recipe. Music, news (see RTL).

## 103.5
### •EUROPE 2
Tel: 47.23.10.63
EUROPE 1 *version jeune.*

## 103.9
### •RFM
Tel: 40.99.15.15
International variety, rock, golden oldies.

## 104.3
### •RTL
Tel: 40.70.40.70
News bulletins on the hour, every hour. The concept here is accessible, popular (games to gogo) and lively— in short, close to millions of hearts nationwide. Unbelievably inane advertising. Nothing really interesting or surprising.

## 104.7
### •EUROPE 1
Tel: 42.32.90.00
News, soft rock, festival coverage, almanacs and DJ-hosted *variété* and entertainment programming. Very informal tone. Not unlike RTL.

## 105.1
### *FIP
Tel: 42.20.12.34
Non-stop music or almost, no ads, above all jazz (every night "Jazz à FIP" at 19h30). Traffic bulletins for Paris region, weather. Suave voices given to satire.

## 105.1
### RADIO NOSTALGIE
Tel: 53.68.80.00
Lots of dippy, purring come-on *chanteurs* & *chanteuses*. All the romantic squish of a sponge dipped in cheap perfume.

## 105.5
### FRANCE INFOS
Tel: 42.30.10.55
Around-the-clock, state-run, commercial-free, nationwide news. Broadcasts in all French cities, albeit on different frequencies. Almost as up-to-the-minute as a wire service. Good to tune in for latest headlines/ reports, but not for excessive listening.

## 105.9
### •M 40
Tel: 40.39.09.09
Extended commercials every 40 minutes. News, quizzes, light music. Records are tested out on the public *"Ça passe ou ça casse"* (Sink or swim).

## 106.3
### FRÉQUENCE PARIS PLURIELLE
Tel: 48.13.00.99
Paris' Afro station plays mix of African, Caribbean and black American music with African news. Commercial-free, cultural programmes, music, art, sites of interest.

## 106.7
### BEUR FM—FÉMININ PLURIEL
Tel: 40.03.97.77
Tel: 49.37.14.14
Féminin Pluriel: varied music, jazz, rock, etc...from 9h to 12h and from 14h to 17h alternating with Beur FM which, from 12h to 14h and from 17h to 9h, puts out modern Maghreb music. Exotic commercials (marabouts, calling cards, mutton, etc...)

## 107.5
### AFRICA N°1
Tel: 45.74.83.83
Africa is the theme of this radio station (transmitted from Libraville in Gabon), news, music, jazz.. Worthwhile tuning in for news (African news of course) in English at approx 13h30 (12h30 *temps universel).*

For news and information in English you can tune in to a range of international English news services, each with its particular ideology. One American professor in Paris used to profess that there was only one real way to learn what's really happening in the world: listen to BBC World Service, Voice of America, Radio Tirana (Albania) English Service, and Radio Moscow English Service and average them out. With the new evolution of the world political order, this system needs revamping. In any case, it's both revealing and amusing tuning in to alternative sources of information. To get the BBC World Service, you need to be able to receive short wave. The frequency moves around depending on the time of day, but from 7 a.m. to 9 p.m. you'll most likely find it at 12095 KHz. It's always a pleasure hearing the hour strike on Big Ben and then hearing the world news from London. BBC Radio 4, serving mostly the northwest part of France, is found on Longwave 198 KHz, and BBC Europe is on Medium wave 648 KHz. To receive BBC Worldwide (formerly London Calling), write or phone BBC, Bush House, PO Box 769 Strand, London, WC2B 4PH, UK, tel: (19) 44. 71. 257-2211. The Paris office does not field inquiries. For BBC teaching products and videos, the BBC has its Omnivox store at 8, rue de Berri 75008 Paris, and a Minitel service: 3614 BBC.

## Press

For a foreign city, Paris has a healthy variety of permanently self-rejuvenating English-language publications, and of course a complete foreign press corps of correspondents. All the major press organizations, publications, and networks represented in Paris are listed in an excellent *aide-mémoire* published by the offices of the *Premier ministre, Média-Sid*. It can be ordered for 130 FF from *La Documentation française*, 29, quai Voltaire, 75344 Paris Cedex 7, Tel: 40.15.70.70. Here is a descriptive listing of what's being published regularly here in English. Those of you who have returned to Paris and are looking for the old city magazine *Paris Passion* should note that the mag folded in 1990 following a takeover by London *Time Out*. Founding publisher Robert Sarner lives in Israel.

### The Biggies:

*International Herald Tribune:* Daily newspaper written and compiled by local staff with the *New York Times* and *Washington Post,* published six days a week in eleven printing plants, catering primarily to the international business community in 181 countries. 9 FF at the kiosk. A special 270 FF for a three-month subscription for students or teachers in France (1950 FF per year).
Daily features include:
Monday: Capital markets by Carl Gewirtz, Q+A with world leaders, plus Sports Page.
Tuesday: International stock markets, Fashion section.
Wednesday: Media markets, London theater reviews.
Thursday: International management, science page.
Friday: Wall Street Watch, Leisure section, and cultural reports.
Saturday: Economic scene with The Money Report, Fine Arts, featuring Souren Melikian's art marketplace.
**International Herald Tribune**
181, av Charles-de-Gaulle
92200 Neuilly-sur-Seine
Tel: 46.37.93.00
Fax: 46.37.93.70
Publisher: Richard McClean
Editor in chief: John Vinocur

*Wall Street Journal Europe:* Published daily out of Brussels, specializing in financial and economic news with a focus on European news and money markets.
**Wall Street Journal Europe**
9, rue de la Paix
75002 Paris
Tel: 42.96.96.44

*USA Today:* The international edition is coordinated in London. This four-color daily brings American news, sports, and events to Europe. No Paris office.
**USA Today**
10 Wardour St.
London WIV3HG
Tel: (44)(71)734-3003

*The European:* English-language weekend newspaper with a particular take on European issues, now under new ownership after the death and demise of its founding publisher, the late Robert Maxwell. Based in London. 15 FF every Friday.

**The European**
42, rue de la Bienfaisance
75008 Paris
Tel: 45.63.03.62
Fax: 45.62.98.34
Bureau Chief: Elisabeth Moutet

## The Freebies

*Paris Free Voice:* The celebrated monthly community-oriented free newspaper with a circulation of over 25,000. Cultural news, features, and local color. Published since the late seventies by community leader, blues guitarist, and Parsons professor of photography, Bob Bishop, out of his basement office in the American Church. Inexpensive and effective classified advertising.

**Paris Free Voice**
American Church
65, Quai d'Orsay
75007 Paris
Tel: 47.53.77.23
Fax: 45.50.36.96
Editor/Publisher: Bob Bishop

*France-USA Contacts (FUSAC):* A well-organized and ubiquitous semimonthly circular of classified advertisements and useful tips, whose growth reflects the commercial anglophone presence in Paris. Free bulletin-board center open from Monday to Friday 10h-19h, and on Saturdays through the window, so bring a pen.

**France-USA Contacts (FUSAC)**
3, rue Larochelle
75014 Paris
Tel: 45.38.56.57.
FAX: 45.38.98.94.
Editor: John Vanden Bos

*Paris City Magazine:* Every two weeks this four-color magazine with Paris as its subject graces the streets and anglophone hangouts. Brainchild of American architect/publisher William Martz and managing director James Pilaar, *Paris City Magazine* has carved an important niche for itself as both an editorial forum for Paris-oriented features and local advertising. Its policy to run free classified ads in 1994 has helped intensify the battle of the give-aways. Its English Language Minitel service—3615 WELCOME—aspires to this mag apart.

**Paris City Magazine**
21, rue Godot de Mauroy
75009 Paris
Tel: 42.66.58.66
Fax: 42.66.69.50
Publisher: William Martz

*Paris Tempo,* The English Language Alternative, published by the Creative Collective of French and anglophone journalists, has started out with a sober-looking but well written newsprint magazine. Too early to say more.

**Paris Tempo**
14, rue Martel
75010 Paris
Tel: 48.00.04.39
Editor: Isabelle Nikolic

**Speaking Small Ads:** Classified ad service by telephone. Main categories include housing, services, lessons, vehicles. The cost is 2,19 FF per minute, charged directly to your phone bill. Tel: 36.68.92.68.

**The Riviera Reporter Magazine**
35, avenue Howarth
06110 Le Cannet
Tel: (16) 93.45.77.19
The most extensive English language publication in the south of France. Also has a very popular radio station.

**Publications/Newsletters**
Paris organizations and clubs often publish newsletters for its members and the public. Here are some of the most significant ones that could be helpful to newcomers. (For full addresses and phone numbers see Organizations.)

*AAWE (Association of American Wives of Europeans)*
*American Chamber of Commerce*
*Democrats Abroad*
*France-Amérique*
*Message Mother Support Group*
*WICE*

**Literary & Art Journals**
*Frank: An International Journal of Contemporary Writing & Art:* A multi-cultural journal of fiction, poetry, literary interviews and contemporary art, published in Paris since 1983. Available at literary book shops in France, the UK, and North America. Edited and published by American writer David Applefield. 220 FF/$35 for four issues.
**Frank: An International Journal of Contemporary Writing & Art**
*Association Les Amis de la Fonderie*
104-106, rue Edouard Vaillant
93100 Montreuil
Tel: 48.59.66.58
Fax: 48.59.66.68

*Paris Transcontinental:* a Magazine of Short Stories. Hosts a Short Story Contest for fiction of 5,000 words or less, the first-prize winner receiving 1000 FF (or $200 US) and publication, or a scholarship to the Annual WICE Paris Writers Workshop.
**Paris Transcontinental**
*Institut du Monde Anglophone*
Sorbonne Nouvelle
5, rue de l'Ecole de Médecine
75006 Paris

*Raw Vision:* Periodical specializing in art brut and primitive art from around the world, published in London.
**Raw Vision**
Sandra Kwock-Silve, Paris editor
22, rue de Turin
75008 Paris
Tel: 43.87.55.08

*Art International:* One of the world's finest quarterlies in English on contemporary art. Edited in Paris by Jill Lloyd and Michael Peppiatt. Well-researched and well-written articles with high-quality reproductions.
**Art International**
77, rue des Archives
75003 Paris
Tel: 48.04.84.54

**Other English-language Press Represented in France**
Here is a rather complete list of major networks, stations, newspapers and magazines in France. For purchasing English and American magazines and newspapers, W.H. Smith, and Brentano's are good sources. The monopoly press distributor NMPP, which runs all Paris kiosks and is owned by the multinational French publisher Hachette, has its own international press shop:
**NMPP**
52, rue Jacques Hillairet
75012 Paris
Tel: 49.28.79.85

*Radio and TV*
Here's a quick list of major anglophone radio and television stations with offices in Paris.
**American Broadcasting Company (ABC)**
Tel: 40.47.80.81
**British Broadcasting Company (BBC)**
Tel: 45.61.23.11 (television)
      45.63.15.88 (radio)

**Central Broadcasting System (CBS)**
Tel: 43.59.11.85
**Cable News Network (CNN)**
Tel: 42.89.23.31
**Canadian Broadcasting Corporation (CBC)**
Tel: 43.59.11.85
**New Zealand TV**
Tel: 43.27.02.75
**Radio France Internationale**
English Service
Tel: 42.30.30.62

*Newspapers*
**Los Angeles Times**
Tel: 49.24.96.65
**New York Times**
Tel: 42.66.37.49
**The Observer**
Tel: 42.74.60.86
**The Times (London)**
Tel: 47.42.73.21
**The Wall Street Journal**
Tel: 47.42.08.06
**Washington Post**
Tel: 42.56.01.80

*Magazines*
**Business Week**
Tel: 42.89.03.80
**Newsweek Magazine**
Tel: 42.56.06.81
**Time-Life**
Tel: 44.95.70.30
**US News & World Report**
Tel: 42.60.34.38

## Computers and Modems

Not long ago, lugging your Mac or PC to Paris posed all sorts of practical and technical hassles. First, there was the obvious drag of carting bulky cartons through airports and train stations. There was similarly the hesitation about customs restrictions, and finally, the obstacle posed by the different electric current, requiring bulky transformer hookups. Almost all of these dilemmas have been cleared up in the last year or two.

Almost all Apple computers today are made with built-in auto-switching electrical currents, so that with a simple adaptor plug you can plug your computer into any electrical socket in Europe, Japan, and North America. Make sure though that your computer has this before you plug-in and fry your machine. One American writer inquired at his Apple outlet in Boston before coming to Paris and was informed that he could just plug his Mac Classic into any French wall. False information, and he had to find a friend flying back to the States to carry the computer back for repair. So, check this out thoroughly.

If your computer—or answering machine, or fax machine, etc. is not equipped for 220 Volts/50 cycle electricity, do not sweat, just march over to the basement of the BHV or another store that carries transformers and adaptor plugs and buy a trans-former to convert the 220 volts into the 110 volts that your machine requires. Then, turn it on.

Another major computer dilemma in the past has been the huge gap in prices between France and the US, American prices having been radically lower for both computers and software. In 1993 and 1994 the gap has seriously closed for hardware, to the point where it no longer really makes sense buying a computer in the US to carry to France, let alone a printer. Software, however, continues to be much cheaper in the US, in that French distributors have a smaller market and are faced with the costly need to localize the product, translate the program, and complete the process of *Frenchification* of the application. As a result, software in the US may be as little as 30% of the prices being asked in France. One American computer programmer in Paris admitted that he often orders software from the US with a credit card, has it sent to an American address, and then forwarded to him in Paris via Federal Express, declared as a NCV (No Commerical Value) Document. This is a dollar-savings subterfuge which circumvents the trade restrictions on products licensed to irate French distributors, who have paid hefty sums for exclusive rights. There are many Apple Dealers (*concessionnaires*) in the Paris area and loads of IBM compatible, PC outlets. Most sales contracts entitle the owner of a computer to international guarantees and service from approved dealers worldwide. For Apple computer information you can call: 69.86.34.00.

In France, like most places, the Mac/PC dichotomy is pretty much the same: 85% PC and 15% Mac, but if you eliminate professional and industrial users, accountants, banks, etc. the split is nearly 50-50. The creative world, however, artists, designers, publishers, journalists, advertising agencies, etc. are heavily invested in Macintoshs. If you hope to rely on a local computer *concessionnaire*, it's a good idea to become a paying client. The dealers most open to anglophone customers all advertise in the local anglophone publications. They are also more sensitive to your technical questions regarding working in English as opposed to French. Be aware that keyboards on French computers are organized in the AZERTY configuration, not the KWERTY, US configuration. American keyboards can be obtained in Paris, and almost all computers have systems that allow the switching of keyboard systems internally.

Most major software companies have user hotline assistance numbers, such as MicroSoft Word and Excel. Most don't require an identification number indicating when and where you bought the program. Sometimes, however, it's ultimately easier and faster to call a service number in the US. You can make all sorts of inter-

esting contacts at the annual *Apple Expo* at La Défense each September, the largest MacWorld fair in Europe, as well as at the InfoMart, which is a permanent fair held in the CNIT building, also at La Défense.

In general, France is highly sensitized to electronics and computerized information transfer, to a great extent due to the Minitel, which has completely revolutionized daily French life and will go down in history as one of the great achievements of the Socialists. The Minitel, which is an on-line computer adapted for any and all households and offices in which telephones are used, has resulted in a popularization (the French sense of the word, implying democratic) of electronic communication and access to information. You can hook up your computer to your Minitel so that your screen becomes the Minitel screen and then access all the services available on Minitel and download anything you want, converting data into Word files, and conversing, ordering, researching on your computer the way you would on a Minitel. This requires a special cable available from dealers for about 350 FF and one of several Minitel emulation software programs, such as Mactel Junior which runs about 600 FF. Modems, except for the very simplest and cheapest, are Minitel-compatible.

As for New Medias, CD-ROM developers, interactivity, etc., most French publishers are racing to get into the electronic CD-ROM market, although many still refuse—with reason—to abandon their belief and reverence for the handwritten manuscript. A new crop of publishers/developers have emerged in Paris, though, such as the US based Voyager, and the younger and innovative Gyoza Media, headed by young American upstart Cory McCloud.

With the explosion of vast public access to E-Mail, Paris may seem much closer to home than ever. For a meager $8.95 US per month for the basic service, you can get hooked up to CompuServe, which has a local Paris access number although administers its European operations out of Germany. The central computer is, of course, in Ohio. You plug your computer with modem into any phone line, log onto the CompuServe computer in Ohio via the automatically dialed local Paris access number and retreive and send E-mail instantly to and from other users worldwide. You'll be billed in US dollars and the monthly fees will be debited directly and appear on your credit card statement. You can sign up when you get to Paris or before you arrive; it's your choice, the computer remains in Ohio. CompuServe users correspond effortlessly with other network users via commercial gateways, such as the massive Internet, which was set up initially to connect all the universities of the world. There is a tiny toll of fifteen cents per message to get through this gateway. CompuServe number in Paris is: 36.63.81.31. Otherwise, in the US call: (800) 848-8990.

| Lexicon | |
|---|---|
| battery | *pile* |
| black and white | *noir et blanc* |
| bromide/camera ready | *bromure* |
| cancel | *annuler* |
| cartridge | *cartouche* |
| character | *caractère* |
| chooser | *sélecteur* |
| clock | *horloge* |
| color | *couleur* |
| computer | *ordinateur* |
| control panel | *tableau de bord* |
| disk | *disquette* |
| document | *fichier* |

| | |
|---|---|
| file | *dossier* |
| film | *typon* |
| hard drive | *disque dur* |
| hide | *masquer* |
| keyboard | *clavier* |
| layout program | *logiciel de mise en page* |
| lazar | *laser* |
| memory | *mémoire* |
| modem | *modem* |
| mouse | *souris* |
| outputting | *flashage* |
| plugged in | *branché* |
| printer | *imprimante* |
| program | *logiciel* |
| scanner | *scanner* |
| screen | *écran* |
| size | *taille* |
| sound | *son* |
| spread sheet | *tableur* |
| to copy | *copier* |
| to cut | *couper* |
| to find | *chercher* |
| to format | *formater* |
| to paste | *coller* |
| to print | *imprimer* |
| to save | *sauvegarder* |
| trash | *corbeille* |
| turn off | *éteindre* |
| turn on | *allumer* |
| type face | *police (de caractères)* |
| word processing | *traitement de texte* |

# Insurance
# and Health Service

## Insurance (Assurance)

Living in Paris, you'll ultimately need to find out the local ins and outs of insurance concerning your home or apartment, your car, and health coverage. These are complicated but essential elements of daily life. Even if your French is perfectly up to snuff, be prepared for alienation and confusion and perhaps exaggerated rates if you don't find an agent willing to render service. For this reason, it's advisable to seek out an anglophone. French insurance agents are not in the habit of fielding a lot of questions by phone, nor responding to a lot of questions in general, and gaining satisfaction with insurance claims can be a difficult and frustrating task. Remember, like everything else administrative and legal in France, everyone begins with *méfiance* (distrust). The assumption is that everyone lies and cheats and

thus it is the responsibility of the individual to prove his or her virtue and just cause. This attitude has a clear impact on the insurance industry, where you must prove with flawless documents that you really owned that Pentax camera that you claim was stolen or that the fireplace in your flat had been cleaned by a chimneysweep within a year before the fire that damaged the apartment on the floor above yours. As one insurance broker in Paris who had lived and worked in the US states: "I prefer to work with Americans because in general they're more honest than the French. I'll commit myself to a car insurance policy on the phone because in almost all cases Americans will send in the check they promised."

In France, insurance policies are renewed automatically each year. You can only cancel them with a written letter sent two months before the annual renewal date. Otherwise, you'll be responsible to pay the next year's premium. If you are unhappy with your current broker or agent, you can replace him or her immediately by signing an "ordre de remplacement", which entitles another broker to take over your policy as soon as the former one has received the letter. The commission will go to the first broken until the annual renewal date comes due, however, the new agent will handle all claims in the interim. One American insurance broker who has been in France for over 25 years and who is noted for his service to English-speaking clients, including general, medical, automobile, fire, accident, and life insurance is Mr. Reuben Giles, Cerise Assurances, 199-207, rue des Pyrénées, 75020 PARIS, Tel: 47.97.64.80. A newcomer to Paris specializing in personalized service concerning motor, home, and life insurance for English speakers is ZAAR Assurance at 46.43.88.50. Ask for Noeleen Loughman; she's Irish and very accommodating. ZAAR is a part of the Irish Life Group and has 34 outlets all over France.

In the last few years, a new insurance agent has emerged on the scene with the logo "Dedicated to Serving Americans in France." No slight to British, Canadian, Australian, Irish, South African, etc. readers is intended. Advantage Insurance has come to the fore in serving both the transient and long-term resident anglophone community. American founder, Vincent Kuhn and his French partner, Anne Deshayes, have demonstrated an understanding of the needs of newcomers. Their emphasis on service is not only helpful; it's refreshing. Rarely in France will you feel that someone who is selling you something truly understands that by saving you money they gain your loyalty and repeated business. Advantage offers a full package of homeowner, theft, water damage, fire, business, bars, shops, restaurant and health insurance policies, answers questions on the phone, corresponds in English, and provides translated copies of procedures and the *Conditions particulières* of policies.

**Advantage Insurance**
Anne Deshayes
57, rue du Fbg. Montmartre
75009 PARIS
Tel: 53.20.03.33 / Fax: 44.63.00.97.
For specific insurance information see Auto Insurance, Health Insurance, and Housing Insurance.

## Health Services

Although France has a highly impressive and widely democratic system of socialized medicine, this might not undo the feelings of loneliness and despair if you fall sick in a foreign country where you are not sure where to turn for sympathy or help. This feeling is compounded, of course, if you are unsure about your language skills. For that reason, services in English have been included here. If you feel like braving the language barrier, you will find that almost any pharmacist is eager and willing to give you advice and to recommend remedies. He or she may go so far as to give you the number of a doctor around the corner. Pharmacists play an essential intermediary role between doctor and patient. And pharmacies are not cluttered with all the non-medical goods found in North American and many British drug stores. Medication comes with two-part stickers *(vignettes)* on the packaging. One part is peeled off and stuck on the orange and white *feuille de soins* used for reimbursement from the *Sécurité Sociale*, the national health administration reserved for salaried employees. Other sectors of professional activity have their own *caisse* (administration) handling the same coverage (see *Working in France*). Prescribed drugs have been traditionally reimbursed at 75%. This has changed somewhat with lower reimbursements on numerous medications. The State is running out of cash. Don't be surprised, however, when you realize that treatment varies from one country to another. You may find yourself using methods you had never even conceived of at home. For instance, the French are keen on the use of suppositories, for many different problems, including a cough. Pharmacists are even trained to know about the mushrooms you find in the woods and will offer free advice on the delicious and deadly.

A lot of misunderstanding about French medical practices is a matter of aesthetics and style. French doctors' *cabinets* (offices) are surprisingly unclinical in feel, and doctors, particularly specialists, appear more like professors than physicians. Doctors' offices in France are not teeming with paramedical practitioners nor do doctors' offices maintain extensive medical records. With children, medical records are maintained in a *carnet de santé* (health book) which accompanies the child throughout his/her life, beginning at birth. Prescriptions are given for tests at local laboratories. You must go for the tests and then pick up the results yourself. You pay for them and are subsequently reimbursed by the *Sécurité Sociale* if you pay contributions into the system. Very little lab work is done in doctors' offices, and the white-coat sterility associated with North American and Scandinavian medical facilities is virtually absent. One does not get the feeling of being dynamically treated; however, there is no denying that French medical procedures are wisely oriented towards prevention rather than intervention. Because the *Sécurité Sociale* reimburses most of the cost of visiting any doctor of choice, people don't wait until they're seriously ill to be treated.

Don't be overly judgmental if the waiting room is drab, there is no air-conditioning and the doctor inspects you in an alcove of his study.

A normal consultation should run between 100-150 FF. Many doctors don't require appointments and simply receive walk-ins during fixed hours. Specialists start at 200 FF an appointment.

## Hospitals

**The American Hospital of Paris** *(Hôpital américain de Paris):* This is a famous, private hospital which employs British, American and French doctors on its staff and is partially bilingual. F. Scott Fitzgerald, among others, spent time here in the pre-renovation days drying out "on the wagon."

It is much more expensive than the French hospitals, but offers excellent health care with a style that you may recognize and appreciate. You can pay with dollars and major credit cards. Those covered by Blue Cross-Blue Shield have their hospitalization covered, provided they fill out the appropriate paperwork first.

**The American Hospital of Paris**
63, bd Victor Hugo
92202 Neuilly-sur-Seine Cedex
Tel: 46.41.25.25
Fax: 46.24.49.38

Another hospital which employs English-speaking doctors and is noted for serving the anglophone community is:

**Hertford British Hospital**
3, rue Barbès,
92300 Levallois-Perret
Tel: 46.39.22.22

## Medical Practitioners

Practitioners in France are either *conventionnés* (abiding by the *Sécurité Sociale* system's schedule of fees) or *non conventionnés* (charging higher rates). Note below that WICE publishes a detailed booklet on health in Paris, the best source on the subject. As for recommendations, The American University of Paris' medical brochure recommends the following English-speaking doctors. Otherwise, ask friends and colleagues.

**General Practitioners**
Dr. Hubert Gamon
20, rue Cler
75007 Paris
Tel: 45.55.79.91

Dr. Claude Guichard
37, rue du Départ
75014 Paris
Tel: 43.22.22.96

Dr. Francis Slattery
32, rue Vignon
75008 Paris
Tel: 47.42.02.34

Dr. Stephan Wilson
44, av de Ségur
75015 Paris
Tel: 45.67.26.53

Dr. Joseph Torkia
54, rue de Paris
93100 Montreuil
Tel: 48.22.22.96

**Chiropractor**
Marc Tourneur, D.C.
44, rue Laborde
75008 Paris
Tel: 43.87.81.62

**Dentists**
Dr. Olivier Bessermann
34, rue de la Victoire
75009 Paris
Tel: 48.78.49.50

Dr. Celine Bismuth
7, rue Bernard de Clairvaux
75003 Paris
Tel: 48.87.61.61

Dr. Chagari
22, rue Cler
75007 Paris
Tel: 47.05.40.10

**Dermatologists**
Dr. Brigitte Marchal
40, av Bosquet
75007 Paris
Tel: 45.51.04.40

**Gynecologists**
Dr. Emile Cohen
118, bd. du Montparnasse
75014 Paris
Tel: 43.35.50.30

Dr. Anne-Fraçoise Neimann
6, av Sully-Prudhomme
75007 Paris
Tel: 45.56.03.30

**Laboratories**
Laboratoire Trivin-Vercambre
14, rue Dupont des Loges
75007 Paris
Tel: 47.05.84.37

Laboratoire d'analyses médicales
16, rue José-Maria de Heredia
75007 Paris
Tel: 47.83.24.13

**Opthalmologists**
Dr. Linda Abitbol
131, rue St. Dominique
75007 Paris
Tel: 45.55.65.45

Dr. Richard Fitterer
9, av Bosquet
75007 Paris
Tel: 47.05.52.43

**Opticians**
Walter's Paris
107, rue St. Dominique
75007 Paris
Tel: 45.51.70.08

**Psychiatrists/Psychologists**
Emmanuel Ansart, M.D.
43, rue La Bruyère
75009 Paris
Tel: 48.78.04.60

Barbara Cox
115, rue du Théâtre
75015 PARIS
Tel: 45.75.74.61

Dr. H.R.S. Nagpal
65, rue Pascal
75013 Paris
Tel: 47.07.55.28

Nancy Sadowsky
12, rue Marie Stuart
75002 Paris
Tel: 42.33.10.07

Joseph Shesko
4, rue Michel Chasles
74012 Paris
Tel: 43.47.19.72

**Sports Medicine**
Dr François Manière
64, rue de Rennes
75006 Paris
Tel: 45.44.03.21

**Free AIDS Testing Clinics**
Centre Anonyme et Gratuit
des Médecins du Monde
1, rue du Jura
75013 Paris
Tel: 43.36.43.24

Centre Médical de Belleville
218, rue de Belleville
75020 Paris
Tel: 47.97.40.49

Dispensaire (City Health Clinic)
3-5, rue de Ridder
75014 Paris
Tel: 45.43.83.78

Hôpital La Pitié Salpétrière
47, bd de l'Hôpital
75013 Paris
Tel: 45.70.21.73

**Reproductive Health**
A prescription is necessary for contraceptive devices and drugs. There is no age limit. Male contraceptive condoms (*préservatifs*) and female contraceptive sponges (*ovules*) are available without prescription. Family planning centers provide information on contraception. Among others, *le Planning Familial* has centers at 10, rue Vivienne, 75002 Paris, *Métro*: Bourse, Tel: 42.60.93.20, and at 94, bd Massena, 75013 Paris, *Métro*: Porte de Choisy, Tel: 45.84.28.25. Do-it-yourself pregnancy tests are available in pharmacies at a cost of about 80 FF. Ask for G-Test, Elle-Test, or Predictor. When positive, these tests can be believed absolutely. When negative, they should be repeated five to seven days later. Abortions are legal in France. You may have heard of the male birth control pill. Like the Lough Ness Monster, one doctor

commented, this pill shows its head in the press from time to time. It's still in the testing stages and is nowhere near the point of being put on the market.

Free, anonymous courses of treatment for venereal diseases are offered by the Institut Prophylactique, 36, rue d'Assas, 75006 Paris, *Métro*: Saint-Placide, Tel: 42.22.32.06; 8h00-15h00 Monday through Friday and Saturday 8h30-12h00; and by the Institut Alfred Fournier, 25 bd Saint-Jacques, 75014 Paris, *Métro*: St-Jacques, Tel: 45.81.46.41.

## Other Health-Related Services
Support Groups

### AIDS Support Group
American Church
75007 Paris
Tel: 45. 50.26.49

### Alcoholics Anonymous
3, rue Fréderic Sauton
75005 Paris
Tel: 47.05.07.99

### Alcoholics Anonymous
American Church
65, Quai d'Orsay
75007 Paris
Tel: 46.34.59.65

### Alcoholics Anonymous
American Cathedral
23, av George V
75008 Paris
Tel: 47.20.17.92

Recorded Information: 46.34.59.65 (Saturdays at the American Hospital: 46.41.25.25)

### American Aid Society of Paris
Talleyrand Building
2, rue Saint-Florentin
75382 Paris Cedex 08
Tel: from 9-12, call 42.96.12.02 ext. 2717; other hours, call ext. 2667 (Office of American Services)
President: Mme Adele ANNIS

### American Women's Group
22bis rue Pétrarque
75116 Paris
Tel: 47.55.87.50

### British and Commonwealth Women's Association
7, rue Auguste Vacquerie
75016 Paris
Tel: 47.20.01.36

### Canada Welcome
24, bd Port Royal
75005 Paris
Tel: 43.37.43.96

### Europ Assistance
1 Promenade de la Bonnette
92633 Gennevilliers Cedex
Tel: 41.85.85.85

### International Counseling Service
65, Quai d'Orsay
75007 Paris
Tel: 45.50.26.49
Mon.-Fri: 9:30-7:00pm/Sat. 9 a.m.- 1 p.m.

**Weight Watchers France**
18, rue Jean Pierre Timbaud
34 BP 87
78392 Bois-d'Arcy Cedex
Tel: 43.57.65.24
Director: D. Brothers

**WICE (Women's Institute for
Continuing Education)**
20, bd Montparnasse
75015 Paris
Tel: 45.66.75.50
Offers courses (in English) in Career
& Personal Development, Arts &
Humanities, Living in France,
Women's Support Group.

For further information on AIDS
*(SIDA),* there is a round the clock
telephone information service at tel:
47.70.03.00 (10 a.m.-7 p.m.) and at
tel: 47.70.98.99 (7 p.m.-11a.m.) or
toll free: 05.36.66.36. More information may be obtained by consulting the Minitel at: 3615 AIDS. Or
this service may be written to, at:
AIDES, 6 Cité Paradis, 75010 Paris.
For more information regarding
English-speaking medical personnel,
a good resource is Health Care
Resources in Paris, a comprehensive
guide in English. Contact WICE at
tel: 45.66.75.50 to order a copy.

## Being Pregnant and Having Babies in Paris

As a foreigner, being pregnant in
Paris and preparing for your *accouchement* (giving of birth) can be both
exciting and a bit scary. On one
hand, you should be very pleased
that, attitudinally, Parisians are very
open and accepting about such natural phenomena as pregnancy and
giving birth. The *accouchement* is not
seen as a medical or surgical intervention; nonetheless, most Parisian
women give birth in hospital *Mater-
nité* wards or private clinics, and a
large percentage opt for the epider-
mie *(péridurale)* procedure of pain-
less but sensitized birthing. The *péridurale* procedure was devised by a
Parisian doctor at La Pitié Hospital,
the largest teaching hospital in
France, located between the Gare
d'Austerlitz and the Porte d'Italie.
Hospital aesthetics in Paris may not
meet the visual expectations of visitors used to more clinically anticeptic
environs. Less attention is given to
the public relations and image of
hospitals in France than in the US.
There are few frills in Paris hospitals,
and it is primarily for reasons of
comfort and not medical ones that
many women have their babies in
clinics. Also, in clinics the post-par-
tum stay can be up to ten days, whereas hospitals keep new mothers for
four or five days, which in itself is
substantially longer than in the US
or UK.

The French practice the use of three or four sonograms *(échographies)* during a normal pregnancy. This is more than is usually prescribed in the US and the UK, which is undoubtedly connected to the cost. In France, of course, the *Sécurité Sociale,* the State health coverage plan, covers this cost completely. On the whole, it is fair to say that in France, medical attention is preventative.

Many women and their men attend midwife *(sage-femme)* birthing classes, which are also reimbursed in part by the *Sécurité Sociale.* Almost all babies are delivered by *sages-femmes,* except in the case of complications or Caesarians. One, absolutely wonderful place for birthing classes with highly trained and culturally sensitive midwives is the *Centre de préparation à la naissance,* 55, rue de la Roquette in the 11th.

Maternity leave is legally 16 weeks, which many working women combine with their five weeks of paid vacation in order to stay home longer. Employers are used to this and do not stigmatize women employees who must go on maternity leaves. Their jobs are secure and they have been paid fully during the leave.

## Pharmacies

To match a prescription from home, be sure to have the following information, since finding the equivalent may be difficult: an up-to-date prescription with the medication's trade name, manufacturer, chemical name, and dosage. If you don't speak French, you may have an easier time if you go to the English and American Pharmacy, since they are used to having to match prescriptions. The pharmacists, aside from speaking English, tend to be very helpful. In most pharmacies, for many prescription drugs, you will be asked to give your address which is noted in a register. This is normal.

**Anglo-American Pharmacy**
6, rue de Castiglione
75001 Paris
Tel: 42.60.72.96

**British and American Pharmacy**
1, rue Auber
75009 Paris
Tel: 47.42.49.40

**Drugstore** (open until 2 a.m.)
149, Bd. St. Germain
75006 Paris
Tel: 42.22.80.00

**Pharmacie Swann**
6, rue Castiglione
75001 Paris
Tel: 42.60.72.96

**Pharmacie des Champs**
(24-hour pharmacy)
84, av des Champs-Elysées,
(passage des Champs)
75008 Paris
Tel: 45.62.02.41

## ALLO Pharma
Tel: 40.54.01.02
Home delivery of medical supplies at night and all day Sundays.

At night and on Sundays you can call the local *commissariat de police* for the address of the nearest open pharmacy and that of a doctor on duty. You can also check the door of a closed pharmacy for the address of the nearest open one.

Note: if you cannot find a prescribed medication at a local pharmacy or you've been told that there is a *rupture de stock* (out of stock), try calling or visiting the *Pharmacie centrale des hôpitaux:*
7, rue du Fer-à-Moulin 75005 Paris. Tel: 43.37.11.00 *poste* 299, *Métro* Gobelins, 9:30-17:30.
This is the central supplier for Paris hospitals.

### Useful Words at the Pharmacy

*ampoules* ...................................................small glass containers
*comprimés* or *pilules* ...................................tablets or pills
*contre-indications* ............warnings (when medicine should not be used)
*cuillère à café* ...................................................teaspoon
*cuillère à soupe* ................................................tablespoon
*diarrhée* ...........................................................diarrhea
*effets secondaires* ..............................................side effects
*gélules* ............................................................capsules
*gouttes* .............................................................drops
*indications* ...........................ailments treated by the product
*indigestion* .......................................................indigestion
*mal des transports* ..........................................motion sickness
*mal de tête, migraine* .........................................headache
*maux d'oreilles* ..................................................earache
*mode d'emploi* ...........................................directions for use
*ne pas dépasser la dose prescrite* ...............do not exceed prescribed dosage
*otite* ...........................................................inner ear infection
*poudre* ...............................................................powder
*posologie* ............................................................dosage
*rhume* ..............................................................a cold
*sachets* ...........................small packets of soluble powder
*sirop* .......................................................liquid or syrup
*suppositoires* ....................................................suppositories
*toux* ..................................................................cough
*voie orale* ..........................................................by mouth

## Natural Medicine

The French are great believers in traditional medicines. *Homéopathie* (homeopathic medicine) uses only herbs and other natural products in very carefully compounded mixtures whose composition is fixed by law. Most pharmacies have extensive homeopathic sections, and many doctors, especially pediatricians, prescribe these natural medicines. In many cafés, *infusions* (herbal teas) are served, largely for complaints such as nervousness, fatigue, weakness, etc. A few of the calming herb teas available in most cafés are *tilleul, camomille, menthe* and *verveine*. There are also a number of *fortifiants* (tonics, mild stimulants) available in pharmacies, as well as preparations for just about any common ailment. Pharmacies specializing in homeopathic medicine will be clearly marked and can be found throughout the city.

## Medical Emergencies

*Police Secours:* Tel: 17.

*Pompiers* (Fire): Tel: 18.

*SAMU ambulances:* Tel: 15 or 45.67.50.50.
Life-threatening situations; detailed information will be required by phone.

*Ambulances de l'Assistance Publique:* Tel: 43.78.26.26.
Handles transportation from one hospital to another.

Burns (severe): Tel: 42.34.17.58
Hôpital Cochin, 27 rue St. Jacques, 75005 Paris.
*SOS Médecins:* Tel: 47.07.77.77 or 47.37.77.77
24-hour emergency medical house calls—150 FF before 19h00, 275 FF after 19h00.

*SOS Dentistes:* Tel:43.37.51.00
24-hour emergency dental help. Similar prices.

*Association des urgences médicales de Paris:* Tel: 48.28.40.04
Sends a doctor in an emergency.

**Anti-Poison Center:**
Tel: 40.37.04.04.
24-hour service.

**SOS Pregnancy:** 45.84.55.91

**SOS Rape:** Tel: 42.34.84.46 or toll free: 05.05.95.95

**SOS Help:** In English.
Tel: 47.23.80.80
Crisis hotline every night from 15h-23h.

**SOS Help:** In French.
Tel: 42.93.31.31

**SOS Drug Center:**
Tel: toll free: 05.05.88.88

*SOS Vétérinaire:* Tel: 47.55.47.00

## Health Insurance

Before coming to France, you should find out whether or not you are insured overseas and in what instances. Certain firms will expect you to pay your bills in France and then reimburse you after you send them the receipt *(feuille de soins)*. It may take several weeks for the reimbursement to come through.

French law requires that students have complete medical coverage during their stay in France. Copies of official documents attesting to this fact are required when you request any visa from the French Consulate in your home country and by the *Préfecture de Police* when you apply for your *carte de séjour*. The law requires that the medical plan provide for the following coverage: hospitalization in Europe, short and long-term, outpatient treatment, visits to the doctor, dentist and laboratory expenses, pharmaceuticals, medical repatriation (transportation back to country of residence), medical recommendation. Most national health plans in European Union countries meet these requirements. Many private plans in the United States and Canada do not. However, if you have substantial coverage by your health plan in North America (inquire for the U.K. and the rest of Europe) and can get a clause to include a provision for medical repatriation, you may meet the necessary coverage requirements.

Several American university programs do provide a special student health insurance plan for students who require it. Students and non-students who are not covered by an employer but who legally reside in France can also take advantage of the French *Sécurité Sociale* (referred to in conversation as the *Sécu*) by paying the annual fee. Inquire at the office of the *Sécurité Sociale* in your *arrondissement* for information.

**Insurance Exemptions for Students:** Those who are covered by European National Health plans (e.g. French Social Security or British National Health), International Organizations or a particularly extensive private plan in North America, may apply for an exemption. You must send a copy of your insurance policy to the Administration or Bursar of your program when paying the tuition fee to determine if your coverage meets exemption requirements. Please note that you will need official copies of your insurance policy translated into French to apply for your visa and your *carte de séjour*. In most cases, exemptions must be approved prior to registration or you may be enrolled in your program's plan automatically. The French *Sécurité Sociale* medical coverage can be purchased for a rather reasonable rate if you are under 26. Above 26, however, the rates are about 12 000 FF a year and only cover you in France, leaving you uncovered elsewhere. Additionally,

# ADVANTAGE INSURANCE
## ·ASSOCIATES·
### DEDICATED TO SERVING AMERICANS IN FRANCE

## INSURANCE MADE EASY ... IN ENGLISH!

When you call Advantage, you'll find the answers to all your questions about insurance in France.

Clear, detailed explanations - in English.

And as we are completely independent, accredited by over 40 French, American and international insurance companies, we can find the best contract at the best price for you.

Your policy documents come complete with full summaries of cover in English ... translations of the claims forms ... and information on exactly what to do should the worst happen.

You'll also be able to call on our full claims service, which will give you all the back-up and assistance you may need.

Whether you need health, motor, home contents, life, personal injury cover, business insurance - or simply want an impartial view on your current arrangements - give Anne Deshayes a call now at 53.20.03.33.

**Advantage Insurance Associates
57, rue du Fbg. Montmartre
75009 Paris**

**Tel: (1) 53.20.03.33  ·  FAX: (1) 44.63.00.97**

the official reimbursement rates of the French *Sécurité Sociale* are set at levels that still can leave you with a hefty bill. (For the average doctor's visitation fee of 140 FF, you can expect a 70% reimbursement, and 40% of the medication bill.) This, of course, is only when you are not working and need to buy this coverage as if it were a private insurance, otherwise, the coverage is a right you have, which you pay for automatically as a percentage of your salary. When you see a specialist and pay 200-250 FF you will still receive back only the 70% of the 140 FF. Citizens of EU countries covered by their own national health plans should file with the *Sécurité Sociale* Form E 111, which is the reciprocal health coverage agreement between European Union countries. For others, Advantage Insurance, for example, offers several helpful health plans for those who don't qualify for the *Sécurité Sociale*, including a "tremendously good" international package, which in many cases is even more advantageous than the official French coverage for those who qualify. This health insurance also meets the French requirements for visas and *carte de séjour* requests, can be paid in US dollars checks drawn off American bank accounts, and is available to anyone not living in his or her own country. For Americans the *tarif confort* is recommended in that it includes coverage in the US as well.

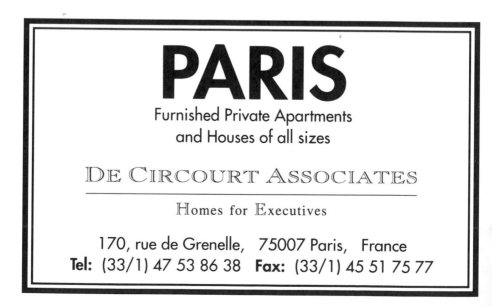

# Housing Accommodations

## Street Signs & Address

In French, your address and phone number are your *coordonnées* (literally, 'coordinates'). Some addresses may seem strange at first, but you'll learn these nuances rapidly. You can live on a *rue*, an *avenue*, a *boulevard*, an *impasse*, a *cour*, a *passage*, a *parc* or a *chemin*. The street number may be a regular whole number like 34 or 7 or 178, but it may also have an extra bit, *bis* or *ter*, which means that the house is attached or adjacent to the property that takes the whole number. Other aspects of the address: *bâtiment* (building name or number), *escalier* (stairway), *étage* (floor), *code* (door code), *à droite* (to the right) or *à gauche* (to the left). When visiting someone, always get as much of this information as possible. People usually will tell you something like this: *J'habite au 35, boulevard du Montparnasse, escalier C au fond de la cour, quatrième étage à gauche* (I live at 35, Boulevard de Montparnasse, stairway C, at the back of the courtyard, fourth floor, on the left). If you see *Cedex* at the end of an address, it simply means that the address is a post office box and the mail is kept at the post office. Most buildings have either a door code, which is activated at night, or a buzzer system outside the building, called an *interphone*. There will always be a button to activate the door, marked *porte*, and, on the inside, a lit button to turn on the timer for the lights in the stairwell. When going to someone's house, always ask if there is a door code, since many buildings now have them on all day and night.

The availability of housing as of 1994 has increased as the economy has softened. Prices, which rose steadily in the 80s, have leveled out and even started declining. Don't feel pressured into taking an apartment you're not sure of or that seems too costly. Commercial space has also become more readily available, with over a million available square meters being empty in Paris in 1992. You can sometimes negotiate rents, commissions, fees and perks but generally the Parisians are not great negotiators and will often keep an apartment empty for a year than rent it at a lower rate. This comes from the fact that it's difficult to get rid of a tenant once he or she is in. Owners always have the right to reclaim their apartments at the end of a lease (most apartments have a standard three year lease) if it is for their own use or for a family member, or if they want to sell it, but otherwise the tenant has the right to renew the lease.

Whether you have a full lease or not, insist on a *quittance de loyer* (rent receipt) every month or quarter. This is your proof of payment and address. As a tenant, you will receive a bill from the city for your *taxe d'habitation* (housing tax). You are obliged to pay this.

As for agents, don't expect much service. You might be surprised to see Century 21 offices all over. American Frank Cluck, formely from Century 21 in Chicago, has over the last decade attempted to revolutionize French real estate agents by introducing a package service. The French caught on to the gold jackets concept (there are some 500 Century 21 offices in France) but still lag way behind in treating customers with courtesy and

efficiency. Be prepared to have to battle for your security deposit back or to get your real estate agent to fix a leaky fancet.

## Hostels

Here are three *auberge de jeunesse* (something between a proper hotel and a youth hostel) in the center of Paris:

**Le Fauconnier**
11, rue Fauconnier
75004 Paris

**Le Fourcy**
6, rue de Fourcy
75004 Paris

**Maubuisson**
12, rue des Barres
75004 Paris
Reservations and information for all three hotels can be sought at Le Fauconnier, or by calling:
Tel: 42.74.23.45. Fax: 42.74.08.93.

### Short Term Housing Options

Miles Turner's *Pauper's Paris* is a great resource for good value hotels and student hostel listings. Here are a few:

**Café Couette**
8, rue d'Isly
75008 Paris
Tel: 42.94.92.00
French "bed and breakfast" association which has rooms throughout France. 190 FF for single and 260 FF for double room.

Ligue Française des Auberges de
Jeunesse (LFAJ)
38, bd Raspail
75007 Paris
Tel: 45.48.69.84
*Métro*: Sèvres-Babylone
Limited to three-day stays for holders of the YHA (Youth Hostel Association) card, and very cheap.

Hôtel Studia
51, bd St. Germain
75005 Paris
Tel: 43.26.81.00
Excellent location at Place Maubert.
275 FF with a *douche* (shower) and
*petit déjeuner* (breakfast).

## Finding an Apartment

Probably the most frustrating aspect
of living in Paris is the hassle of
searching for a place to live. The
options are numerous, from finding
other people to live with to cloister-
ing yourself in your own small room.
Remember, however, that the competition at certain times of the year
can be tough and that those who rise
early and call first have the best
chance. The competition is at its
worst during September and October when the Parisians come back
from a month of vacation and students need to find accommodations.
The simplest and cheapest way to
find accommodations is to look for
individuals who have apartments or
rooms to rent. In some cases, avoid-
ing the agencies will save you a lot of
paperwork, not to mention paying
high commission fees, which is
usually a month's rent, and a required two-month deposit plus one
month's rent in advance. There are
several newspapers you can consult
which carry housing ads *(petites
annonces)* from individuals. *J'annonce*
comes out weekly on Wednesday
morning and *De Particulier à Particulier* comes out every Thursday
morning. These two papers also have
Minitel services which are updated
daily. The French daily *Le Figaro* also
has extensive listings. To recognize
ads not placed by agencies, look for
the words *propriet. loue* placed by the
owner. For those who yearn for the
security of going by the book, you
can make an appointment with
someone at the City Hall of your
district to receive free legal advice.
This service, called AILAP, can be
used to verify your contract or lease
and any other "suspicious" extra fees
your landlord or landlady may
conveniently—and convincingly—
inform you of after signing the
contract. Normal extra fees include
the *taxe d'habitation* paid by whom-
ever is in the apartment as of January
1 of that year, *droit de bail*, a small
tax split by the owner and the
tenant, and tenants insurance which
is mandatory in France. You can also
rent the services of a *huissier de justice*
(notary) from a housing agency for
about 200 FF/hour before you move
into your new apartment. He will

insure that everything is done to the letter, and in under a couple of hours.

*FUSAC, Paris Free Voice,* and *Paris City Magazine* list housing opportunities as well as all sorts of services and some job opportunities. These are available at most English language bookstores, public places and restaurants. The *International Herald Tri-*

*bune* also advertises apartments but these tend to be rather up-market. Here is a sample housing ad followed by a translated explanation.

17e ROME. 4p. cuis. bns. ref.nf. 6300. 44435111

*17th arrondissement* near *Métro* Rome, 4 rooms, kitchen, bathroom, newly remodelled. 6300 FF a month. Call 44.43.51.11

---

## Column Headings in the Newspaper

| | |
|---|---|
| *Immobilier* | Real Estate |
| *Achats et Ventes* | Wanted/Offered for Sale |
| *Location Offres/Demandes* | Offered/Wanted to Rent |
| *Meublé* | Furnished |
| *Vide* | Unfurnished |

## Helpful Terms

| | |
|---|---|
| *agences s'abst.* | no agencies |
| *asc. (ascenseur)* | elevator |
| *bns. (bains)* | bathrooms |
| *bal. (balcon)* | balcony |
| *box* | parking space |
| *calme* | quiet street, building |
| *carac. (caractère)* | with character |
| *caution* | security deposit |
| *ch. (charges)* | supplementary monthly fee in addition to rent |
| *chb. (chambre)* | bedroom |
| *chambre de bonne* | maid's room |
| *chambre indépendante* | independent room |
| *charm.* | charming |
| *chauf. cent.* | central heating |
| *com.* | agent's commission |
| *cft. (confort)* | "comfort"—i.e. private bath, carpeted rooms, equipped kitchen |
| *coq. (coquette)* | cute |
| *cour* | courtyard |
| *cuisine eq. (equipée)* | equipped with major appliances |
| *dche. (douche)* | shower |

*et. el. (étage élevé)* ...................................................................upper floor
*except.* ...............................................................................exceptional
*garçonnière* ...........................bachelor's apt; small studio or room
*grenier* ..................................................attic, room under roof
*imm.* ......................................................................building
*imm. mod.* ...........................................................modern building
*imm. nf.* ..............................................................new building
*imm. p de t (pierre de taille)* ...........................cut stone building
*imm. rec.* ..............................................................new building
*imm. anc.* ...............................................................old building
*interméd.* ......................................................................agent
*jar./jdn.* ...........................................................................garden
*kit.* ...................................................kitchenette, not separate
*loue, je loue* ...........................I am offering for rent (i.e. no agency)
*lux.* ..............................................................................luxurious
*loyer.* ...................................................................the rent
*m² (mètre carré)* ...........................square meter (about 10 square feet)
*moq.* ..................................................................wall-to-wall carpeting
*part à part (particulier à particulier)* ........private party to private party;
                                                                              no agency
*p. (pièce)* ...........................................rooms, not including bathroom
*pierre de taille* ...........................cut stone building (nicer than ciment)
*poss. (possibilité)* ................................................possibility of
*pr. cpl.* ..........................................................couple preferred
*poutres apparentes* ..........................................beamed ceilings
*rav. (ravissant)* ....................................................delightful
*ref. nf. (refait neuf)* ....................................newly remodeled
*r. (rue)* ...........................................................................street
*slle. (salle)* ..........................................large or formal room
*salle de réception* .........................................large living room
*salle à manger.* ...............................................formal dining room
*salle d'eau* .................................................................sink
*salle de bains* ....................................with shower or bath
*ss. (sans)* ....................................................................without
*stdg. (standing)* ...."status" or "high class" building, fashionable address
*gd. stdg., tr. gd. stdg.* ......................................................deluxe
*studio* .............one room apartment, usually with bath and kitchenette
*s/ (sur)* ...........................................................................on
*tél* ....................................................................telephone
*terr.* ...............................................................................terrace
*ttc (toutes charges comprises)* ....................................all charges included
*w.c.* ..............toilet, in room separate from bath and sink; water closet

There are also many bulletin boards scattered all over Paris. Try the following for finding housing:

**The American Church in Paris:** 65, Quai d'Orsay, 75007 Paris, *Métro*: Alma-Marceau or Invalides. Tel: 47.05.07.99. Open Monday-Saturday 10h-22h00; Sundays 10h-19h30.

**FUSAC** (France-USA Contacts) Bulletin Board: (*Centre d'annonces et bureau*): 3, rue Larochelle, 75014 Paris, *Métro*: Gaîté or Edgar Quinet. Open from Monday to Saturday 10h-19h, Saturday 12h-17h.

**The American Cathedral:** 23, av Georges V, 75008 Paris, *Métro*: Georges V, Alma-Marceau. Tel: 47.20.17.92.

**Shakespeare and Company:** 37, rue de la Bûcherie, 75005 Paris, *Métro*: St. Michel. Open noon-midnight seven days a week.

**Centre d'Information et de Documentation Jeunesse:** 101, Quai Branly, 75015 Paris, *Métro*: Alma-Marceau.

**Minitel 3615 Welcome.**

Many *laveries* (laundromats), *boulangeries* (bakeries), large grocery stores (Prisunic, Monoprix, etc.) and gyms also have bulletin boards.

## Relocation Firms

**Executive Relocations**
3 rue Berryer
75008 Paris
Tel: 40.74.00.02

**Iris Difference**
25 avenue Gabriel
92000 Nanterre
Tel : 47.25.70.00

## Short and long-term housing service

**Apalachee Bay**
25, rue Keller
75011 Paris
Tel: 40.21.39.67

**Mr. and Mrs. Z. Szabo** (proprietor, therefore no agency fee)
7, rue Charles V
75004 Paris
Tel: 42.72.49.02

## Types of Housing Contracts

• Short term furnished contracts can be for one year or less and are renewable at the option of the landlord.
• Long term unfurnished contracts are for three years and are hard for landlords to break without a just reason. Both can be broken by the renter with 1-3 months notice, depending on the contract.
• Commercial leases are traditionally 3-6-9, meaning the *bail* (lease) can be sold or yielded in three, six or nine years.

## Housing Insurance

French law requires that anyone occupying space in France (an apartment, a maid's room, a studio or a room in someone else's home), be covered by property insurance. The landlord will assume that you have proof of this coverage. Renters are responsible for any fire or water damage originating from their apartment—not just for their premises, but for the entire building. This is so well known that your landlord may not ask for it, but you are legally liable so this must not be overlooked. More likely you will be asked to provide a photocopy of your policy each year to the owner or agent.

Your minimum legal liability policy covers you for damage to the Owner's property. To be covered for your property you need a "multi-risk" policy which covers water damage, fire or explosion, and theft. In all cases, contact your insurance agent immediately by phone and by registered letter. In the case of theft you're going to have to prove what was stolen. Receipts, inventories, guarantees, and photos are very helpful. Note that this applies for your home only. Your camera or jewelry for example is *not* covered on the street.

Make sure you pay for your insurance on time, because it's hard to collect for losses when a policy hasn't been paid. A *constat de dégât des eaux* for water damage is a form you fill

out with a neighbor if one's apartment has damaged the others. A copy is sent to both your insurance agent and to theirs. In case of fire call your agent and ask him to order a personal expert for you. Again, Advantage Insurance has pre-prepared forms in English for its prospective clients.

For particularly wealthy homeowners, Chubb Insurance offers its "personal asset protection" policy, Masterpiece, which is adapted for art collectors, antique buffs, etc. with replacement value reimbursement, a rare feature in French insurance practices. In general, premiums are not necessarily higher in France than in the US, but the services and reimbursements are also more limited.

**Furnished/Unfurnished Apartments**
First, consider the amount of time you are planning to stay in Paris. When looking through rent ads, note whether the apartment is furnished or unfurnished. If you are only staying for a short time, a furnished place will be much more suited to your needs, even though the rent may be higher. If you plan to stay for a while, however, consider taking an unfurnished place since you can most likely obtain a standard three year lease *(un bail de trois ans)* and will want to get set up with your own stuff. The advantages of having a three-year *bail* (lease) include a set percentage over which your rent may not increase annually, the right to

sublet for one year, and the right to break your contract if you give your landlord three months notice by registered letter (*lettre recommandée avec accusé de réception*). On the other hand, you have the right to six months notice from the landlord before having to move out, and the reasons for asking you to leave are limited by law.

When you do find an apartment, the *propriétaire* (landlord) will want a *caution* (security deposit) as well as some proof that you are financially able to pay the rent. A letter in French from a parent or sponsor stating financial support will normally suffice, but as the economy worsens, agencies are taking no risks and might insist on proof of income as much as four times the monthly rent as well as a solid employment record. One executive employed at Euro Disney from the day it opened was denied an apartment by the Century 21 office in Vincennes because he'd been with the same employer for less than two years! Some of these agents can be real creeps. Don't lose your cool if you really want the apartment. Remember everything in France depends on one's ability to *séduire* (seduce) or charm. Yes, they'll make you feel like they're doing you a favor to take your money. It'll baffle you why the customer must be apologetic. Asking to see the supervisor is a sure way to lose the battle. Eat humble pie or move on.

If you do get the apartment, you will probably be asked to sign a lease. Under French law, minors (under 18) cannot sign contracts, and if you are under this age the landlord or his agent may insist that your parents or some responsible adult sign for you. If you sign a lease, ask for an *état des lieux* or an *inventaire détaillé* (detailed inventory) of the apartment and its contents, and make two copies. This way the landlord can't hold you responsible for damage done to the apartment before you moved in.

In any case, you should keep in mind that some landlords and almost no agencies will accept a guarantee of financial support from outside of France, since tracking down the tenants to pay for damages would be impossible.

## The French Apartment

*L'entrée*
Often the best apartments are in the most unlikely places, so don't be influenced by the building's street-side appearance; the grungiest looking building with a seedy stairwell may have a beautiful garden in the courtyard and an entirely different look behind the front door. On the other hand, a well-kept entranceway with bourgeois details, polished brass, etc. indicates immediately that the building is of high *standing*, a term the French have borrowed. New laws have been passed permitting old buildings to be gutted as

long as the street façade remains unchanged. You'll come to feel that the entranceway and stairwells of Parisian buildings possess an aesthetic quality that is particularly Parisian—the worn, wooden steps, the old tile, the snaking bannisters. At first what you might feel as old and seedy will grow on you, if you let it.

## La cour

Most French urban structures are built in a square, around a courtyard. The Paris everyone can see is but a portion of what is there: behind the average front door may be a formal garden complete with fountain, a stone-paved walkway leading to a private residence, hidden behind the walls of the *bâtiment* (building) or parking lot. It may also be just a playground for the children of the *concierge* or a passageway to the back section of the building. Often it'll host a series of *ateliers* (workshops).

## La concierge

The *concierge* in Paris, almost always a Portuguese or Spanish wife and husband team crammed into a tiny apartment in the entranceway of the better Parisian apartments, plays a unique role in daily French life. The Law of 1948 imposed rent controls which has limited the rapid improvement of buildings and thus helped institutionalize the *concierge*. He or she is the onsite representative of the organization or group of owners in an apartment building (*syndic*). He/she knows all, hears all, tells all, and is an essential person to get along with. Their principal tasks include shining the brass in the entranceway, distributing the mail in the building, cleaning the stairwells, doing minor repairs, carting out the garbage cans, receiving packages, etc. When you move in, and at Christmas, it is a good idea to tip your *concierge* as much as you can afford (100 FF is normal) and according to the amount of extra work you make for them. *Concierges* are very valuable allies and very powerful enemies. If problems arise over such things as noise after 22h, your concierge can often prevent or instigate much unpleasantness. Almost all buildings, even commercial and public ones, have live-in concierges or *gardiens*, who keep an eye on things. North Americans find it unusual to see a family live in a small flat off the lobby of a public school. With the increased installation of securite systems, *digicodes*, *interphones*, and modern elevators, concierges are becoming redundant with over 2000 positions being eliminated each year in Paris.

## Les toilettes (WC)

WC means "water closet," and that's what it is, a closet-sized space with a toilet. The WC (also called *le water*, pronounced as if the word was French) is very often a separate room. Although this may seem odd at first, it's rather practical. The WC is colloquially referred to as *les chiottes* (the crapper). Don't use the word too lightly. Other classic bathroom functions are performed in the *salle de bains*.

### La salle de bains

*Bidet* : You may be perplexed on your first trip to a French bathroom to find this little fixture. Historically designed to serve aristocratic women as a hygienic aid, today the *bidet* can be used for lots of things, from relieving the pain of hemorrhoids, hand-washing delicate clothing, bathing a baby, or soaking your feet. Fresh water enters the fixture through a vertical spray in the center of the bowl, through a flushing rim or integral filler or through a pivotal spout that delivers a horizontal stream of water. A pop-up drain allows you to fill it with water. New bathrooms often do not have these.

### Le bain/la douche.

Expect anything. Although on the rise, showers are not as classically standard in daily French life as baths. Consider yourself lucky if you end up with a large enough space to stand up and lather up, let alone possess a shower curtain. This seemingly essential bathroom fixture is not seen as essential to the French. Invariably, a shower is taken via a metal hose running from the bathtub spout, and dexterity is a must to prevent splashing, especially since you will probably not have a place to hang the nozzle on the wall. But washing your hair with one hand has got to be charac-

ter-building. In the older buildings you'll have to get used to tiny tubs, sitting tubs *(baignoires-sabots)*, and other microscopic means of washing. Remember to be careful. You are responsible for water damage to any and all floors below if it comes from your apartment (See *Housing Insurance*). The bathroom sink is called a *lavabo*, but a kitchen sink is an *évier*.

### La cuisine

Parisian kitchens tend to be an exercise in space utilization. They often have tiny but efficient appliances, especially refrigerators *(le frigo)* and gas stoves. Unfurnished apartments almost never come with appliances, and often don't even have kitchen cabinets. Get used to the *chaudière*, the hearth of the French home, the gas apparatus that heats on command the water for the kitchen and bathroom. Appliances that you may not be familiar with include the deep fryer, *la friteuse* and the pressure cooker (*cocotte minute*). Also note that Parisian kitchens are very often where you house your washing machine or dryer, if you have one. In recent years, most French households have caught on to dishwashers (although small) and microwave ovens. The king of French appliance stores is Darty noted for its *service après vente* (after sales service).

### Moving In

When you have found your apartment and are ready to move in, keep in mind that the electricity and gas will probably have been turned off. Contact your local EDF-GDF office (*Electricité de France/Gaz de France*) to reactivate the service. Bring proof of address—your rental agreement, for example. And make sure to take the meter reading as you move in to avoid being charged for previous tenant's bills. You might need these to avoid paying for renters before or after you as well as proof in the case of dispute over cost of electric and gas.

To obtain a telephone, call *renseignements téléphoniques* (information—dial 12) to find out at which France-Telecom office in your *arrondissement* you must make your request. The surest bet to have the service and number activated is to go in person. If you can bring the former tenant or at least his or her last bill with you, you might facilitate matters. This usually happens within one or two days. You may rent one of many snazzy models of phones or you may purchase your own. Similarly, you will be offered a Minitel, instead of phone directories. Take it, it's essential. If there is already a phone line, the landlord may insist that you list the number under your name, which is a smart move, since you would not want to pay for the previous tenant's calls, making your first bill an unpleasant surprise. If the phone is under the landlord or previous tenant's name, your access to 19 (international calls) or 16 (regional calls) may be blocked. If you are

sharing the apartment with other people, it is always best to restrict the phone to local calls. You can request a special service that gives you an access code from any phone. You dial 3610 and your code, followed by the number. The call will appear on your bill. For four people calling internationally, it is not uncommon to have bills up to 6,000 FF ($1,100 US) or more. As an alternative, reserve long-distance calls for your *télécarte* (see *Communications*), so you can gage how much you are spending, since it can be more costly to telephone from France than from North America or Asia.

If you want an itemized bill of all calls (*une facture détaillée*) you must request this from the start. It's 8 FF a month extra. The bill comes every two months and you have two weeks to pay. Late bills are subject to a 10% penalty. And it's virtually impossible to contest items on the bill. Again caution on billing errors due to cordless phones; unlike in the US, it's almost impossible to be credited for billing errors. Neither do you get credit for wrong numbers.

### Moving Out

Before leaving, ask for a *relevé spécial* (special reading) of the electricity, gas and telephone from the local EDF-GDF and Telecom agencies listed on your bills. At the EDF-GDF center, your charges can be computed immediately from the meter readings, though the telephone company takes about one or two days. Don't forget to return your phone and minitel, or you will be billed for them. If you need a mover, the local give-aways often run private adds for inexpensive moving. Otherwise, a small firm called F.T.E. offers a very reasonable and reliable service for any sort of move. Tel: 44.62.78.78. Another mover specializing in fine art is:

**Grospiron International Movers**
15 rue Danielle Casanova
93300 Aubervilliers
Tel : 48.11.71.71
International moving, packing (fine arts), storage, customs, insurance.

### Room with a French Family

You can also rent a room in an apartment with a French family or, more often, an individual *propriétaire*. This housing arrangement usually consists of a private room with limited access to the kitchen, telephone and bathroom facilities. Each situation offers varying degrees of privacy. Some landlords have more than one room to rent in their apartments, making it possible for two students to live together. Others have large rooms that can be shared by two people. There are varying degrees of comfort (private or shared bathroom, television, personal phone) and the price fluctuates accordingly. Landladies and couples are usually interested in some cultur-

al exchange, which can help enable the student to ease his/her way into daily French life. This is an arrangement that can often be made through particular university housing offices.

### Chambre de bonne

The most inexpensive form of accommodations is usually a *chambre de bonne* or *chambre de service* (maid's room). This is usually a converted maid's room on the top floor of a bourgeois apartment building. It often has a separate entrance from that of the landlord (very often a 6th or 7th floor walk-up) via a service entrance. It is usually a small room with mansard ceiling for one person with a sink and a hot plate. Many independent rooms do not have private showers or full kitchens, but shared shower and bathroom facilities are usually available in the hallway. Some landlords offer the use of the shower in their apartment. This doesn't sound too glamorous but it can have its charm for a while. With simple accommodations you can focus more time and money on Paris itself. The view can be memorable.

### Au pair

Another alternative to finding an apartment is to look for an *au pair* position. *Au pair* arrangements are available primarily but not exclusively for female students. This work often consists of baby-sitting, housework, English lessons, mother's helper chores, collecting children at school, or any combination thereof in exchange for room and board and a small salary. It often entails some evening or weekend work. Students must generally have some knowledge of French and be willing to work a regular schedule. Though the conditions of such positions can vary, the following agencies will arrange *au pair* positions. They require that students be at least 18 years old and under 30 years of age, have a valid student visa and be enrolled in classes, and will ensure that students are paid pocket money (not salary) of about 1600 FF a month plus room and board in exchange for up to 30 hours a week of work. For full-time students with a heavy workload, it is wise to find *au pair* work for not more that 10-20 hours per week. You should keep in mind that *au pairs* are often treated as paid help rather than members of the family. The quality of this experience depends wholly on the household that you work in. Some experiences can be wonderful, especially when the host family is not only friendly, open, and instructive, but also has a country house in Normandy or Burgundy or ask you to accompany them on vacation to the Alps or Riviera.

During the school year, a minimum stay of three months is required. The regular program stay is normally one year, but it can be extended to a maximum of 18 months. A student may stay with more than one family during the *au pair* period, but the total stay cannot exceed 18 months. There are also summer *au pair* programs of one to three months. In these cases, the requirement that the *au pair* be taking French courses is waived if the student has completed at least one year of college-level French studies.

Most families provide their *au pair* with a *carte orange*, a monthly pass valid for the *métro*, buses and suburban trains, but they are not always required to do so by the Ministry of Labor regulations.

The family must declare the *au pair* as *stagiaire aide familiale* to the French Social Security Administration (URSSAF) and make the monthly contribution (*cotisation*) so the *au pair* will receive social security benefits in case of illness or accidents.

After arrival in France with a visa, the classic *au pair* must apply within eight days for a residence permit (see section on Residence Permits and *cartes de séjour*).

Along with his/her work contract, the *au pair* must present evidence of registration in a French language school (Alliance Française, the Sorbonne, etc.). Evening classes are not acceptable.

Having obtained an *au pair* position, the *au pair* returns to the *Service de la main d'œuvre étrangère* to receive a temporary work permit (*autorisation provisoire de travail*). The permit is normally valid for six months and is renewable.

**Accueil familial des jeunes étrangères**: 23, rue du Cherche-Midi, 75006 Paris, *Métro*: Sèvres-Babylone. Tel: 42.22.50.34. Open Monday-Friday from 10h-16h and Saturday from 10h-noon.
**Arche**: 7, rue Bargue, 75015 Paris, *Métro*: Volontaires. Tel: 45.45.46.39. Open Monday-Friday from 9h 17h.
**Géolangues**: 25, rue de Navarin, 75009 Paris, *Métro*: Place Clichy. Tel: 45.26.14.53. Open Monday-Friday from 9h30-19h30.
**Inter Séjour**: 179, rue de Courcelles, 75017 Paris, Tel: 47.63.06.81. Open Monday-Friday 9h30-17h00.
**Relations Internationales**: 20, rue de l'Exposition, 75007 Paris, *Métro*: Ecole Militaire. Tel: 45..50.23.23. Open Monday-Friday from 9h-12h30 and from 14h-18h30.

Here are a few more places to try when looking for housing and/or *au pair* positions:

**A.C.I.S.J.F.**
63, rue Monsieur-le-Prince
75006 Paris
Tel: 43.26.92.84
*Métro*: Odéon
Hours: Monday and Wednesday only 2-6 pm; closed August
**Alliance Française**
101, bd Raspail
75006 Paris
Tel: 45.44.38.28
*Métro*: Rennes, St. Placide
(For their students only) Hours: Monday—Friday 9h00-18h00.

**Institut Catholique**
21, rue d'Assas
75006 Paris
Tel: 45.48.31.70
*Métro*: Rennes
Hours: Monday -Friday 9:30 a.m.— 5:30 p.m. (closed 12—2:30). Saturday 9:30—11h30 Open all year round except Saturdays in July and August.
**Foyer le Pont**
86, rue de Gergovie
75014 Paris
Tel: 45.42.51.21
*Métro*: Pernety
(Six-month students only. Financed by the German Government, the Foyer is open to others as well) Hours: Monday to Thursday 10h00—18h45 p.m., closed 12 noon—14h00. Friday 9 a.m.—12 noon.
**A.P.E.C.**
39, rue Gounod
92210 Saint-Cloud
Tel: 46.02.90.83
Places foreign students who want to learn French in France.
There are also several housing Mini-tel services. 3615 APPART specializes in finding apartments.

*Cité Universitaire*
This lovely campus complex has rooms available at very reasonable rates in 30 different *maisons* (houses) for university students (under 30) studying in Paris. If you are an architecture buff, you might want to investigate the two *maisons* designed by Le Corbusier: the Swiss Founda-

tion and the Franco-Brazilian Foundation. Make sure to call or write far in advance of your arrival date if you are considering this option. Rooms go fast, and can only be booked for a year-long period. A single room goes for 90 FF per day, and 1200 FF per month; monthly double room rates are 1500 FF, depending on the *maison*. This could also be a good alternative to a hotel while you are looking for other accommodations —rooms are available to anyone with an International Student Identity Card at 80-100 FF per night during the summer and in September before the beginning of the school year. Accommodations are usually provided in the *maison* of the country from which the student originates; some houses prefer graduate students only. A list of all the houses is available from the central office at the following address:

**Cité Universitaire**
19, bd Jourdan
75014 PARIS
Tel: 45.89.68.52

Or try contacting one of the following directly:

**Fondation des Etats-Unis**
Cité Universitaire
15, bd Jourdan
75690 Paris Cedex 14
Tel: 45.89.35.77 (administration)
Tel: 45. 89.35.79 (students)
Director: Terence Murphy

**Maison des Etudiants du Canada**
31, bd Jourdan
75014 Paris
Tel: 40.78.67.00

## Neighborhoods

To give you an idea in advance of the difference between neighborhoods, a general idea of Paris' principal areas and a brief, highly subjective description of each of the 20 *arrondissements* and surrounding suburbs is provided here. Use the enclosed map to locate these areas.

**Opéra:** 1st, 2nd and 9th *arrondissements*
**Les Halles:** 1st
**Le Marais:** 3rd and 4th
**Ile Saint-Louis:** 4th
**Quartier Latin:** 5th
**Saint Germain:** 6th
**Champ-de-Mars/Invalides:** 7th
**Etoile/Faubourg St-Honoré:** 8th
**Bastille:** 11th, edge of 12th
**Chinatown:** 13th
**Parc Monceau:** 17th
**Montparnasse:** 14th and 15th
**Victor Hugo/Palais de Chaillot:** 16th
**Montmartre:** 18th
**Belleville/Ménilmontant:** 19th and 20th.

### Paris by *arrondissements*
There is of course quality housing with charm in every *quartier*, but a notion of each area might be helpful in deciding where to look and what

to consider. The following comments should be especially useful when having to select a neighborhood sight unseen. One of your first purchases in Paris should be a small square red or black book called *Plan de Paris par arrondissements*, which includes detailed maps, a street and *métro* index, and bus routes. It'll cost you around 100 FF. This is indispensable for finding your way around Paris. Trust this advice, you'll need a *plan*. Carry it at all times.

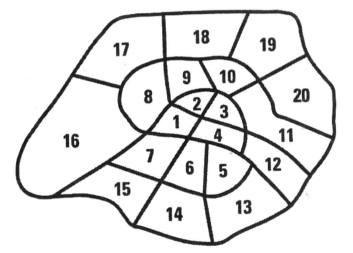

**1er**—Central Paris, well connected by *métro* and bus. Tends to be pricey and very busy. Not a great place if you have a car. Châtelet is very congested, but very central. Once chic and trendy around Les Halles, now a bit overrun and seedy at night. The park Palais-Royal is a bastion of undisturbed Parisian elegance.

**2e**—Also central but more commercial in the sense of wholesale outlets. Sentier is the core of Paris' garment district. You may find unusual places to live here but it's more the exception than the rule. The parts near the Opera and Madeleine are very high rent districts and not especially inviting as far as daily Parisian neighborhood life. The streets between Les Halles and the Grands Boulevards are some of the oldest, truly Parisian and most enchanting you'll find. The rue Montorgueil, the oldest market street in Paris, is worth a detour. Also contains the fashion-chic Place des Victoires.

3e, 4e—Very central with many lovely little streets, cafés, shops, etc. Congested, but worth it. Expensive. The Marais has lots of living advantages. One of the most desirable areas of Paris, for those who insist on old buildings with character and multi-cultural exposure. Rue des Rosiers is the heart of the Jewish quarter.

5e—Left Bank, the Latin Quarter. This is where you get the chic, the classy, the cultural, and the commercial. The areas down by St. Michel are tight and noisy. The areas closer to the 13ᵉ are more residential, well connected to the center of Paris and very pleasant. You can't go wrong in the 5th. Tends to be expensive, but great little finds are not impossible.
6e—Left Bank, St. Germain des Prés, Odéon. This is for the stylish wealthy and artistic. Many bookshops, galleries, cinemas, up beat cafés, restaurants and publishers. Between St. Germain and the Seine, prices are sky high. The 6th extends to Montparnasse and to Duroc. Lots of wonderful little streets.

7e—Tends to be expensive, high class, conservative and residential. Also houses most of the government ministries including the Assemblée Nationale and the Quai d'Orsay (Foreign Ministry). Not very lively at night, although very pleasant and pretty. The street behind Les Invalides, the avenue de Tourville, is the most expensive property in the French version of Monopoly. The Esplanade des Invalides offers sprawling lawns that are not off-limits for frisbee-playing and picnicking. The market on the rue Cler is particularly pleasant and filled with high quality shops.
8e—Right bank. Financial and corporate territory. Champs-Elysées. Very high rents and a lot of pomp. Lots of motion and money. Some surprisingly quaint and quiet streets. The rue St. Honoré has to be a highlight for extravagant Sunday window shopping.

9e—This includes Pigalle and Clichy. More *populaire*, meaning working-class. This can be fun. Depends on particular street and apartment. Don't exclude this. The covered passageways wait to be discovered. The streets taking the names of foreign cities, north of the Gare St. Lazare, are pleasant.

10e—There are some great spots near La République and along the St. Martin canal, although along the major boulevards and St. Denis, an element of tackiness and sleaze is present. Lots of Turkish and North African restaurants. Definitely worth checking out. Less expensive than nearby 3ᵉ and 4ᵉ.

11e—In the last ten years this district has emerged as perhaps the best combination of new "in places,' great apartments, artists spaces, and intriguing passageways. Not too far from things and still filled with great finds, but hurry up. Close to the Bastille on one end and Nation on the other. The 11ᵉ has a lot to offer without the pretentions of the Marais. Excellent for artists, restaurants, and lively evolving neighborhoods.

12e—Similar to the 11ᵉ; up and coming around Bercy, the former wine village, and Gare de Lyon, areas that were rather run-down and depressed. Not the most beautiful district, but you may find more space for less francs here than elsewhere. New construction tends to be hideous although the new Bercy business park flanking the Seine offers some of the most expensive and highly sought commercial properties in Europe. The new American Center is located next to the Bercy Palais Omnisport.

**13e**—The heart of Chinatown. Here you can find quaint streets with little houses next to horrible rows of Miami Beach style high rises. Some excellent, authentic Chinese restaurants. The areas near the 5ᵉ are very desirable. The district is growing rapidly along the Seine and the Tolbiac Bridge area with the new Bibliothèque de France complex dominating the scene.

**14e**—Denfert, Montparnasse, Porte d'Orléans. On the major north south axis. Many popular neighborhoods and great markets, particularly the one on the rue Daguerre. Without a doubt some of the best residential living in Paris. The area around the Parc Montsouris is lovely.

**15e**—Highly sought-after residential district among Parisians. Comfortable and not without its share of trees. The parts near the Seine host an unlikely outcrop of Japanese tourist hotels (to be avoided). The rue du Commerce captures the essence of daily Parisian family life. The streets around La Motte-Piquet are particularly lovely.

**16e**—Etoile, Trocadéro, etc. Perhaps the most boring and bourgeois area of Paris, yet one of the richest spots on earth. Many international students end up here, falsely attracted by the nearby Champs-Elysées, prestigious address and safety (a mistake). The streets, although pretty, are dead quiet at night and there

is nothing to do. Street life is absent except around the rue de Passy. Many lovely small museums and private streets.

**17e**—The most schizophrenic district of Paris. Half as bourgeois as the 16e, Parc Monceau is absolutely exquisite to stroll around. The other half near La Fourche is *populaire*, real and even funky. A bit far from the heart of things but this could be worth it if you want to really experience Paris life. Prices vary dramatically.

**18e**—Kind of far from central districts, although this depends if you're on a good *métro* line. More immigrants than elsewhere. Less expensive, so you definitely can get more for your money. Lots of things to discover. Encircles Montmartre. Some great markets.

**19e**—Probably the least known of all the Paris districts, mainly because it is so isolated. Not very convenient in most cases, but again, you may find a great space near a *métro*. Check it out. The Stalingrad area has become a bit tainted by druggies and dealers.

**20e**—A lively mix of races and ethnic groups, Africans, Antilleans, etc. Some excellent work spaces and artists' ateliers. Less expensive than the middle of town, working class, and less prestige, but it all depends on what you want.

**21e**—Not yet a reality, but discussion and some advanced advertising is already circulating. This district will include parts of the north east quadrant of Paris around the canals near La Villette and Pantin where new neighborhoods are being carved.

## A Word on the *Banlieues*

You may find yourself living in the Parisian suburbs, which can be either pleasant or grim, depending on your expectations and the actual town you're in. The closest suburbs which touch Paris, and are well-served by *métro* and bus lines, are called the *proche banlieue*. The most "exclusive" and desirable include Neuilly, Boulogne and St. Cloud to the west, and St. Mandé and Vincennes to the east. The little towns in the Vallée de Chevreuse, served by the RER, are the most desirable southern *banlieues*. The towns to the north tend to be the poorest and what the French would describe as sad *(triste)*. The northern suburbs and scattered others have experienced increases in crime, drugs, and delinquency in public places and housing projects called *cités* or *zones*. Bands or gangs of bored youth called *les casseurs* from these suburbs have on occasion invaded student demonstrations and vandalized and looted sections of Paris. The "Red Suburbs" signify the municipalities governed by the Communist Party and include Montreuil, Bagnolet, Bobigny, Kremlin-Bicêtre, Malakoff, etc. These communities, although not very different from the others, tend in theory to cater to the needs of the working class. In towns like Montreuil, which houses the headquarters for the CGT (powerful left-wing worker's union), there are large Arab and African communities. The town is conveniently located on the #9 métro line and has in recent years attracted hundreds of creative people and young families. Montreuil's dynamic *Deputé-Maire*, Jean-Pierre Brard, has set a tone for his town, the third largest in the region after Paris, as a place where multiculturism is celebrated, and cultural policies are progressive. Assistant mayor René Foulon and his cultural director Jean-Michel Morel administer a cultural program that would put to shame even large American cities. Montreuil hosts part of the annual Banlieue Bleues music festival, the largest children's book fair in France, a municipally subsidized art cinema, a literary bookshop, art opening literary conferences and the only jazz club in the *département, les Instants chavirés.* Apartments and work spaces here can be cheaper and more spacious than anywhere in Paris. Speculators are not encouraged.

The more distant suburbs (*grandes banlieues*), such as Versailles, St. Germain-en-Laye and Chantilly, are served by RER and commuter trains. The eastern line of the RER has recently been extended to Marne la Vallée to better serve Euro Disneyland.

The choice to live in the suburbs is a highly personal one depending on how important it is for you to be in the vicinity of Paris with its cafés and night life. The suburbs tend to be quiet at night and provincial in feel.

Often there seems to be little difference in being 10 kilometres or 200 kilometres from Paris. Offsetting this are the very vibrant cultural programs such as the Banlieue Jazz and Banlieue Bleues Festival in Seine-Saint-Denis, and the public theater in Bobigny.

## Doing Laundry in Paris

*One Californian reader of a previous edition of* Paris Inside Out *wrote to point out the guide book's Achilles heel, doing laundry in Paris. This short section attempts to respond to that past flaw.*

Admittedly, laundromats, those great American hang-outs, Maytag Meccas, those linty and egalitarian public spaces that would have thrilled the gizzards of de Tocqueville are not very numerous nor very complete in Paris, although certainly in a state of transition. Some improvement has already occurred; more and more laundromats are being created. The laundromat concept has been so rooted to the idea of self-autonomy that the concept in France has been slow to catch on. Anything that permits the public or the individual to make their own rules, Parisians find suspect. People are unaccustomed to go out and do laundry after hours and stand around with strangers and separate colors from whites and fold underwear in public. It just isn't French. Nonetheless, there are laun-

dromats, but you have to look for them, check out their hours, and facilities. Bring a long novel in that Parisian machines plow through lots of cycles and take over an hour to wash and numerous 2-franc coins to dry. The washing machines are calibrated by weight with the five or six kilo machines being the standard and the mega ten or fifteen kilo machine being the ones for blankets, slipcovers, drapes, etc. The machines usually take tokens (*jetons*) which are bought in machines for anywhere from 18 FF to 30 FF. Bring pockets of assorted change.

The common and traditional solution to dirty laundry is the local *blanchisserie* or cleaners which is usually combined with a *nettoyage à sec* or dry cleaners. These are relatively convenient but wildly expensive compared to North American and British standards. Rarely will you find a "same day" or even "next day" service, but this is not a steadfast rule. The white button-down shirt you were used to having cleaned and pressed in a day for a buck and a half will set you back either 20 FF if they send it out to some 3 or 4 day industrial service or 25 FF if they do it on the spot. If you opt for the industrial solution be prepared to sacrifice a button here or there, or sometimes find that a new button or thread that doesn't match has been sewn on for you at the plant.

When you pick your clothes up, you might be surprised to see how the garments are wrapped and folded in either plastic or brown paper. The laundry retains the wire hangers.

Many Parisians have small washers in their apartments, usually in the kitchen or bathroom, because no space for bulky utilities had been anticipated in the master scheme of things Parisian. Dryers are rarer, and masses of Parisians are used to draping wet clothes over chairs, on clothes lines over the tub, and across radiators. As for cleaning supplies, the French are addicted to their *eau de javel*, bleach, which they dilute and use to wash, disinfect, and bleach with. Woolite is commonly found but pronounced "Wooleet". To clean surfaces and especially floors, the French love their *serpillère*, absorbent cleaning rag often wrapped around the head of a broom or mop.

---

### Lexicon

| | |
|---|---|
| a stain | *une tache* |
| a sweater or pullover shirt | *un pull* or *pull-over* |
| an iron | *un fer à repasser* |
| button down shirt | *une chemise* |
| cotton | *coton* |
| hem | *un ourlet* |
| ironing board | *une planche à repasser* |
| jeans | *un jean* |
| laundry/dry cleaner | *un pressing, une blanchisserie* |
| sewing shop | *une mercerie* |
| dye shop | *une teinturerie* |
| pants | *un pantalon* |
| socks | *une paire de chaussettes* |
| starch | *amidon* |
| to iron | *repasser* |
| to knit | *tricoter* |
| to sew | *coudre* |
| wool | *laine* |
| zipper | *une fermeture éclair* |

# Banking & Money

*Journalist Philip Crawford whose articles regularly grace the pages of* The Money Report *in* The International Herald Tribune *contributed to this overview of banking in Paris.*

Despite the progress made in harmonizing trade and financial service regulations within the 12-country European Union, since certain aspects of the Maastricht Treaty took effect on January 1, 1993, hopes for a single currency by the end of the decade now seem rather unrealistic. New diplomatic obstacles to an ECU-spending Europe seem to crop up everyday. Nevertheless, French banks will have to begin offering more complete services for international customers at competitive prices. Your reactions and experiences with French and international banks in France will undoubtedly vary depending on what you're accustomed to. Remember one thing—France has never really been a service-oriented society. Things do not run around the omnipresent operating practice that the customer is always right. Although money and financial gain play an important role in France, as in all Western societies, the French are unwilling to sacrifice everything for the sake of profit. A shopkeeper may refuse to stay open slightly after closing time, even to make a sale. Businesses often don't answer phones at lunch time. Real estate brokers will wait for you to call back. All this can be both enchanting and annoying. Learn to be enchanted—the quality of daily life wins out over more aggressive commercial practices. Take the longer meal.

In banks, you will probably not have a personal first-name-basis relationship with your banker. He or she will not close each transaction with a drippy but sincere "Have a Nice Day." You will experience this everywhere from banks to restaurants. If you receive moderately polite and efficient service in a bank consider yourself lucky. And don't expect toaster ovens or Walkmans for opening an account! Patience is not a commodity found in abundance when the thick Plexiglas *guichet* (window) service is involved. No one in any particular branch of any bank will ever have the authority to credit your account one *centime* without first passing on your written request to *la Direction* (management) of the bank. All operations, complaints, modifications and verifications are slow and tedious and, when possible, should be avoided. It is a good idea to get yourself known by at least two bank employees at your branch. That way when one is *en vacances* (on holiday) you still have a chance of better service if needed. This will save you time and aggravation in that a number of bank operations run smoother when you're recognized and don't have to provide identification each time.

Over the last five years, France has become highly *informatisée* (computerized) in everything from banking to dating. *Guichets automatiques* (ATMs, automatic teller machines for withdrawing cash) abound. Between your *Carte Bleue* bank payment card and the Minitel, the private citizen in France essentially has access to all sectors of commercial life. This computerization comes as much from the French love of form (or, systems and structures) and aesthetics (or, style) as from a search for greater efficiency.

So, service in France is improving in business as less and less is required from human interaction. In the last few years, some banks have understood that customer service is the way to go. Barclays Bank has opened up branches all over and have confronted the French banking system head on by trying to offer interest bearing checking accounts, something French banks have never done and French customers have never demanded. In fact, French consumers never demand anything; they accept. This stems from an old world mentality that is so grateful and content already with the luxury of individual freedom and the availability of goods that price and service are inconsequential. Americans take the first two for granted; only price and service matter. The French consumer hasn't yet discovered the power of his pocketbook. Getting back to banks, everyone has his or her own horror story. One American businessman nearly went out of business in 1992 when his local branch of a large French bank neglected to deposit a large foreign check for four weeks because the document needed a 4 FF *timbre fiscal* (tax stamp) to make the transaction required. By the time the customer complained, the maker of the check, an international company, had gone bankrupt and the American in Paris had lost $35,000 US due to the bank's incompetence. Stories like this abound. Young banking personnel are often narrowly trained technocrats. Stay on top of your bank, court a personal relationship with at least two different bankers if you're doing business in France, and scream like crazy if—when—they foul up.

As for daily banking you'll probably have a few early questions: How do I change money? How can I receive money from abroad? What do I need to open a bank account? Which banks are the best? Where can I cash travelers checks? And what about credit cards? These are all answered here.

A society's relationship to money reveals much about that society. If you're coming from the United States, where banking (except currency conversion in small banks) is a relatively easy and flexible activity, you may be frustrated at first when even attempting simple transactions. In France, the banks are a highly regulated industry. The State has played an increasingly present role in matters of banking since 1983, when Mitterrand nationalized much of the industry. There are a handful of huge and omnipresent banks that have hundreds of branches all over Paris and in a majority of towns in the provinces. The largest French banks, and thus the ones with the most branch offices, are Crédit Agricole, Banque Nationale de Paris (BNP), Crédit Lyonnais and Société Générale. These are the most visible and the easiest to work with concerning overseas transfers, but they don't necessarily provide better service than the smaller banks. In 1993, the BNP reverted from being a state bank to being a private bank in Prime Minister Balladur's move to privatization which also included the insurance company, UAP and industrial giant, ELF.

When selecting a bank, first consider the branch's location in terms of convenience to your home, place of work, or school. Insist on service. If you're displeased, go elsewhere; there are plenty of banks and almost as many answers to your questions as there are banks. Don't forget that in France the post office (la Poste) also serves as the largest banking facility in the country, issuing checking, savings, and money management accounts that are often advantageous with regards to income taxes. One reason la Poste is popular is that every post office is a branch, the hours extend from 8 a.m. to 7 p.m. (till noon on Saturdays), and every transaction is confirmed with a receipt by mail. This makes for easy bookkeeping. One possible snag: La Poste often requires that its banking customers have résident status.

Here are a few key banks well-adapted for foreigners, where you'll be able to change money and ask questions.

**American Express International**
11, rue Scribe
75009 PARIS
Tel: 47.77.77.07
Travel agency, exchange service,

clients' mail and travelers' checks. Open 9h-17h Monday-Saturday for clients' mail, currency exchange and travelers checks and 9h-17h30 Monday-Friday for travel agency. In cases of stolen credit cards during hours of closure, call 47.77.72.00. For lost travelers checks call AMEX at telephone number 05.90.86.00 (free call—all 05 calls, *numéros verts*, are automatically collect). American Express *green* card holders, that is, the normal card, can write checks off their accounts up to $1,000 per week, and for those with gold cards, the limit is $2,000 per week.

**Crédit Commercial de France (CCF):**
115, Champs-Elysées
75008 Paris
*Métro*: George-V
Hours: Open every day, 8h45-20h and in July, August and September on Sundays from 10h15-18h.
Tel: 40.70.27.22 or 40.70.77.17

**Banque Nationale de Paris (BNP)**
2, Place de l'Opéra at rue du Quatre Septembre
75002 Paris
*Métro*: Opéra
24-hour VISA automatic cash machine and automatic changer for foreign notes.
Tel: 44.94.53.99

**Barclays Bank**
24 bis, av de l'Opéra
75001 Paris
*Métro*: Opéra
9h30-16h, Monday-Friday and
6, Rond-Point des Champs-Elysées
75008 Paris
Tel: 44.95.13.80
*Métro*: Champs-Elysées-Clemenceau
Barclay checks only, and travelers checks. 7,50 FF commission on checks up to £100.

**Citibank**
30, av Champs-Elysées
75008 Paris
Mondays to Fridays 9h-18h45, Saturdays 10h30-13h15, 14h30-18h30.
Tel: 40.76.33.00

Banking Hours: generally 9h00-16h30 or 17h00 on weekdays, closed on weekends. Foreign banks close at 16h00. The currency exchange closes for lunch.
Foreign Currency Exchange: Open nightly on weekdays until 20h00 at the Gare St. Lazare and the Gare de L'Est, everyday at the Gare du Nord and Gare de Lyon until 21h00 and 23h00, respectively. Many banks also have exchange windows, usually open during select hours (never during lunch). The Crédit Commercial de France, 113 av des Champs-Elysées, is open on Saturdays from 8h30-20h00.
Exchange rates and commissions vary greatly in France. So, don't be too hasty. One British visitor recently found that the CIC Banque which advertises to be anglophone-friendly,

wanted a 32 FF commission, plus a 1,2% fee to change a £20 sterling bank note! A branch of the BRED bank offered 8,05 FF per pound with a 25 FF fee while the post office across the street paid 8,39 FF with no fee whatsoever. Some, major post offices do offer a foreign exchange service. In that they are slow to change their rates day to day, when official rates drop you can actually gain by using La Poste's service. Many branches of banks do not handle foreign currency exchange, and in tourist areas of town, often stick a handwritten note in the window: NO CHANGE.

Many private exchange services have opened all over the city, most in response to the five million tourists who came for the bicentennial and the new Japanese presence in France. One change outfit with a major presence in Paris is Exact Change with 17 key locations. Another popular one is called Chequepoint (Head Office, 150, av des Champs-Elysées), which accepts Eurocheques and personal checks drawn on British bank accounts. Remember you can always negotiate a slightly better exchange rate with these walk-up change bureaus, especially if you're changing large sums. If they won't budge, go elsewhere. Be wary of individual money changers in that numerous travelers and students have reported being victims of short change artists. Some have even ended up with fists full of worthless Polish *zlotes*.

## Opening an Account

There has been some ambiguity as to the procedures for foreigners to open accounts in France. This stems from the curious fact that rules, regulations and formalities vary greatly from not only bank to bank but between branches of the same bank. As a new resident, you'll want to remember that the way you're handled is highly discretionary. So, it's to your advantage to present yourself well, convey stability, respectability and the certainty and regularity of deposits. If you hit a small snag, don't fight or lose sleep; try another branch, or another bank—there are plenty.

In most cases, you'll be asked for a *carte de séjour* and proof of address (EDF/GDF strikes again). However, even this fluctuates. One Société Générale manager stated confidently "just a passport will do." The BNP, although one of the largest banks, tends to require a lot of paperwork. The Société Générale may ask for fewer documents to begin with, but tends to be cautious in issuing checkbooks and *Carte Bleue* bank payment cards. Some of the smaller banks like BRED and the Crédit du Nord may prove to be the easiest in opening up accounts and offering services but have fewer branch offices. Many banks will only let you open accounts if you live or work in the neighborhood of the branch. Friends have reported that at one large bank's branch they were told that they had to maintain a 20000 FF minimum in the account at all times. The fact that they produced a certified letter from an American banker testifying that they had $100,000 US on deposit in the US didn't help matters.

For your first two years in France you will be entitled to a *compte non-résident* (non-resident account) unless you are from an EU country. Previously, the *compte non-résident* limited you to making deposits from outside of France. These regulations have been dropped. So essentially there is no difference between a *compte non-résident* and a *compte résident* for deposits up to 50,000 FF. You can withdraw and deposit funds of any currency without limit. Note that although it's easy to deposit foreign currency checks and cash, hefty and seemingly illogical fees and commissions, and TVA (sales tax) on the fees and commission, may be debited from your account and a delay of up to four weeks may occur before payment is completed. In most cases, you'll receive your *chéquier* (check book) in 2-3 weeks, and, if you request one, your *Carte Bleue* bank payment card. Cards must be picked up in person while check books may be sent to you via registered mail at your expense. When you leave France, you might want to maintain your account in that after two years you'll qualify for a *compte résident*. This is easier than starting everything over should you

decide to return and an easy way to settle bills that arrive later.

*La Poste* offers both checking and saving account facilities, which are convenient in that every post office becomes a branch of your bank, and check deposits can be made by postage-free mail. *Immo'Poste* is a postal banking product whereby savings investments reap immediate tax deductions. And *Audioposte* is a service whereby you have 24-hour access to your CCP (*compte chèques postal*) balance by phone.

### Checking Accounts

Although eclipsed by the *Carte Bleue* as the most used form of payment, the personal check still plays a vast role in daily French life. You will most certainly want to get yourself *un compte-chèques* (a checking account) and *carnet de chèques* or *chéquier* (checkbook), in that paying by check is a widely accepted and easy form of handling your affairs in France. Everywhere from restaurants to gas stations, the personal check is readily accepted. You can even pay for your monthly *métro* pass with a check. All stores accept checks. The post office accepts checks, too. You will often, but not systematically, be asked to show some form of identification when you pay by check. The reason for the widespread acceptance of checks stems from the fact that checks in France are not negotiable or even cashable as they are in the

US, Canada, and to a great extent, the UK. Most checks in France are *barrés*, meaning they have two lines or bars pre-printed across the front of each check. This simply signifies that the check cannot be signed and re-endorsed for payment to a third party. All checks thus must be deposited into the bank account of the person whose name appears on the face of the check. So, be wary of accepting a personal check from someone if you do not have a bank account yourself. You will not be able to go to the maker's bank and cash the check. It must be deposited. This means that all payments by check are officially recorded and thus are easily controlled by bank inspectors, accountants, and eventually the *fisc* (tax collectors). Most salaries in France are paid directly into the employees bank account via *virement* (electronic bank transfer). Similarly, bank mortgages, utility payments, telephone bills, etc. are often deducted automatically from the recipient's account (*prélèvement automatique).* A *relevé d'identité bancaire* (RIB) is the printed form at the top of your monthly statement that gives all the codes of your account, bank and branch. These are demanded of you when payment is to be wired directly into your account. Restrictions limit the mobility of money in French society, but also reduce seriously the degree of fraud and the frequency of bounced checks or bad checks (*chèque en*

*bois*—wooden check). It can be difficult to stop payment on a check (*faire opposition à un chèque*) and French law is unrelenting concerning writers of bad checks, although as the economy tightens, more and more bad checks are in circulation. The strictest penalty is being reported to the national Banque de France, where your name goes on a list of people not allowed to have checking accounts in France.

### Savings Accounts

*Un compte d'épargne sur livret* (savings account) can also be opened. Most banks will pay modest interest on funds left in savings accounts for extended periods. Your current balance will be noted in *le livret* (passbook) after each deposit or withdrawal. In France, many people also have a PEL (*Plan d'épargne logement*), a government-subsidized, low-interest bearing savings account designed to accrue credits toward a future low-interest loan to be used exclusively for the purchase of a house or apartment or a home improvement project. Minimum monthly deposits of 300 FF for at least four years are required to benefit from this account. *La Poste* also offers other beneficial savings plans. The private bank, Cortal, has attempted to compete with the commercial banks which offer little or no interest, by offering safe and attractive banking facilities that function like a money market account based on SICAVs (French treasury bills). Cortal, 131, av. Charles de Gaulle, 92571 Neuilly-sur-Seine.

**Credit Cards**

In France the *Carte Bleue* (CB) offered by each bank has truly become an institution in daily life. The French attraction to computerized systems has been married to this centralized form of payment. The CB (part of both the VISA and Mastercard/ Eurocard network) is widely accepted, although it is not really a credit card; it's a payment card. Purchases and automatic cash withdrawals are debited from your checking account on a fixed date of the month. Thus, you do not really get true credit. You do not receive a monthly credit card statement although you do receive a monthly accounting and you cannot run up large bills. You do not have a credit line other than the overdraft limit permitted by your bank. Your use of the card is debited automatically. The idea of real credit, that great and abusive invention that permits people to live painlessly beyond their means, is still rather foreign in Europe. The main advantage of the *Carte Bleue* is its surprisingly wide acceptance. You can use your card at any ATM machine regardless of which bank the card belongs to although the withdrawal limits vary. You can pay your tolls on the *autoroute* with your CB; you can pay all your supermarket purchases with your CB as well as pay automatic underground parking lots; you can even stick your CB into a ticket machine in selected *métro* stations to buy your monthly *Carte Orange*, or purchase a museum admission ticket in the lobby of the Louvre with your CB. Many stores require a minimum purchase of 100 FF. The list continues. CB cards now contain not only a magnetic band which permits users to draw up to 1800 FF cash (amount can depend on your bank) per week from any bank's automatic teller machines, but also a circular micro chip *(puce)* into which your four digit access code (PIN) is inscribed. This system has eliminated the need for customers to sign bills as most restaurants, gas stations, hotels, etc. now have portable, cordless machines that read the *puce* and check it against the number the customer punches in. CB cards sometimes malfunction and need to be rubbed with a clean cloth. And keep the card away from keys. When using the automatic tellers note that they only accept cards issued on French banks, so don't stick your Visa, Mastercard, or American Express cards into one of them. It may retain the card and you'll have to return the next day with your passport to retrieve it. Cards eaten by machines in the *métro*, etc. take several weeks before being returned to your bank branch. Note that the ATM machines will often be marked with stickers indicating they are part of the Plus, Cirrus, and NYCE ATM networks. American banks often tell customers that their American cards will work in France. This is not yet the case. The cards are not compatible. However, ATM cards issued in France will work in many other ATM machines around Europe. Some French ATM machines now carry the American Express "Express Cash" logo and these will work with Amex cards.

All major credit card companies are represented in France. Here are phone numbers in case of lost or stolen cards:

**American Express**
Tel: 47.77.70.00
Lost cards: 47.77.72.00

**Diners Club de France**
Tel: 47.62.75.00 (Info)

**(Mastercard) Eurocard**
Tel: 45.67.53.53
Lost cards: 45.67.84.84

**(Visa) Carte Bleue**
Tel: 42.25.51.51
Lost cards: 42.77.11.90 (Paris)
(16) 54.42.12.12 (provinces)

## Transferring Funds From Abroad

### Getting Cash Fast

One of the most important questions you may someday have about banking is: "How can I get money quickly from home?" Despite assurances made by many issuing banks in other countries, the majority of money orders and inter bank checks—and all personal checks—must normally be cleared through the issuing bank before they can be credited to your account. This can take weeks. Other, quicker possibilities include:

• Wire transfer: the sender can wire money directly to a French franc account, specifying the branch name and the address of your bank—this normally takes 48 hours. Always note the *siège* (branch) number and *clé RIB* (bank code). Having money telexed to your Paris bank account can be done quickly if the issuing bank is directly affiliated with the receiving bank so that the money does not have to go through intermediaries. For example, money telexed from the Société Générale in New York will go directly into your account in a Parisian branch if the branch name and account number are specified. If you plan to receive a regular transfer of funds over a period of time, and if the issuing bank is not directly affiliated with your bank in Paris, count on the transfer to take as long as four weeks. Therefore, it is a good idea to ask your home bank if it is affiliated with a French bank before you open an account. Most banks have an electronic bank transfer system called SWIFT, which doesn't always live up to its name, in that although the actual transfer takes one day, some banks may take a day to send the order from one branch to a larger one, and then another to process the transfer. When weekends and holidays interfere money can be slowed down tremendously. Depositing foreign fund checks into a French bank account can take weeks to clear and cost you high fees. It's usually better to group small checks and deposit them together. On some occasions a small sum like ten dollars or ten pounds might cost you less not to deposit. Depositing *Eurochèques* in either French francs or foreign currency will cost you at least 30 FF per check plus the commission and exchange charge and TVA sales tax.

• American Express: if you have no account in France, a wire transfer can be made through American Express—one of the most rapid systems. A "Money-gram" allows one to send or receive cash instantly; the minimum being $100 US and the maximum being $7500 US. The American Express Bank on the Champs Elysées is not for currency exchange. At the rue Scribe address, you can draw French cash against your American Express card.

• Western Union Worldwide Money Transfer. You can send money to any of Western Unions 19000 agents from the US and Canada. You can charge this transfer by phone to your VISA or MasterCard, 7 days a week. In the US call 1-800-325-6000. A trick: call from Paris and send yourself money against your credit card. In France, 40.23.95.79.

• Bank checks in francs: have the sender purchase a bank check drawn in French francs at your Paris bank's foreign branch and send it to you through the mail.

• One American translator in Paris contends that the Washington D.C. bank, Riggs National Bank, offers a convenient service for check depositing and cashing, and currency conversion through their US Embassy Office:

Riggs National Bank
US Embassy
2 av Gabriel
75328 Paris Cedex 8
Tel: 47.4237.22
Fax: 47.42.38.10

Citibank is the only American bank with retail operations in France. Equipped to handle your banking in the US, and open accounts prior to your arrival in France, Citibank offers full service in English for all long-term French banking needs. *(See inside back cover.)* For more information, write to Mr. Becvar, Citibank-PIO, 19 Le Parvis, 92073 Paris-La Défense.

# Working in France

France's attraction not only as a place to visit and live, but as a country to work in, continues to mount, especially among anglophones. Americans continue to be attracted by the quality and style of life as well as the ripeness of Paris commercially in certain sectors of activity. AT&T, for example, was thrilled in the mid-80s to discover the untapped possibilities of direct mail campaigns to sell products and services. As the new commercial Europe continues to develop, more and more companies send executives and their families to France. Additionally, EU nationals from the UK and Ireland continue to arrive with the ability and expressed wish to both work—legally—and to profit by the culturally exciting style of life.

Being able to work successfully in France requires a certain number of legal steps as well as an understanding of the local work culture. The working environment in France,

Paris in particular, has changed dramatically over the last decade. First of all, it's harder to find work since 1993 when the economy worsened and a new set of laws intensified restrictions on non-EU foreigners. On the other hand, traditions that once limited the mobility of the French workplace have broken down to a certain degree and a receptivity to new commercial ideas and marketing strategies has increasingly grown. A glance at the advertising give-aways reflect this growth. In terms of the economy, in Paris one always talks of the *reprise*, the bounce back, as if the high unemployment picture, high prices, and stagnant growth rate, is a very short term thing. The reality is that more people are out of work in 1994 than at any other moment in history since World War II, with official unemployment at over 13%. Paris streets and *métros* are beginning to host the ubiquitous presence of no longer just *clochards* but homeless, down and out, and economically deprived individuals. The city isn't dangerous but the despair that one associates with large American cities has begun to encroach on the French capital. The homeless, referred to as SDF (*Sans domicile fixe*), along with the jobless, have at least three major semi-monthly newspapers which they peddle incessantly and competitively in the *métros* for 10 F (they pay 3 to 4 FF)—*Le Réverbère, La Rue,* and *Macadam,* as well as the publication of the great humanitarian leader, l'Abbé Pierre, *Faim de siècle.* This is a sign not to be ignored. The French tend to be less mobile when it comes to career in general, and now in a tight economy, people are increasingly reluctant to change or to risk. Security is more important in France than salary, although a move to reduce the minimum wage *(le SMIC)* for students to 20% lower than the adult SMIC led to massive and violent demonstration. Young people in particular feel insecure and threatened by the lack of an economically promising future. Banks are not lending as they once had, and on the whole it's not the easiest moment to launch new entrepreneurial undertakings. Having stated all this, you can proceed to note nonetheless some of the cultural highlights of the Parisian employment scene, as well as a host of practical tips on job-looking. First, though, a mini-tour of the legal requisites for working in France.

Note, first of all, that EU nationals have the right to work in France, and so not all of the legal discussion below will pertain to them.

## Work Status

In France, you are always given a status which regulates your working possibilities. For example, you can't simply start up your own business and invoice clients. For that you need to be either a *travailleur indépendant,* which means that you are a declared self-employed individual paying your own social charges, or you have to set up a legally-constituted company, a SARL or a SA. There are other work opportunities, but they require preparation and greater self-initiative. Read on. Much depends on what you want from your job, and what your needs are.
For non-EU nationals here are the types of working status available in France.

**Employee** *(salarié)*: This means that you work for a company for a monthly salary. Salaries in France are always calculated on a monthly basis. You do not have the right to invoice someone else for your services. Your employer pays your social charges and you are entitled to numerous legal benefits. It is difficult for a non-EU person to obtain this status unless you are being sought by a company who offers you a work contract with a salary of at least 22000 F per month, or unless you already possess a 10-year *carte de séjour* or *carte de résident* with the right to work. You will receive a monthly *fiche de paie* or payslip that details your earnings and deductions. Your salary will most likely be deposited directly to your bank account electronically on the day you contractually get paid. Very few people in France are paid regularly by check, and checks in France cannot be cashed; they can only be deposited into the account of the person named on the check. There is no third party checks and you can never collect cash for a check by presenting the check at the bank on which the check is drawn. Your *fiche de paie* will spell out how much has been taken out for the social security, retirement, unemployment, and numerous other administrations. Note that when the French government needs to raise more cash, it creates and implements new withholdings from salaries.

### Self-employed
### (*Travailleur Indépendant*)
Once in France legally and having obtained the *carte de séjour* (see Administrative Matters), you can proceed to request status as a *travailleur indépendant*, or self-employed person if your activity of work falls into this category. *Travailleurs indépendants* are usually writers, translators, consultants, professions that

don't work permanently for one company, etc. This cannot be done as a student. With *travailleur indépendant* status you'll be obliged to pay monthly sums to the URSSAF, the Social Security administration for self-employed individuals, or to one of the other organs *(Caisses)* administering *Sécurité Sociale*. Authors, for example must contact the AGESSA; musicians, the SACEM; artists, the *Maison des Arts;* and journalists, the *Syndicat des Journalistes*. Most, though, go through URSSAF *(Union pour le Recouvrement des Cotisation de Sécurité Sociale et d'Allocations Familiales)*. The URSSAF fees *(charges)* for the first two years are around 700 FF per trimester, and 5.4% of your invoiced earnings after that.

### URSSAF
3, rue Franklin
93100 MONTREUIL
Tel: 49.20.10.10 / 48.51.75.75

Although this may seem like an expensive option in the beginning, it gives you the ability to work legally and benefit from social advantages offered in France. Also, as a *travailleur indépendant* you'll increase your employment chances in that employers are not obliged to pay the high social charges for employing you, nor are they locked into a potentially expensive permanence. This is a particularly useful option for individuals whose professional activities lend themselves to freelance work. Note that it seems like every expatriate you meet will have his or her own story on how he or she maneuvered through the system. Without exaggeration, there are no absolutes when it comes to working in France; you have to get out there and ask questions, supply documents, and ride with the tide. You'll be told one thing one day, another thing the next. Don't despair; give 'em what they want or pick a new strategy. The system is oppressive, but porous.

**Student (*étudiant*)**
American and other foreign students in France can, under certain conditions, obtain a temporary work permit (*autorisation provisoire de travail*) for part-time (*mi-temps*) work during the summer vacation months or during the regular school year. Students at the Sorbonne's "*Cours de civilisation française,*" the Alliance Française and the Institut Catholique and at any other school which does not provide French social security medical care coverage of students are not eligible for temporary work permits.
Part-time work during the school year is limited to a maximum of 20 hours per week, and during the summer vacation, a maximum of 39 hours per week. Each year, the French Government issues instructions during the last trimester of the academic year governing part-time employment from June 1 of the cur-

rent year through May 31 of the following year.

*Part-Time Employment During the Summer Vacation*
The following categories of foreign students can be considered for summer employment if they have completed one year of study in France.
• Students pursuing higher (university) studies, including *établissements d'enseignements supérieurs, facultés, grandes écoles* and *écoles de préparation aux grandes écoles.*
• Students, 16 years and older, in secondary and technical schools (*collèges* and *lycées*).
• Students aged 14 and 15 (light work only).
Summer work cannot exceed three months and must fall within the time frame of June 1 to October 31, except for a maximum of 15 days each for the Christmas and Easter holidays. The work period for students aged 14 and 15 is limited to one-half of their school vacation time.

*Part-Time Employment During the School Year*
Part-time employment during the academic year is restricted to foreign students attending French universities and other institutions of higher learning. A student must submit his or her current card (*carte d'étudiant*) in order to be eligible. Secondary and technical school students are not eligible.

Temporary work permits are usually given to students who do not have sufficient private resources to pursue their studies. Thus, recipients of grants and those who have sufficient means are not authorized to have temporary work permits. Students wishing to work part-time during the school year must, in addition to the usual documents (see below), submit a letter justifying the need to work as a student.

The part-time work must fall within the academic year. The temporary work permit is valid for three months and may be renewed upon presentation of evidence of continuing studies.

Foreigners attending French universities in Paris should apply at:
*Ministère du Travail*
Service de la Main d'Oeuvre
Etrangère
80, rue de la Croix Nivert
75015 Paris
Tel: 45.31.10.03/40.56.60.00
Hours: 9:30 a.m.-11:30 a.m.
and 1:30 p.m.- 4:30 p.m.
Métro: Commerce.

Aside from a list of documents including a letter from an employer stating the following,
-name and address of applicant
-position of job description
-number of hours to be worked
-wages offered
-place of work
-length of employment
secondary school students may be asked for a *certificat de scolarité* in lieu of a *carte d'étudiant.*

You will probably also be required to prove that you are not a French *boursier* (French State Scholarship Recipient) by picking up a waiver form at: CROUS, 6 rue Jean Calvin, 5e, Métro Censier. Open 13h30-16h. This might seem silly but it's necessary while being simple to obtain.

Otherwise, three-month work permits are issued to students at CIEE at 1, Place de l'Odéon 75006 Paris for the fee of 950 FF. In that regulations and fees are subject to change, it is wise to always verify latest information.

### *Au Pair* Positions

Although being an au pair in France seems like an informal working arrangement, it actually is a highly formal work contract, regulated by French law. *Au pairs* usually are pursuing their studies at the same time as their work contract with a family. Responsibilities vary, but always include looking after children, some housework, bringing kids to school and fetching them after school, and some baby-sitting. *Au pairs* work 30 hours per week, receive room and board, a *Carte Orange* métro pass, and 1600 FF per month on average.

## Other Situations that May Grant Working Status

A number of situations may or may not afford you the right to work in France. Each case must be examined and evaluated. In addition, with the new immigration laws being implemented, it is difficult to say in advance which cases will apply to which laws. Much discretion is being left in the hands of local municipal authorities, le *mairie* of each jurisdiction, and so what might work for one may fail for another. Be warned. Here is a short list of situations that may help guarantee your right to work in France.

• Marriage to a French national.
• Being an accompanying family member of someone able to work in France.
• Short-Term transferees from foreign companies with offices in France.
• Having a French or French-nationalized child.
• Marriage to a British Commonwealth national.
• Marriage to a EU National.

## Working Culture

Laws and procedures can always be learned by reading books and hiring professionals. It's the atmosphere in the workplace, the underlying attitudes about life, work, money, etc. that requires personal knowledge and experience. The working environment in France is radically different than those in the US, UK, or for that matter Germany, or Japan. It takes a good, long time to figure out how people think and communicate. You just have to know. French employers find Americans to be too direct, bold, and to the point for their taste. The French care more about the individual's ability to integrate, to work together, to respect protocol, to grow patiently with the job. In that the French enjoy greater job security, they can concentrate on building long-term structures. They are less in a hurry to make money, although a new breed of young French managers have been influenced by the American model and seem to be attempting to get everything at once. Although the French understand profit and the accumulation of wealth, they are less comfortable showing wealth. There is still something vulgar about money in the French mind-set. The French also prefer to maintain a sense of formality among employees and with management even after having worked many years together. People *se vouvoient* each other for what may seem like forever. Use *vous*. One American journal editor continued to *vouvoyer* the printer he worked with for seven years. Finally, he risked it and told Monsieur Claude that he could *tutoyer* him. Politely, the Frenchman agreed, but continued to *vouvoyer* his client for another two years. Remember, the French are in love with form. Don't be too loud, gregarious, or familiar too quickly. Business is done at a culturally recognized pace. One American metals dealer from Boston was stunned when he took along an experienced translator friend to help him sort out a nasty snag in a deal with the director of a large French importer. The American had one hour to resolve the problem and catch his plane at Charles de Gaulle airport. The first thirty minutes of the meeting were devoted to chatter about the director's summer house in the Loire, wine, his son's interest in studying in the US, and other assorted blabber. Only when the director was comfortable and a rapport had been established, did the conversation turn to the details of the metal shipment that had gone amuck. The director proposed a compromise slightly better than what the American had expected. Everyone shook hands, conversation returned to the Loire for a minute, then proper good-byes were exchanged, and the American made his plane with 15 minutes to spare. The key was to respect the local cadence. Always wait for the other to start in on the serious stuff. The French, at best, will understand your eagerness and directness because you're Anglo-Saxon, but they will not really like it.

# Doing Business
## Forming a Company

This is potentially complicated—for assistance, consult the US Embassy Foreign Commercial Service at 2, av Gabriel, 75382 Paris Cedex 8, Tel: 42.96.12.02, Fax: 42.66.97.83. Additionally, information and support can be obtained from the American Chamber of Commerce in France, 21, av Georges V, 75008 Paris, Tel: 47.23.80.26 or 47.23.70.28. The Chamber of Commerce publishes a business directory and a magazine called *Commerce in France* and a pamphlet on small companies in France as well as its directory of members. A third resource is the French-American Chamber of Commerce located at 7, rue Jean Goujon, 75008 Paris, Tel: 42.56.05.00. For a list of lawyers see *Paris Anglophone.* American lawyers often consulted in the community include Samuel Okoshken, who lectures at WICE, 51, av Montaigne 75008 Paris, Tel: 44.13.69.50, Daniel Lapres, 11, rue Jules Chaplain, 75006 Paris, Tel: 43.26.77.90, Catherine Kessedjian, 27, rue des Plantes 75014 Paris, Tel: 45.40.86.27, and John Fredenberger, 109, av Henri Martin, 75116 Paris, Tel: 45.04.10.10. According to the British Consulate, law firms capable of helping British citizens include:

**Wise and Mercer**
203bis bd St. Germain
75007 Paris
Tel: 45.48.40.79

Marion Matthey
213 bd St. Germain
75007 Paris
Tel: 45.49.15.47

Herbert Smith & Co
41 av Georges V
75008 Paris
Tel: 47.23.91.24

A word on lawyers: ask enough questions to make sure the lawyer you have consulted understands your precise needs and your budgetary restrictions. The range of legal advice concerning legal status in France and means of setting up a business in France varies greatly depending on the experience and preference of the lawyer you consult. Find out your options before you commit. And ask for a written estimate (*devis*) before you start. If you have the time and the energy, many of the administrative procedures required to satisfy legal guidelines can be done by you, initial searches can be made on the Minitel, etc. You can also receive free or low cost legal counsel at your city hall (*mairie*) one evening a week. Trade unions and professional organizations also provide legal assistance to its members. The cost of creating an infrastructure for a business in France is higher than in the US or UK, and it is easy to start off with a great idea, lots of energy and enthusiasm, and a bit of money, only to get discouraged fast by the red-tape and the cost of retaining your lawyer

and accountant. Think this through before you jump into the deep end. For really small businesses, a non-profit *association de 1901* may be a better option for you at first than setting up an SARL, an option lawyers don't usually suggest.

## Types of Companies

**SARL** *Société à responsabilité limitée.* This is the equivalent of the US Inc. or the British Ltd. It is the easiest and most common corporate structure in France. It requires an initial capitalization of a minimum of 50000 FF which is deposited at a bank by the shareholders in the name of the company and cannot be touched until the company is officially registered and receives its papers of incorporation or K-Bis. The company will receive a *SIRET* number as well which must appear on the company's letter head along with the amount of the capitalization and the legal address (*siège*). There must be at least two shareholders (*associés*) but not more than 50. The legally responsible person for the company is the *gérant*, and he or she, among other legal, administrative, and fiscal responsibilities, must keep the register of the *assemblée générale*, or the official minutes of the company's meetings of shareholders. The *gérant* must have a *carte de commerçant*, a 10 year *carte de séjour* or be an EU national. If you don't fit into this category, you'll have to hire a *gérant* for your company. To set up a

SARL, lawyers normally bill from 10000 FF to 15000 FF as a basic fee.

**SA** *Société anonyme:* This is a larger corporation with a minimum capitalization of 250000 FF. It carries more weight with banks. It must have a least seven shareholders and a board of directors, and more serious accounting and auditing is required. Companies with numerous employees often opt for the SA.

**EURL** *Entreprise unipersonnelle à responsabilité limitée:* This is essentially a SARL with one shareholder. For an independent or a free-lancing individual, this solution may make sense in that personal assets are free from risk, although banks are increasingly requiring personal guarantees on loans made to EURLs. There are major tax implications on this and other forms of companies. Careful discussion should preceed all decisions to incorporate in France.

***Association de loi de 1901*:** This is not a company, but a non-profit organization, created legally for a clearly described reason, usually cultural, artistic, or humanitarian, but not necessarily. The legal, administrative, and fiscal tasks of setting-up and running an association are reasonable, although the size and budget of the *association* determines everything. The American University of Paris fore example is a non-profit organization with over 150 employees. An *association* cannot make profit but it can buy and sell, hire employees, invest earnings, etc. If your project contributes to the cultural, educational or scientific life of France, and your intentions don't go further than being able to make the project come alive with an honest salary for yourself and your collaborators, an *association* is the easiest, cheapest, safest, and least frustrating legal structure available to you in France. On the other hand, an association gains its working capital from its members, and membership by law is open. Members vote. Banks are not too keen on lending capital to *associations.* If you need major funding and need to maintain a business profile, the *association* won't do. On the third hand, if you hope to receive subsidies or funding from a government ministry or one of its organs, you need a non-profit organization, thus an *association.*

## Accounting in France

A certified public accountant in France is an *expert comptable.* A *comptable* is a simple accountant, and someone who just does the *comptabilité* is a bookkeeper. Companies almost always hire an *expert comptable* or a *cabinet d'expert comptable.* Individuals may or may not depending on the size and complexity of their earnings and holdings. If you do set up a business in France, make sure that the accounting side is established from day one. It is imperative that books are kept impeccably according to French accounting principles. There will be no reasoning with an accountant later why the books were kept in some other fashion, and he or she will spend countless hours (around 400 FF/hour) getting every *centime* to match up with a scrap of paper, receipt, bank statement, invoice. You may have to spend a thousand francs to make fifty francs accountable. So, find out how to keep your accounts straight *à la française*. At times, it'll feel like you are working for your accountant. Don't throw anything away and always ask for a receipt (*reçu* or *fiche* or *facture*) showing the TVA. As of 1992, the French have allowed the recovery of TVA on restaurant bills. The recovery *(récupération) of* TVA in general is a national pastime in France. The advantage of working *au noir* (under the table) or undeclared (*non-declaré*) is the TVA savings (18,6%). Highly illegal. TVA is very serious business in France. Don't ignore it.

## Taxes (*Impôts*)

US citizens can earn up to $80000 US of tax-free foreign earned income. Whether you earned money or not in France you are obliged to file a US tax return. Available at the US Consulate on the rue Florentin. US citizens residing in France are automatically granted an extension from April 15 to June 15 to file.

To help you understand the complicated French tax laws, Price Water-house offers a booklet entitled *The French Pocket Tax Book* as well as legal and tax advice, available at: 18, Place Henri-Bergson, 75008 Paris Tel: 41.26.40.00. For a discussion of TVA (sales tax) see the section on Duty Free. American lawyer Samuel Okoshken's office offers US and French tax services. Similarly, the British Embassy publishes a list of accountants competent in both British and French taxes.

Here's a quick overview of French fiscal taxes and fees:

*Impôt sur le revenu* : income tax—tax returns due each year usually in February or March. Payments are made on an annual, trimestrial, or monthly basis. For an average income count on about one month's salary in income taxes.

*TVA (taxe sur la valeur ajoutée):* sales tax—built-in tax of 18.6% on most goods and services. 33% on luxury items. 5.5% on books. There is talk of creating a unified TVA for Europe set at 15%.

**CSG** (*Contribution sociale généralisée*) —a tax of 2.3% of your gross income used to subsidize the government's social welfare program. This is deducted directly from your *fiche de paie*.

*Taxe foncière:* property tax—an annual tax on the value of land and housing to be paid by the owner.

*Taxe professionnelle:* professional tax—a sum levied on all businesses for the right to conduct business based on surface space being used for professional purpose.

*Taxe d'habitation (impôts locaux):* municipal housing tax—an annual local tax imposed on housing payable to the town by both owners and renters.

*Vignette:* motor vehicle registration sticker—purchased each autumn at any *tabac* in the *département* in which the vehicle is registered. Price is based on year of car and size of engine.

## Minitel

The Ministries of the Economy and Budget offer a line of Minitel services concerning finance matters:

3615 Finances: taxes, fees, customs, prices, statistics.

3615 Irservice: a program to calculate your taxes.

3614 Consom: consumer protection information.

3517 Sirene: instantaneous identification of all companies in France.

## Tax Breakdown

The French tax authorities report that this is how the State spends every 1000 FF:

| | |
|---|---|
| 224 FF | education/professional training/culture/research |
| 151 FF | defense |
| 132 FF | social programs/health/ employment/housing |
| 116 FF | municipal and regional aid |
| 109 FF | interest on the public debt |
| 109 FF | security and judicial system |
| 105 FF | economic initiatives |
| 54 FF | France's contribution to the EU budget |

## A Word on Applying for Jobs

Your résumé (CV or *curriculum vitae*) should always be neatly typed, but your cover letter must be hand-written. The French place great importance on the handwriting of a candidate; it reflects and reveals all sorts of information about the character of the applicant, his or her stability, reliability, adaptability. It has been said that it is better to write in black ink, leave correct margins, make sure not to change styles in mid-letter, and sign in a natural and full manner. French companies regularly hire or consult graphologists to submit reports on applicants, based on the cover letter or writing samples. There are of course cultural and educational factors in hand-writing that graphologists take into account. Americans tend to have legible signatures, whereas the French sign in a hurried way that leaves a mark or symbol, but is rarely readable.

**Free Non-Conventional Freelance Ideas, Free of Charge**

There are many ways to manage working in France even if you do not qualify for the legal status discussed earlier. The legal and administrative nuances you'll have to investigate for yourself, but these ideas could help generate a productive way to remain in France.

**Stringer:** Contact your local or hometown newspaper about sending in articles about aspects of Parisian life.

**Representative:** Find a company or organization in your home country that might be interested in having a Parisian representative or contact at no risk and little fixed overhead cost. You could be paid on commission or receive a retainer.

**Tourist officer:** Offer to your home city, county, or state to represent it or them in France. For example, the city of Omaha, Nebraska or Newcastle, England could use you and your address as its Paris address. You could distribute information and promote that city among French tourists and businesses.

**Be home while you're away:** With faxes, modems, E-Mail, Fed Ex, etc. if you're self-employed you might be able to continue your business, although with some modifications, while you live in Paris.

**Win the Loto:** Yes, lotteries can change things.

The key to these ideas is that they reflect jobs that require no administrative entanglements with the French government. You have an activity but you do not get paid in France, nor do you benefit from the labor advantages of working in France. But, you're here and you're earning a living.

---

### French Business, Financial, and Accounting Terms

| | |
|---|---|
| *achats* | purchases |
| *actif* | assets |
| *actionnaire* | shareholder |
| *administrateur* | company director |
| *agent de change* | stockbroker |
| *bail* | lease |
| *banqueroute, faillite* | bankruptcy |
| *bénéfice net* | net income (profit) |
| *biens de consommation* | consumer goods |
| *bilan* | balance sheet |
| *brut* | gross |

| | |
|---|---|
| *cadre* | executive |
| *caution* | guarantee |
| *chiffre d'affaires* | turnover |
| *contrôle des comptes* | audit |
| *créances* | accounts receivable |
| *deposer le bilan* | to file a petition for bankruptcy |
| *détail* | retail |
| *dettes à court terme* | accounts payable |
| *devise* | foreign currency |
| *émission* | issue |
| *filiale* | subsidiary |
| *fiscalité* | taxation |
| *gros* | wholesale |
| *hors taxes* | net of taxes |
| *offre publique d'achat (OPA)* | takeover bid |
| *passif* | liabilities |
| *procuration* | proxy |
| *redressement judiciaire* | period of court-supervised financial recovery |
| *risques divers* | contingencies |
| *valeur vedette* | blue chip |

# CULTURAL PARIS

# Education
# & Cultural Exchange

## The French System

Formal education in France begins for many at the age of three months in the state-run *crèches* (nurseries). These tend to be remarkably well-organized and pedagogically-sound institutions. Aside from the shared colds and minor illnesses, *crèches* seem to offer only positive factors for French society. Mothers return to their secured jobs and the kids emerge as well-adjusted individuals. The education of the French palate too begins in infancy, as the toddlers begin to be fed a complex menu of everything from filet of sole to calves' brains, artichoke *purée* to *Port Salut* cheese. And Evian or Volvic for a beverage. Between the ages of three and six years, the child can attend his or her neighborhood *école maternelle* (pre-school) which is also state-run and municipally administered.

Classes in French public education through university run like this:

Ecole maternelle ...*petite, moyenne, grande section* ......................3-6 years old
Ecole primaire.......CP *(cours préparatoire)* ...................................6 years old
CE 1 ..................*(cours élémentaire,* first year) ...........................7 years old
CE 2 ..................*(cours élémentaire,* 2nd year).............................8 years old
CM 1 ..................*(cours moyen,* first year) .................................9 years old
CM 2 ..................*(cours moyen,* 2nd year) .................................10 years old
Collège .................(6ᵉ, 5ᵉ, 4ᵉ, 3ᵉ) ...............................11-14 years old
Lycée....................*(Seconde, Première, Terminale (Bac)*.............15-18 years old
Université, Grande Ecole, preparatory school, special school ...............19 +3

Education is compulsory from six to sixteen and is free in state schools. Eighty three percent of children are in state education; the remainder go to private schools, most of which are run by the Catholic Church. Private education does not carry with it much prestige and can even imply the opposite. The French educational tradition emphasizes encyclopedic knowledge and memorization. The rigidness of former years, however, has loosened somewhat and great battles, student strikes, and debates over pedagogic issues have played a major roll in the French political climate since 1968. In general, all children attend the same kind of state day schools, and the tenacious go on to study for the *baccalauréat, (bac or BAC),* which is roughly equivalent to a level of studies one year beyond the American high school diploma. This *bac* is a highly important indicator of a student's potential choices in life. At age 15 or 16 the more academic children go to a *lycée* (high school) to prepare for the *bac,* usually earned at age 18 or 19. The *bac* is more of a means to get into a university than a job qualification in itself. Passing the *bac* is essential for access to all upper-level jobs. Failure is a negative status symbol and source of shame in some socially well-placed families.

There are almost a million university students in France. Unlike in the United States, admission to a state-run university is not selective, but guaranteed to everyone who has passed the *bac.* Student/teacher ratios are high. There is little personal contact between professors and students, and professors see their jobs as confined to the classroom. The system is centralized, tightly-controlled, highly politicized, and ridden by life-sapping internal regulations. The Sorbonne's international reputation stems from the quality of the minds who teach there. The archaic organization of the university, however, might dissuade you for life. On the other hand the place might fill you with the sensation of participating in a great and celebrated tradition. Think positive. It has been the focus of many political debates and upheavals in the past two decades.

In brief, the French university system is organized into three cycles: the *1ᵉʳ*, *2ᵉ*, and *3ᵉ*. The first cycle is usually two or three years, and comprises the *DEUG* and the *Licence.* The second cycle, or *Maîtrise,* is roughly equivalent to the American Master's degree. The third cycle, and clearly the most prestigious in the French system, is the Doctoral program, which not long ago offered three different doctoral diplomas. More recently the long and painfully serious *doctorat d'Etat* was replaced by the *doctorat d'université* modelled after the American Ph.D. A unique, although disruptive quirk in the university cycle system is the fact that prescribed programs are subject to modification with governmental and ministerial changes. For all questions of recognized transferable credits, you must submit in writing a *dérogation* (appeal) to the universities' *Service des équivalences*. Remember to bring original diplomas. French universities need to see the stamped document itself.

In 1968, in keeping with the international climate, there were a series of nationwide demonstrations, walkouts and riots staged by French university students demanding an overhaul of the dated and archaic university system. Since then the scene has relaxed somewhat and universities have now been split up into smaller, more manageable units.

Thus, the Sorbonne is now simply a building, beautiful at that, which houses a part of the amorphous *Université de Paris* system. There are a number of programs in Paris run by American colleges which include the possibility of study at one of the Paris campuses. They can also be contacted directly. A complete list of all universities and schools in France, public and private, is published by *L'Etudiant* magazine, called *Le Guide des études supérieures*. Another source of information are French consulates around the world, which provide information on specific areas of study in France through their Cultural Services office.

---

### Major Paris Universities

*Université de Paris Panthéon Sorbonne—Paris 1,*
12, place du Panthéon, 75231 Paris Cedex 05. Tel: 46.34.97.00

*Université de Paris 2 (Droit, Economie et Sciences Sociales)*
12, place du Panthéon, 75231 Paris Cedex 05. Tel: 46.34.97.00

*Université de la Sorbonne Nouvelle—Paris 3*
17, rue de la Sorbonne, 75005 Paris. Tel: 45.87.40.00

*Université de Paris- Sorbonne—Paris 4*
13, rue de Santeuil, 75230 Paris Cedex 06. Tel: 40.46.22.11

*Université René Descartes—Paris 5*
12, rue de l'Ecole de Médecine, 75270 Paris Cedex 06. Tel: 40.46.16.16

*Université Pierre et Marie Curie—Paris 6*
4, place Jussieu, 75230 Paris Cedex 05. Tel: 43.29.29.29

*Université de Paris 7*
2, place Jussieu, 75251 Paris Cedex 05. Tel: 44.27.44.27

*Université de Paris Dauphine—Paris 9*
Place du Maréchal-de-Lattre-de-Tassigny, 75775 Paris Cedex 16. Tel: 45.05.14.10

*Institut National des Langues et Civilisations Orientales*
(Langues O or INALCO), 2, rue de Lille, 75007 Paris. Tel: 49.26.42.00

## Art Schools

*Ecole du Louvre*
34 quai du Louvre
75041 Paris Cedex 01
Tel: 42.60.25.50, 42.60.39.26

*Ecole nationale supérieure
des Arts Décoratifs (ENSAD)*
31, rue d'Ulm
75005 Paris
Tel: 43.29.67.31

*Ecole nationale supérieure
des Beaux-Arts (Beaux-Arts)*
17, quai Malaquais
75272 Paris Cedex 06
Tel: 49.23.12.12

*Les Ateliers—Ecole nationale
supérieure de création industrielle*
48, rue Saint-Sabin
75011 Paris
Tel: 43.38.09.09

## Architecture Schools

*Ecole d'architecture
Paris—Belleville*
78-80, rue de Rebeval
75013 Paris
Tel: 42.41.33.60

*Ecole d'architecture
Paris—la Seine*
14, rue Bonaparte
75006 Paris
Tel: 42.61.81.11

*Ecole d'architecture
Paris—La Villette*
144, rue de Flandre
75019 Paris
Tel: 40.36.79.70

*Ecole d'architecture
Paris—Tolbiac*
5, rue du Javelot
75645 Paris Cedex
Tel: 44.06.85.10

*Ecole d'architecture
Paris—Villemin*
11, quai Malaquais
75272 Paris Cedex 06
Tel: 49.27.99.54

*Ecole spéciale d'architecture*
245, bd Raspail
75014 PARIS
Tel: 40.47.40.47

## Grandes Ecoles

The difference between a university and one of the *Grandes Ecoles* is vast. There are about 250 small, autonomous, and elite *Grandes Ecoles*. They train high-level specialists in engineering, applied science, administration and management studies. The entrance exam for French students requires two or three years' rigorous preparatory study in special post-bac classes at the *lycées*. Extremely few foreigners are admitted to the *Grandes Ecoles*. Only 10% of the students are women. These schools turn out a high proportion of senior civil servants and industrial and business leaders. One of the most prestigious is the *Ecole Polytechnique,* founded by Napoleon to train engineers for the armed forces. It is still run by the Ministry of Defense and is headed by a general. Other *Grandes Ecoles*: *Ecole Centrale, Ecole des Hautes Etudes Commerciales,* and *Ecole Nationale d'Administration,* which trains future high-level political types.

### L'Institut d'Etudes Politiques

More than 800 of the 5000 students at *L'Institut d'Etudes Politiques de Paris,* or *Sciences-Po,* are foreign. You must speak and write French to be admitted. There are several possibilities for courses of study:

Those who already have a master's degree in a related field (Political Science, Economics, History, etc.) can enter the *troisième cycle* and obtain a *doctorat* for further research work in the field or a *diplôme d'études supérieures spécialisées* for preparation for more professional work.

Those who already have three years of university work can enter the *deuxième cycle* by passing an entrance exam. They receive the *diplôme de l'institut* after two years of study.

The *cycle d'études internationales* is suitable for those on Junior Year Abroad in American University programs; no preparation for diploma.

The *certificat d'études politiques* is a one-year program for international

students concentrating on studies of modern France, and prepares those who wish to enter the *deuxième cycle.* Further information can be obtained by contacting:

**Fondation Nationale des Sciences Politiques**
27, rue Saint Guillaume
75341 Paris Cedex 07
Tel: 45.49.50.50
Fax: 42.22.31.26

---

## French Language Schools

*Newly arrived American, Lisa Glazer, set out to investigate and decipher the multitude of ways to learn French in Paris. Here are her findings.*
Living in Paris without speaking French is a little like being myopic in the Louvre: you can feel your way around in a stumbling, bumbling kind of way—but deep down you know you're missing the essential beauty of the experience.
Because of this, learning French is the key to truly appreciating Paris. And despite all the headaches, embarrassments, excruciating silences, garbled tenses and gender mutilations, figuring out how to communicate in French is immensely rewarding—and necessary. Shopkeepers and bureaucrats are friendlier, the complications of life in a new city are less overwhelming and the language offers endless insights in French culture and

thinking. Most importantly, if you speak even a little French you can start to make French friends, a crucial step towards understanding and enjoying Parisian life.

But how to go about learning French? The most obvious answer is enrolling in a language school, but it's also possible to meet with a tutor, teach yourself with self-study books, or plunge right in by living or working with French people.

Of the five million foreign visitors each year, more than 50,000 people come to Paris from all over the world each year just to study French, and there are about 30 French language schools, scores of private tutors and numerous get-togethers that exist solely to help foreigners in Paris become conversant in the local language. The trick is finding out what's best for you. This is especially important for people who need a student visa because you have to register and make a down payment before you even set foot in France—with a valid student visa (see visas).

Because there's so much choice—and because the choice you make will probably influence your whole experience here—it's important to consider all your options carefully. To do this, you have to be realistic with yourself. How much French do you have already? How much time and money are you willing to commit to learning French? Are you more interested in spoken, written or professional French? Do you learn better in groups or on your own? Do you want to achieve perfect French or will French that will just get you around suffice? Would you rather learn by classic schoolroom techniques or through interaction with other people?

This chapter has general information about three of the largest and most well-known language schools: the Alliance Française, the Cours de Civilisation française located at the Sorbonne, and the French language program at the Institut Catholique de Paris, as well as one smaller school, Accord. The larger schools were chosen because of their size and reputation, while the smaller one was chosen as a sample at random. There's also a section on how to study with a tutor or on your own, and a lengthy but far-from-definitive list of schools that teach French to foreigners.

It's recommended to check out a number of the schools that are listed. Although the larger schools often come with a reputation, they also tend to offer big classes, and with careful research, you can probably spend the same amount of money, attend a lesser-known school and receive a lot more personal attention—or learn with a new or unusual teaching tools such as interactive CD ROMs. But be careful: schools that teach French to foreigners are usually private and completely unregulated by the government so it's important to check what type of teaching credentials the instructors have and how long the school has existed. One more note: please remember that all prices listed are subject to change.

*Alliance Française:*
### The People's Choice

For a sound grounding in the basics and a lively, friendly welcome to Paris, the *Alliance Française* is the institution of choice. Founded in 1883, this private, non-profit teaching organization sprawls between two buildings in the St. Germain neighborhood and is probably the largest French-teaching school in the world. More than 20,000 students attend classes each year in Paris and when you add up their students worldwide, the figure is a whopping 300,000. Many lifelong friendships have been made here and the amount of couples that found each other at the Alliance is pleasingly considerable.

Because of its size and solid reputation, many people automatically choose *Alliance Française*, with good reason. Many of the 135 teachers are excellent, there's a language lab, a 15,000 book library, a housing service, notice boards with job and housing information, organized sightseeing tours, free conferences on French history, art and literature, a film society, a restaurant, a welcoming service that matches students with French families for a meal or regular chats, and the cacophonous, exciting atmosphere created by stud-

ents from 140 countries. As Markovic Aleksandar, a 22-year-old from the former Yugoslavia says, "the best thing is learning with people from all over the world. I've been studying here for a year and a half and now I have friends from all the continents." However, the Alliance's explosive success has its drawbacks. Classes can have as many as 22 students and the relatively large class sizes means there's room for a frustratingly wide range of abilities in a single class and shy students can be drowned out amid the hubbub. Still, many say the Alliance suits them just fine. Tammy Deacon, a British 21-year-old, has a class of just 15 students and a superb teacher. "We're learning about grammar by talking about it—it's a very good way to learn the grammar and improve your speaking ability at the same time," she says.

Marc Bailly, an *Alliance Française* administrator, explains that the school's teaching leans toward practical, everyday, spoken French, although advanced classes spend more time on grammar and writing skills. Students say teachers use a variety of teaching methods spanning role-playing and sit-down learning, and homework usually doesn't take more than an hour. In most classes, students sit in a circle, and although the teachers keep attendance records, it's no disaster if you miss a few classes. The ambiance is relaxed and bantering, most students are between the ages of 18 and 30, and Americans, Japanese and Germans are the largest nationality groups.

Graduates of Alliance Française repeat one nugget of advice: Not all the teachers are stellar, so keep searching until you find someone that makes you keen to study. The school may balk if you make more than a few changes, but once you've paid it's your right to find a teacher you like. Another important point is that enrollment occurs monthly, which means you'll have new classmates and sometimes a new teacher every four weeks. This is an excellent system for people in France for a short period of time, or those who travel frequently, but if you want to study continuously for six months or more, the disruptions can become a nuisance.

### Alliance Française
101, bd Raspail
75270 Paris Cedex 06
Telephone: 45-44-38-28
Fax: 45-44-89-42

The *Alliance Française* offers a great variety of courses for beginners, intermediates, professionals, French teachers and others. Placement tests are free and prices for classes vary according to the times and type of course chosen. Four weeks of standard language classes for seven and a half hours a week is 1250 FF. Four weeks of classes for 17 and a half hours a week is 2500 FF. There's also a 220 FF enrollment fee.

### Higher Learning:
### *Cours de civilisation française de la Sorbonne*

The Sorbonne name and the marbled corridors of the institution itself evoke academic images of devotion to the pursuit of higher knowledge. So it's entirely appropriate that the *cours de civilisation française*, which is located at the University of Paris-Sorbonne—but not formally connected to the university—has acquired a reputation for rigorous study that includes French culture, literature and civilization as well as grammar, phonetics and writing.

"Our specialty is written texts and the history of literature more than conversation," explains Jean-Louis de Boissieu, the assistant director. However, he adds, "We are adding some conversational courses because the students ask for this."

The academic style here is reflected in the enrollment requirements: students must be at least 18, they must have the equivalent of a French *baccalauréat* (a high school diploma), and they usually have to sign up for four-month semesters. The teaching methods are resolutely traditional. Students sit in rows in front of a teacher who writes on the blackboard, there's lots of homework, and grammar and vocabulary tests take place frequently.

Many people, especially those with a university education, thrive in this environment. "The program is very good. It's very thorough, very comprehensive," says Lisa Waldo, a 23-year-old American who studied French in college and is spending a year in Paris perfecting her language skills and working as an *au pair*. But for those who prefer conversational French, this is not the place to be. As Petra Wunderle, a 20-year-old German student, adds, "The teachers give us excellent explanations but we don't speak much in class—I don't like that."

Although it's not huge like the Alliance Française, the *cours de civilisation française* is still large. There are about 120 teachers, about 8,500 students annually and class sizes vary between 15 and 25. The average student is university age, 22, and the greatest numbers of students come from the United States, Japan and Sweden. As noted earlier, the *cours de civilisation française de la Sorbonne* is a private, non-profit program that is located within the famous university but operates independently. However, its sister program, the *centre experimental d'étude de la civilisation française*, which is for graduate-level students, does have a formal connection with the Sorbonne and uses some of their professors.

Besides the regular courses during the university year at the *cours de civilisation française*, there are also a variety of special summer and winter French courses. Of special interest is the three-month, five-hours-a-day crash course that takes place through July, August and September. Many

foreigners who live in France and now work in French swear by this as a swift, sure ticket to fluency.

One final note: the course calendars for the *cours de civilisation française* are incomprehensible if you don't have any French skills and confusing even if you do. What's more, some of the secretaries who answer information inquiries over the phone have that haughty, harried Parisian attitude that can make someone with beginner's French feel like hiding under a stone. But if you want first rate French, don't let these barriers hold you back.

### Cours de civilisation française de la Sorbonne

47, rue des Écoles
75005 Paris
Telephone: 40-46-22-11, extensions 2664 and 2675
The program here includes a variety of courses, conferences and seminars. A basic language course of between 10 and 15 hours a week for four months is 4700 FF. The intensive summer session of 25 hours a week between July 5 and September 24 is 10000 FF.

### The Middle Road: *L'Institut Catholique*

Just up the street but worlds away from the bustle of the Alliance Française is the *Institut Catholique de Paris*, a private Catholic university with a reputable language program. Within the university lies the *Institut de langue et de culture françaises,* formed in 1948 with just 15 students and now educating about 3,000 students a year. The *Institut Catholique* offers a quiet, serious, but convivial learning atmosphere—a middle ground between the challenges of the Sorbonne and the rough-and-tumble of *Alliance Française.*

The language program has 45 teachers and class sizes range between 18 and 25 students. The largest group of students here come from Japan, with Germany and Poland close behind. Director Jean-René Rouquette says that when the program started, most students only took classes six hours a week but since then the school has changed its approach, following some of the Sorbonne's methods. Now students usually come for a year or a summer and their learning commitment is much deeper.

I sat in on an afternoon class of 13 very attentive students, mostly Asians, ranging from teenagers to an older woman graciously pushing 70. The chairs in the small, cosy classroom were arranged in a circle and the teacher was careful to give everyone a chance to talk. After nearly two hours of solid grammar instruction, with students copying and reciting verb tenses, the rest of the class was devoted to active role-playing and language games.

It was hard to find someone with less-than-glowing reviews of the school. Dalia Yarhi, an Israeli 39-year-old, says, "When I first came to Paris I went to *Alliance Française* for three months but I didn't learn anything. I was in a very big class and I just couldn't keep up. It was a very bad experience. Then I waited a year and a French friend who lives here told me this is the best school. I came in July and I was very happy and I'm still here." Reem Alhaddad, 25, heard the same superlative assessment of the *Institut Catholique* from her husband, a cultural attaché at the Kuwaiti embassy. "He told me it was the best school in Paris," she says—and so far, she's had no reason to doubt his judgment.

## Institut de langue et de culture françaises

*Institut Catholique de Paris*
21, rue d'Assas
75270 Paris Cedex 06
Telephone: 44-39-52-68
Fax: 45-44-27-14

The *Institut Catholique* has a variety of courses on French language, culture and civilization and an intensive summer program. Standard intensive language courses of 15 hours a week for four months are 7800 FF. Extensive courses of six hours a week for four months are 2800 FF.

## Accord: Something Completely Different

Just a hop and skip from the Centre Georges Pompidou are the classrooms of the Accord language school, where you can hear strange and wonderful sounds: singing, giggling, acting and debating, all in beginner's French that seems remarkably unstilted.

This may well be due to the philosophies of the schools founders, Christine Mestra and Marie-Claude Vacherie, who opened Accord's doors in 1988. "We believe that everyone has the capacity to learn languages but many people are inhibited. Our role is to use our tools as teacher to encourage them," she says. "We want to create a special environment for teaching, to focus on the individual, to create a place where people can feel good and learn well."

In line with this theory, few grammar books are used at Accord. Instead, there's a plethora of talking, reading and listening using excerpts from film, television, radio and newspapers. Student speeches are videoed with camcorders and some courses include a weekly theater class. But most importantly, the classes are small—between seven and 14 students—so everyone can speak at length. "First we work on oral development, with a lot of work on pronunciation," adds Mestra. "We try and build a good dynamic within the class."

With less than a dozen full-time teachers and only about 1000 adult students a year, Accord offers the benefits and drawbacks of a small school. I observed two classes where students sat in semi-circles in white, airy classrooms, and each had a lovely ambiance: it was clear that the students were very comfortable with each other and their teacher. However, there aren't extensive library facilities and if you don't like your teacher you don't have many options for changing. Interestingly, many of the students come from Spain and South America, and the age range is very mixed. French beginners take note: the English-language pamphlet for Accord is refreshingly easy to follow.

Again, students here seem content with their choice. "I researched a lot of different schools and I chose this one because they use an audiovisual method, because it's in the center of Paris and because we talk in the class about real, everyday topics and we do lots of games. I really like it," says Sonia Fuentes, 42, a Venezuelan television director living in Paris for the year.

Ryusaku Kubota, a Japanese florist now working in Paris, is equally positive. "I decided not to go the Alliance Française because there were too many Japanese there. I'm very happy here. You have a lot of opportunity to talk in class, to ask questions."

### Accord

72, rue Rambuteau
75001 Paris
Telephone: 42-36-24-95
Fax: 42-21-17-91
Classes of 20 hours a week for a month are 2600 FF. Classes for 10 hours a week for a month are 1600.

Plus there's a registration fee of 100 FF.

### The Roads Less Traveled

Before you plunk down a hefty enrollment fee and get ready to return to the classroom, stretch your imagination for a moment. With a bit of gumption, creativity and self-discipline, you can probably design your own personalized language program—and get a crash course in contemporary French society at the same time.

It goes without saying that very best way to learn a language is total immersion. So try and dream up ways to install yourself in the middle of a French family. Do you know people who live in the country? Offer to paint their roof in exchange for meals, lodging and kindly pronunciation corrections. Work as an *au pair* in a French family, or make a list of your useful skills—bookkeeping, computer layout, driving or woodworking, for example—and set up an unpaid internship in French business or a local non-profit group. The all-time best method, of course is falling in love with someone French. It works!

For those who don't find their very own French teacher, it's back to the more structured learning track. Another effective approach is hiring a tutor, but this calls for astute decision-making because prices and quality vary enormously. For only 60 or 80 francs an hour, you might find a tutor who's an undergraduate French literature student at the Sorbonne, an under-employed journalist or an out-of-work refugee from the publishing business. But for between 100 and 200 francs an hour you'll have access to dedicated, well-qualified professionals who can develop a teaching program specially for you. To find a tutor, scan the copious listings in the bi-monthly newsletter *France-USA Contacts*, the monthly *Paris Free Voice* and *Paris City Magazine*, the notice-board at The American Church and the classified pages of the other English-language publications in Paris. Make sure to search widely, ask for references, and, to save money, ask for free or half-price introductory lessons. Don't forget to think carefully about how you connect with the person: in a one-on-one teaching situation personal chemistry plays a big role.

The only real drawback to hiring a tutor is the expense, but an easy way to get around this is to find a few friends at your learning level and develop your own classes in the comfort of your home or *chambre de bonne*. Divided between two or three people, the hourly costs for a tutor can become reasonable.

### Some other tips:

•Set up a weekly language swap with a Parisian anglophile wanna-be. This type of language exchange involves a bit of chance: you might end up meeting with someone who becomes

# INSTITUT PARISIEN DE LANGUE ET DE CIVILISATION FRANÇAISES

The Institut Parisien specializes in teaching French to foreigners, welcoming throughout the year students from over 80 different countries. After taking a free placement test, students may enroll in one of the three course options:

### GROUP CLASSES
**Extensive:** 4-1/2 or 9 hours per week offered during the academic year. Extensive class options: French for Business, French for Tourism and Hostellery (preparation for the Paris Chamber of Commerce Certificate.)
**Intensive:** 15 or 25 hours per week offered throughout the year. Maximum 15 students. Students may enroll the beginning of each week.

### INDIVIDUAL INSTRUCTION
Courses "à la carte," individually designed for each student.

### PRIVATE GROUPS
Specially tailored programs for schools, universities, and corporations, as well as professional training for French teachers.

- The Institut Parisien also offers French Civilization courses on history, art, and literature.

- Certificates and diplomas can be obtained upon completion of courses.

- The Institut Parisien is an Etablissement Libre d'Enseignement Supérieur (Rectorat de Paris, No. 556) and as such has an agreement for continuing adult education credits.

- Housing service is available upon request.

**Institut Parisien de Langue et Civilisation Françaises**
87 Bd. Grenelle    75015 Paris

Tel: (33/1) 40.56.09.53        Fax: (33/1) 43.06.46.30

a friend for life...or a total nut. When this works, it's an ideal way to learn French, but there have also been some stories circulating about women who have met men for language swaps and got more than they bargained for. So be warned: always arrange the initial meeting in a public place, like a café or park, *not* in your home. Scan the local announcements for the names and telephone numbers of Parisians searching for language swaps.

•The Centre Georges Pompidou Centre has a free language lab that is open to the public six days a week on the ground floor of the *Bibliothèque publique d'information (BPI)*. This resource is a real gem: there's a copious catalogue of teaching cassettes and videos on topics ranging from neighborhood life in Paris, the French revolution and those tough-to-acquire telephone conversation and answering machine skills. Plus, if you're interested, you can also take a stab at any of about 100 other languages you might be interested in. Maori? Yiddish? Armenian? Provençal? You can learn them all here—just turn up, decide which cassette or video you desire, then sign for it and listen or watch in one of the many snazzy lime-green language lab booths. The only limitations: use of the language lab is restricted to an hour per day for each person and there are often long lines to get into the library.

•Local publications also list French-English get-togethers for a small fee, as well as a multitude of pleasant ways to learn French. You can study French cooking, French cinema history, theater techniques or simply hang out in a beautiful country estate, all the while speaking French. If you've got time and money, all of these options are worth checking out.

•The Assimil bookstore, famous for its method *French with ease*, has scores of self-study books, cassettes and CDs.

•Read the papers, listen to the radio, go to the movies or watch TV all day!

*Bon Courage !*

## Language Schools

### Accueil Franco-Nordique
7, rue de Surène
75008 Paris
Tel: 42-66-53-02
Fax: 42-66-53-32
A French-Norwegian organization where both languages are taught. About 160 students per year, formed in the 1970s. Many students are *au pair*.

### Berlitz France S.A.
Six offices in Paris
Champs-Elysées address is:
35, avenue Franklin D. Roosevelt
75008 Paris
Tel: 40-74-00-17
About 300 teachers, individual

classes and small group classes. Started in France in 1907. The Berlitz method, taught all over the world, teaches languages "instinctively", the way a child learns a language, without focusing on grammar. The majority of the students at Berlitz France learn English, but about 15 percent learn French. The method, which is not cheap, is mostly used by business people.

## Business Talk France
134, Boulevard Haussmann
75008 Paris
Tel and Fax: 49-53-91-83
Formed in 1990, about 200 students each year, four teachers, individual classes and group classes of between three and six students. Focus on business French at all levels. Teaches French and other languages.

## Centre parisien de formation permanente
20-22, rue Richer 75009 Paris
Tel: 45-23-35-68
Fax: 45-23-16-60
This school has about five to 10 students in group classes.

## C.E.R.C.L.E.
16, rue Meslay
75003 Paris
Tel: 42-78-54-11
Fax: 42-78-70-88
Formed in 1988, about 350 students for French classes, about 12 teachers. Classes are for individuals or in groups of up to seven.

## Centre international linguistique Bouchereau
196, Bd. Haussmann
75008 Paris
Tel: 42-56-14-96
Fax: 42-56-14-92
In-company language courses.
Created in 1985, up to 25 teachers, classes are individual or groups of four or five. Goal is teaching functional French as opposed to written French.

## Chambre de commerce et d'industrie de Paris
28, rue de l'Abbé-Grégoire
75279 Paris Cedex 06
Tel: 49-54-28-76
Individualized, made-to-measure French classes, mostly used by business people organized by the Paris Chamber of Commerce.

## DCR International
22, rue Legendre
75017 Paris
Tel: 47-63-19-49
Fax: 44-15-95-55
Formed in 1976, about 20 teachers. Classes are individual or with between four and six students. They use an audiophonique method that teaches French through the sound of the language. Students wear oversized headphones and speak into a microphone—you have to get their catalogue to truly understand the method.

**Ecole de langues de Neuilly**
114 Avenue Charles de Gaulle
92200 Neuilly-sur-Seine
Tel: 46-37-56-41
Fax: 46-37-33-61
Formed in 1992, about 350 students, 40 teachers. Individual courses, group classes are usually two or three people, maximum of eight. This school has a multi-media resource center with computers that use interactive CD ROMs and video disks. They also produce multimedia resources for other language schools.

**Ecole Nickerson**
26, rue de la Tremoille
75008 Paris
Tel: 47-23-36-03
Fax: 40-70-12-71
Formed in 1962, about 20 students for French classes, four teachers, individual classes.

**EF Institute**
3, rue de Bassano
75016 Paris
Tel: 42-96-57-46
Fax: 47-20-18-80
Formed in 1965, about 500 students annually and five teachers. Individual teaching.

**Elysées Business International**
102, av des Champs-Elysées
9th floor
75008 Paris
Tel: 42-94-21-98
Fax: 42-93-79-78

**Eurocentres**
13, passage Dauphine
75006 Paris
Tel: 43-25-81-40
Fax: 46-34-65-34
Formed in 1973, about 1,800 students annually, 20 teachers. Maximum of 15 in a class. Focus on oral expression.

**Executive Language Services**
25, Bd. de Sébastopol
75001 Paris
Tel: 42-36-32-32
Fax: 42-36-62-55
Formed in 1982, about 100 students a year for French, five teachers for French. Classes are one-on-one. Teaching English is their specialty but they also teach French and other languages to executives. Classes are adapted to the needs of the student.

**Fomalanguages**
106, Bd. Haussmann
75008 Paris
Tel: 45-22-99-12
Fax: 45-22-08-25
About 3,000 students a year, 80 teachers, classes are one-on-one or in groups of up to six students.

**France Langues**
2, rue de Sfax
75116 Paris
Tel: 45-00-40-15
Fax: 45-00-53-41
Formed in 1976, about 3,500 students per year, up to 30 teachers, between 12 and 18 students in each

class. Their specialty is teaching French to foreigners.

### French Courses for Executives
Tel: 46-33-39-72
Fax: 46-33-38-04
Formed in 1991, one teacher, about 100 students a year, and classes are one-on-one or in small groups of up to five students. The teacher works on-site at businesses, does some teaching by telephone, and sends corrected homework to students by fax.

### Idelfle
66, rue René Boulanger
75010 Paris
Tel: 42-03-00-25
Fax: 42-03-27-40
Formed in 1990, about 120 students a year and four teachers, maximum of 12 students per class.

### Inlingua Rive Gauche
109, rue de l'Université
75007 Paris
Tel: 45-51-46-60
Fax: 47-05-66-05
Formed in 1978, about 45 teachers, classes are one-on-one for in groups of up to seven students. Classes are for adults.

### Institut de langue française
15, rue Arsène
75008 Paris
Tel: 42-27-14-77
Fax: 44-09-02-33
Formed in the late 1980s, about 2,000 students per year, 30 teachers,

15 students maximum in a class. "Classic" teaching method.

### Institut parisien de langue et de civilisation françaises
87, boulevard de Grenelle
Tel: 40-56-09-53
Formed in 1988, about 2,000 students each year, 14 teachers, 15 students maximum in a class. Uses the "Le Nouveau Sans Frontières" teaching books.

### Institute of Applied Languages
41, rue de Turenne
75003 Paris
Tel: 44-59-25-10
Fax: 44-59-25-15
Language training center of the Franco-British Chamber of Commerce. Formed in 1978, 2000 students per year, 35 teachers, one-on-one classes or group classes with up to five students. Mostly teaches English but also teaches French and other languages.

### Language and Communications Center
11, Pl. du Beffroi
95260 Beaumont-sur-Oise
Tel: 34-70-38-38
Formed in 1980, up to three teachers for French, individual classes or groups classes with a maximum of five students.

**Langues-Plus**
C.I.E.L.F
15, rue d'Hauteville
75010 Paris
Tel: 48-00-06-93
Fax: 42-46-92-62
About 150 students each year, up to five teachers, 15 students maximum in a class.

**Language Studies International**
350, rue Saint-Honoré
75001 Paris
Tel: 42-60-53-70
Fax: 42-61-41-36
Formed in 1965, about 600 students per year, four permanent teachers but up to 12 or 13 teachers in the summer. Up to nine students in a class. Focus on grammar as well as conversation.

**Languages F.I.A.P.**
30, rue Cabinis
75014 Paris
Tel: 45-65-05-28
Formed in 1991, about 1,000 students a year, 14 teachers, 12 students maximum in a class. Emphasis on conversational French.

**Quai d'Orsay Language Center**
67, Quai d'Orsay
75007 Paris
Tel: 45-55-78-23
Fax: 45-51-87-14
Formed in 1985, now has several thousand students, 10 teachers, individual lessons or groups of three to four students. Classes are designed for transferred executives and their spouses.

**Transfer**
20, rue Godot-de Moroy
75009 Paris
Tel: 42-66-14-11
Fax: 42-66-31-89

**13e Sans Frontières**
16 bis, rue E & H Rousselle
75013 Paris
Tel: 45-89-52-00
Fax: 45-88-69-32
Formed in 1985, about 1,000 students annually, 20 teachers, and about 12 students in a class.

**Other Key Sources**

**Bibliothèque publique d'information (BPI)**
**Centre Georges Pompidou**
19, rue Beaubourg
75197 Paris Cedex 04
Tel: 42-78-44-32
Open Monday, Wednesday, Thursday and Friday from noon to 10h. Saturday, Sunday and public holidays from 10h to 22h. Closed Tuesday. No inscription required. Expect long lines to get in.

**Assimil Bookstore**
11, rue des Pyramides
75001 Paris
Tel: 42-60-40-66
Sells self-taught methods (books and cassettes).

**FUSAC**

FUSAC can also be obtained in the United States at France Contacts, 104 W. 14th Street, New York, NY 10011-7314. Tel: (212) 929-2929 Fax: (212) 255-5555

## Foreign & Exchange Programs in Paris

There are more than thirty university exchange and foreign study programs in Paris in English and a handful in the rest of France. Additionally, there are a number of English-language universities based in or with campuses in Paris, the largest and most complete being The American University of Paris and Schiller International University. The list of higher education programs (in alphabetical order) is found below and is followed by a list of schools and alumni associations. Note that a number of American programs have closed their Paris programs in 1993 due to drops in enrolment. The famous hub of university exchange programs, Reid Hall, has lost a good amount of its tenants. The Dean of The American University of Paris, William Cipolla, has reported that this drop of enrolment in Paris reflects a trend in American education and culture in general away from interest in European study. More exchange students are going to Africa and Asia, notably Vietnam, to study French, a phenomenon rooted to an increased focus in US life on multiculturalism.

**University Programs**

For a full listing of elementary and secondary schools, as well as French schools offering English-language instruction, you may consult *Paris-Anglophone.*

**Academic Year Abroad**
Reid Hall
4, rue de Chevreuse
75006 Paris
Tel: 43.20.91.92

**Alma College**
c/o Alliance Française
101, bd Raspail
75006 Paris
Tel: 45.49.08.16
Director: Mme Bounoure

**American Business School**
15, av de la Grande Armée
75016 Paris
Tel: 45.01.96.01
FAX: 40.67.96.96
Academic Director:
Ms. Nazila Amirkhosvari

**American Institute for Foreign Study**
10, rue du Docteur Blanche
75016 Paris
Tel: 43.22.11.91
Director: Mrs. Marthe B. Cooper

**American School of Modern Music**
117, rue de la Croix-Nivert
75015 Paris
Tel: 45.31.16.07

The American University of Paris
31, av Bosquet
75007 Paris
Tel: 40.62.06.00
Fax: 47.05.33.49
President: Glenn Ferguson
Dean of Academics:
Mr. William Cipolla
Dean of Students:
Mr. Paul Marcille
(American university education;
B.A./B.S. degree; all classes in English)

Admissions/Development Office
20, av Rapp
75007 Paris
Tel: 40.62.07.20
Director of Admissions:
Ms. Kathy Nance

The American University of Paris
Division of Summer and Continuing
Education
34, av New York
75116 Paris
Director: Ms. Susan Kinsey
Summer Program:
Ms. Camille Hercot
Tel: 47.20.44.99

Boston University in Paris
64, rue Pierre Charron
75008 Paris
Tel: 42.56.81.54
(offers Masters degrees in International Relations)

California State/Denver/CUNY
MICEFA
101, bd Raspail

75006 Paris
Tel: 40.51.76.96

Center for University Programs
Abroad (CUPA)
21, rue Cassette
75006 Paris
Tel: 42.22.87.50
Tel: (315) 853-6905 Clinton,
N.Y, USA
Directors: Elliot Chatelin
Pascale Bessières

Central College (Iowa)
214, bd Raspail
75014 Paris
Tel: 43.20.76.09
Director: Inge Drapper

Chicago Overseas Program
Fondation des Etats-Unis
15, bd Jourdan
75014 Paris
Tel: 45.89.35.77
Director: Terence Murphy

Collège Irlandais
5, rue des Irlandais
75005 Paris
Tel: 45.35.59.79

Columbia University
Reid Hall
4, rue de Chevreuse
75006 Paris
Tel: 43.20.24.83
Associate Provost:
Danielle Haase-Duboc
Director of Studies:
Brunhilde Biebuyck

**Architecture Program Jan-June**
4, rue de Jarente
75004 Paris
Tel: 42.78.53.44
Director of Studies:
Meredith Sykes

**EDUCO/Duke/Cornell**
23, rue du Montparnasse
75006 Paris
Tel: 42.22.34.66

**European University**
137 av Jean Jaures
92140 Clamart
Tel: 46.44.39.39
Director: Mr. Ledent

**European University of America**
17/25, rue de Chaillot
75016 Paris
Tel: 40.70.11.71

**Hamilton College**
Reid Hall
4, rue de Chevreuse
75006 Paris
Tel: 43.20.77.77

**Hollins College**
4, pl de l'Odéon
75006 Paris
Tel: 46.34.59.85

**Institut Franco-Américain
de Management**
19, rue Cépré
75015 Paris
Tel: 47.34.38.23
Director: Mme Marie-France Joseph

(B.A., M.B.A. and French *diplôme* programs; associated with Hartford University, Northeastern University, Boston University and Pace University)

**Inter-Univ. Center for Film
and Critical Studies**
1, place de l'Odéon
75006 Paris
Tel: 46..33.85.33

**MBA Insead**
Bd de Constance
77305 Fontainebleau Cedex
Tel: 60.72.40.00
telex: 690 389
Fax: 60.72.42.42
(10 month graduate MBA program)

**MBA Institute**
38, rue des Blancs-Manteaux
75004 Paris
Tel: 42.78.95.45

**Middlebury College**
Reid Hall
4, rue Chevreuse
75006 Paris
Tel: 43.20.70.57

**New York University**
56, rue de Passy
75016 Paris
Tel: 42.88.52.84
Fax: 42.24.03.73
Director: Mme Walther

**Paris American Academy**
9, rue des Ursulines
75005 Paris
Tel: 43.25.08.91
and
Pavillon Val-de-Grâce
277, rue St. Jacques
75005 Paris
Tel: 43.25.35.09
Director: Richard Roy

**Parsons Paris School of Design**
10-14, rue Letellier
75015 Paris
Tel: 45.77.39.66
FAX: 45.77.10.44
Director: Janice Nagourney

**Reid Hall**
**Centre universitaire Americain**
4, rue de Chevreuse
75006 Paris
Tel: 43.20.33.07
(eight American Academic Year
Abroad programs located here)

**Sarah Lawrence College**
Reid Hall
4, rue de Chevreuse
75006 Paris
Tel: 43.22.14.36

**Saint Xavier University—Chicago**
Graham School of Management
*(executive MBA program)*
20, rue de St. Petersbourg
75008 Paris
Tel: 42.93.13.87
Fax: 45.22.12.65

**Southern Methodist University**
Reid Hall
4, rue de Chevreuse
75006 Paris
Tel: 43.20.04.86

**Schiller International University**
32, bd de Vaugirard
75015 Paris
Tel: 45.38.56.01
Fax: 45.38.54.30
Director: Heidi Miller

**Skidmore College**
142, rue de Rivoli
75001 Paris
Tel: 42.36.02.55

**Smith College**
Reid Hall
4, rue de Chevreuse
75006 Paris
Tel: 43.21.65.54

**Southern Methodist University**
Reid Hall
4, rue de Chevreuse
75006 Paris
Tel: 43.21.65.54

**Stanford University**
79, av de la République
75011 Paris
Tel: 49.23.20.00

**SUNY Stony Brook**
1, Place de l'Odéon
75006 Paris
Tel: 43.20.33.07

**Sweet Briar College**
101, bd Raspail
75006 Paris
Tel: 45.38.79.30

**Tulane University/Newcomb**
4, rue de Chevreuse
75006 Paris
Tel: 43.21.35.85

**University of Hartford Business School**
8, Terrasse Bellini,
Paris-La Défense 11
92807 Puteaux Cedex
Tel: 49.00.19.61
Fax: 47.76.45.13
Paris Contact: Ms. Pamela Meade
or Office of Graduate Studies

**University of Illinois at Chicago**
Centre Franco-Américain
33bis, rue de Reille
75014 Paris
Tel: 45.88.26.52

**University of Southwestern Louisiana**
I.A.C. Cycle Int'l
71, rue de Fbg. St Honoré
75008 Paris
Tel: 42.66.66.82

**Wesleyan University Reid Hall**
4, rue de Chevreuse
75006 Paris
Tel: 43.22.12.47

**Willamette**
23bis bd Berthier
75017 Paris
Tel: 42.67.52.28

*Schools*

**American School of Paris**
41, rue Pasteur
92210 St-Cloud
Tel: 46.02.54.43
Headmaster: M. Juse

**British School of Paris**
38, Quai de l'Ecluse
78290 Croissy-sur-Seine
Tel: 39.76.29.00
Headmaster: M. A. Slesser

**Ecole Active Bilingue Jeannine Manuel**
• Ecole Internationale de Paris
70, rue du Théâtre
75015 Paris
Tel: 45.75.62.98
• 39, av de la Bourdonnais
75007 Paris
Tel: 45.51.20.84
• 141, av de Suffren
75007 Paris
Tel: 47.34.27.72
Director:
Mme Jacqueline Roubinet

**International School of Paris**
• Grades K-5
96 bis, rue du Ranelagh
75016 Paris
Tel: 42.24.43.40
• Grades 6-12

7 rue Chardin
75016 Paris
Tel: 45.27.50.01

**Institut de l'Opéra**
41, Bd des Capucines
75002 Paris
Tel: 42.61.58.51

**Lycée international
de Saint-Germain-en-Laye**
230, rue du Fer-à-Cheval
78104 Saint-Germain-en-Laye
Tel: 34.51.74.85
Director (American Section):
Mme Nancy Magaud

**Marymount School**
72, bd de la Saussaye
92200 Neuilly-sur-Seine
Tel: 46.24.10.51
Headmistress:
Sister Maureen Vellon

**United Nations Nursery School
Association Paris**
40 rue Pierre-Guerin
75016 Paris
Tel: 45.27.20.24
(international bilingual school for
children 2-6; summer school in July)

**Wilson Learning Performance SA**
30, av Am. Lemonnier
78160 Marly-le-Roi
Tel: 39.16.21.11

**Women's Institute for Continuing
Education (WICE)**
20 bd Montparnasse
75007 Paris
Tel: 45.66.75.50
(Offers courses in Teaching English
as a Foreign Language, Career Development, Self-Development, Living
in France, Arts, Humanities. Has
career services, a monthly newsletter,
a volunteer service, etc.).

**Exchange Programs**

**Aspect Foundation Exchange
Programs**
53, rue du Fbg. Poissonnière
75009 Paris
Tel: 48.00.06.00
FAX: 48.00.05.94

**Council on International
Educational Exchange (C.I.E.E.)**
Centre Franco-Américain Odéon
1, place. de l'Odéon
75006 Paris
Tel: 440.75.95.10

**Experiment in International Living**
89, rue Turbigo
75003 Paris
Tel: 42.78.50.03
Director: M. Gilbert Guillemoto

**Fondation des Etats-Unis**
15, bd Jourdan
75690 Paris Cedex 14
Tel: 45.89.35.77 (admin.)
Tel: 45.89.35.79 (students)
Director: M. Terence Murphy

**Franco-American Commission
for Educational Exchange**
(Fulbright Commission
Scholarships)
9, rue Chardin
75016 Paris
Tel: 45.20.46.54/44.14.53.60
Director: M. Collombert

## The American Center

51, rue de Bercy
75592 Paris Cedex 12
Tel: 44.73.77.77
Fax: 44.73.77.55
After years of being situated in a beautiful building on the bd Raspail, the American Center, a private non-profit cultural organization, has relocating to Bercy, a former wine producing village of the last century tucked into the *12e*. The new Frank Gehry building is scheduled to open in 1994 four years and over 50 million dollars of time and money later. Although not very much has been announced in the way of specific programming and dates, and the organization has been reported to have been plagued by budgetary and personnel issues (directors Henry Pillsbury and Judith Pizar are no longer at the helm), The American Center promises a rich program of visual arts, theater, dance, music, film, video, workshops and conferences. The building itself offers a 400-seat proscenium theater, a cinema, classrooms, exhibition galleries and terraces, dance and art studios, black-box studios, a restaurant, a bookstore, a documentation center and 27 apartments for visiting artists, musicians, writers and scholars. Everyone is waiting to see what this, the largest American cultural center in Europe, will produce.

## Anglo-American Clubs & Organizations in Paris

For a complete list consult *Paris Anglophone.*
*Note that with the closing of Pershing Hall at 49, rue Pierre Charron to many service organizations, many groups have scattered around Paris. You can call Pershing Hall at 42.25.37.31 to find the new whereabouts of groups not listed below.*

**American Club of Paris**
34, av New York
75016 Paris
Tel: 47.23.64.36

**American Friends of Blérancourt, Inc.**
34, av de New York
75016 Paris
Tel: 47.20.22.28
President: Eugenie Angles

**American Joint Distribution Committee**
33, rue Miromesnil
75008 Paris
Tel: 42.68.05.68

**American Catholic Women's Organization (ACWO)**
St. Joseph's Church
50, av Hoche
75008 Paris
Tel: 42.27.28.56
President: Elizabeth Van Reisenfelder

**American Chamber of Commerce in France**
21, av George V
75008 Paris
Tel: 47.23.70.28 / Fax: 47.20.18.62

**American Women's Group in Paris (AWG)**
22bis rue Pétrarque
75116 Paris
Tel: 47.55.87.50

**American Library in Paris**
10, rue du Général Camou
75007 Paris
Tel: 45.51.46.82
FAX: 45.50.25.83
Assistant Director: Adele Witt

**Amis du Jardin Shakespeare du Pré-Catelan (AJSP)**
1, place Wagram
75017 Paris
Tel: 42.27.39.54
Chairman: M.L. Hemphill

**Association of American Residents Overseas (AARO)**
BP 127
92154 Suresnes Cedex
Tel: 42.04.09.38

**Association of American Wives of Europeans (AAWE)**
BP 127   92154 Suresnes Cedex
Tel: 47.28.46.39
President:
Ms. Marisa Roufosse

**Australian Women's Group**
Australian Embassy
4, rue Jean Rey
75015 Paris
Tel: 40.59.33.00
Community Liason Officer: Jane Lee

**Amnesty International**
4, rue Pierre Levée
75011 Paris
Tel: 49.23.11.11
Minitel: 36.15 Amnesty

**British European Centre**
5, rue Richepanse
75008 Paris
Tel: 42.60.35.57

**British Institute**
11, rue de Constantine
75007 Paris
Tel: 45.55.71.99

**Business Connexions**
*profession networking group*
BP 15
25 rue Ducouédic
75014 Paris
Tel: 43.27.89.52
Fax: 43.20.47.02
Director: Brigitte Cassigneul

**British and Commonwealth
Women's Association
(BCWA)**
7, rue Auguste Vacquerie
75116 Paris
Tel: 47.20.01.36
President: Jane Maurin

**British Community Committee**
9, rue d'Anjou
75008 Paris
Tel: 42.65.13.04
Chairman:
Christopher Mitchell-Heggs

**Canadian Women's Group in Paris**
5, rue de Constantine
75007 Paris
Tel: 45.51.35.73

**Canadian's Women's Group in Paris**
Ile de la Jatte
3, allée Claude Monet, apt. L2-24
92300 Levallois-Perret
Tel: 47.48.91.25
Vice-President: Lynn Trapnell

**Canadian Cultural Center**
5, rue de Constantine
75007 Paris
Tel: 45.51.35.73
FAX: 47.05.43.55
Represented by: Lynn Trapnell

**Club culturel franco-américain**
12, rue Villehardouin
75003 Paris
Tel: 46.30.71.37
Fax: 46.31.46.80
Represented by: Catherine Aubin

**Democrats Abroad (France)**
5, rue Bargue
75008 Paris
Tel/Fax: 45.66.49.05
Contact: Joseph Smallhoover

**English Speaking Union France**
21, rue Michel-Ange
75016 Paris
Tel: 46.51.55.24

**Focus on the Family**
St. Michael's Anglican Church
5, rue d'Aguesseau
75008 Paris
Tel: 47.42.70.88
Chairperson: Jill Lea

**France-Amérique**
9-11, av Franklin D. Roosevelt
75008 Paris
Tel: 40.75.00.97
President: Mr. André Ross

**France-Canada**
5, rue de Constantine
75007 Paris
Tel: 45.55. 83. 65

**France-Etats-Unis**
6, bd de Grenelle
75015 PARIS
Tel: 45.77.48.92

**Holy Trinity Church**
Art and Architecture Group
15, av Charnot
78600 Maison-Lafitte
Tel: 39.62.34.97
Represented by: Reverand Ben Eaton

**Junior Guild
of the American Cathedral**
23, av George V
75008 Paris
Tel: 47.20.17.92
President: Patti Cumming

**The Liberal Democrats Association
(UK)**
Founded in 1988 to provide a focus
for all those interested in truly democratic politics in Britain and in participating in the democratic development of Europe as part of a
European network of Liberal Demo-
crat groups.
31, rue Brunel
75017 Paris
Tel: 48.76.90.29 or 44.09.71.20

**Lions Club International**
295, rue Saint-Jacques
75005 Paris
Tel: 46.34.14.10
Secretary: Mr. Raymond Fages

**Message Mother Support Group**
10, rue du 8 mai 1945
78290 Croissy-sur-Seine
Tel: 34.80.05.88
Fax: 43.80.92.68

**Musée d'Art Américain**
99, rue Claude Monet
27620 Giverny
Tel: (16) 32.51.94.65
Fax: (16) 32.51.94.67
Represented by:
Maylène Crossley

**Organization for Economic
Cooperation & Development
(OECD)**
2, rue André-Pascal
75016 Paris Cedex 16
Tel: 45.24.82.00
Secretary: Mr. Jean-Claude Paye

**OECD British Delegation**
19, rue Franqueville
75016 Paris
Tel: 45.24.98.28

**OECD Canadian Delegation**
15bis, rue Franqueville
75016 Paris
Tel: 45.27.62.12

**OECD US Mission**
19, rue Franqueville
75016 Paris
Tel: 45.24.74.77
Head: Ambassador Denis Lamb

**Office of American Services**
2, rue Saint Florentin
75042 Paris Cedex 1
Tel: 42.96.12.02

**Ontario General Delegation**
Ontario House
109, rue du Fbg. St. Honoré
75008 Paris
Tel: 45.63.16.34

**Paris Embassy Group (PEG)**
2, av Gabriel
75008 Paris
Tel: 42.96.12.02
President: Andy Searls

**Paris Welsh Society**
10, rue de l'Armée d'Orient
75018 Paris
Tel: 46.06.76.13
President: Nesta Pierry

**Rotary Club of Paris**
40, bd Emile Augier
75116 Paris
Tel: 45.04.14.44

**Salvation Army**
76, rue de Rome
75008 Paris
Tel: 43.87.41.19

**Swedish Women's Educational
Association (SWEA)**
22, av Taillevent
78100 St-Germain-en-Laye
Tel: 39.73.51.80
President: Ingela Henricksson

**TOCH Association**
14, av de Joinville
94130 Nogent-sur-Marne
Tel: 48.73.48.37
Represented by: Doris Leck

**UNESCO**
7, place de Fontenoy
75700 Paris Cedex 07
Tel: 45.68.10.00
Director: Mr. Mayor Saragoza

**Volunteers of the American
Hospital of Paris**
63, bd Victor Hugo
92202 Neully-sur-Seine
Tel: 47.47.53.00
**Women of the Church (WOC)**
American Church of Paris
65, Quai d'Orsay
75005 Paris
Tel: 47.05.07.99

**WICE**
20, bd du Montparnasse
75015 Paris
Tel: 45.66.75.50
Fax: 40.65.56.53
Represented by: Marylea Van Daalen

**YMCA/YWCA**
22, rue de Naples
75008 Paris
Tel: 45.22.23.49

Alumni Associations

*Numerous American university alumni associations have chapters in Paris. However, in that membership tends to be highly transient and presidents come and go using their personal addresses for the group, no definitive list is possible. However, France-Amérique (Tel: 43.59.51.00) houses a cluster of alumni associations and can provide an up to date list of their members, which include Stanford, MIT, Northwestern, and others. The US Embassy also has a list. Contact these two places and/or your own alumni office to find out if your alma mater has a chapter in Paris. Here are some chapters to start with. Others that have been present in Paris in the near past include: Mount Holyoke College, Princeton, and Tufts.*

**Amherst College**
47, av George Mandel
75116 Paris
Tel: 45.53.99.01
Rep: Axel Baum

**Harvard Club of France**
c/o France-Amérique
9 et 11, av Franklin D. Roosevelt
75008 Paris
President: Ms Sally Williams Allen

**Harvard Business School Club of France**, c/o France-Amérique
9 et 11, av Franklin D. Roosevelt
75008 Paris
Tel: 42.56.20.98
President: Mr. François Bujon de l'Estang

**Yale Club of Paris**
7, rue de l'Odéon
75006 Paris
Tel: 46.33.37.50
President: Ms Regine Lussan

---

## Bookstores

### ENGLISH

Paris is a sheer delight in its proliferation of small bookshops. Additionally, Paris wouldn't be Paris without its rows of *bouquinistes* (book stalls) most of which line the Left Bank *(rive* or *quai)* of the Seine. These are independently-owned, mainly by individuals who have a passion for used or rare books. In recent years the quality of the offering has dwindled to include tacky postcards and cheap prints, but fortunately the integrity of the traditional buying, selling and browsing on nice days along the Seine has remained intact.

The book as object plays a sacred role in Parisian life. In general, the quality of book production is higher in France than in North America, with serious covers reserved for quality literature, although now the marketing advantage of flashy jackets has become apparent to literary publishers who often opt for commercial jackets wrapped around somber covers. The most prestigious literary publishing houses in France include the classic Gallimard, le Seuil, Grasset, Calmann-Levy, etc. but there are scores of excellent publishers of literary, political, social and pure science books. Some of the most significant small to medium size literary publishers include Actes Sud, directed by Hubert Nyssen in Arles, which has introduced hundreds of contemporary world authors into the French language, Editions de Minuit, directed by Jerôme Lindon, a pillar in French intellectual history of this century, POL, founded by Paul Otchakovsky-Laurens, a model of the new crop of small but brilliant literary publishers, and Christian Bourgois, a dynamic iconoclast who reflects the Parisian flare and daringness to still take artistic risks. Despite contemporary economic pressures, much effort is made in France to protect the life of the small bookshop and the small publisher. The retail prices of books are regulated so that large outlets, department stores and supermarket chains cannot simply slash prices. The most you'll ever find a new book marked down is 5%. There are remainder chains where prices on coffee table books are greatly reduced. But French law prevents publishers from selling books for lower than cost price. The FNAC (see department stores) has one of the most exhaustive collections of French and foreign language books in Paris, and is particularly well-stocked with travel books.

As English-speakers and readers you'll probably be more directly interested in sources of English books in Paris. Fortunately, there are a lot of resources at hand. If you're not already aware you should be— Paris has an illustrious and important tradition of English and American expatriate writers, poets and artists, as well as editors and publishers who have made fabulous contributions in Paris with their work. Although this tradition may not be the source of your inspiration for coming to live and/or study in Paris, it certainly does generate much of the aura and myth about Paris that attracts tourists and long term visitors each year. And if this glorious past is what drew you to Paris, you might be disappointed to find a changed Paris. For in-depth discussion of Paris' expatriate literary and artistic history see: Ernest Hemingway's *A Moveable Feast*, Noel Fitch Riley's *Sylvia Beach and the Lost Generation*, and *Literary Cafés*, Brian Morton's *Americans in Paris*, Maurice Girodias' *The Frog Prince*, Hugh Ford's *Published in Paris*, Dougald McMillan's *transition*, Christopher Sawyer-Lauçanno's study of post-war Paris, and John Calder's *Garden of Eros*, an intimate history of expatriate literary Paris which is forthcoming from Simon & Schuster.

There are a few things to remember regarding books. First, in most cases, new ones are a lot more expensive than what you are probably used to. The price in francs is not a simple conversion from dollars or pounds; each bookstore has its own conversion mark-up rate to compensate for shipping and customs charges. So, for those special copies of books dear to your heart you might want to carry or have them shipped to you from home. There are, of course, libraries (see Libraries).

The English language bookshops in Paris contribute to the vitality of the literary scene. You'll probably want to renew your contact with your language and culture by frequenting some of the following shops on a regular basis:

### Abbey Bookshop:

29, rue Parcheminerie 75005 Paris, Tel: 46.33.16.24. Fax: 46.33.03.33. This Canadian-owned, small but well-organized and pleasant shop in the Latin Quarter has carved an important place for itself in the English-language literary scene in Paris in the last few years. One of its real advantages is the shop's ability to procure titles from North America in record time. Owner Brian Spence offers his clients plenty of service, including an up-to-date ROM bibliographic search and efficient mail order capacity. Strong in fiction, poetry, and the humanities. On occasion the Abbey also has readings, usually concentrating on Canadian writers.

### Albion:

13, rue Charles V, 75004 Paris, *Métro*: St. Paul. Tel: 42.72.50.71. Closed Sunday and Monday mor-ning. Classical and contemporary Anglo-American literature, some history and science.

### American University of Paris Bookstore:

Located in the basement of the American Church, 65, Quai d'Orsay, 75007 Paris, Tel: 40.62.05.92. (Ask for bookstore) principally serves the university community. The bookstore has expanded its operations to function as a local source of academic and trade titles. New titles from the US or UK can be ordered with surprising efficiency. Although a university bookshop, it's open to walk-ins.

### Attica:

64, rue de la Folie Méricourt, 75011. *Métro*: Oberkampf. Tel 48.06.17.00. Attica is an old standby for English books in Paris. More British-oriented than American, Attica in its new location is a densely packed space for new fiction, poetry, journals and guides. The store also caters to French students looking for English titles for their university English courses, thus a lot of classics and 19th century fiction. Students get a small discount upon request.

### Book Cellar

23, rue Jean de Beauvais, 75005 Paris, Tel: 46.34.62.03. *Métro*: Maubert.

English books and papers.

**Brentano's:**
37, av de l'Opéra, 75002 Paris, *Métro*: Pyramides. Tel: 42.61.52.50. Fax: 42.61.07.61. Open daily 10-19h. Closed Sunday. Anglo-American literature, art books, magazines and newspapers. Brentano's rides on a long and illustrious reputation. Today it greatly serves the French anglophile market and business and tourist crowds interested in English paperbacks and best-sellers. Although less connected to the indigenous anglophone population than some of the other literary bookshops, Brentano's is the only English bookshop in the neighborhood of the Opéra. The back entrance area hosts a large selection of English-language periodicals. Other areas of speciality include American hobbies, arts and crafts, sports, and an impressively complete selection of children's books. Brentano's also hosts signatures for prominent authors in Paris and services important events including Bloom, Expolangues, and diverse charities fairs. Brentano's offers an efficient international magazine subscription and mail order book service.

**Cannibal Pierce Australian Bookshop:**
7, rue Samson 93200 Saint Denis, Tel: 48.09.94.59. Irregular hours and by appointment. The regularly scheduled readings, openings and performances have been reduced to the occasional. Call first.

**Galignani:**
224, rue de Rivoli, 75001 Paris. *Métro*: Tuileries. Tel: 42.60.76.07 Closed Sunday. Books, guidebooks, maps, newspapers, and magazines. This bookshop is actually the oldest English bookstore on the continent. Its selection of fiction, travel and art books is extensive.

**Nouveau Quartier Latin (NQL):**
78, bd St. Michel, 75006 Paris. *Métro*: Luxembourg. Tel: 43.26.42.70. Closed Sunday. Only new titles. Here's a store that you can call to find out if they have what you need. Well-organized and highly modern, NQL specializes in Anglo-American literature and guide books and also distributes to its network of bookshops through France.

**Shakespeare & Company:**
37, rue de la Bûcherie, 75005 Paris, *Métro*: St. Michel. No telephone. Open daily from noon until midnight. George Whitman's Shakespeare & Company is by far the single most celebrated bookshop on the continent. The shop and its owner have remained loyal to the cause of international literature and the solidarity of those who write. Much of this reputation comes from Sylvia Beach's original Shakespeare & Company which was located nearby on the rue de l'Odéon in the Twenties and Thirties. It was there that James Joyce's *Ulysses*, published by Beach in 1922, first saw the light of

day. Ernest Hemingway, Gertrude Stein and a whole stable of luminous literati congregated there. Beach's store was shut by the Germans at the beginning of the Occupation. George Whitman, the self-acclaimed illegitimate grandson of Walt Whitman (his father was also Walt, but a writer of science books in Salem, Massachusetts) resurrected the name in the spirit of the original enterprise, tagging on "the Rag and Bone Shop of the Heart." Everything you hear about Shakespeare & Co. is true. It can be unruly, chaotically organized, overrun at times by weirdos and dubious writers, but the bookshop is a living legend and continues to be a wealthy storehouse of fabulous first editions and signed copies of novels and volumes of poetry whose authors came through Paris and gave a reading or book party under the supervision of poetic and iconoclastic George. He is often offering tumblers of iced tea or plates of Irish stew to visiting writers, wanderers and the mildly down and out. The store has thousands of used books and a spotty selection of new titles. It's impossible to predict what you'll find. The prices are high for the new stuff, but can be excellent for used and obscure hardcovers. George will buy your used books and pay you cash if you bring identification. In the warm months, the sidewalk in front of the store—exquisitely set in the Latin Quarter opposite Notre-Dame—becomes a favorite hang-out for visitors, backpackers and local riffraff, a scene which will give you a good whiff of the state of contemporary Bohemia. And if you are writing poetry or fiction ask George to be slotted into the Monday night reading series—a good way to test your voice. The shop sells its own mag called *Paris Magazine*. There are practically no traces of the 1990 fire that destroyed much of the shop and many rare books. A landmark!

**Tea and Tattered Pages:**
24, rue Mayet, 75006 Paris, Tel: 40.65.94.35. Fax: 44.49.94.12. Open daily, 11-19h, even in August. This cozy and friendly spot owned and run by former Californian beachcomber Christy Chavane de Dalmassy, near *Métro* Duroc specializes in used and inexpensive paperbacks. The selection has grown rapidly over the last two years—over 10000 books. The prices warrant a visit—so do the brownies and other American edibles. Weekend brunches.

**Village Voice:**
6, rue Princesse, 75006 Paris, *Métro*: Mabillon. Tel: 46.33.36.47. Fax: 46.33.27.48. Closed Sunday. Monday open from 2-8, Tuesday-Saturday 11-8. Founded in 1982 by French owner Odile Hellier, the Village Voice (no connection to the newspaper) has evolved into one of the most significant literary English bookshops in Europe. Tucked into a small

street just off the Boulevard Saint Germain, the store hosts a lively reading series that has included some of the most important American, Canadian, British and French authors writing today, including Don Delillo, William Kennedy, Alison Lurie, Mavis Gallant, and Louise Erdrich. These readings are free and often conclude with wine and discussion. Odile, assisted by her nephew Yann, diligently attempts to stock a rich collection of the newest literary titles from both the US and the U.K. in her bright and pleasant store. Additionally, the collection is vast in modern and contemporary fiction, poetry and translations as well as works in the social and political sciences, philosophy, and women's studies. The store also has a wide variety of literary journals and intelligent magazines—*The Village Voice, Times Literary Supplement, New Yorker, Harper's, Paris Review, Frank, Granta*, etc.

**W.H. Smith:**
248, rue de Rivoli, 75001 Paris. *Métro*: Concorde. Tel: 44.77.88.99. Closed Sunday. Part of the major British bookstore chain. Anglo-American literature, cookbooks, guidebooks, maps, magazines and newspapers. This large, well-stocked and busy store offers a broad selection of contemporary titles and gift books as well as a vast display of English-language publications. Well situated at the Place de la Concorde. The up-

stairs tearoom no longer exists. The staff is very helpful and highly knowledgeable about the selection of books available. Hosts book signings and special events.

**Unesco (Librairie de l'):**
9, place de Fontenoy, 75007 Paris. *Métro*: Ségur. Tel: 45.68.10.00. Closed Saturday and Sunday. Newspapers and UNESCO publications (Education and Science).

**Virgin Megastore**
52, av des Champs-Elysées 75008 Paris. Tel: 49.53.50.00. Virgin offers a huge selection of English and French books, records, and CDs. Largely in the press in 1993 for its controversial challenge of the French law which forbids stores to remain open on Sundays and 24 hours. Recently opened another store with kiosk of international press at the new mall at the Louvre.

**FRENCH BOOKSTORES**
As for French literary bookshops, there are scores of excellent ones, with a high concentration in the fifth and sixth *arrondissements*. A few well-known ones include *La Hune*, 170, bd St. Michel, and *Le Divan* at 37, rue Bonaparte, near the Place St. Germain-des-Prés in the 6th *arrondissement*, and *Flammarion* at the Pompidou Center. The *l'Œil de la Lettre* group of literary bookstores are first class, one of which is *Librairie Compagnie* on the rue des Ecoles

next to the Sorbonne and the excellent *Mille Pages* in Vincennes.

The FNAC, the largest retail cooperative of electronic, stereo and photographic equipment, also has the most extensive collection of books and records in France.

**FNAC Micro**
71, bd St. Germain
75005 Paris
Tel: 44.41.31.50

**FNAC Forum des Halles**
1, rue Pierre Lescot
75001 Paris
Tel: 40.41.40.00

**FNAC Montparnasse**
136, rue de Rennes
75006 Paris
Tel: 49.54.30.00

**FNAC Etoile**
26, av des Ternes
75017 Paris
Tel: 44.09.18.00

**Espace Hachette Evasion**
77, Bd St. Germain
75006 Paris
Tel: 46.34.89.51
Fax: 46.34.65.45
Guides, maps, and travel titles of all sorts.

**Joseph Gibert**
26 bd St. Michel
75006 Paris
Tel: 46.34.21.41

An especially useful address for students is the Parisian institution, Joseph Gibert, a three-store operation that specializes in academic and university texts and school supplies, and buys used books on the fourth floor.

**Gibert Jeune**
5, place Saint-Michel
75006 Paris
Tel: 43.25.70.07
Son of the above, he opened his own store.

**SPECIALIZED BOOKSTORES:**
*Cinema*
**Librairie de la Fontaine**
13, rue Médicis
75016 Paris
Tel: 43.26.76.28

*Photography/Theater*
**Association Liko**
161, rue de Rennes
75006 Paris
Tel: 45.48.69.49
**La Chambre Claire**
14, rue St. Sulpice
75006 Paris
Tel: 46.34.04.31

*Women*
**Femmes Savantes**
73bis, av Niel
75017 Paris
Tel: 47.63.05.82
**Librairie des Femmes**
74, rue Seine
75006 Paris
Tel: 43.29.50.75

*Science Fiction/Bande Dessinée*
*(Comic Books)*
**Cosmos 2000**
17, rue Arc de Triomphe
75017 Paris
Tel: 43.80.30.74

*Music*
**La Librairie Musicale de Paris**
68bis, rue Réaumur
75003 Paris
Tel: 42.72.30.72

*Politics*
**Librairie des Sciences Politiques**
30, rue St. Guillaume
75007 Paris
Tel: 45.48.36.02

*Third World*
**Librairie l'Harmattan**
16, rue des Ecoles
75005 Paris
Tel: 43.26.04.52

*Cars and Motor Vehicles*
**La Librairie du Collectionneur**
4, rue Cassette
75006 Paris
Tel: 42.22.34.08

*Cuisine*
**Librairie Gourmande**
4, rue Dante
75005 Paris
Tel: 43.54.37.27

*Government Publications*
**Librairie de la Documentation**
**Française**

29/31, Quai Voltaire
75007 Paris
Tel: 40.15.70.00

*Spanish/Latin American*
**Ediciones Hispano-Americanas**
26, rue Monsieur Le Prince
75006 Paris
Tel: 43.26.03.79
**Librairie Espagnole**
72, rue de Seine
75006 Paris
Tel: 43.54.56.26

*Russian*
**Librairie du Globe**
2, rue de Buci
75006 Paris
Tel: 43.26.54.99
**Les Editeurs Réunis**
11, rue Montagne Ste Geneviève
75005 Paris
Tel: 43.54.74.46
**Librairie Russe**
9, rue Eperon
75006 Paris
Tel: 43.26.10.60

*Arabic*
**Al Manar Librairie**
220, rue St. Jacques
75005 Paris
Tel: 43.29.40.22

*German*
**Calligrammes Librairie**
8, rue Collégiale
75005 Paris
Tel: 43.36.85.07

Marissal Bucher
42, rue Rambuteau
75003 Paris
Tel: 42.74.37.47

*Indian*
**Adi Shakti Tapovan**
9, rue Gutenberg
75015 Paris
Tel: 45.77.90.59

*Italian*
Librairie Italienne
Tour de Babel
10, rue du Roi de Sicile
75004 Paris
Tel: 42.77.32.40
Librairie Italienne
54, rue de Bourgogne
75007 Paris
Tel: 47.05.03.99

*African*
Présence Africaine
25bis, rue des Ecoles
75005 Paris
Tel: 43.54.15.88

*Japanese*
**Tokyo Do**
8, rue Ste. Anne
75001 Paris
Tel: 42.61.08.71
**Espace Japon**
9, rue de la Fontaine au Roi
75011 Paris
Tel: 47.00.77.47

*Polish*
Librairie Polonaise

123, bd St. Germain
75006 Paris
Tel: 43.26.04.42

*Portuguese*
Librairie portugaise
Michel Chandeigne
10, rue Tournefort
75005 Paris
Tel: 43.36.34.37

## Libraries (bibliothèques)

The largest library complex in France is being built on the left bank in the 13th *arrondissement* and promises to be the most extensive research facility in the country. In the great tradition of politicians aspiring to leave their mark via great architectural achievements (*Les Grands Projets*), the *Bibliothèque de France*, has been added to the cityscape. Popularly known as the TGB or *Très Grande Bibliothèque*, it is slated for a 1996 opening, at a cost of 7.2 billion francs, and will house books, recordings, film, videotape, and 9-12 million catalogued files; in addition there will be spaces for 3500 readers who will have access to 11 million books arriving at 150 delivery stations through an 8 kilometer long monorail system.

**Bibliothèque de France:** 1, pl. Valhubert, 75013 Paris, Tel: 44.06.30.00 Fax: 44.06.32.98 (*Numbers may change when library finally opens*).

You may find in dealing with the libraries in Paris the same sort of inconvenience as you did in other areas of daily life, such as shopping. The inconvenience in this case stems from a certain degree of inaccessibility and inherent lethargy which takes a little time to adjust to. If you are coming from a small university where you had your own desk at which you could camp out until early morning hours, you may find the adjustment difficult. You may have to keep a more civilized schedule when it comes to your treks to the library. The libraries frequently have quite limited hours. One exception is the *Bibliothèque Publique d'Information* at the Pompidou Center which is open until 22h but can be so jammed that you'll give up hope.

Limited hours are not the only handicap in getting research done or a term paper finished, for most libraries do not allow you to borrow books. So be prepared to take good notes. Laptop computers can be helpful here. These libraries only offer *consultation sur place* (books don't leave the library). You may or may not find working photocopy machines. The one machine in the Sorbonne library requires one franc per copy!

Some libraries require that you register and obtain a card to enter and consult books. Be prepared to have to wait in a line when you go. You'll need some identification, such as your passport and proof of address and a couple of photographs. Another thing to be aware of is that in many libraries you are not free to browse through the stacks. Instead, you must go to the *salle des catalogues* and fill out a description of what you are looking for (*fichier*). An employee, in one of those omnipresent blue smocks that sets workers apart from white collar employees, will look for the book and send it to the *centre de distribution*, where you collect it.

The library at the Sorbonne is a fascinating place to visit but a frustrating place to use. It can take up to twenty minutes to obtain each book, depending on which *guichet* your book is filed under. Of course, don't expect to do much research around lunchtime. In addition, special permission must be obtained from the "president" of the *salle* for access to the reference section. There are a number of excellent libraries though in Paris with extensive collections and priceless resources and archives. Here are the major libraries:

• **American Library in Paris:** 10, rue du Général-Camou, 75007 Paris, Tel: 45.51.46.82. The largest collection of English language books in Paris. Open Tuesday-Saturday from 10h-19h. Membership allows you to check out books, but is required for admittance. Annual membership fees are as follows: 500 FF for the individual rate, 400 FF for students, and 700 FF for a family card. You need to bring a recent photo, student identification, proof of residency in Paris (such as telephone bill) and another piece of identification. If you do not want to be a member, you may spend the day in the library for 30 FF but you cannot check out books. AUP students are automatically members. This library owns over 80,000 volumes and over 700 periodicals and journals. Also holds a diverse reading series of leading writers.

• **American University of Paris Library**: 9, rue de Montessuy, 75007 Paris, Tel. 45.51.44.31. This library is physically connected to the American Library in Paris. It is open more hours than any other library in France —seven days a week for a total of eighty hours per week. It has over 50,000 titles, primarily English, and adds close to 3000 titles every year. Reserved for members of The American Library and AUP students (but they cannot check things out).

• **Benjamin Franklin Documentation Center**: 2, rue St.-Florentin, 75001 Paris, Tel: 42.96.33. 10. 9,000 volumes in English. Housed in the US Consulate building, Tallyrand, at place de la Concorde. Open 13h-18h Monday-Friday. Extensive documentation on the USA. Open to university students. Bring your passport. Minitel: 3614 DOC USA.

• **Bibliothèques et Discothèques de la Ville de Paris**: 31, rue des Francs-Bourgeois, 75004 Paris, Tel: 42.76.40.40. This is the central administration of the City of Paris' 55 municipal public libraries. They can give you information on your local libraries.

• **Discothèque des Halles**: Forum des Halles, 75001 Paris, Tel: 42.33.20.50. Huge library of music, records, CDs.

• **Bibliothèque de France**: 1, Place de Valhubert, 75013 Paris, Tel: 44.06.31.86 (information). Currently under construction. Will be open to both researchers and the public in late 1996. (See beginning of section.)

• **Bibliothèque Nationale de France**: 58, rue de Richelieu, 75002 Paris, Tel: 47.03.81.26. Minitel: BIB NAT. *Métro*: Bourse or Palais Royal. Open Monday through Saturday 10h00-19h00. Known as the BN, this library houses one of the world's most important and complete collections of books, periodicals, manuscripts and archives. Dark, dense and serious, the BN is accessible to doctoral students and researchers with letters of accreditation. The BN also has its own bookstore located in the Galerie Colbert.

Gaining access to the BN's *salles de lecture* may be a vital step for many of you who've come to Paris to do research. A *carte de lecteur* is required for regular entry. A *laissez-passer* can be obtained for a one-time entry, upon presentation of identification and two photos. Good for two consecutive days. The *carte de lecteur* requires a letter from a university or official organization justifying your need to use the BN, along with your ID, and student card, if applicable. A card allowing 8 entries in a year costs 35 FF, 24 entries costs 80 FF, and is valid two years. Half price for students under 27. The number of people allowed at one time in the sumptuous Grand Hall is limited and constantly controlled. You may have to wait in a small ante-chamber at the entrance for someone to leave.

• **Bibliothèque Publique d'Information**: Centre Georges Pompidou, 19, rue Beaubourg, 75004 Paris, Tel: 42.77.12.33. Minitel: 3615 BPI. Open Mon, Wed, Thursday and Friday from noon to 10h. Saturday, Sunday, and public holidays from 10h00 to 22h00. Closed Tuesday. *Consultation sur place.* Free access to books. No inscription required.

• **Bibliothèque Sainte Geneviève**: 10, place du Panthéon, 75005 Paris, Tel: 43.29.61.00. Open Monday-Saturday from 10h-13h. Personal library card is required, which you can obtain Monday-Friday before 17h30 and on Saturday between 14h-17h30. Bring a photo and identification, no charge. *Consultation sur place.* Distribution center.

• **British Council Library**: 9-11, rue de Constantine, 75007 Paris, Tel: 49.55.73.00. Open daily 11h-6h. Saturday from 10h30-16h. Membership costs 230 FF a year (with passport and photo) and allows you to check out books. Otherwise you may use the library at 25 FF a day. Mainly books from or about Britain.

• **English Language Library for the Blind**: 35, rue Lemercier, 75017 Paris, Tel: 42.93.47.57.

• **Université de la Sorbonne**: 13, rue Santeuil, 75005 Paris, Tel: 43.31.53.94. This library is closed for much needed renovations until September 1994.

### OTHER LIBRARIES
**Agence Culturelle de Paris**: 6, rue François Miron, 75004 Paris, Tel: 44.78.80.50.

**Bibliothèque Internationale de Musique Contemporaine**: 52, rue Hôtel de Ville, 75004 Paris, Tel: 42.78.67.08.

**Bibliothèque de Géographie**: 191, rue St. Jacques, 75005 Paris.

**Bibliothèque de l'Opéra**: place Charles Garnier, 75009 Paris, Tel: 47.42.07.02.

**Bibliothèque de l'Union des Arts Décoratifs**: 109, rue de Rivoli,

75001 Paris, Tel: 42.60.32.14. Open Tuesday-Saturday, 10h-17h30; Monday 13h45-17h30. Closed Sunday. No registration is needed. More than 100,000 works, from the origins of art to the highly contemporary.

**Bibliothèque des Arts:** 3, place de l'Odéon, 75006 Paris, Tel: 46.33.18.18.

**Bibliothèque Musicale Gustave Mahler:** 11bis, rue Vézelay, 75008 Paris, Tel: 42.56.20.17.

**Bibliothèque Polonaise:** 6, Quai d'Orléans, 75004 Paris, Tel: 43.54.35.61.

**Bibliothèque Roumaine Pierre Sergesco Marya Kasterska:** 39, rue Lhommond, 75005 Paris, Tel: 43.37.82.74.

**Bibliothèque Russe Tourgenev:** 11, rue Valence, 75005 Paris, Tel: 45.35.58.51.

**Bibliothèque Ukrainienne Simon Petlura:** 6, rue Palestine, 75019 Paris, Tel: 42.02.29.56.

**Centre Information Documentation Israël Proche Orient:** 134, rue Fbg. St. Honoré, 75008 Paris

**Centre Protestant d'Etudes et de Documentation:** 46, rue de Vaugirard, 75006 Paris, Tel: 46.33.77.24.

**Institut de France, Bibliothèque Thiers:** 27, place St. Georges, 75009 Paris, Tel: 48.78.14.33.

**Institut Supérieur des Arts Cinématographiques:** 135, av Félix Faure 75015 Paris, Tel: 44.25.25.19.

**Institut des Hautes Etudes de l'Amérique Latine:** 28, rue St. Guillaume, 75007 Paris, Tel: 44.39.86.79.

**La Joie Par Les Livres:** 8, rue St. Bon, 75004 Paris, Tel: 48.87.61.95.

**Métrolire:** 6, place Nation, 75012.

**Service Information Documentation Juifs-Chrétiens:** 73, rue Notre Dame des Champs, 75006 Paris. Open Monday to Friday from 14h30-18h.

**Société Asiatique de Paris:** 3, rue Mazarine, 75006 Paris, Tel: 46.33.28.32.

**Université Paris I, Bibliothèque Centre Pierre Mendès-France:** 90, rue Tolbiac, 75013 Paris, Tel: 40.77.18.14.

**Ville de Paris:** 2, rue Guadeloupe, 75018 Paris, Tel: 46.07.38.25.

## RECORD/CD LIBRARIES

About 26 Parisian libraries specialize in lending records, cassettes, or CDs. Contact the *Direction des Affaires Culturelles* at the *Mairie de Paris* to find out the *discothèques* in your district. Tel: 42.76.40.40. They publish a booklet entitled *Bibliothèques Discothèques de La Ville de Paris* specifying which libraries have this option. Some *discothèques* require that you present the needle from your turntable for inspection before they lend you records.

## Religion

Although France is a traditionally Catholic country, religion does not play a highly visible role in Parisian life or values. Church and State formally separated in 1905, and the debate over public *(laïque)* vs. parochial education in France flares up periodically. A recent government decision to permit municipal mayors to decide whether they will allocate public funds to private schools, polarized the nation.

The Paris area, of course, has some of Europe's most astonishing cathedrals and churches, although these treasures are more architectural and art monuments than religious sites. They are also important for their series of classical and sacred music concerts. Attending Mass in Nôtre Dame or l'Eglise de St. Germain-des-Prés, for example, however, can be memorable and highly spiritual. Just being in the presence of the stained glass windows at Chartres is a religious experience.

As in all big cities, the opportunities for worship are numerous. Here's a list of what Paris offers in English.

### American Church in Paris
65, Quai d'Orsay
75007 Paris
Tel: 47.05.07.99
Pastor: Larry Kalajainen

(services for all Protestant denominational)

### American Cathedral of the Holy Trinity
Church of the Holy Trinity
23, av George V
75008 Paris
Tel: 47.20.17.92
(Episcopalian/Anglican services)

### Christian Science Church
36, bd St. Jacques
75014 Paris
Tel: 47.07.26.60

### Church of Jesus-Christ of Latter-Day Saints
23, rue du Onze Novembre
78110 Le Vesinet
Tel: 39.76.55.88
Leader: James Johnson

### Church of Scotland
17, rue Bayard
75008 Paris
Tel: 48.78.47.94
Reverend: Bill Reid

### Consistoire Israëlite de Paris (synagogue)
17, rue St. Georges
75009 Paris
Tel: 40.82.26.26

### Emmanuel Baptist Church
56, rue des Bons-Raisins
92500 Rueil-Malmaison
Tel: 47.51.29.63 or 47.49.15.29
Pastor: Dr. B.C. Thomas

**Great Synagogue**
44, rue de la Victoire
75009 Paris
Tel: 45.26.95.36

**International Baptist Fellowship**
123, av du Maine
75014 Paris
Tel: 47.49.15.29 or 47.51.29.63

*La Mosquée* **(Moslem)**
Place du Puits de l'Ermite
75005 Paris
Tel: 45.35.97.33

**Liberal Synagogue**
24, rue Copernic
75016 Paris
Tel: 47.04.37.27
Rabbi Michael Williams

**Living Word Christian Fellowship**
21, rue Gallieni
78230 Le Pecq
Tel: 39.76.75.88

**Quaker Society of Friends**
114, rue de Vaugirard
75006 Paris
Tel: 45.48.74.23
(Sunday silent meditation service)

**St. George's Anglican Church**
7, rue August-Vacquerie
75016 Paris
Tel: 47.20.22.51
Chaplain: Martin Draper

**St. Joseph's Roman Catholic Church**
50, av Hoche
75008 Paris
Tel: 42.27.28.56
Father Paul Francis Spencer

**St. Mark's Anglican Church**
31, rue du Pont Colbert
78000 Versailles
Tel: 39.02.79.45
President Chaplain: Rev. Marshall

**St. Michael's Church** (Anglican)
5, rue d'Aguesseau
75008 Paris
Tel: 47.42.70.88
Venerable Brian Lea

**Unitarian Universalist Fellowship of Paris**
1, rue de l'Oratoire
75001 Paris

# Art in Paris

*This newly elaborated section of* Paris Inside Out *was penned by Sandra Kwock-Silve, Paris art critic, historian, hula dancer, and president of the Hawaii Association in Paris. She has curated numerous art exhibitions in France; and her articles appear regularly in the* Paris Free Voice *and various art publications.*

Since the late 18th century when the Louvre was first opened to the public, this world-famous museum has ranked high on most visitors' lists of "things to see in Paris." Recent renovations, coupled with I. M. Pei's impressive glass pyramid have given the Louvre a more contemporary look. Parisians and visitors from around the world flocked in record numbers to the grand inauguration ceremonies in December 1993 of the "New Louvre," the Richelieu wing of the palace, which was the former home to the Department of Finance offices (now at Bercy), which has now been incorporated into the museum as a whole. Its renovation has allowed a further 12000 works to be shown, including French sculpture, oriental, and Islamic antiquities, medieval and rennaissance objects, and French, Flemish, German, and Dutch paintings from the 14th to 17th centuries. For the adventurous spirits, however, classic art museums like the *Musée du Louvre* and the *Musée d'Orsay* should suggest only the beginning of a serious museum sampling. There are nearly one hundred museums to discover in and around Paris. Prestigious private and public collections highlight just about every subject imaginable. There are serious museums devoted to the history of wine, fashion, new technology and the arts from every era, country and culture. Something is sure to capture your interest in Paris' rich museum world, whether it's a glimpse of the future at *La Villette*, or an afternoon stroll through the sculpture garden at the *Musée Rodin*. Visits to the artist's studios will take you to some interesting neighborhoods off the beaten tourist track. And the city's eccentric collection of counterfeits, locks, and spectacles (to name but a few) will keep you exploring.

Major museum exhibitions are an important part of the Paris art scene all year round. The weekly publications *Pariscope* and *Officiel des Spectacles* have extensive museum and gallery listings of current exhibits. For historical information, the Michelin guide to Paris and the Hachette "*guide bleu*" are considered the best sources available.

Consider going on a museum spree with the *Carte des musées et monuments*. This special pass allows unlimited access to over 60 museums and monuments without having to wait in line for tickets. Card prices range from 85 FF for one day to 175 FF for a five day period. Cards can be bought at the tourist office (121, av Champs Elysées), *métro* stations or Museums. Some museums are free, or half price on Sundays. Check for interesting student/teacher rates. Teachers are usually free. As a general rule, national museums are open 9h45h-17h00 every day except Tuesday. Municipal museums keep the same hours, but are closed on Monday. Many museums are closed on public holidays, and smaller collec-

tions may close during the the month of August.

A list of major museums is followed by a selection of diverse thematic collections such as "artists' studios" or suggested "museum outings for children."

## Major Museums

• *Centre Georges Pompidou (Beaubourg):* 19, rue Rambuteau, 75001 Paris (*Métro*: Châtelet /Les Halles). Tel: 42.77.12.33. Open weekdays: 12h00-22h00 weekends and holidays: 10h00-20h00 closed Tuesday. Museum entrance fee: 30 FF, 20 FF for those under 25 (proof of age is required); free on Sunday from 10h00-14h00. Contemporary galleries 20 FF.

• *Musée de l'Armée:* Hotel des Invalides, 75007 Paris (*Métro*: Latour-Maubourg). Tel: 45.55.37.70. Open daily from 10h00-17h00. Closed on holidays. Entrance fee: 34 FF, 24 FF.

• *Musée d'Art moderne de la Ville de Paris*: 11, av Pres. Wilson, 75116 Paris (*Métro*: Iéna). Tel: 47.23.61.67. Open daily from 10h00-17h30 and until 20h30 on Wednesday. Closed Monday. Entrance fee: 28 FF, 14 FF.

• *Musée des Arts africains et océaniens*: 293, av Daumesnil, 75012 Paris (*Métro*: Porte Dorée). Tel: 43.43.14.54. Open weekdays from 10h00-12h00 and 13h30-17h30. Weekends from 12h30-18h00. Closed Tuesday. Entrance fee: 27 FF,

14 FF. Sunday 16 FF, 8 FF. Aquarium open daily except Tuesday from 10h00-18h00. Under 18 free.

• *Musée des Arts décoratifs:* 107-109, rue de Rivoli, 75001 Paris (*Métro:* Palais Royale). Tel: 42.60.32.14. Open daily from 12h30-18h00. Closed Monday and Tuesday. Entrance fee: 25 FF, 16 FF. Admission to Dubuffet donation 20 FF.

• *Musée des Arts de la mode:* 109, rue de Rivoli, 75001 Paris (*Métro:* Palais Royale). Tel: 42.60.32.14. Open daily from 12h30-18h00. Closed Monday and Tuesday. Temporary exhibitions. Entrance fee: 25 FF, 13 FF. *Closed until 1996 for major renovation work.

• *Musée national des Arts et Traditions populaires:* 6, av du Mahatma Gandhi, 75116 Paris (*Métro:* Sablons). Tel: 40.67.90.00. Open daily from 9h45-17h15. Closed Tuesday. Entrance fee: 20 FF, 14 FF.

• *Musée Carnavalet:* 23, rue de Sévigné, 75005 Paris (*Métro:* Saint Paul). Tel: 42.72.21.13. Open daily from 10h00-17h35. Closed Monday and holidays. Entrance fee: 26 FF, 14 FF.

• *Musée Guimet* (Asian Art): 6, Place d'Iéna, 75116 Paris (*Métro:* Iéna). Tel: 47.23.61.65. Open daily from 9h45-17h15. Closed Tuesdays and holidays. Entrance fee: 26 FF, 17 FF.

• *Musée de l'Histoire de France:* Hotel de Soubise, 60, rue des Francs Bourgeois, 75003 Paris (*Métro:* Saint-Paul). Tel: 40.27.62.18. Open daily from 13h45-17h45. Closed

Tuesdays and holidays. Entrance fee: 15 FF, 10FF.

• *Museum national d'histoire naturelle:* Jardin des Plantes, 57, rue de Cuvier, 75005 Paris (*Métro:* Monge). Open daily from 10h00-17h00. Weekends: 11h00-18h00. Closed Tuesday. Zoo: Tel: 43.36.19.09. Open daily from 9h00-18h00. Entrance fee: 25 FF, 15 FF.

• *Musée de l'Homme:* Palais de Chaillot, Place du Trocadéro, 75116 Paris (*Métro:* Trocadéro). Tel: 45.53.70.60. Open daily from 9h45-17h15. Closed Tuesdays and holidays. Entrance fee: 25 FF, 15 FF.

• *Institut du monde arabe:* 23, Quai Saint-Bernard, 75005 Paris (*Métro:* Jussieu). Tel: 40.51.38.38. Open daily from 13h00-20h00. Closed on Monday. Entrance fee: 40 FF.

• *Musée de Jeu de Paume:* Galerie Nationale (Temporary exhibitions-Contemporary art). place de la Concorde, 75001 Paris (*Métro:* Concorde). Tel: 47.03.12.50. Open daily from 12h00-19h00; Tuesday until 20h30. Closed Monday. Entrance fee: 40FF.

• *Musée du Louvre:* rue de Rivoli, 75001 Paris (*Métro:* Palais-Royal Louvre). Tel: 40.20.51.51. Open every day except Tuesday. Permanent exhibitions: 9h00-18h00. Wednesday until 21h45. Temporary exhibitions 12h00-20h00. Entrance fee: 40 FF, 20 FF.

• *Musée de la Marine:* Palais de Chaillot, Place de Trocadéro, 75116 Paris (*Métro:* Trocadéro). Tel:

45.53.31.70. Open daily from 10h00-18h00. Open holidays. Closed Tuesday. Entrance fee: 31 FF, 16 FF.
• *Musée Marmottan*: 2, rue Louis-Bouilly, 75016 Paris (*Métro*: La Muette). Tel: 42.24.07.02. Open daily from 10h00-17h30. Closed Monday. Entrance fee: 35 FF, 15 FF.
• *Musée de la Mode et du Costume:* Palais Galliéra, av Pierre-1er-de-Serbie, 75116 Paris (*Métro*: Iéna). Open daily from 10h00-17h40. Closed Monday.
• *Musée de la Monnaie*: 11, Quai de Conti, 75006 Paris (*Métro*: Pont-Neuf). Tel: 40.46.55.35. Open daily from 13h00-18h00; Wednesday until 21h00. Closed Monday. Entrance fee: 20 FF, 15 FF. Free on Sunday.
• *Musée national des Monuments français*: Palais de Chaillot, place de Trocadéro, 75116 Paris (*Métro*: Trocadero). Tel: 47.27.35.74. Open daily from 9h00-18h00. Closed Tuesday. Entrance fee: 20 FF, 13 FF.
• *Musée national du Moyen Age—Thermes de Cluny* (ex-Cluny), 6, place Paul-Painlevé, 75005 Paris (*Métro*: Saint Michel). Tel: 43.25.62.00. Open daily from 9h30 - 17h15. Closed Tuesday. Entrance fee: 20 FF, under 18 free.
• *Musée de l'Orangerie des Tuileries*: place de la Concorde, 75001 Paris (*Métro*: Concorde). Tel: 42.97.48.16. Open daily from 9h45-17h15. Closed Tuesday. Entrance fee: 23 FF, 12 FF.
• *Musée d'Orsay*: 62, rue de Lille, 75007 Paris (*Métro*: Solférino). Tel: 40.49.48.14. Recorded message: Tel: 45.49.11.11. Program information: 40.49.48.48. Open daily except Monday from 10h00-18h00; Thursday until 21h45; Sunday 9h00-18h00. Entrance fee: 36 FF, 24 FF; Sunday; 15 FF, under 18 free.
• *Musée du Petit Palais:* av Winston Churchill, 75008 Paris (*Métro*: Champs-Elysées-Clemenceau). Tel: 42.65.12.73. Open daily from 10h00-17h40. Closed Monday and holidays. Entrance fee: 26 FF, 14 FF.
• *Palais de Tokyo (Centre de la Photographie)*: 13, av du Président Wilson, 75116 Paris (*Métro*: Iéna). 47.23.36.53. Open daily from 9h45-17h00. Closed Tuesday. Entrance fee 25 FF.
• *Musée Picasso*: Hôtel Sal, 5, rue Thorigny, 75003 Paris (*Métro*: Saint-Paul). Tel: 42.71.25.21. Open daily from 9h15-17h15; Wednesday until 22h00. Closed Tuesday. Entrance fee: 26 FF, 17 FF.
• *Musée de la Poste*: 34, bd de Vaugirard, 75017 Paris (*Métro*: Montparnasse). Tel: 42.79.23.45. Open weekdays and Saturday: 10h00-18h00. Closed Sunday and holidays. Entrance fee: 26 FF, 12,50FF.
• *Musée de la Publicité*: 18, rue du Paradis, 75010 Paris (*Métro*: Château d'eau). Tel: 42.46.13.09. Open daily from 12h00-18h00. Closed Tuesday. Entrance fee: 18 FF.
• *Musée des Sciences et de l'Industrie*: Parc de la Villette, 30, av Corentin-Cariou, 75019 Paris (*Métro*: Porte de

la Villette). Tel: 46.42.13.13. Open daily except Monday from 10h00-18h00. Entrance pass: 45 FF, 35 FF. Cité and Géode: 85 FF., 72 FF

## Museums in Artists' Homes

• *Musée Henri Bouchard*: 25, rue de l'Yvette, 75016 Paris (*Métro*: Jasmin). Tel: 46.47.63.46. Open Wednesday and Saturday from 14h00-19h00. Entrance fee: 25 FF, 15 FF. A tour of this official sculptor's studio is given the first Saturday of each month at 15h00. Bouchard lived from 1875-1960. Academic and decorative sculptures and medals are on view in changing exhibits.

• *Musée Bourdelle*: 16, rue Antoine-Bourdelle, 75015 Paris (*Métro*: Montparnasse). Open daily from 10h00-17h40. Closed Monday and holidays. Entrance fee: 25 FF, 18 FF. The artist's studio contains a large collection of sketches and sculptures in many styles. Bourdelle lived from 1861-1929. Family portraits, *maquettes* and casts are on view.

• *Fondation Le Corbusier*: 8-10, square de docteur Blanche, 75016 Paris (*Métro*: Jasmin). Tel: 45.27.50.65. Open during the week from 10h00-12h30 and 13h30-18h00. Closed on weekends. Entrance fee: 5 FF, under 12 free. A fine collection of Le Corbusier's *Esprit Moderne* paintings and sculpture is housed in Villa La Roche, designed by the great architect in 1923. Research library.

Theme exhibitions organized each year.

• *Musée Delacroix*: 6, place de Furstenburg, 75006 Paris (*Métro*: Saint-Germain-des-Prés). Tel: 43.54.04.87. Open daily from 9h45-12h30; and 14h00-17h15. Closed on Tuesday. Entrance fee: 19 FF, 16 FF. Delacroix's studio and living quarters can be visited to view a collection of prints, drawings and documents. Theme exhibits are organized at times. Charming garden. *Closed for renovation work until 1995.

• *Fondation Jean Dubuffet*: 137, rue de Sèvres, 75007 Paris (*Métro*: Duroc). Tel: 47.34.12.63. Open weekdays from 14h00-18h00. Free Entrance. Changing exhibitions contrast different periods of this prolific artist's work. The charming house once contained Dubuffet's famous *Art Brut* collection. Research library.

• *Musée national Hébert*: 85, rue du Cherch-Midi, 75006 PARIS (*Métro*: Vaneau). 42.22.23.82. Open daily except Tuesday from 12h30-18h00; Weekends from 14h00-18h00. Entrance fee: 12 FF, 8 FF. Drawings, watercolors, and paintings of Hébert (1870-1908). Fine decor and furniture. Special exhibitions feature late 18th century art.

• *Musée national Jean-Jacques Henner*: 43, av de Villiers, 75017 Paris (*Métro*: Malsherbes). Tel: 47.63.42.73. Open daily except Monday from 10h00-12h00; and 14h00-17h00. Entrance fee: 14 FF,

10 FF. A large collection of paintings and drawings by Henner (1829-1920). The exotic decor is a perfect setting for works by this celebrated second empire artist.

• *Musée Gustave Moreau*: 14, rue de la Rochefoucauld, 75009 Paris (*Métro*: Trinité). Tel: 48.74.38.50. Open daily except Tuesday from; 10h00-12h45 and 14h00-17h15; Wednesday 11h00-17h15. Entrance fee: 17 FF, 10 FF. Moreau's house and studio contain an extensive collection of paintings and drawings, including *"Salomé"* and *"Les Licornes"*. During the 1890s it was here that the noted symbolist painter taught future greats like Matisse and Rouault.

• *Musée Rodin*: 77, rue de Varenne, 75007 Paris (*Métro*: Varenne). Tel: 47.05.01.34. Open daily from 10h00-17h00. Closed Monday. Entrance fee: 26 FF, 17 FF. An important collection that includes some of Rodin's most famous works like *"The Thinker"* and *"The Kiss"*, with works by Camille Claudel. Housed in the stunning 18th century Hotel Byron, this museum is surrounded by a large formal garden.

• *Musée de la Vie Romantique*: Maison Renan-Scheffer, 16, rue Chaptal, 75009 Paris (*Métro*: Saint-Georges), Tel: 48.75.95.38. Open daily from 10h00-17h45. Closed Monday. Entrance fee: 35 FF, 25 FF. The house of Dutch artist Ary Scheffer (1795-1858) is the setting for temporary exhibitions that feature the 19th century Romantic movement.

There is a permanent exhibition on the writer George Sand.

• *Musée Zadkine*: 100 bis, rue d'Assas, 75006 Paris (*Métro*: Vavin). 43.26.91.90. Open daily from 10h00-17h40. Closed on Monday. Entrance fee: 12 FF, 6,50 FF. Free on Sunday. Works on paper and sculptures by the Russian artist Ossip Zadkine are on permanent exhibition in the house where he lived untill 1967. A lovely sculpture garden.

## Museums With Unusual Themes

• *L'Aracine (Musée de l'Art Brut)*: Château Guerin, 39, av de Gaulle, 93330, Neuilly-sur-Marne, (RER Neuilly-Plaisance). Tel: 43.09.62.73. Open Thursday-Sunday from 14h00-18h00. Entrance fee: 15 FF. Important *Art Brut* collection founded by three marginal artists. Fine temporary exhibitions and an excellent permanent collection with works by major figures such as Wölfi, Van Genk, Lonné and Rattier.

• *Musée de l'Avocat*: 25, rue du Jour, 75001 Paris (*Métro*: Louvre). Tel: 47.83.50.03. Open during the week. An appointment must be made to visit the collection of authentic documents and works of art. The correspondance between Zola and Dreyfus' lawyer Labori can be seen, as well as a bust of Gerbier known as "the eagle of the bar."

• *Musée Cernuschi*: 7, av Vélasquez, 75008 Paris (*Métro*: Villiers).Tel: 45.63.50.75. Open daily except Monday from 10h00-17h45. Entrance fee: 25 FF,18 FF. Free admission on Sunday, except for temporary exhibit. Henri Cernuschi's private collection was unique at the end of the 19th century. The treasures include neolithique terracottas, ancient bronzes, funerary pieces and fine examples of calligraphy. An impressive collection on the edge of Parc Monceau.

• *Musée de la Chasse et de la Nature*: 60, rue des Archives, 75003 Paris (*Métro*: Rambuteau). Tel: 42.72.86.43. Open daily from 10h00-12h30; and 13h30-17h30. Closed Tuesday and holidays. Entrance fee: 25 FF, 13 FF. Stuffed trophies from around the world; including big game hunts from Africa. Guns and art celebrate the hunt in a beautiful historic house.

• *Musée du Cinéma Henri-Langlois*: Palais de Chaillot, place du Trocadéro, 75116 Paris (*Métro*: Trocadéro).Tel: 45.53.74.39. Visits with a guide every hour from 10h00-17h30. Open daily except Tuesday and holidays. Closed between 13h00-14h00. Entrance fee: 25 FF, 15 FF. The history of the Cinema (1895 to present) is illustrated with documents, stage sets, posters and costumes worn by Greta Garbo, John Wayne and others.

• *Musée de la Contrefaçon*: 16, rue de la Faisanderie, 75016 Paris (*Métro*: Port Dauphine).Tel: 45.01.51.11.

Open Monday and Wednesday from 14h30-16h00 and Friday from 9h30-12h00. Free admission. The art of forgery is celebrated in all its forms going back to the Romans. Creators have always worried about imitation of original products; you can smell the difference between perfumes, and compare Chanel in Paris with Sanel in Turkey.

• *Musée Dapper*: 50, av Victor Hugo, 75016 Paris (*Métro*: Etoile).Tel: 45.00.01.50. Open daily from 11h00-19h00. Entrance fee: 15 FF, 7,50 FF; Wednesday free. This private house in a bamboo thicket highlights the traditional precolonial arts of Africa. The changing exhibitions on diverse themes such as Pygmie Tapa cloth or Fang masks and sculpture are always superb. The research library can be used by appointment.

• *Musée d'Ennery*: 59, av Foch, 75116 Paris (*Métro*: Porte Dauphine).Tel: 45.53.57.96. Open Thursday and Sunday from 14h00-17h00; closed in August. Free entrance. A private collection of Asian art that highlights Netsuke and Kogos fom Japan. Chinese dragons and furniture encrusted with mother of pearl create the perfect atmosphere to enjoy this electric collection.

• *Musée de l'Holographie*: Forum des Halles, level 1, Grand Balcon, 75001 Paris (*Métro*: Châtelet-Les Halles). Tel: 40.39.96.83. Open daily from 10h00-19h00; Sunday and holidays from 13h00-19h00. Entrance fee: 32 FF, 26 FF. Changing exhibitions of

three dimensional works in this new medium by contemporary artists. Lasers and holograms combine technology and art in exhibits that feature new develpments.
• *Musée Kwok-On*: 41, rue des Francs-Bourgeois, 75004 Paris (*Métro*: Saint-Paul). Tel: 42.72.99.42. Open during the week from 10h00-17h30. Closed weekends and holidays. Entrance fee: 15 FF, 10 FF. This collection from Hong Kong focuses on all aspects of the theater in Asia with masks, puppets, instruments and costumes from many different countries. There are changing exhibitions and a fine permanent collection, as well as a documentation center. Closed until 1995.
• *Musée des Lunettes et Lorgnettes*: Pierre Marly, 2, av Mozart, 75016 Paris (*Métro*: La Muette). Tel: 45.27.21.05. Open daily from 10h00-18h00. Closed Sunday, Monday and holidays. Free entrance. An eccentric private collection (housed in a boutique) of several thousand pairs of reading glasses, monocles and binoculars. An opticians paradise; with rare 13th century examples and new trends.
• *Musée de la parfumerie Fragonard*: 9, rue Scribe, 75009 Paris (*Métro*: Opéra). Tel: 47.42.04.56. Open daily from 9h00-17h30. Closed Sunday. Free entrance. This elegant collection tells the story of perfume through the ages. Beautiful glass flacons, vanity cases and a display that explains the process of extracting oils from plants to create a fragrance.

• *Musée de la Serrure*: 1, rue de la Perle, 75003 Paris (*Métro*: Chemin-Vert). Tel: 42.77.79.62. Open daily from 14h00-17h00. Closed Sunday and Monday. Entrance fee: 10 FF, 7 FF. Keys and locks through history are featured in this fine Marais house. Ancient bronze keys, gothic locks, and pieces with Dianne de Poitier's emblem are on view. There is a reconstructed locksmith's workshop in the courtyard.
• *Musée du Vin*: 5, Square Charles Dickens, 75016 Paris (*Métro*: Passy). Tel: 45.25.63.26. Open daily from 12h00-18h00 and 20h00-23h00 for dinners. Entrance fee: 26 FF, 20 FF. Entrance free for diners in museum restaurant (meals with wine from 100 FF). This museum evokes the process of wine making with wax figures. Documents and objects illustrate the long history of wine in France. A glass of wine is included with the visit. Oenological courses are conducted there.

## Museum Visits For Children

Most major museums have workshops, tours, and special art initiation programs for children. These activities include an introduction to the world of robots at La Villette, calligraphy courses at the Institut du Monde Arabe, painting at the Centre Pompidou and art appreciation tours at the Musée d'Art Moderne de la Ville de Paris.

These programs change each season. For complete information contact the individual museums, or the following offices:

• *Affaires Culturelles de la Ville de Paris*: Hôtel d'Albret, 31, rue des Francs-Bourgeois, 75004 Paris (*Métro*: Saint-Paul). 42.76.67.00. Open 8h45-18h00. Closed Saturday.

• *Direction des Musées en France*: 34, Quai du Louvre, 75001 Paris (*Métro*: Louvre). Tel: 42.60.39.26. Open daily from 9h45-18h30. Closed Tuesday.

Check through this guide's listings for subjects of special interest to your child. Some of the eccentric collections listed under "Unusual Theme Museums" will certainly appeal. The thousands of spectacles and the pair of bronze dragons that guard the Cernuschi museum are a big hit with young children. Classics like the *Musée de l'Homme* or the Aquarium at the *Musée des Arts Africains et Océaniens* will enthrall toddlers as well as adolescents! There are some wonderful museums in artists' homes too; everyone loves the *Musée Rodin*! The following is a list of major museums conceived for children:

• *Halle-Saint-Pierre (Musée Max Fourny)*: 2, rue Ronsard, 75018 Paris (*Métro*: Anvers). Tel: 42.58.74.12. Open daily except Monday from 10h00-17h30. Entrance fee: 22 FF, 16 FF. School groups: 15 FF; studio workshop: 25 FF. Two museums: a large collection of naive paintings and sculptures from around the world, and a second space created to initiate younger children to museum viewing.

• *Musée Grévin*: 10, bd Montmartre, 75009 Paris (*Métro*: Rue Montmartre). Tel: 47.70.85.05. Open daily, including holidays from 13h00-19h00. Open during school vacations 10h00-18h00. Entrance fee: 48 FF, 34 FF. This famous wax museum, similar to Mme. Tussaud's in London, traces French history and highlights 20th century figures. There is also a half-hour magic show (*Palais des Mirages* or *Cabinet fantastique*), that runs each day.

• *Musée en Herbe*: Jardin d'Acclimatation, (*Métro*: Sablons). Tel: 40.67.97.66. Open daily from 10h00-18h00. Entrance fee: 15 FF, 12 FF, workshops: 20 FF. This museum was created as a "hands on" experience to introduce children of all ages to museums. Special theme exhibits are animated by games and diverse activities. Past exhibits have included: "*Uluri; les Aborigènes d'Australie*," and "*Sur les Pavés de Paris.*"

• *Palais de la Découverte*: av Franklin-Roosevelt, 75008 Paris (*Métro*: Franklin Roosevelt). Tel: 43.59.18.21. Open daily from 10h00-18h00. Entrance fee: 22 FF, 11 FF; Planetarium: 15 FF, 10 FF. This fine science museum has been overshadowed by the Cité des Sciences at La Villette, but still has a lot to offer in terms of changing exhibits on everything from solar energy to biology. All children love the planetarium.

## Galleries

Paris' gallery scene has truly become a moveable feast. During the 70s and 80s innovative galleries established mushrooming art districts in both the Marais and the Bastille areas, bringing new life to an art world formerly restricted to distinct neighborhoods on either bank of the Seine. In spite of difficult financial times in recent years, "the city of light" continues to shine as a lively art center. Artists and artlovers are still drawn to Paris. Many Parisian art dealers have developed creative strategies to continue showing (and selling) fine art during the slump. Hard times have favored an increase in serious attention to photography and experimental work being done with computer technology.

Although the Paris art scene lost numerous galleries in recent years, there is still an overwhelming choice of fine gallery exhibits each month.

To have a sense of what is going on in the Paris art world today, one should visit the four main gallery districts...and compare art works, trends and the unique atmosphere associated with each area. In 1977 the area around the newly opened Centre Pompidou quickly became a hot-spot for avant-garde galleries promoting the newest trends in the international art world. More recently, during the 80s, contemporary art stormed the Bastille. The city now counts close to 200 serious galleries showing early modern and contemporary art!

The following list, though far from complete, will give you a good overview of the four main gallery districts. You will find the Right Bank galleries to be more traditional. This is an area noted for art dealers specialized in old masters and 19th century paintings. There are several galleries of historic interest, such as *Bernheim-Jeune*, which was founded in 1863.

Major post-war art movements from the 50s and 60s were launched in Left Bank galleries. Several scandalous Dubuffet exhibits are associated with the rue de Seine. An historic Yves Klein event took place in the rue Visconti during the early 60s. The neighborhood is still talking about how he blocked cars and pedestrian traffic for hours with a wall of stacked oil-drums!

Galleries in the Marais (and Les Halles) often highlight major artists and international movements, while many Bastille galleries have continued to feature Paris based trends.

Paris galleries are open Tuesday through Saturday during the afternoon from 14h00-19h00. All galleries close on Sunday and Monday. Double-check morning hours by phone, as they vary greatly.

Look for the "*Association des Galeries*" listing of exhibitions which is distributed for free in most major galleries. You can also check the *Pariscope* and *Officiel des Spectacles* for information on current exhibitions.

**Right Bank** (*Métro:* Miromesnil)
• *Galerie Ariel:* 140 Bd Haussmann, 75008 Paris, Tel: 45.62.13.09. This gallery recently celebrated its 30th anniversary. Since 1964 Jean Pollack has been showing works by Alechinsky, Appel, Lindstrom, Corneille, and Riopelle, to mention just a few of the now famous "école de Paris" artists associated with the gallery since the 60's.
• *Artcurial:* 9, av Matignon, 75008 Paris, Tel: 42.99.16.16. A unique commercial center on several levels with a museum-like gallery that features 20th century masters (Magritte, Picasso, and Saura to name but a few), as well as a fine book store, decorative arts department, jewelry boutique and poster shop.
• *Marcel Bernheim:* 18, av Matignon 75008 Paris, Tel: 42.65.22.23. Specializing in late 19th century painting and early 20th century works (Monet, Renoir, Utrillo, Van Dongen). This gallery opened in 1912 and is still going strong.
• *Bernheim-Jeune:* 83, Faubourg Saint-Honoré, 27, av Matignon, 75008 Paris, Tel: 42.66.60.31. Another historic gallery responsible for launching the careers of some impressionists; later showing works by Chagall and Matisse.
• *Louis-Carré:* 10, av de Messine, 75008 Paris, Tel: 45.62.57.07. This important gallery shows museum-quality works by 20th century greats like Calder, Chaissac, Léger and Geer Van Velde.

• *Mathias Fels:* 138, bd Haussman, 75008 Paris, Tel: 45.62.21.34. Fine gallery that features works by New Realists Artists from the 60s like Cesar, Rotella, and Spoerri, as well as Kudo, Louis Cane, and Combas.
• *Fanny Guillon-Laffaille:* 4, av Messine, 75008 Paris, Tel: 45.63.52.00. This art dealer is specialized in works by the *Ecole de Paris* artists of the 50s like Doucet, Estève and Poliakoff, as well as contemporary works by Chasse-pot, Charpentier and Tal-Coat.
• *Lelong:* 12-13, rue de Téhéran, 75008 Paris, Tel: 45.63.13.19. This gallery was originally part of an international art network founded by Aimé Maeght (of the Maeght Foundation in the South of France). Internationally known contemporary artists like Alechinsky, Bacon, Judd, Penck, Serra, Tapiès and Voss show in this superb space.

**Left Bank** (*Métro:* Odéon)
• *Claude Bernard:* 7-9, rue des Beaux Arts, 75006 Paris, Tel: 43.26.97.07. An important figurative gallery that opened during the 60s. Major international names like Balthus, Botero, Tibor Csernus, David Hockney, Lindner and Andrew Wyeth.
• *Down-Town:* 33, rue de Seine, 75006 Paris, Tel: 46.33.82.41. Decorative arts of the 40s and 50s as well as works by Pincemin, Claude Viallat, BP and Takis in this original gallery.

• *Arlette Gimaray*: 12, rue Mazarine 75006 Paris, Tel: 46.34.71.80. This gallery shows different tendencies in abstraction with artists such as Debré, Degottex, Hartung, Lanskoy and Zao Wou-Ki.
• *Albert Loeb*: 12, rue des Beaux-Arts, 75006 Paris, Tel: 46.33.06.87. This respected gallery shows figurative works in all mediums by Caballero, Guinan, Lam, Jeanclos and other established artists of today.
• *Adrien Maeght*: 42-46, rue du Bac, 75007 Paris, Tel: 45.48.45.15. A gallery that has become an institution; showing 20th century masters like Braque, Giacometti, Kandinsky, and Matisse while launching a new generation of artists. Contemporaries include Delprat, Gasiorowski, Kuroda and Labauvie.
• *Darthea Speyer*: 6, rue Jacques Callot, 75006 Paris, Tel: 43.54.78.41. An American gallery with an electric selection of high quality works in all media. Some of the artists associated with the gallery are Sam Gilliam, Roseline Granet, Stanly Viswanadhan and Zuka.
• *Stadler*: 51, rue de Seine, 75006 Paris, Tel: 43.26.91.10. This well-established gallery opened in 1955, promoting non-figurative works by Tapiès, Bluhm, Domoto and the Gutai group. Today major artists include Saura, Arnulf Rainer, Huftier and Rühle.
• *Galerie 10*: 10, rue des Beaux-Arts, 75006 Paris, Tel: 43.25.10.72. A fine exhibition program in limited space.

This gallery actively launches their discoveries: artists such as Lavocat, Lepoureau, Teffo and Cehes.

## Beaubourg/Le Marais
(*Métro*: Hotel de Ville)
• *Beaubourg*: 23, rue du Renard, 75004 Paris, Tel: 42.71.20.50. and 3, rue Pierre au Lard, 75004 Paris, Tel: 48.04.34.40. Important gallery promoting contemporary French art, with strong links to the cultural ministry's programs. Major French artists include Arman, Ben, Buren, Garouste, Hains, Klein, Nikki de Saint-Phalle and Villeglé.
• *Farideh Cadot*: 77, rue des Archives, 75003 Paris, Tel: 42.78.08.36. Avant-garde gallery with many American artists. Among the first to open in the Marais. Artists associated with the gallery include Connie Beckley, Joel Fisher, Rousse, Tremblay and David Hodges.
• *Gilbert Brownstone*: 26, rue Saint-Gilles, 75003 Paris, Tel: 42.78.43.21. An American gallery, highly active in the field of conceptual work. Promotes the works of Albers, Fontana, Gottfried Honneger, Jesus-Raphael Soto and Raynaud.
• *Jean Fournier*: 44, rue Quincampoix, 75004 Paris, Tel: 42.77.32.31. A well-respected gallery that shows abstract works by an international group of artists. Much support surface work by Hantaï and Viallat as well as works by Bishop, Sam Francis, Shirly Jaffé and Joan Mitchell.

• *Galerie de France*: 52, rue de la Verrerie, 75004 Paris, Tel: 42.74.38.00. A beautiful space on several levels showing works by well known artists like Domela, Degottex, Matta, Soulages and Keiichi Tahara.

• *Nikki Diana Marquardt*: 9, place des Vosges, 75004 Paris, Tel: 42.78.21.00. An American gallery that opened in 1986. Young contemporary French and European artists.

• *Christian Mollet-Viéville*: 26, rue Beaubourg, 75003 Paris, Tel: 42.78.72.31. Telephone or write for an appointment. This well known dealer promotes minimal and conceptual works by artists such as Carl André, Buren, Sol LeWitt and Weiner.

• *Alain Oudin*: 47, rue Quincampoix, 75004 Paris, Tel: 42.71.83.65. Lively, active program with installations and performance work as well as painting and sculpture. International artists include Marie Chamant, Thierry Cauwet, Matsutani and Turin.

• *Daniel Templon:* 30, rue Beaubourg, 75003 Paris, Tel: 42.72.14.10. Well known gallery specialized in minimal and conceptual art, (Judd, Flavin and Morris), as well as more exuberant works by Alberola, Ben, Chia, Fetting, Rauchenberg and Salle.

• *Pierre-Marie Vitoux*: 3, rue d'Ormesson, 75004 Paris, Tel: 48.04.81.00. A small space with big talents. The gallery represents Hadad, Ben-Ami Koller, Linström, Mazliah and Maurice Rocher.

• *Zabriskie*: 37, rue Quincampoix, 75004 Paris, Tel: 42.72.35.47. This branch of the famous New York gallery opened in 1977 to feature photography. Photos by Klein, Friedlander and Stieglitz can be seen as well as works in other mediums by Tony Long, Poivret and Shirly Farb.

Bastille (*Métro*: Bastille)
• *A.B. Galleries (Formerly Galerie du Génie)*: 24, rue Keller 75011 Paris, Tel: 48.06.90.90. This gallery showcases video work, computer paintings and electronic installations. An international group of artists including major names associated with the fluxus movement as well as Catherine Ikam and Bernard Roig.

• *Franck & Hervé Bordas:* 2, rue de la Roquette 75011 Paris, Tel: 47.00.31.61. This gallery space highlights original prints produced inhouse at the Bordas' reputed lithographic printing studio. Original works by such international names as Pierre Alechinsky, James Brown, and Roberto Matta. Artist's books by Jean-Charles Blais, Jean Dubuffet, and Robert Wilson.

• *Durand-Desert*: 28, rue de Lappe, 75001 Paris, Tel: 48.06.92.23. One of the most recent arrivals in the Bastille, this fine gallery boasts five levels to showcase monumental sculpture as well as works on paper. Artists include: Beuys, Boltanski, Haacke, Flanagan and Tosani.

• *Espace d'Art Yvonamor Palix,* rue Keller, 75011 Paris, Tel: 48.06.36.70. Recently inaugurated, dynamic new gallery that highlights conceptual art and experimental photography from the United States, Europe, South America. Artists include Paloma Navares, Jorge Orta, and Sandy Skogland.

• *Jacqueline Felman:* 8, rue Popincourt, 75011 Paris, Tel: 47.00.87.71. This renovated factory space opened in 1985 to promote contemporary figurative work by younger artists. Artists include: Michel Coquery, Buffoli, Hours and Riccardo Licata.

• *Lavignes-Bastille:* 5 & 27, rue de Charonne, 75011 Paris, Tel: 47.00.88.18. Spacious, well established gallery that often has simultaneous exhibits that contrast a wide range of styles from neo-expressionism to abstraction. Artists include: Fraser, Grataloup, Rauchbach, Sandorfi and Vostell. Don't miss the experimental space for launching new talents within the courtyard at 5, rue de Charonne.

## Salons

Modern art history begins with the rejection of the impressionists by the official French academic *salon*. Significant *salon* events are many during the late 19th century. The *Salon des Refusés* rocked the Paris art world, and some years later the famous Fauve scandal heralded a new era of modern painting at the *Salon d'Automne* in 1905.

It is curious to remember that the *Salon d'Automne* (considered the most traditional *salon* today), was originally created as a rather violent reaction against the prevailing academic criteria of the time. In 1903, artists Rodin, Jourdain, Renoir and Cézanne founded a new *salon* that was to serve as an alternative exhibition space for a new generation of artists whose experimental work was not deemed acceptable by the official *salons*.

At the end of the 20th century, art history repeats itself with the emergence of off-shoots from established *salons*. Artistic quarrels seem to be a lively part of the *salon* tradition, and today there are at least 35 *salons* in and around Paris. A current example of this principle is the highly successful *salon* MAC 2000, which began as a splinter group from the *Salon de la Jeune Peinture*.

The launching of young artists is an important part of of the *salon* tradition. Painters and sculptors from other countries envy the opportunities French *salons* offer to Paris-based artists. Today the *salon* tradition continues to interest a large audience of art lovers. Each *salon* is highly publicized by posters about town and on a giant billboard in front of the Grand Palais. The following list includes the most important of the French *salons* held in the Grand Palais. Application requirements and fees vary. Individual *salons* should be contacted for further information.

• *Grand Palais:* 2, av Winston Churchill, 75008 Paris (*Métro:*

Champs Elysées-Clemenceau). Tel: 42.89.23.13. This immense, domed exhibition hall was built at the same time as the Petit Palais for the Universal exhibition of 1900. There are several exhibition spaces to receive major retrospectives and temporary theme exhibits. The Grand Palais is also "home" for most Paris *salons*. Exhibitions are open daily excepting Tuesday, from 10h00-20h00; Wednesday until 22h00. Entrance fees vary. The Grand Palais will be closed for important renovation work until 1995.

• *Salon d'Automne*: Porte H, Grand Palais, 2, av Winston Churchill, 75008 Paris, 43.59.46.07. (15h00-18h00). A historic *salon* which maintains the great *salon* tradition. Annually, each November.

• *Salon des Artistes Décorateurs*: Porte H, Grand Palais, 2, av Winston Churchill, 75008 Paris, Tel: 49.59.11.10. Every aspect of interior design. A professional *salon* that involves manufacturers/artists/designers and decorators. Once every two years during autumn.

• *Salon Comparaisons*: Grand Palais. President: Bernard Mougins, 5, rue du Général de Maud'huy, 75014, Paris, Tel: 43.39.45.06. International *salon* featuring diverse trends. Once every two years in June.

• *Salon Figurations Critiques*: Grand Palais. President: Mme Dors-Rapin, 1, rue Louis-Gaubert, 78140 Vélizy-Bas. A *salon* that promotes figurative work. Held during September.

• *Salon de la Jeune Peinture*: Grand Palais. President: Katerine Louineau, 143, bd Jean-Jaurès, 92110 Clichy, Tel: 47.31.66.37. A post-war *salon* founded in 1949 that supports painted works by emerging talents. Annual. February.

• *Salon des Indépendants*: Porte H, Grand Palais. Tel: 42.25.86.39. Historic *salon* founded in 1884. Exhuberant but often very crowded. Highly eclectic selection. Annual. Held during winter (February or March).

• *Salon de la Jeune Sculpture*: Porte d'Austerlitz, 75013 Paris, Tel: 43.04.68.86. Association de la Jeune Sculpture, 10, Square de Port-Royal, 75013 Paris. A bi-annual *salon* that takes place during the spring and fall to promote contemporary sculpture of all *tendances*.

• *Salon de Mai*: Grand Palais. Secretary: Jacqueline Selz, 8, av Victorien Sardou, 75016 Paris, Tel: 42.88.44.01. A *salon* that highlights artists of repute as well as emerging talents. Annual. Held in May.

• *Salon Grands et Jeunes d'Aujourd'hui*: Grand Palais. President: Marylène Dénoval, 12 bis, rue de l'Etoile, 75017 Paris, Tel: 43.80.38.75. A well-respected *salon* with a rigorous selection policy that provides a fine overview of contemporary trends. Annual. October.

• *Salon MAC 2000*: Grand Palais. President: Concha Benedito, 28, rue du Sergent Godefroy, 93100 Montreuil, Tel: 48.59.19.30. A unique *salon* that features a series of one person shows for confirmed artists. Careful selection and high quality work. Annual. Held in November/December.

• *Salon de Montrouge*. Centre Culturel et Artistique de Montrouge. Tel: 46.56.52.52. President: Nicole Ginoux-Bessec, 32, rue Gabriel Péri, 92120 Montrouge. The most important of the *salons* outside of Paris; well known for launching artists. Fine quality of work. Annual. During Autumn.

## Off the Beaten Track: Art Factories

The *Bateau Lavoir* in Montmartre and *La Ruche* on the edge of the 15th *arrondissement*, in which the Cuban painter Alvarez-Rios currently resides, are two classic artist studio complexes that housed a number of modern masters early in the century. Since that nostalgic period, Paris' real estate has soared and an artist's studio in Paris has gone from being a high-priced commodity to a nearly extinct species. Increasingly, contemporary artists of the 90s are gathering in reconverted factories and warehouses to produce their art.

Most of these large abandoned spaces are to be found in the grimmer parts of the city, or the nearby suburbs. Social security sources suggest there may be more than 40,000 (declared) professional artists living in the Paris region. This staggering figure would account for the growing edge to an already competitive art scene, and the increasing sense of alarm over the scarcity of studio space. In recent years, artists' *squats* have called media attention to these pressing problems of space.

The following is a list of art factories that may be visited by the general public. There are exhibition programs and open studio visits. It is best to call for an appointment.

• *Quai de la Gare*: 91, Quai de la Gare, 75013 Paris, Tel: 45.85.91.91. A former refrigerator warehouse situated between the train tracks and the Seine. Over 250 artists work in diverse mediums in private studios. Lively open studio events several times a year.

• *La Base*. 6 bis, rue Vergiaud, Levallois, (*Métro*: Louise-Michel), Tel: 47.58.48.58. A reconverted factory with a fine exhibition space and an artists-in-residence program. An art center with an international scope, showcasing works produced on the spot by major talents from around the world.

• *Hôpital Ephémère*: 2, rue Carpeaux, 75018 Paris (*Métro*: Lamarck-Caulaincourt), Tel: 46.27.82.82. The former Bretonneau Children's Hospital in Montmartre has been transformed into studios, exhibition halls, photo labs and theaters. Space for 40 artists. On-going exhibition program.

• *Art Factory at Asnières*: 93, bd Voltaire, Asnières, (*Métro*: Asnières), Tel: 46.27.82.82. Newest space funded (in part) by the Ministry of Culture. Studios and exhibition space.

• *La Fonderie*: 104-106, rue Edouard Vaillant, 93100 Montreuil (*Métro*: Croix de Chavaux), Tel: 48.59.66.58 /Fax: 48.59.66.68. This private initiative (*Les Amis de La Fonderie*), launched by David Applefield and John Calder, highlights literary creation as well as providing studio and exhibition spaces for serious artists. Open house exhibitions and poetry readings (many in English) are part of an active program.

## Cinema/Film

*American film critic Lisa Nesselson, who moved to Paris from Chicago in 1978, regularly edifies readers on Paris' celluloid scene with her film reviews and profiles in* Variety, The Paris Free Voice *and* Le Magazine. *A former Radio France International DJ, Satellite News Channel correspondent and one-time voice for Cartier perfume, Lisa saw 351 feature films in 1993 and has never owned a television set. Here are her comments on the Paris film scene.*

As the devout make pilgrimages to Mecca or Jerusalem, so should the true believer in cinema come to Paris. For although movies may be made in Hollywood, only in France are they worshipped. The French themselves are surprised to hear it but, in terms of sheer variety and accessibility to the movies of many lands, Paris is the viewing capital of the world.

As the commemorative plaque at 14, boulevard des Capucines indicates, history's first public projection of motion pictures for paying customers (courtesy of France's own Lumière brothers) took place in the *Salon Indien* of the Grand Café on December 28, 1895. So, as the world gears up for the centenary of motion pictures, Paris, with its film archives, ciné clubs, repertory cinemas and fabulous concentration of commercial movie houses, is the perfect place to catch up on nearly ten decades of the 7th art.

Say, why do they call it that, anyway? Glad you asked. It was in Paris, in 1911, that the Italian critic Ricciotto Canudo declared the Cinema to be "the 7th art," next in line after architecture, music, painting, sculpture, poetry and dance. (Every so often someone has the temerity to suggest that television/video might be the "8th art" but such people are usually found—bound with celluloid and gagged with cathode ray tubes—at the bottom of the Seine.)

Paris, with 314 commercial screens for a population of roughly two million (Manhattan, by comparison, has less than half as many screens) sports some of the best-equipped theaters on the planet. French audiences still respect the notion that a public theater is not a private living room—i.e. extraneous comments and play-by-play accounts ("He's got a gun! - He's going to shoot her! - Look, he shot her!") are practically unheard of. Reverence toward projected celluloid is particularly acute at the Cinémathèque Française, the hallowed-yet-happening film archive where generations of film buffs (including the gents known collectively as the French New Wave) have studied Saint Cinema in the dark. Your chances of coming across a film crew or even bumping into a major director or actor while walking down the street, riding the *métro* or standing in line for a movie are excellent. And, although refreshments are served at many theaters, you'll never find gum stuck to the floor.

That's the good news. The bad news is: movies aren't cheap. The average admission price is over 40 FF. But the CNC, the government body that regulates all film production and exhibition in France, wants everybody to be able to afford to go to the movies at least once a week. From 1980-1992 ticket prices were 30% cheaper for one and all on (traditionally slow) Mondays. In 1992, "cheap day" officially migrated to Wednesday, the day on which new films come out. After a year of experimentation, most theaters retain Wednesday as discount day. But be sure to check the listings: several independent art houses discount seats on Mondays *and* Wednesdays and a few theaters have reverted to Mondays only.

With official documentation, there are discounts (*tarif réduit*) for the unemployed, military personnel, senior citizens, families with three or more children and students. A valid student I.D. card (local or international) is worth its weight in gold since hundreds of theaters offer a 30% reduction to students at daytime shows and some (including the Action cinemas, which pioneered the practice, and the three-screen Entrepot in the 14th) extend the privilege to every show, seven days a week. There are other alternatives to paying full price, which will be discussed further along.

Since films change on Wednesdays, that's when the weekly entertainment guides hit the newsstands. (These are a better bet than the daily papers for complete addresses and showtimes). *L'Officiel des Spectacles* is neatly organized and costs only 2 FF. Some folks prefer *Pariscope* (3FF) which offers listings by "category" (Westerns, Comedies, Horror films) as well as by neighborhood, and sports an insert in English.

When you're scanning the weekly listings or spontaneously ducking into a theater, pay special attention to whether a given film is being presented in "V.O." or "V.F." V.O. (for *version originale*) means the film will be shown with its dialogue intact (be it English, Danish or Pig-Latin) accompanied by

French subtitles. V.F. (for *version fran-çaise*) indicates that the film has been dubbed into French. Most of the theaters in the Latin Quarter and along the Champs-Elysées specialize in V.O. prints. The Montparnasse area deals in both dubbed and subtitled fare. The theaters of the Grands Boulevards and Montmartre are almost all purveyors of V.F. films. If, as is increasingly the case, a French-speaking director (Jean-Jacques Annaud) has made an English-language film (*The Name of the Rose*, *The Lover*), you may come across the designation V.A. (*version anglaise*).

As for titles, it's not difficult to deduce that *9 semaines et demie* is *9 1/2 Weeks* but if you don't know your directors and actors, it might be hard to guess that *Voyage au bout de l'enfer* (Journey to the End of Hell) is actually *The Deer Hunter*, *Aux portes de l'enfer* (At the Gates of Hell) is *Angel Heart*, *Personne n'est parfait* (Nobody's Perfect) is *Torch Song Trilogy* and *Un cadavre sous le chapeau* (A Cadaver Under the Hat) is *Miller's Crossing*.

Most cinemas list two show times for each presentation. The first, known as the *séance*, consists of anywhere from 10 to 40 minutes of coming attractions and commercials. Theoretically, the house lights are to be only partially dimmed, leaving patrons the option of reading Proust, conjugating irregular verbs or otherwise ignoring the ads. However, if you hail from a country where it would probably not occur to the telephone company to use topless women in its advertising campaigns, you may want to direct your attention to the screen, where you're also likely to see a buck naked hunk romping in the surf on behalf of a popular brand of men's underwear. Condom ads tend to be clever.

Sometimes sex references turn up in the most unlikely places. A few years ago one of the major French banks used an instrumental version of Lou Reed's "Walk on the Wild Side" to accompany its commercials. One wonders if the bank's officers had any idea when selecting a melody to convey fiscal responsibility that the song's lyrics refer to unbridled male hustlers and at least one transsexual administering oral sex from coast to coast.

On weekend nights or during the first few days of a film's run you should arrive for the *séance* to be assured of a good seat. (Some theaters, including the Max Linder Panorama will sell you a ticket for a specific show up to a week in advance, at the box office or via Minitel).

Otherwise, if the movie's not a runaway hit, you can generally safely plan to arrive just before the second time listed, for the *film* itself.

The ubiquitous usherette or *ouvreuse*, (so named because the base of the seats in legitimate theaters had to be unlocked—*ouvrir* being the French verb "to open"— and the usherette, who had the key, was loathe to do so unless assured of a tip) has, in recent years given way to salaried personnel. In the heyday of regular movie-going, working for tips at one of the bigger theaters was considered such a plum position that jobs were jealously guarded and "sold" for elevated sums. The ushers at the major theater chains (Pathé, Gaumont, UCG) no longer expect a tip, but those at art houses and a few first-run cinemas still rely entirely on your generosity. A minimum *pourboire* of 2 FF is polite. Although some multiplexes have installed vending machines or built concession stands, in many theaters the usherettes walk the aisles before the show carrying straw trays stocked with ice cream bars and candy. Take the precaution of opening any potentially noisy wrappers before the feature starts—patrons have been seen coming to blows over one too many crinklings of cellophane.

Ticket prices range from 35 to 50 FF, with student (*réduction étudiant*) and senior citizen discounts running roughly 10 FF cheaper. Interestingly enough, you can expect to pay the same amount of money for an art house revival of *Citizen Kane* as you would for the very latest Hollywood fare. (Afterall, the reasoning goes, art is art, whatever its vintage). Stanley Kubrick's *A Clockwork Orange*, made in 1971 and last shown in French theaters in the mid-80s, was one of the top box-office performers of early 1992.

Although American films are often released at roughly the same time in North America, in France, there is sometimes a gap of at least several months. Disney animated features hit French screens as much as one full year later. Some films, however, come out in Paris *before* they are released in American theaters. Examples include *Highlander II*, Clint Eastwood's *Bird* and *White Hunter, Black Heart*, Jim Jarmusch's *Night on Earth*, Woody Allen's *Shadows and Fog*, Michael Mann's *The Last of the Mohicans*, Jennifer Lynch's *Boxing Helena*, Bernardo Bertolucci's *Little Buddha*, and *Robocop 3*.

Although Parisians can be relied upon to smoke everywhere else, smoking is not permitted in cinemas. Depending on your tolerance for tobacco fumes, this in itself could be a major incentive to spend time at the movies.

### Discounts

If you're planning to do a lot of mainstream film-going, you may want to invest in the magnetic debit cards offered by Gaumont (150 FF for five admissions) and UGC (120 FF for four individual admissions or 180 FF for 6 admissions for a maximum of two people at a time) which also entitle bearers to priority entry. (UGC does not offer reductions to students.)

At 25-29 FF, noon shows also represent terrific savings. Bargain matinees are offered at the Forum Horizon (starting as early as 10:30 AM),

Forum Orient Express and Gaumont Les Halles (in the 1st *arrondissement*), the Ciné Beaubourg (in the 3rd), the Epée de Bois and the Reflet Médicis Logos, (in the 5th) the Saint-Germain-des-Prés, Racine, and Luxembourg (in the 6th) and the UGC George V (in the 8th).

For just 25 FF, the Grand Action (5, rue des Ecoles in the 5th) shows a different classic film weekly at noon, excluding Sundays and holidays.

The somewhat scruffy but very well programmed Ciné Beaubourg Les Halles (next door to the Pompidou Center) opens for business at 10h20 and charges only 29 FF until 13h.

Certain independent theaters reward repeat customers with one free ticket for a specific number of paid admissions. Ask for a free *carte de fidélité* at the Action cinemas (the Ecoles and Grand Action in the 5th, the Christine in the 6th and MacMahon in the 17th) and enjoy a free movie after five paid visits.

Other practitioners of the buy-five-get-one-free policy are: Studio Galande (5th), the Denfert and the Entrepôt (14th) and the Grand Pavois (15th). The recently revamped Balzac, in the 8th, antes up one free seat after *six* paid admissions.

Other individual theaters give quantity discounts. The Latina two-plex (the only movie theater in the 4th *arrondissement*) specializes in films from Latin America and sells cards good for 5 admissions for an unbeatably low 100 FF. The quaint and historic Studio 28 is the only V.O. outpost in the 18th and offers a five-admission card that's valid for two months for 120 FF.

## Archives (Non-commercial and Miscellaneous Film)

*La Cinémathèque française: Palais de Chaillot,* Place de Trocadéro (Avenue Albert de Mun and Avenue du Président Wilson, in the 16th) *Métro*: Trocadéro. Palais de Tokyo, 13 Avenue du Président Wilson, 75016 *Métro*: Iéna. Tickets 25 FF. For members, 15 FF. Recorded program: 47.04.24.24

The *Cinémathèque Française* has remodeled its 400-seat theater in the left-hand wing of the *Palais de Chaillot* (from 1986-1992, the seats had no armrests) and two different films a day are programmed there on weekdays increasing to three on weekends. While the *Palais de Tokyo* down the block undergoes a radical facelift (projected re-opening as the *Palais de l'image* in 1995), the C.F., has provisionally replaced its theater there with a screen at the Republique cinema (18, rue du Fbg-du-Temple in the 11th—same prices, same phone number.)

The now legendary *Cinémathèque* was founded in 1936 by film fanatics Georges Franju and Henri Langlois when they were barely out of their teens. Langlois (1914-1977), who believed that every film was a potential masterpiece and collected accordingly, is largely responsible for the grudging acknowledgment that the movies can be art as well as entertainment. Don't be daunted by the pasty-faced regulars affectionately known as "the rats of the *Cinémathèque.*" Although generations of film lovers have come to the *Cinémathèque* to see what could not be seen elsewhere, you needn't be a walking encyclopedia of film trivia to feel comfortable on the premises. Past retrospectives have been devoted to Russ Meyer, Frank Capra and Clint Eastwood as well as lesser known and downright obscure filmfolk.

**Musée du Cinéma-Henri Langlois:** Palais de Chaillot (45.53.74.39) *Métro*: Trocadéro. Admission: 25 FF. You know how you can see your favorite movies over and over and appreciate them a little more each time? Well, the same principle is at work in the fabulous museum that Langlois designed to display a portion of the Cinémathèque's peerless collection of cinemabilia. Original cameras, costumes, posters, set designs (sketches, scale models and mock-ups) and props from all over the world serve to illustrate Langlois' brilliantly eclectic vision of the evolution of moving images. Guided tours only (in French) at 10h, 11h, 14h, 15h, 16h. Closed Tuesday. (As we go to press, there are tentative plans to close the museum in mid-1994 for restoration, so call ahead.) **Salle Garance:** Centre Pompidou (42.78.37.29) *Métro*: Rambuteau or Hôtel de Ville. Tickets: 25 FF.

The Salle Garance (entrance to the rear of the main floor of the Pompidou Center) is a no-frills theater that hosts excellent comprehensive retrospectives at reasonable prices. Pick up a program at Beaubourg's information desk or check the weekly entertainment guides. Garance is also the site, each March, of the *Cinéma du Réel* festival of ethnographic films.

**Vidéothèque de Paris:** 2 Grande Galerie: porte Saint-Eustache - Forum des Halles. (40.26.34.30) *Métro*: Châtelet-Les Halles. Tickets 22 FF (per day). Memberships available.
Opened in 1988 as a public-access archive of film and video documents concerning Paris, the *Vidéothèque*, located underground, offers individual video consoles for research (a state of the art robot can select any of the 4000 + films on tap in under a minute). Despite its name, the *Vidéothèque* projects as many as seven feature films daily (always preceeded by an appropriate newsreel or film trailer) in its impeccable (if sterile) screening rooms. Chunks of programming are loosely organized around themes (children, music, public transportation). One of the advantages here is that titles are repeated on different days and at different times in the course of a retrospective, which gives you more than one chance to catch a given film. Pay 22 FF and stay all day or become a member and reserve a video console via Minitel.

### Outstanding, Unusual and Historic Theaters

For technical excellence and sheer hipness, the Max Linder Panorama (24, boulevard Poissonnière in the 9th) is the grooviest theater in town. With its jet-black walls, 700 seats (each named for a film personality or movie title) on three levels, enormous slightly curved screen and ultra sharp optics and sound system, it may be said that one would be an utter dolt to see a given film elsewhere if it's playing at the Max Linder. (What's more, their first show of the day—and sometimes the Saturday night midnight show—costs only 30 FF.)

At a whopping 24 meters across, the screen that graces the *Grande Salle* of the Gaumont Grand Ecran Italie in the 13th is very impressive, even if the setting itself is a bit sterile. The theater, which hosted the "director's cut" re-releases "Blade Runner" and "The Abyss," introduces each show with a worth-seeing-once laser light extravaganza that is equal parts "Oh, neat!" and "Gee, that's dinky."

Other satisfyingly large screens with a good distance ratio of seats-to-screen include that at the Gaumont Kinopanorama (60, avenue de la Motte-Piquet in the 15th), all six screens but especially the THX salle at the Forum Horizon (underground at 7, place de la Rotonde in the Nouveau Forum des Halles shopping mall in the 1st) and the main auditorium of the spiffy, pleasantly retro Escurial Panorama (11, boulevard de Port-Royal in the 13th). As a general rule, any screen listed as *grande salle, salle prestige,* or Gaumont Rama should deliver a large viewing area, comfortable seating and high standards for projection and sound.

The Trianon in the 18th is a registered landmark that was built in 1902 and has been showing movies since 1939. Until recently home to cheap martial arts double features, the theater now hosts art films and concerts. Proceed up the once-elegant staircase to the foyer with its bar and Versailles-style windows, pause to examine the cherubim on the ceiling and enter the nicer-than-you'd-think auditorium through one of the port-holed doors flanked by topless ladies made of plaster. Trianon: 80, boulevard Rochechouart, 75018. Tel: 46.06.63.66.

La Pagode, the only cinema in the 7th (57 bis, rue de Babylone), is, as the name belies, housed in a pagoda, complete with miniature rock garden and Oriental tea room. The *salle japonaise* is an exquisite setting, but the room is long and narrow and the screen is on the small side.

In October 1988 over a dozen people were seriously injured when religious fanatics firebombed the Saint-Michel movie theater because it dared to show Martin Scorsese's *The Last Temptation of Christ*. Declaring that no attack on a filmmaker's freedom of expression would be tolerated, the government vowed to help rebuild the theater. It took a while, but the all-new Espace Saint-Michel opened in October of 1991 sporting two screens and a pleasant restaurant/exhibit space. Espace Saint-Michel, 7, place Saint-Michel, 75005. Tel: 44.07.20.49. The Café Ciné, in the Passage du Nord-Ouest in the 9th (13, fbg. Montmartre, tel: 47.70. 81.47), opened in late 1991 and has caught on as a concert and film space. The Café Ciné functions as both a movie theater and a café. This was a common configuration in several European countries both before and during WWII—and, in a throw-back to that era, smoking is permitted. The programming—often made up of short films—is willfully offbeat. The summer of 1993, for example, was devoted to "The Strange Film Festival."

Studio 28, 10, rue Tholozé. *Métro*: Abbesses or Blanche. (46.06.36.07) Tickets 35 FF/reduced 28 (except weekends), 120 FF for 5 entries, valid for 2 months.

If a recent film got yanked before you had a chance to see it, keep your eye on the listings for one of the most charming movie houses in Paris, if not the world. Founded in its namesake year of 1928, the marvelous cinema Jean Cocteau dubbed "a masterpiece among theaters, the theater of masterpiece" was trashed by hooligans when Salvador Dali and Luis Bunuel's *L'Age d'Or* premièred there in 1930. The Studio programs a different film (in V.O.) every two days. In honor of Studio 28's 60th anniversary, veteran art director Alexandre Trauner (who died at age 87 in December of 1993) redecorated the slim lobby of this family-run enterprise, which displays molded footprints of film celebrities. The kitschy duncecap lamps in the auditorium and the homey little bar and courtyard are just a few of the reasons to visit Studio 28. Closed on Mondays and most of August.

As its name suggests, the Latina (20, rue du Temple in the 4th) shows films mostly from Spanish-speaking countries. Images d'Ailleurs (21, rue de La Clef in the 5th) specializes in movies by black and third world filmmakers. The Utopia (9, rue Champollion in the 5th) often programs outstanding Iranian films. The Europa Pantheon (13, rue Victor-Cousin in the 5th) is dedicated to showing fare from the nations that make up the new united Europe. The greatest concentration of movies for kids can be found at the Saint-Lambert (6, rue Péclet in the 15th), an adorable neighborhood theater.

Every Christmas season, The Grand Rex—the city's biggest theater at 2,800 seats—presents a kitschy show involving dancing fountains and colored lights. (For reasons unknown, programming jets of water to bob and spurt to music is something of a French art form.) The only true "atmospheric" movie palace left in operation (the star-sprinkled ceiling with projected clouds is meant to approximate an exotic evening under the open sky), the Rex sometimes shows features in *Grand Large*, meaning that a colossal retractable screen takes up most of the extremely comfortable main floor, forcing patrons to scurry into the balcony for a momentous view. The only drawback to the Grand Rex is that foreign films are almost always dubbed into French.

Rex (only the "Grand Rex" is of interest—the other 7 Rex theaters are run-of-the-mill), 1, bd Poissonnière in the 3rd.)

If your lifestyle calls for regular exposure to *The Rocky Horror Picture Show*, the 92-seat Studio Galande (42, rue Galande in the 5th) keeps the tradition alive on Thursday through Saturday nights.

And if you've never seen Marcel Carné's masterpiece *Les Enfants du Paradis* (Children of Paradise), it plays regularly at the magnificent 19th century Ranelagh, the only movie house in the 16th apart from the *Cinémathèque*.

The Action cinema chain celebrated its 25th anniversary in 1992. Founders Jean-Marie Rodon and Jean-Max Causse display almost flawless programming taste, strike fresh prints of film classics and survive in a tough field by having the good sense to honor student I.D. cards 7 days a week. They also offer a discount to people under twenty who don't happen to be attending school.

## Film Festivals & Special Events

There is a film festival going on in one or more French towns or hamlets nearly every weekend of the year. The "International Festival of Films and Horses" (held in October in the Ardèche region because, as the director once stated, "The people around here like movies and they like horses") even hosts a competitive "screenplay-writing marathon" during which pre-selected writers work around the clock for three days and three nights to turn out scripts that are eligible for production money.

The celebrated Cannes International Film Festival takes place each May (47th edition in 1994). Unless you have friends to put you up and some legitimate connection to the film industry, a trip to the Fest could be both costly and frustrating.

That said, a certain number of tickets *are* sold to the general public (or given away by generous souls) for the so-called "parallel sections," (Directors' Fortnight, Critics' Week, A Certain Regard, *Cinémas en France*) whose line-ups can prove more interesting than the films in the Official Competition. Throughout the Festival, the cultural center called "Studio 13," (roughly a 20 minute walk uphill from the *Palais des Festivals),* welcomes the general public to meet fest filmmakers and view their work for very reasonable fees. The *Fédération française des ciné-clubs* organizes two "cultural expeditions" to Cannes during the Festival and secures accreditation for participants. (Request details from: FFCC, 5, passage Magrou, 34500 Béziers. Tel: (16) 67 31 27 35.

In recent years, the *Vidéothèque de Paris* and the *Cinémathèque française* have shown many of the parallel section films immediately following the Festival. Since the *Vidéothèque* has a 'pay once and stay all day' policy, for just 22 FF, the devoted film fan can recreate the Festival-goer's diet of four pics a day and still sleep in his or her own bed.

The annual Fête du Cinéma (end of June in 1994) is a cross between trench warfare and the proverbial free lunch. Every theater in town participates: customer pays full admission price at the first movie he or she attends that day. For each subsequent film, customer pays only 10 FF. Wear comfortable shoes, pack sandwiches and water, plan your itinerary with stopwatch in hand and you may be able to fit in five current releases for the price of two.

In late February, City Hall runs a grand week-long event called "18 heures/18 FF." What this means is that the show that begins closest to 6 pm (18h on the 24-hour clock) costs only 18 FF.

The annual International Women's Film Festival, held in the nearby suburb of Créteil, is completely geared to the general public and assembles outstanding female film talent from all over the world. The 16th edition is scheduled for April 1994.

Films de Femmes, Maison des Arts, Place Salvador Allende, 94000 Créteil Tel: 49.80.38.98.

The annual French-American Film Workshop (11th edition slated for the first week of July 1994) in Avignon is a model of everything a manageable, unpretentious mini-festival should be.

Under the sharp eye and pungent cigar of octogenerian American legend Sam Fuller, *les Rencontres cinématographiques franco-américaines* is dedicated to the independent spirit in filmmaking on both sides of the Atlantic. Varied intelligent programming and lively bilingual panel discussions make this casual event an outstanding way for film buffs to meet and talk with filmmakers (past guests include Louis Malle, John Sayles, Agnes Varda, Nicholas Roeg, Theresa Russell, and Quentin Tarrantino) producers and distributors. Avignon is a quick four-hour train trip from Paris on the TGV. For information contact: Jerome Rudes, The French-American Film Workshop, 10, Montée de la Tour, 30400 Villeneuve-les-Avignon. Tel: (16) 90.25.93.23. Fax: (16) 90.25.23.24.

### Reading Matter

For those who read French, there are dozens of monthly magazines devoted to the cinema, with *Studio, Première, Positif* and *Cahiers du Cinéma* being the best known. *Cinéphage* is an entertaining newcomer. *ActuaCiné,* given away free in theaters, provides a non-critical overview of upcoming releases. Gaumont and UGC each produce glossy freebies, on display in their respective lobbies. The American edition of *Première* magazine is readily available at the more cosmopolitan news kiosks.

The André Malraux public library maintains a good cinema reference collection and subscribes to all of the major film periodicals.

Bibliothèque André Malraux, 78, boulevard Raspail, 75006. Tel: 45.44.53.85 Open 14h-19h Tues.-Fri. and 10h-12h/14h-17h on Saturday. For serious film research, the library of the *Cinémathèque française* is open to the public on weekday afternoons. Its reading room high atop the Palais de Chaillot affords an excellent view of the Trocadéro gardens and the Eiffel Tower.

### Paris and the Performing Arts

You don't have to be in Paris very long to notice that the French pay much more attention to the sensual side of life than to the practical side. This is not good news only for the late night *bon vivant* who likes to wander home through the empty streets at dawn after a night of major-league clubbing. The daylight hours, too, are often packed with possibilities for tasting a bit of what the Parisians call *"la qualité de la vie."* It would take a very dull mind and a seriously withered heart to be bored in this city.

The great battle in Paris over the last two centuries, in art and in life, has been between the avant-garde and classical: the Impressionists, for example, shocking the academics in the 1800s, the Dada and Surrealist movements shocking the bourgeoisie in the 1920s and 30s, the writers of the *nouveau roman* shocking the reader in the 1950s and 60s. The avant-garde and the classical act like tides that ebb and flow, one temporarily conquering the other. The waves caused by their inevitable clashes tend to keep things bubbling, and interesting for the casual observer and leisurely partaker of all kinds of entertainment, French or foreign. Though much has changed over the decades, Paris remains a place where the new and strange are not only tolerated, but welcomed and even proudly displayed. When it comes to the performing arts, this is still in evidence, just as it is in fashion—which in Paris has become a performing art of its own.

## Music in Paris

Choices run from the upper-crust, tuxedo and *escargot* atmosphere of the old *Opéra Garnier* to the merely crusty, like the head-bashing rock club *le Gibus* near République. There's a lot in-between—like jazz, for instance. Paris is one of the world's most jazz-appreciative cities, and France actually has a state-funded National Jazz Orchestra. Even in the years before World War II, black

American musicians found the Parisians a better audience than anything in the US, and the trend continues today. The city sponsors a *Festival de Jazz* each fall (usually in October) but year round you can watch and listen to some of the best American and international acts at intimate cellar clubs like *New Morning*, the two *Petit Journal* clubs at Saint Michel and Montparnasse, the *Petit Opportun* at Châtelet and a number of others scattered across the city. Every Spring, the suburban *département*, Seine St. Denis (93), sponsors an impressive gathering of international blues and jazz artists in a festival called *Banlieues Bleues*, with popularly priced gigs strewn all around the *département* from Bobigny to Montreuil. Call 48.13.12.10 for information and maps (see The Pop Scene).

Experimental, electronic, and avantgarde composition of music and sound occurs year round at the underground attachment to the Pompidou Center, IRCAM, which attracts musicians, composers, and researchers each year from around the world.

Parisians are serious jazz afficionados. Most clubs are small, crowded, smoky and fairly expensive. There is usually a cover, and the price of drinks can seriously unbalance the average checking account. But people don't come to these places to drink, they come for the music, which begins at about 22h, lasts long and loud through multiple sets and ends about 4h on weekends. Lots of people stay for the duration. When the band breaks, it's time for a cigarette and loud conversation, in the honorable Paris tradition. And unlike most American establishments, no obnoxious waiter will force drinks on you and give you the bum's rush if you don't consume enough.

Paris is particularly open to street and *métro* musicians, although the RATP asks musicians playing underground to register first. Parisians are usually receptive to those who pass the hat—that is, if the music is good.

## Classical Music and Opera

The classical music scene is Paris is so rich that one doesn't really know where to start describing it. A free, monthly newspaper devoted to classical music and concert recitals is available at all concert halls, and offers the best listings and news. To obtain a copy or to subscribe, contact: *Cadences*, Editions Firca, 7-9, rue Anatole-France, 94140 Alfortville Tel: 43.96.54.77.

### Opera

*Irish opera-lover Sheila O'Leary, with British publisher and opera afficionado, John Calder, who has personally attended close to 900 operas in his life, and publishes a series of opera guides, has added here several editorial comments on the Paris opera and classical music scene.*

Paris now has two operas, the ornate *Opéra Garnier* which could easily pass for a wedding cake if it were not so large, and the new state-of-the-art *Opéra de la Bastille*, which looks more like a postmodern ocean liner, only bigger. Created in 1989 to coincide with the *bicentenaire* as an "opera for the people" by the Mitterrand government, it has become the main venue for opera in Paris. The *Opéra Bastille* specializes in productions of the repertory and modern classics, 16 operas per season from September through January, while the old Opera house now features mostly ballet and other forms of dance. Each is well worth the visit, although not always the steep ticket prices. Both offer simutaneous subtitles to librettos in English and French. The *Palais Garnier*, finished in 1868, is a marvel of architectural romanticism—lots of gold paint, red velvet and swarming cherubim. Guided tours of both opera houses are available.

The *Opéra Bastille* accepts casual dress and offers modern interpretations of both classics and new operas. Inexpensive tickets are available; the cheapest currently at 60 FF. To get seats at this low price, go to the ticket office on the ground floor of the Opéra Bastille exactly two weeks prior to the performance you wish to see. The ticket office opens at 11 am (closes 18h30) but if the production is a popular one and tickets are hard to get, then you should consider turning up at the door of the Bastille anytime after 7 am, (for the divas you should camp overnight) where someone will deal you a numbered ticket and you must return on the hour every hour until 10 am when you form a line according to your ticket number and wait for the *guichets* to open at 11h. This is really the only way of ensuring you get cheap tickets though it's always worth asking at any time if all the cheaper tickets have been sold. Tickets range in price from 60 FF-570 FF. For more information, call into the opera house and pick up the annual programme or telephone 44.73.13.99.

The venerable *Opéra comique* in the Salle Favart, architecturally a typically old-style Italian theater, also hosts many visiting operas and dance companies. Tel: 42.86.88.83, as do the *Théâtre du Châtelet*, tel: 40.28.28.40, the *Théâtre de la Ville (Sarah Bernhardt)*, tel: 42.74.22.77, which was formerly called the *Opéra lyrique*, and the *Théâtre des Champs-Elysées*, which presents mainly touring theater, opera and dance companies all year round except August.

Many modern works are performed in the suburban theaters or *Maisons de la culture*, which are reachable by métro or RER and often perform American works by John Cage, Philip Glass or John Adams.

### Concert Halls

Major spots for an inspiring dose of Bach or Beethoven include:

*Salle Pleyel*: the major hall in Paris for large scale symphonic concerts and celebrity artists. 252, Fbg. St. Honoré 75008 Paris, Tel: 45.61.06.30.
*Salle Gaveau*: mainly chamber concerts and recitals. 45, rue La Boétie, 75008 Paris, Tel: 49.53.05.07.
*Salle Olivier Messiaen*: In the Maison de Radio France, this concert hall functions with the radio for musical broadcasts. Over in the 16th, Radio France, the national radio network, offers concerts at very reasonable prices in this spacious and comfortable auditorium. Radio France. Tel: 42.30.15.16.
*Théâtre des Champs-Elysées*: 15, av Montaigne, 75008 Paris, Tel: 49.52.50.50.
*Théâtre Musical de Paris/Châtelet*: 2, rue Edouard Colonne, 75001 Paris, Tel: 40.28.28.28.
*Pavillon Baltard*: Musical theater, symphonies, and international traveling operas. Tel: 43.94.08.00.
*Churches*: Certain churches around the city make good use of their excellent acoustics and sponsor concerts throughout the year, especially in the summer, during the annual Festival Estival. Churches include: La Madeleine, Saint Sulpice, Saint-Séverin, St. Germain-des-Prés, Eglise Sainte-Geneviève, La Sainte Chapelle, St. Augustin, and of course Notre Dame.
*IRCAM*: And for the very latest in contemporary compositions, there is the famous *Ensemble Intercontemporain* led by Pierre Boulez, based in their underground studios next to the Centre Pompidou at IRCAM.

This venue is mostly devoted to experimental and avant-garde works and 20th century classics. Tel: 44.78.48.16.

One particularly nice way to spend an evening of classical or jazz music, drinks and/or dinner is at:
**OPUS Café**
Café de la Musique
et des Arts Lyriques
167, quai de Valmy 75010 Paris
Tel: 40.38.09.57 or 40.38.36.14
(for recorded program)
Nightly 20h-2h00, except Sunday.

## The Pop Scene

*Mike Zwerin, Paris' resident anglophone music journalist, whose articles appear regularly in the* International Herald Tribune, Paris City Magazine *and elsewhere, assembled the following data on pop music.*

Going out to hear live popular music in Paris is more often than not either expensive, uncomfortable or futile (though not so dangerous as New York). It is possible to avoid some of these calamities, and we'll try to advise how, but frankly the odds would be better if you switched on the cable, where there are plenty of good live and taped concerts. *Canal Jimmy, Paris Première* and of course *MTV* are the places to look. Take your shoes off and zap.
If you still want to go out, here goes.

For the kind of people who used to buy junk bonds, who like high risks and high rewards, the best bet is to search out that category with the hideously pejorative name "*World Music*" or "Third World," a euphemism for "ethnic". Chalk it up to Developed-World mass-marketing imperialism. Although one would prefer the name "World's Music," whatchamacallit is one of the most interesting musical events of our time and Paris is its capital.

The most realistic, if least efficient, way to approach this wide-ranging music artificially stuffed into a category is to look in the rock, jazz or folk categories in any of the city's entertainment guides. Search for African, Asian or Latin American names you've never heard of. Names like Senem Diyici, Safy Boutella, Papa Wemba or Sheikh Hamza Shakour. If they've been able to travel, they are either the best or the brightest or at least the most ambitious at home. From wherever they come, these people generally end up in Paris, which, xenophobic twitches notwithstanding, takes pride in its cultural variety. Some journals, including *Télérama*, the best of them, list World Music separately (*Musiques du Monde*).

The most consistently creative World Music programming can be found at *Le Passage du Nord-Ouest* at 13, rue du Fbg. Montmartre in Pigalle. It is a pleasant room which holds 500-600 people, mostly seated at tables on tiers, with a reasonable admission and minimum consumption price structure. They also book fusion jazz, New Age flirts like John Surman and Ageing Hippies like Hot Tuna. Tel: 47.57.24.24.

*La Chapelle des Lombards* on 19, rue de Lappe presents salsa and Brazilian music. It starts late, around 11 pm, it's usually packed with smoking Latinos and it can swing. Tel: 47.70.81.47.

The *New Morning* on 7, rue des Petites Ecuries in the 10th can no longer be called a jazz club. It has one of the most interesting and varied programations in town. You must join a disorderly mob outside about an hour before the band hits (the French are not very good at lining-up) if you want a table (it's smarter to wait for the second set, around 10:30 pm, when sleepy squares are heading toward beddie-bye). Many of the 400-500 people the place holds stand in the back. The ventilating system is inadequate and in the summer the smell of armpit can be lethal. Tel: 45.23.51.41.

Although presenting more World Music recently, *The New Morning* is still more jazz-oriented than *Le Passage*. People like Archie Shepp, Pat Metheny and Foley favor the friendly ownership and management team headed by Madame Fahri, an Egyptian lady of some class who grew up in Cairo with Benny Goodman and Count Basie records and likes to book musicians she likes. Before his death, Chet Baker was a regular here. Even though he sometimes wouldn't show up or fell off his chair stoned, Fahri thought he was a "sweet man and a great artist." Armpit or no armpit, you've got to support a place like this. (His Royal Badness Prince likes it, occasionally sneaking in to listen or for a surprise recital.)

Going down the line in venue importance, we come to the *Olympia*. Jimi Hendrix opened for Johnny Hallyday here in days of yore. Thelonious Monk and Nina Simone worked here. It's a monument. Artistically, it's been more or less downhill since the death of owner Bruno Cocatrix in the 80s. Now mostly French variety music stars are featured. Of course some people like that kind of thing, including Cultural Politicians who are lobbying to increase the quota of French music on the media up to 40%. Yes, there is a quota but nobody has been able to define exactly what "French" means. Vanessa Paradis singing in English is French, long-time resident Americans-in-Paris singing in French are apparently not. The fight goes on. Stay tuned.

*La Cigale, L'Elysée Montmartre* and *Le Bataclan* are three halls where what Ahmet Ertugon called *ruckoids* can hear rock, funk and reggae attractions too new or intelligent to draw more than 1,500 customers—people like P.J. Harvey, Four Non Blondes, Alpha Blondy and John Hiatt. *La Cigale* is somewhat less *sauvage* than the others (you sit down). It helps to be young to survive the out-front sidewalk mob scene, which is often suffocating, and the volume inside, which can blow your ears. Entering all three you are body-searched by in-your-face muscle, and once in you get stoned on weed just breathing.

You can find the best local blues bands, about half of them American, seven nights a week in the cave of *The Front Page* at 58 rue St. Denis (or eat an overpriced hamburger on street level). As Brian Eno said, the blues is "25 million people singing the same song." At least those who play here try to swing and it is a clean and cheap place to meet young people of the opposite sex.
Tel: 40. 39.92.77.

As far as jazz goes, it doesn't go very far. The "Round Midnight" days of the romantic caves of Saint-Germain-des-Prés with Jean-Paul Sartre and Juliette Greco listening to Bud Powell and Dexter Gordon are over. Some caves remain, but they mostly present French cats. This is not to say that the French can't swing. Oh no, I'd never say that. Jazz is, however, the poor relation of pop music so you rarely catch it barefoot at home on the cable. There's no choice; out the front door we go.

The most prominent, authentic and expensive jazz cave is the plush, intimate and usually jammed (reserve in advance) *La Villa*, just down the rue Bonaparte from place Saint-Germain-des-Prés at 29 rue Jacob, 75006, not far from where Racine once lived. They book interesting groups led by such people as the current jazz queen of song Shirley Horn, Ravi (son of John) Coltrane and Teddy Edwards (who used to accompany Tom Waits). You can't get out of there for much less than 200 FF per person. Tel: 43.26.60.60.

*Les Latitudes*, *Le Montana* and *Le Bilboquet* are also just off place Saint-Germain, on Rue St Benoit in back of the Café de Flore. Generally (there are exceptions) they feature journeyman French jazz at high prices. They are not recommended.

Let's cross the river.

Laid-back, a musicians' hangout, a place to go no matter who plays there, the street-level *Le Duc des Lombards*, 42 rue des Lombards, 75001 Paris, will cost you 25% of *La Villa* and the service is thrice friendlier. You may not be familiar with the names, but the management knows how to book. The odds are with you. There's a friendly dining room upstairs with inexpensive respectable food. Tel: 42.33.22.88. Metro: Châtelet.

On the same street, which is a short one near Châtelet in the middle of town, lies *Le Sunset*, 60, rue Lombards, 75001 Paris, a bit more formal and expensive than *Le Duc* and more like a tunnel than a cave where you can hear good music if you choose beforehand. Both book a sprinkling of Americans. Tel: 40.26.46.60.

If you don't mind a little ride, one of the best jazz clubs in, or rather out of, town is the *Manhattan Jazz Club* in the Hotel New York at Euro Disney theme park. You get there quicker and easier than you might think by going to the end of the Marne-La-Vallée RER line and then walking ten minutes. It's comfortable, the sound system is excellent, you can drink for only 60 FF or eat reasonably priced Cajun dishes while listening to people like the Arkansas bebopper Bob Dorough, Buddy De Franco, Hermeto Pascoal and the wonderful Antillais bebop pianist Alain Jean-Marie. Tel: 60.45.73.00.

*The Jazz Club Lionel Hampton* in the Hotel Méridien Etoile, near Porte Maillot, 81, Bd. Gouvion St. Cyr, 75017 Paris, is a well laid-out, acoustically agreeable and ass-friendly if somewhat pricey venue to hear jazz, gospel and the blues. Reserve in advance and you sit at tables with good sight and sound lines to the likes of legendary New Orleans singer/songwriter/producer Allen Toussaint, the post-bebop funk of T.S. Monk and Linda Hopkins with her "Black and Blue Band." The room is off-lobby and you can hear for free, sitting in one of their very-easy-indeed leather easy chairs (possibly next to a napping Japanese businessman). Tel: 40.68.30.42.

The most complete and reliable French-language jazz and rock listings are also in the mass-circulation *Télérama*, which comes out every Wednesday; they include short descriptions of the music. In English, the bi-monthly *Paris City Magazine* and the monthly *Paris Free Voice* do the same, though they are mostly found in Tex-Mex restaurants and other temples where Anglo-Saxon tourists cluster.

For those of you looking to buy good and/or hard to find used records, there's Crocodisc at 46 rue des Ecoles and its sister shack Crocojazz on the nearby rue Montaigne St. Génévieve, both in the 5th *arrondissement.* If you're looking to pick up an instrument or have one repaired, try the area around the Pigalle métro stop, the Paris equivalent to New York's 48th Street, where the shops, especially those with electric intruments, are clustered. (The area around the métro Europe near the Conservatoire in the 8th is studded with classical music instrument shops.)

For the visiting musician looking to jam, both the Sunset and Duc des Lombard have weekly jam sessions. Show up with your horn and most likely you'll get to blow.

Okay? One, two...*un, deux, trois, quatre.....* swing!

### New To the Block
**Hot Brass at Parc de la Villette.**
New space devoted to hot jazz, salsa, blues, etc.
211, av Jean Jaures, 75019 Paris. Tel: 42.00.14.14. Nightly Tues-Sat. Opens at 20h00. 90 FF entry, 60 for students under 26. Drinks from 28 FF up. Metro: Porte de Pantin.

---

### Quick Reference Guide to Clubs with Live Music

*Le Passage du Nord-Ouest* 13, rue Fbg. Montmartre. 75009 Paris. Tel: 47.57.24.24.
*La Chapelle des Lombards* 19, rue de Lappe 75011 Paris. Tel: 47.70.81.47.
*New Morning* 7, rue des Petites Ecuries 75010 Paris. Tel: 45.23.51.41.
*The Front Page* 58, rue St. Denis 75003 Paris. Tel: 40.39.92.77.
*La Villa* 29, rue Jacob 75006 Paris. Tel: 43.26.60.60.
*Le Duc des Lombards* 42, rue des Lombards, 75001 Paris. Tel: 42.33.22.88.
*Le Sunset* 60, rue Lombards, 75001 Paris. Tel: 40.26.46.60.
*Manhattan Jazz Club* New York Hotel at EuroDisney. Tel: 60.45.73.00.
*The Jazz Club Lionel Hampton* Hotel Méridien Etoile, Porte Maillot, 81, Bd. Gouvion St. Cyr, 75017 Paris. Tel: 40.68.30.42.

---

## The Rock Scene

For Paris rock, the choice is between the *salle* where you pay to sit and the club where you pay to dance. There's live rock in either spot, but the livelier nights tend to be in the clubs. The big venues for live bands start at the massive Palais Omnisport de

Bercy, one of the city's few buildings that has to have its walls mowed, to the belle-epoquish, more human-scale *Le Zénith, La Cigale, L'Olympia* or *L'Elysée-Montmartre*, and the *salles les plus à la mode, Le Passage du Nord-Ouest* or *L'Araphao*. In general, Paris is not one of the essential stops on every band's concert tour, mostly because of the lack of big-profit-generating stadiums and the policy of Paris municipality which is not concerned with rock music except in closing clubs and/or in unauthorizing gigs in others, so the selection for live bands is less than you'd see in some smaller North American cities. But the big acts make it through town at one point or another.

The best way to get your ticket entrance is to buy them at the main FNAC stores (Forum, Montparnasse) or at Virgin Megastore.

### Arapaho
30 avenue d'Italie
75013 Paris, *Métro*: Place d'Italie
Tel: 43.48.24.84

### Le Bataclan
50 bd Voltaire
75011 Paris, *Métro*: Oberkampf
Tel: 48.06.21.11

### Palais Omnisports de Paris Bercy
8, bd Bercy
75012 Paris, *Métro*: Bercy
Tel: 43.42.01.23
for reservations, call 43.46.12.21
Minitel: 36.15 BERCY

### La Cigale
120, bd Rochechouart
75018 Paris, *Métro*: Pigalle
Tel: 42.23.15.15

### Théâtre Dunois
108, rue Chevaleret
75013 Paris, *Métro*: Chevaleret
Tel: 45.84.72.00

### L'Olympia
2ter, rue Caumartin
75009 Paris, *Métro*: Madeleine
Tel: 47.42.25.49

### Elysée-Montmartre
72, bd Rochechouart
75018 Paris, *Métro*: Anvers
Tel: 42.52.25.15

### Le Passage du Nord-Ouest
13 rue du Fbg Montmartre
75009 Paris, *Métro*: Rue Montmartre
Tel: 47.70.81.47

### Le Rex
44, rue Poissonnière
75002 Paris, *Métro*: Bonne-Nouvelle
Tel: 40.28.08.55

### Le Zénith
211 avenue Jean Jaurès
75019 Paris, *Métro*: Porte de Pantin
Tel: 42.08.60.00

## Clubs

The Paris club scene is lively and varied, the beat for fashion zombies, celebs and apprentice celebs, and people who just like to get out and move it around. There are the "classic" joints that have been on the scene for years, like *le Palace* (almost a Paris institution) and *Les Bains*, where people-watching is at least as important as dancing. And then there are the African clubs, like *le Tango, Mambo Club* and *Keur Samba*, for some serious shaking and a taste of the exotic.

And, of course, there are the high-tech discos like *la Scala*, lots of glass, aluminum, lasers and decibels in the auditory-damage range. The bouncers in these places tend to be numerous and over-trained in rapid intervention, which is fine if your primary concern is protecting your designer clothes from some drunken *zonard,* but bad news if you're not on best behavior. As a rule, North American clubs and discos tend to be a lot rowdier than the Paris version. Public drunkeness or other overt signs of altered behavior are in *très mauvais goût* (very bad taste) here.

Not to be missed on the music and dance scene is the tiny rue de Lappe near the Bastille, home of *le Balajo,* one of this area's several ex-tango ballrooms that date from the nineteenth century. The atmosphere on certain nights is surreal in its mix: fortyish prostitutes dancing with African immigrants, French sailors on leave and on the prowl, the young and hip *branché* (connected or plugged-in—the now dated French word for "in") crowd moving to live and recorded music, sometimes retro, sometimes rock. It's an experience. Note: Not that long ago, the very *branché* use the invented language *verlan* (the syllabic reversal of *l'envers,* meaning "backwards," thus *chébran* for *branché*) to communicate their hipness. This, for the time being, has dropped out of mode, and is considered rather *ringard* (embarrassingly dated).

As a general rule, the club scene in Paris gets started late, rarely before 23h, and doesn't get rolling until the tiny hours, sometimes, depending on the club, around 3h or 4h. The hard core spill out at dawn.

*La Locomotive*
90, bd Clichy
75018 Paris
Tel: 42.23.55.00

*Les Bains-douches*
7, rue Bourg l'Abbé
75003 Paris
Tel: 48.87.01.80

*Le Tango*
15, rue Jules Lamant et Fils
93330 Neuilly-sur-Marne
Tel: 43.08.20.49

*Keur Samba*
79, rue de la Boétie
75008 Paris
Tel: 43.59.03.10

## Theater in Paris

*American theater director and founder* of the Compagnie du Horlà, *Dana Burns Westberg, has been living and working in Paris since the mid-80s. Here, he has penned a few comments on the Paris theater scene for* Paris Inside Out *readers.*

If you like theater, you've come to the right city. There are about a hundred and fifty theaters in and around Paris within *métro* distance, and some two hundred shows a night in the high part of the season. France's rich theatrical tradition, like England's and Italy's, goes back to the late Middle Ages. Today the quantity is not always matched by the quality, but there's a lot to savor no matter what your taste. These days, along side the conventionality of French theater, there is a tendancy to make theater of anything (translation: any text), so be prepared to expand your pallette.

The three companies of international renown, although not listed in order of size, are Peter Brook's *Centre international de créations théâtrales,* at the *Théâtre des Bouffes du Nord,* Ariane Mnouchkine's *Théâtre du Soleil,* which performs in the *Cartoucherie* in the Bois de Vincennes, and the *Comédie française.* The three companies are heavily subsidized, maintain a standing troupe of actors, and tour extensively; the latter two characteristics distinguish them from the pack. But all similarities between them stop here.

### Peter Brook—Les Bouffes du Nord

Peter Brook's most recent work is characterized by his forays into deconstructed opera, the nine-hour Indian epic *The Mahabharata,* and the international nature of his acting company - many whom have been with him since he abandoned England, set up shop in Paris over twenty-five years ago, and undertook perhaps the most famous theater renovation in modern times. No Parisian theater-goer or self-styled culture vulture hasn't passed through the door of Les Bouffes du Nord and seen a production by the author of the slim volume masterpiece *The Empty Space.* And listened to the melting pot of *francophonie* which is Brook's company. While certain critics still privately whine about the indignity of their French, few dare to question the genius of their enterprise, or that Brook is probably the most important and influential theater artist in any language of the second half of the century.

### Théâtre du Soleil

Discovered during the student and worker uprisings in May 1968, Ariane Mnouchkine's *Théâtre du Soleil* is now a French institution, housed in the Cartoucherie, a former ammunitions depot in the Bois de Vincennes on the eastern border of Paris, and known for their kabuki-influenced Shakespeare productions, Hélène Cixous' contemporary 'history plays' on Cambodia and India, or their recent cycle of Greek tragedies. They are currently working on a piece which investigates the contaminated blood scandal/AIDS crisis in France. Communally organized, and influenced by Eastern music and culture, the *Théâtre du Soleil* has broken new ground while amassing enormous popular support. Their cavernous playing space in the *Cartoucherie* is transformed for each production, the actors apply their make-up and dress as the audience enters, and the company doubles as ticket-takers, ushers, barmen and waiters before, during and after each show. No stars, they have also built the sets and costumes, and maintain the space. Not to be missed.

## Comédie Française

In another vein, the *Comédie française*, the famous "*Maison de Molière*," was founded more than three centuries ago by Louis XIV. Productions and costumes are lavish, and two or three plays rotate in repertory throughout the season in its luxurious Salle Richelieu, named after the Cardinal who was Louis' top cop for culture. Molière, Racine, Corneille, Marivaux and Musset are the bread and butter of the company. But at the end of the 80s, Antoine Vitez bravely expanded the repertory to include modern playwrights (Sartre's *No Exit* was performed, for example), and openings were made for francophone playwrights and directors from the Caribbean, Africa and North Africa. Since Vitez' untimely death, the direction of the *Comédie Française* has changed twice amidst shifting political winds. In 1993, *Le Français* (as you will hear insiders call it) took over the legendary and recently restored *Théâtre du Vieux Colombier*, to create a home for modern and contemporary work.

## Sites

The spirit of Jacques Copeau still roams the *Vieux Columbier*. Those interested in visiting the theaters associated with other French directors who championed the modernist cause can go see productions in their legendary haunts - the *Théâtre de l'Atelier* still dominates the pictoresque Place Charles Dullin in Montmartre; Louis Jouvet's *Théâtre de l'Athénée* now houses two salles near the Opéra; and Lugné-Poë's *Théâtre de l'Oeuvre*, where Alfred Jarry's *Ubu roi* harbingered the chaos of the 20th century, continues on the rue de Clichy. Jean Vilar's home for the influential *Théâtre national populaire* is now the *Théâtre national de Chaillot*, housed within the massive marble interiors of the Palais du

Trocadéro in the shadow of the Eiffel Tower. With a little scratching around and footwork, theater buffs can easily discover the Paris of Antonin Artaud, Etienne Decroux, Jean Cocteau, Sartre, Camus, Ioensco, Roger Blin and Samuel Beckett. The recently deceased Jean-Louis Barrault fought for thirty years along with his wife and partner Madeleine Renaud against government indifference and cultural fads to maintain a home for their internationally-known troupe in places such as what is now the *Musée d'Orsay*, the impressive *Théâtre de l'Odéon*—now home to the *Théâtre de l'Europe*—and the *Théâtre du Rond-Point* at the bottom of the Champs-Elysées.

### Trends

The *Théâtre national de la Colline* near Place Gambetta has probably the clearest artistic direction of all the Parisian institutional theaters, concentrating on contemporary European work. Parisian theater is divided into government-subsidized and private, or commercial, theaters. But the marriage of public support and private sponsorship, and an ever-increasing infatuation with "showbiz" has blurred the distinction between the two in recent years. Market pressure's impact on a long tradition of cultural responsibility has created an uneasy ideal of *"rentabilité culturelle"*, and a flurry of heavily-subsidized/privately-sponsored productions with well-known actors in the leading roles, top-heavy publicity budgets, and questionable creativity. Not all have worked. The private, commercial theaters are making increasing efforts to support new work, but are constrained by their fiscal responsibilities. It is very difficult to produce new work or reinvigorated classics with unknown actors and directors; both private and subsidized theater directors are playing it very safely these days, and seek clear, marketable commodities. Production and promotional costs scare all but the very hearty, and these often fall short of cash before they can muster the public attention necessary to sustain a run. Fewer theaters create new work, increasing numbers buy and sell it, once established. There are interesting public theaters in the close suburbs that ring the city, like Saint-Denis, Aubervilliers, Gennevilliers and Bobigny.

The Parisian "boulevard" theaters still exist, and their fare can range from beguiling revivals of Guitry and Feydeau to distracting contemporary comedies and farces of varying interest. Ticket prices are very steep, and production values don't always follow suit. It's fairly standard stuff, not so different from that offered up in the capitals of most other countries.

### Theater and the Press

The French press is a willing partner in the heavy, expensive publicity and promotion machinery of Paris theater, and is often neither objective nor terribly thorough: the large institutions and big-budget productions compete for decreasing space in newspapers and magazines - and for radio and television time - the same press and media that they are often also solliciting for sponsorship. Show biz, *quoi. Le Figaroscope,* the Thursday cultural supplement to *Le Figaro* newspaper, is the best place to find out what's happening on the fringes, and does a very responsible and fair job of covering the shows which don't have the budget to attract the 'front-line' critics or the financial ambitions of the main-stream cultural venues.

## Pocket Theaters

There are pocket theaters galore, where the hearty vye for attention and public with the comedy-orientated "*café-théâtres*" (something of a French institution). The quality can vary greatly, but excellent work can be discovered with a little determination and a sense of adventure. Many of these venues present as many as three or four shows a day (there is quite a good deal of children's theater presented on Wednesday and Saturday afternoons, by the way). The worst of these venue directors are indifferent, absentee landlords, but some work without recognition to promote the companies they take in. The fare can range from the almost forty-year, uninterrupted run of Ionesco's *The Bald Soprano* and *The Lesson* at La Huchette (where some of the five original cast members still

perform), to plays in English, German, Spanish and Italian, and student companies.

## Theater in English

Paris is one of the few European capitals without an established English-speaking theater. But there is a long-dating underground community of English-speaking theater artists, some of whom work in French as well, and whose work is often of the highest quality. The names of the companies change constantly, as recent French business-*cum*-cultural regulations are making it harder for them to continue. But continue they do. The level of acting is very high indeed. There is a minimum of production values. Particularly well-suited to plays by Harold Pinter, Paris is the unknown Pinter capital of the English-speaking world, and he a very unofficial resident playwright *in absentia.*

In summary, short-timers in Paris as well as the here-for-the-duration crow, should definitely take in Brook at the *Bouffes du Nord,* the *Théâtre du Soleil* and the *Comédie française,* and something in their mother tongue. The avid and the lifers will see Beckett plays in Paris (and maybe think of doing the same in Dublin), investigate the fringes of the theater scene, and run into Neil Simon and Woody Allen on the *boulevard.* Childrens theater abounds around holidays and school vacations, and

Wednesday and Saturday afternoons. *Pariscope* and *L'Officiel des Spectacles* are the best and cheapest sources of listings. *Pariscope* includes a several-page pull-out from London's *Time Out* in English. The Comédie française offers one of the best ticket deals in town; fifteen minutes before curtain, you can get upper balcony seats for next to nothing. The state-run theaters have subsidized ticket prices, and good seats are available for 100 to 150 FF, sometimes less. Private and boulevard theater seats are more. Smaller pocket theaters don't always have *small* prices. Student discounts are often available, and group rates and bookings abound, particularly at the beginning of runs. You should have yourselves a pretty good time.

## Major Theaters in Paris

**Amandiers de Paris (Nanterre)**
Tel: 46.14.70.00
**Athénée Louis Jouvet**
Tel: 47.42.67.27
**La Bastille**
Tel: 43.57.42.14
**Bouffes du Nord**
Tel: 46.07.34.50
**Comédie française**
Tel: 40.15.00.15
**Comédie de Paris**
Tel: 42.81.29.36
**Huchette**
Tel: 43.26.38.99
**Espace Cardin**
Tel: 42.66.17.30

**Le Gymnase**
Tel: 42.46.79.79
**Lucernaire Forum**
Tel: 45.44.57.34
**Madeleine**
Tel: 42.65.07.09
**Marigny**
Tel: 42.56.04.41
**Mathurins**
Tel: 42.65.90.00
**Montparnasse**
Tel: 43.22.77.74
**Palais des Glaces**
Tel: 42.02.27.17
**Palais Royal**
Tel: 42.97.59.81
**Paris Villette**
Tel: 42.02.02.68
**Théâtre de l'Europe, Odéon**
Tel: 44.41.36.36
**St. Georges**
Tel: 48.78.63.47
**Théâtre des Champs-Elysées**
Tel: 49.52.50.50
**Théâtre Grévin**
Tel: 42.46.84.47
**Théâtre de l'Est Parisien**
Tel: 43.64.80.80
**Théâtre de la Main d'Or**
Tel: 48.05.67.89
**Théâtre National de Chaillot**
Tel: 45.05.14.50
**Théâtre National de la Colline**
Tel: 43.66.43.60
**Théâtre de Paris**
Tel: 48.74.10.75
**Théâtre de la Ville**
Tel: 42.74.22.77
**Théâtre du Vieux Colombier**
Tel: 44.39.87.00

## Theaters for English-speakers

*Théâtre Marie Stuart*
Compagnie Robert Cordier
4, rue Marie Stuart
75002 Paris
Tel: 45.08.17.80
Director: Robert Cordier
An institution in contemporary anglo-franco productions in Paris, Robert Cordier's company has vitalized Paris bi-lingual theater scene for a decade, gaining much attention for its performances of Sheppard, Joyce Carol Oats, Sartre, Duras.

*ACT (English Theatre Company)*
20, rue du Ct. René Mouchotte
75014 Paris
Tel: 43.21.48.02
Performs at Théâtre de la Main d'Or and hosts an annual festival of English language theater companies.

*Compagnie du Horlà*
21, rue Henri Regnault
92210 St-Cloud
Director: Dana Burns Westberg
Tel: 47.71.23.46
Versatile company that plays the work of American playwrights in French. Horlà has performed at the Avignon Festival for several years, and is introducing Oyamo into France.

*On Stage*
27, rue de la Beaune
93100 Montreuil
Director: Nick Calderbank
Tel: 48.59.41.50
Performs anglophone plays in V.O.

*Dear Conjunction*
6, rue Arthur Rozier
75019 Paris
Tel: 42.41.69.65
Contact: Patricia Kesseler
Founded in 1991 by Barbara Bray. Performs Pinter, Friel, Wodehouse and Coover in both English and French.

*The Gare St Lazare Players*
No fixed address
Contact Bob Meyer
Tel: 43.14.04.96 or 42.59.41.37
This troupe floats around town playing at diverse venues from the cellars of bars to the Théâtre Marie Stuart. Works by O'Neill, Pinter, Beckett, etc. and by writer/ director/artist Bob Meyer.

*Voices (Assoc. of English & American Actors)*
13, rue Chambéry
75015 Paris
Tel: 45.31.65.48
Collective of international actors.

*Sweeney Irish Pub*
18, rue Laplace
75005 Paris
Tel: 46.33.36.37
Houses a series of well produced one act plays in its *cave*.

Additionally, the Royal Shakespeare Company and the British National Theatre perform for several weeks during the Summer.

## Dance in Paris

The French dance scene is a very healthy one these days, and there's lots of activity in Paris and the close suburbs. The *Théâtre de la Ville* programs the big, internationally known dance companies throughout the year. The *Opéra Garnier* features the work of the *Ballet de l'Opéra de Paris*, as well as another in-house group, *Groupe de recherche chorégraphique*, formerly headed by Rudolph Nureyev, that is more experimental in nature. Both do very high-quality work. Elsewhere, on a less exalted level, there is some very interesting dance work shown at the *Théâtre de la Bastille*, usually during the beginning of the year, as well as at the *Ménagerie de verre* and the *Café de la Danse*, both in the Bastille neighborhood. The Centre Georges Pompidou programs some interesting avant-garde companies from France and abroad. The numerous smaller dance companies based in and around Paris perform at various locations, sometimes in theaters, often in dance studios scattered across the city. The *Studio regard du cygne* and the *Atelier de la danse* offer some of the most exciting modern and contemporary programs in Paris.

Quick Reference—Dance

*Atelier de la Danse*
16, av Junot, 75018 Paris.
Tel: 46.06.44.44.
*Centre Georges Pompidou*
19, rue Beaubourg, 75004 Paris.
Tel: 44.57.42.15.

*Opéra-Palais Garnier,*
Place de l'Opéra, 75002 Paris
Tel: 47.42.53.71.

*Studio Regard du Cygne*
210, rue de Belleville, 75020 Paris.
Tel: 43.58.55.93.

*Théâtre Contemporain de la Danse*
9, rue Geoffroy-l'Asnier, 75004 Paris.
Tel: 42.74.44.22.

*Théâtre de la Bastille*
76, rue de la Roquette, 75011 Paris
Tel: 43.57.42.14.

*Paris Villages*
Of a far more rustic nature is the city's annual summer program called *Paris Villages*. In some neighborhoods, mostly the ones on the eastern side of the city, a bandstand is set up in one of the squares, party lights are strung up, and a retro band complete with accordion and female vocalist plays the old French favorites while everybody from the baker to your *concierge* comes out for a drink and a dance. It's lots of fun, very *vieux Paris*. Not to be missed are the local Bastille Day dances held at

every fire station (called *Sapeurs-Pompiers*) the night of July 13th. Here you can dance the night away to live music that is usually so bad, it's an experience in itself. Everyone in the neighborhood comes out for these, from infants to the elderly. The wine flows, there are games and prizes, neighbors who steadfastly refuse to speak to each other during the rest of the year are suddenly great friends, while the firemen gallantly dance with every available woman or young girl. You will probably learn more about the French character in one evening like this than in a year's worth of observation and study. And you can work off your *gueule de bois* (hangover) the next day by watching the parade on the Champs-Elysées.

# Sports & Recreation

It is true that more and more Parisians are becoming fitness conscious, but the fact remains that the role of recreational sports in Parisian life has not yet approached the levels they enjoy in America or even Britain. The closest you'll see in Paris to the jogging phenomenon in New York's Central Park or along Boston's Charles River is in Luxembourg Gardens. The air quality in Paris is not ideal for running, although the Bois de Vincennes and Bois-de-Boulogne are vast, lush, relatively pollution-free and well-marked for runners.

In France, you're either *"sportif"* (athletic) or *"non-sportif."* So make up your mind. *Non-sportifs* outnumber the *sportifs* and most smoke cigarettes. The *sportifs* tend to be very *sportif* and often belong to clubs, where they regularly swim, ride, work out or play tennis or squash. Other *sportifs* only "spectate" *le foot* (football/soccer) matches and horse racing, read *l'Equipe*, and hang around the special cafés where PMU (off-track betting) is marked on the awning.

Several sports events in France are of great importance. The *Tour de France* international bicycling race; Paris-Dakar international car rally; the French Open tennis matches at Roland Garros; the Paris Marathon for runners; and Europe Cup soccer matches are a few highlights.

Certain sports such as cycling have a historic significance in France and are widely practiced by amateur specialists. Throughout the French countryside you'll see cyclists with their skin-tight outfits and colorful beenies pedalling up and over the hills. The French also care deeply about car racing with Alain Prost attaining near hero status. Horse racing, too, is popular with major tracks located in the Bois de Vincennes and in the Bois de Boulogne.

Sports, in general, still maintain the remnance of social and class order. Golf, for example, which is on the rise in France, is still an elitist sport, and remains prohibitively expensive. Golfing in France for your average North American "hacker" can be an alleviating and highly serious experience. One "duffer" from New Jersey invited by a French colleague to play at her club was sent away because he didn't have a handicap and, worse, hadn't purchased golfing insurance, a requirement for all those wishing to tee-up in France.

Basketball has gained tremendous status over the last few years, capturing the popular imagination of the country's youth, following the widely televised "Dream Machine" at the 1992 Olympics in Barcelona. At a time when more and more idle, urban youths find themseles on Paris (and suburb) streets, more and more hoops are going up. The body skills though have been replaced by the Jordanesque desire to dunk (*smatch*). For pickup basketball games, go to the courts in the Champ de Mars on Sunday mornings. The Saturday morning games at the American Church are no longer up and running. For up-to-date sports information, including upcoming sporting events, call *Allô-Sports* (Tel: 42.76.54.54)—a recorded phone line operating from 10h30-17h Monday-Thursday and 10h30-16h30 on Friday.

In the last few years the French have become more interested in playing American baseball and football. The Japanese have organized a complete league of baseball players in Paris and play in the Bois de Vincennes. Canal Plus regularly broadcasts Monday Night Football and other sports events.

Since the popular ascent of Yannick Noah, now a pop singer, tennis has become more and more available to the masses. Pick up the application form for a *Carte de Paris Tennis* at your local *mairie* which you will need to book a court at one of the numerous public tennis complexes around the city. It's not that easy to get a court where and when you want one; the only way to ensure you get the court you want is to phone (or book by Minitel: 3614 Paris) early in the morning exactly one week before, which is the most in advance you can book your court. Each reservation costs around 20 FF which you pay when you turn up for your game. Otherwise, it is possible to join a sports club that has tennis facilities, but like in any city, this can prove expensive.

## University Sports

Team sports at French universities are organized by clubs and student organizations. They tend to be only moderately organized and modestly equipped. There are no large scholarships to entice middle linebackers to the Sorbonne. University sports can be serious, but rarely obsessively played, other than insisting that all participants have proper enrolment cards, health certificates, and insurance forms. If you show up at a university sports complex in your gym clothes but have forgotten your active student card, a guardian at the door will most likely not let you in. Always carry identification with you. A few years back the starting five for the basketball team for the Sorbonne included two short Americans, a scrappy Mexican, a Japanese forward who owned no white socks, and a lanky French student who was more or less flat-footed. So, playing organized sports for a French university team can be fun and recreational, but it won't be ruthlessly competitive. University exchange programs have a variety of facilities available to them and organize games and matches with French university teams and sports clubs.

**Listing of Sports Contacts in the Paris Area:**

### Baseball

Baseball Club de France
Tel: 42.50.50.01

### Basketball, etc.

Espace Vit'Halles
48, rue Rambuteau
75003 Paris
Tel: 42.77.21.71
(Saturday mornings at 11 am at nearby gym)

Marché St. Germain
75006 Paris
Tel: 43.29.90.97

### Bowling

Bowling Club de Paris
Jardin d'Acclimatation
Bois de Boulogne
75116 Paris
Tel: 40.67.94.00

Paris Université Club (PUC)
31, av Georges Bernanos
75005 Paris
Tel: 43.26.97.09

Bowling Mouffetard
73, rue Mouffetard
75005 Paris
Tel: 43.31.09.35
(everyday 10h-2h, Fr. and Sat. until 4h)

Bowling de Montparnasse
25, rue du Commandant-Mouchotte
75014 Paris
Tel: 43.21.61.32
(Mon-Fri, 10h-2h. Saturday and Sunday until 4h)

### Boxing

Fédération Française de Boxe de l'Ile de France
Tel: 47.42.82.27

### Cycling

Bicyclub de France
8, place de la Porte de Champerret
75017 Paris
Tel: 47.66.55.92

## Fencing
Ligue d'Escrime de
l'Académie de Paris
Tel: 44.85.34.61

## Football
Fédération Française
de Football Américain
13bis, av Général Gallieni
92000 Nanterre
Tel: 47.29.22.03

## Golf
American Golf
14, rue du Regard
75006 Paris
Tel: 45.49.12.52

## Horseback Riding
Bayard UCPA Centre Equestre
Bois de Vincennes
75012 Paris
Tel: 43.65.46.87

Centre Hippique du Touring Club
Route de la-Muette-à-Neuilly
75016 Paris
Tel: 45.01.20.88

## Ice Skating
Patinoire des Buttes Chaumont
30, rue Edouard-Pailleron
75019 Paris
Tel: 42.39.86.10

Fédération Française des Sports
de Glace
Tel: 40.26.51.38

## Roller Skating
La Main Jaune
rue Caporal Peugeot
75017 Paris
Tel: 47.63.26.47

## Rugby
Fédération Française de Rugby
Tel: 43.42.51.51

American Rugby Company
171, rue St. Martin
75003 Paris

Comité de l'Ile de France de Rugby
Information on amateur clubs
and organizations
Tel: 43.42.51.51

## Soccer
Information
Tel: 47.20.65.40

Stade Olympique de Paris
90, rue Jeanne d'Arc
75013 Paris

## Squash
Stadium Squash Club
66, av d'Ivry
75013 Paris
Tel: 45.85.39.06
(every day 14h-2h)

Squash Quartier Latin
17, rue Pontoise
75005 Paris
Tel: 43.54.82.45

Squash Puc Pontoise
19, rue de Pontoise
75005 Paris
Tel: 43.54.82.45

Squash Rennes Raspail
149, rue de Rennes
75006 Paris
Tel: 45.44.24.35

Sporting Club Loisir
24, rue Richard-Lenoir
75011 Paris
Tel: 43.67.13.98

## Swimming

Note: the famous Seine-side Piscine Deligny was destroyed by fire and sank in 1993!

Piscine Pontoise
19, rue de Pontoise
75005 Paris
Tel: 43.25.52.58

Piscine Buttes-aux-Cailles
5, place Paul-Verlaine
75013 Paris
Tel: 45.89.60.05
(Art-deco pool built in 1910)

Aqualand
91, Gif-sur-Yvette
Tel: 60.12.25.90
(Outdoor pool with waves)

Aqua boulevard
4, rue Louis Armand
75015 Paris
Tel: 40.60.10.00

## Health and Sports Clubs

Over the last several years, there has been a dramatic upsurge of interest in health clubs and fitness centers. Garden Gym is well-adapted for younger people, with seven locations around Paris, while Gymnase Club, with its 15 locations, is the largest and thus a bit more impersonal. A series of discounts are available to company employees, students and others. Currently, Gymnase Club offers a 12 month membership to students at 1400 FF. There are several other alternatives. Most university programs, organizations, and companies have been offered special discounts for their members, employees, or students. Note that the Paris gym club scene can be overcrowded and less than comfortable. The finer touches that often are found at even moderately priced American clubs- abundant, clean towels, hair dryers, private lockers, saunas and steam rooms etc.— are frequently not part of the deal. Check out the club first. One advant-age to these chains is that you can frequent any locations with your membership card. Here are some numbers for inquiries.

Garden Gym Beaugrenelle
208, rue de Vaugirard
75015 Paris *Métro*: Volontaires
Tel: 47.83.99.45
Open Mon-Fri 7h30-9h30, Sat 9h-14h.

Garden Gym Quartier Latin
19, rue Pontoise
75005 Paris
Tel: 43.54.82.45

Garden Gym Elysées
65, av des Champs-Elysées
75008 Paris
Tel: 42.25.87.20
*Métro*: Franklin D. Roosevelt
Open Mon-Fri 9h-22h, Sat. 10h-17h.

Gymnase Club Denfert Rochereau
10, rue Victoire
75009 Paris
Tel: 48.74.58.49

Gymnase Club Denfert Rochereau
28, av du Général Leclerc
Les Portiques d'Orléans
75014 Paris
Tel: 45.42.50.57

Gymnase Club Nation
16, rue des Colonnes du Trône
75012 Paris
Tel: 43.45.93.12

## Parks

Paris has fabulous parks for strolling, sunning and passive recreation. The idea of the park in France differs from its North American equivalent in that Parisian green spaces are aesthetically planned, surveyed, and regulated. Lawns are for looking at, not walking on or sporting picnics. A uniformed guard with a whistle will let you know if you are stepping out of line or using the public space for ball playing or frisbee. Sports are for the *bois*, not the parks. Parks are for strolls, for reflection, reading, lovers' rendezvous, concerts... Paris parks usually close at dusk and are locked. The following are some of the major parks in Paris:

• **Bois de Boulogne:** 16e, *métro*: Porte de Neuilly, Porte Dauphine or Les Sablons. This park has existed as a green wooded space for centuries, and once stood just inside the fortified boundary of Paris. Now it has been transformed into 2000 acres of varied terrain which includes a rose garden, a museum, two world-famous race courses, a small zoo, a polo ground, a "Shakespeare Garden" where all the plants mentioned in the bard's plays can be found and the plays are staged in the summer, two lakes, broad avenues for riding and paths for biking. You can even stay here in the campground. The *Jardin d'acclimatation* has a little zoo, a playground, and a restaurant where you can share your table with the goats and chickens on Wednesdays. Nearby is the *Musée des arts et traditions populaires*. There are boats for hire in the Lac Inférieur, and the Parc de Bagatelle is nearby with its castle, flower garden, and pick-up softball games. At night the park changes character though. Crime and vandalism are not unheard of, and a most interesting variety of outdoor prostitutes and a hybrid of

Brazilian transvestites flourish. Recently, the police have begun an unprecedented crack-down on the prostitution in this park, due to the increased number of AIDS cases.

• **Bois de Vincennes:** 12e, *Métro*: Porte de Charenton or Château de Vincennes. Noted for its Parc Floral, *hippodrome* and stables, this park has two lakes with rowboats for hire, biking and jogging paths, a medieval castle, playing fields, three fine restaurants. and Paris' largest zoo. There is also an annual ecological fair called *Marjolaine*.

• **Jardin des Plantes:** 5e, *Métro*: Jussieu or Gare d'Austerlitz. This lovely park houses a formal garden, a botanical greenhouse, the Natural History Museum, a hidden gazebo and a *ménagerie* (zoo).

• **Jardin du Luxembourg:** 5e, *Métro*: Luxembourg. Located at the edge of the Latin Quarter along the bd St. Michel, this garden/park captures the contrasts of modern Paris, with its joggers, wooden toy sailboats, wrought iron park chairs, *Guignol* (matinee puppet shows), pony rides, tennis courts and *pelouse* (lawn) specially designated for infants. The gardens are formal in the classical French style, with long open vistas and a popular central fountain. On the north side, the Château du Luxembourg, built by Marie de Medicis in 1615 (and which served as German headquarters during the Occupation) now houses the French Senate and a museum of art.

• **Palais Royal:** 1er, *Métro*: Palais-Royal. In the classic but now out-of-print and difficult to find *Nairn's Paris*, Ian Nairn describes the "luminous melancholy" of the elegant home and gardens of the Duc d'Orléans as "surely among the greyest joys in the world."

• **Parc des Buttes-Chaumont:** 19e, *Métro*: Buttes Chaumont. Lesser known to tourists and visitors, but very charming, with two restaurants, exotic trees, and deep ravines.

• **Parc Monceau:** bd de Courcelles, 8e, *Métro* Monceau. One of the loveliest spots in Paris, set amidst exemplary bourgeois apartments. You'll find artificial waterfalls and ponds, glades and romantic statuary in this park. Nearby (63, rue de Monceau) is the Musée Nissim de Camondo, a completely preserved 18th-century mansion.

• **Parc Montsouris:** 14e, *Métro*: Cité Universitaire. Elegant formal park located near the Cité Universitaire, the residential campus for international students in Paris. The unusual temple-like structure, *pavillon du Bey*, that the park was known for, was destroyed by fire. The *cité universitaire* is the closest one will find in Paris to the American style university campus, organized according to national "houses," such as the Fondation des Etats-Unis, Casa de Cuba, Sweden House, etc.

• **Jardin des Tuileries:** 1er, *Métro*: Tuileries. Contains over 20 original Rodin sculptures.

## Children in Paris

Paris is a wonderful city for children. And for adults as well trying to stimulate, entertain, and educate kids in Paris. In fact, children are the best catalyst for adults to learn about and participate in a foreign culture. (There are over 2 million inhabitants of Paris under the age of 18, with about 5 million more visiting each year.) First, you must appreciate the fact that the city is not dangerous. You don't have to clutch your kids in fear as you do in large American cities. The French don't have to print pictures of missing kids on milk cartons, fortunately. Occasionally, there are cases of violence and perversion that make the national news. However, you can feel relatively secure about bringing up children in Paris or visiting the city with your little ones.

Children are more often than not included at dinner parties and are regularly taken to restaurants. Children's menus exist in many, but not most, restaurants and consist of a slice of ham or two strasbourg sausages, *frites*, and an orange juice. Let the kid pick *à la carte!*

Several books exist on experiencing Paris with children, most notably in French, *Découvrir Paris est un jeu d'enfant* (Editions Parigramme), *Le Paris des Tout-Petits* (Editions Annabelle), *Le Guide de l'Enfant à Paris* (MA Editions), and in English, *Kidding Around Paris* (John Muir Publications). Better than those, is a local guide written and published by *Message*, a group of anglophone parents who formed an organization to support bringing up children in Paris. Tel: 39.73.48.61. One expert parent, Bonnie France, has written a book, *Children of Paradise: 100 Fun Things to do with Your Children in and around Paris*, which, although still unpublished, is packed with great ideas. Tel: (203)655-7190 in the US. One American father swears by the Labyrinth play area for kids in the park above Les Halles. It's wildly inventive, physically stimulating, and only 4 FF. Kids up to 12 can enter and exit on the hour only.

The bird market, stamp market and flower market, along with the annual Marjolaine ecology fair are all wonderful activities. For the more adventurous, the *Egouts de Paris* (Paris sewers) (entrance on the Pont d'Alma) and the *Catacombes* make for memorable and interesting visits for children and parents alike.

No Paris apartment/house bans kids and almost none forbids pets.

If you want to take your child fishing there are possibilities but the rules and licensing fees, which depend on the site and the kind of fish you're angling for tend to kill all the excitement of being out in the open air. But you can dangle your rod in the Seine without much hassle.

Childrens clothes in Paris are beautiful and well made but very expensive. Good finds for clothes can be made at the flea markets.

Someone named Madeleine Deny has recently launched an *Agence des enfants* and a catalogue of goods and services for children, called *Si tu veux*. Tel: 42.60.45.42. Some of the best things to do with kids include the *Jardin d'Acclimatation* in the Bois de Boulogne, the Jardin du Luxembourg, which has old-time *manège* (merry-go-rounds) and pony rides, the Parc Floral in the Bois de Vincennes. The theme parks are always a treat, although expensive and time-consuming. Aside from Euro Disney (see section) there is Mirapolis and the very French Parc Astérix about an hour north of the city.

Ménilmontant district is the Paris of *The Red Balloon*, a children's classic. The museums make for superb outings. The Egyptian collection at the Louvre, the sculpture garden at the Rodin Museum and of course the *Musée de l'Homme* and *Musée des Arts africains et océaniens* are all sure bets. One single father discovered after taking his four year old to the Louvre that kids can read hieroglyphics! They're pictograms. Only the educated minds of schooled adults find that ancient form of writing culturally alienating. (See Museum section for Children.)

Wednesday afternoons (14h and 16h) there are the traditional *Guignols* (marionette) shows in many small theaters in the major parks. Bring your kids to these and you'll really feel like you're participating in the Paris you came to discover. And you'll improve your French by learning the esoterica of the infantile world.

The *Cité des Sciences* at La Villette offers an excellent simulated *chantier* (work site) —off-limits for adults— for kids to play and "work" in.

As for schools, the public *crèche* system starts at three months. The system is excellent, the food remarkable —baby food for a toddler might include *purée* of sole, Port Salut cheese, Evian mineral water and *compote* of *Anjou* pears (no wonder the French palette is so refined)—and the pedagogy is highly humane and pychologically sound. Only 4 out of 10 kids find places in the *crèches*; parents almost need to start in motions the *dossier* for enrolment and then try to conceive. Enrolment takes place at the local *crèche* and the *mairie* of your *arrondissement*. Be persistent.

*Ecole maternelle* starts at 3 years old and continues until six when the child moves on to the *école primaire* where little kids have to lug heavy book bags on their backs to and from school. Note: schools are closed on Wednesdays, but many have classes on Saturday mornings.

### Euro Disneyland

On April 12, 1992, compulsively on schedule, Euro Disneyland opened its imported pearly gates in the Marne Valley, 32 kilometers east of Paris, on a land site that is said to be a fifth the size of the capital. In what was one of the largest press campaigns in the history of the world, this fantasy theme park opened to the buzz of rampant media attention, popular conversation and mild debate. One radical French intellectual called Euro Disney a "cultural Chernobyl," which the press also enjoyed and which then Euro Disney Chairman Fitzpatrick dispelled as a disillusioned communist response. Attracted by the wave of 12000 new jobs, a revved up local economy, and the coming of state of the arts technology couched in inoffensive family entertainment, the French-officials and the public had shown much enthusiasm and optimism for the park, despite the high entry prices—up to 290 FF for adults/175 FF for children per day. The northern European market of 400 million potential visitors certainly helped the Euro Disneyland resort go public in the USA a year before the opening date. In days, all shares were gobbled up. Believe it or not, these mega-powerful American fantasy brokers even managed to get the RER commuter train network to extend its A line directly to the site, and re-do its maps, graphics, poster campaign and information brochures in order to instruct Euro Disney visitors. In May 1994, the SNCF opens a TGV train station on the premises to serve Brits who'll be zooming over by rail through the EuroTunnel in a record three hours.

In 1993, EuroDisney announced dreadful financial news, a runaway deficit which sent the stock tumbling and rumours of collapse echoing throughout the world. No one really knew if the park was in the trouble they claimed or if they were crying wolf as part of some larger marketing/financial strategy that would ultimately translate into even greater profits for the company. Part of the growing pains comes from Euro Disney's less attractivenss during the off-seasons and the French reluctance to spend a day at a theme park that doesn't serve wine or beer in its restaurants. Puritan values were never greatly appreciated by the French, especially Parisians. In any case, the organization seems to have pulled out all stops and introduced new features to the park, rendering the experience even more complete. Undeniably, the Disney people are good at what they do, and even the most hostile individual to American commercialism can't help but be impressed by the technology and grandeur of the Disney vision.

The resort so far features a theme park with 35 attractions, 6 hotels, a camp ground, 27-hole golf course, a jazz club and a night time entertainment center with nightclubs, restaurants and shops.

Since opening in 1992, the park has added a dozen new attractions, including *Indiana Jones et le Temple du Péril*, the first looping roller coaster in Disney history. In 1995, the park will take the classic Disney attraction "Space Mountain" a step further into the next century. "Discovery Mountain," as the European version is called, will send visitors through loops, corkscrew turns and even a shower of meteorites —all in the darkness of deep space. If the park offers slices of European, hand-woven Aubusson tapestries, Victorian gas lamps and better cuisine than its American counterparts, the neighboring hotels and *festival Disney* entertainment center are definitely American. *Festival Disney* has a country-western saloon, New York-style deli complete with lox and bagels, 1950s-type diner with waitresses in poodle skirts (without the poodles) and roller skates, a Sports Bar with American beer and snacks, etc.

To complete with Paris hotels, Disney built six hotels on American themes like Manhattan, New England, Santa Fe and the Wild West with corresponding food, decoration, etc. Prices aren't cheap but rooms are for a family of four. Hotel prices change with the seasons and so does park admission—another first in a Disney park. The US parks are so firmly established that admission— and long lines are the same year round. Since it's new and is trying to build its off-season business, Euro Disneyland charges less between September and April, except at peak Christmas time. That's also the best time to try the *Temple du Péril,* Big Thunder Mountain Railroad, Star Tours flight simulator, Peter Pan and other top attractions that generate those awe-inspiring and annoying

lines. The best days to visit are Tuesdays and Thursdays, when French kids are back in school, hairdressers and shop-keepers back in their salons and shops, and nobody is thinking about a long weekend of fun.

Reaching the resort is not as complicated as it may seem (Paris *métro* authorities decided not to name the RER station "Euro Disneyland"). Instead, you have to follow signs on the RER A line for "Marne-la-Vallée/Chessy." Once you've landed there (30-45 minute ride from Paris stations), the park is a two-minute walk away. If you're driving, it's best to follow the "Georges Pompidou Express" road past Bercy and the Gare de Lyon to hook up to the A4 highway. It's about a 45-minute drive to exit 14, "Parc Euro Disneyland."

Since Euro Disney is still adapting to its new home in Europe, it's best to call ahead for the latest opening hours, admission prices, etc. Call 64.74.30.00 for park information, or 49.41.49.41 (or in the USA (407)-W-DISNEY) for hotel information and reservations. For information call Euro Disney at Tel: 64.14.43/00 or 36.15 on your Minitel. Hotel reservations can be made by calling 49.41.49.41 or writing:

**Euro Disneyland:** BP 100
77777 Marne-la-Vallée Cedex 4

# Culinary Paris & Shopping

Eating in France is a ritual that can reach religious proportions. No city in the world has a greater density of eating establishments per square meter than Paris. Nothing of importance happens in France where food, somehow, is not included. Amidst the French adoration of quality-filled form exists another important but unwritten rule: ANYTHING YOU DO AT THE TABLE THAT ENHANCES YOUR ENJOYMENT OF A MEAL IS PERMISSIBLE. Remember if you're motivated by pleasure and aesthetics, you'll never be ill-judged.

For advice and information on everything food-related in Paris, Patricia Wells' *The Food Lover's Guide to Paris* is an excellent resource. It has information on shopping for food, restaurants and cafés, as well as comprehensive restaurant recommendations, including hours of operation, restaurants open on weekends, restaurants open after 23h, restaurants open in August, and restaurants with sidewalk tables or outdoor terraces, as well as cross-listings by price, regional specialties, and location. Her book is a must for frequent restaurant-goers and food lovers.

## Café Culture

Cafés are places where people go to be among friends and acquaintances. They are meeting places, solariums (the French are notorious sun-worshipers) or shelters from bad weather; places to sit, talk, dream, make friends, make out or eat. They are also handy for their telephones and toilets. Café and bar-sitting are an integral part of daily French life. Knowing a little about how cafés function will save you from a lot of surprises. First of all, the large, well-situated cafés on the Champs-Elysées, on the boulevard Saint Germain at

Saint-Germain-des-Prés, at Montparnasse, along all the major boulevards, and in the Latin Quarter are expensive. But remember, you are not paying for your cup of coffee or glass of beer as much as for your right to sit in a pretty spot for as long as you like and talk, read, watch, or daydream. If you're spending 15 FF for an *express* or 20 FF for a *demi* (half a half of a pint of draught beer), think of it as rent for the time and space. You should know that the prices of drinks in cafés depend on whether you're standing at the bar (*comptoir*) or *zinc* (counter bar) or sitting, and then, of course, where you're sitting. Drinks are less expensive if you are served at the bar. The outside terrace is always the most expensive. And then don't forget that the prices of drinks go up after 20h. Also, you can order some drinks at the bar which you cannot order sitting down. A glass of draught lemon soda (*limonade*), the cheapest drink available and very refreshing on warm days, can only be ordered when you're standing at the bar. Otherwise you get the more expensive and overly sweetened bottled lemon soda. No matter where you're sitting or when, the tip is always included. Although not required or even really expected, it is customary to leave the copper-colored coins *(la ferraille)* in your change as a little extra tip. At the counter, you'll be presented with a little plastic dish for payment, which is then flipped over to signify that the barman has collected from you. At the tables, the *serveur* leaves a slip of paper from the cash register indicating what you owe. Usually, you pay at the end of your stay, but sometimes the *serveur* (not to be called *garçon*, even though old guidebooks will still indicate so) will come around to collect as he goes off duty. When you've paid he'll crumple or rip slightly the paper indicating that you've paid. *Chacun son style !*

Cafés are open very early for coffee and *croissants*. One of the more delightful and simple practices is to

---

### Quick Guide to Café Coffee

*café noir, un café (express)*..................classic strong coffee served in a tiny cup
*café noir double* or *double express*............................twice the dose of an *express*
*café au lait* .................................................*express* with mostly steamed milk
*petit crème* ...................................................*express* with steamed milk
*grand crème*.................................................larger version of the *petit crème*
*café noisette*..................................................*express* with a dab of milk.
*café allongé*.................................................*express* with extra hot water,
also called *un café long* or *un café américain*
*café serré*...................................*express* with half the normal amount of water.
Note: Very weak coffee is humorously labelled *jus de chaussettes* (sock juice).

ask for a *tartine*—a buttered stick of *baguette*—to dunk in your coffee. *Très Parisien.*

The most common beverage in a café is obviously *un café* (coffee), and the nuances need enumeration and explanation: when you just want to sit and talk, read, write or pass away the time and you don't want to spend much, order *un café*. Note that although French coffee in cafés is notably stronger and more flavorful than American or British coffee, it is widely understood that the café coffee is not excellent in quality. Go to a *brûlerie* to buy the best quality coffees.

In the daily cycle of most cafés, there are three periods of peak activity: at breakfast time (before 9h30); at lunch (between 12h00 and 14h00); and before dinner at the *heure de l'apéritif (apéro)* (cocktail hour) from about 17h30 to 19h30. It is not unusual to see two different sets of regulars at different times of day, one at breakfast and lunch and the other at the *apéritif* hour. Between the peak periods customers come for a rest from their work, to meet other people or simply to sit alone with their thoughts.

The choice of beverages in a Parisian café is superb. The French make popular drinks by mixing syrups with either Vittel mineral water or milk. Thus, you can order a *Vittel menthe* (or *menthe à l'eau*) or *Vittel grenadine*, or a *lait fraise* or *lait grenadine*. As for beer, you can order *un*

*demi* (8 ounces), *un sérieux* (pint), or *une formidable* (liter). Or a *panaché* (a mixture of draught beer and draught lemon soda), a popular drink in the summer and one that foreigners acquire a taste for after four or five tries. A final twist on the *panaché* is called a *pinochet*, which is a *panaché* with grenadine.

**Popular drinks include**
*thé citron*, tea with lemon
*thé nature*, plain tea
*thé au lait*, tea with milk
*chocolat froid*, chocolate milk
*chocolat chaud*, hot chocolate
*citron pressé*, fresh-squeezed lemon juice (comes with water and sugar)
*orange pressée*, fresh orange juice (comes with water and sugar)
*jus de fruits*, fruit juice

Many cafés will specialize in a certain brand of beer on tap *(pression)*, usually marked clearly on the café's awning.
*un demi, un demi pression*, a quarter liter of draft beer
*un demi Munich*, a quarter liter of German beer
*une bière*, a beer in a bottle.

Wine: You should not judge French wine by what is served in most cafés other than the nouveau Beaujolais when it comes out each fall. Cheap café wine is seldom very good, and the caraffed rosé is often very bad.

Cafés normally serve wines in two sizes of glass, *un ballon* (large) and *un petit* (small). For a more complete discussion see the section on Wine.

---

**Popular wine drinks include**

*un blanc sec* (*petit* or *ballon*), dry white wine

*un kir,* white wine and *crème de cassis*

*un kir clair,* white wine with just a touch of cassis

*un kir royal,* a *kir* with champagne instead of white wine

---

There are a variety of *aperitifs* served in cafés, usually served over ice with a twist of lemon. These drinks are mixed with water and sometimes *sirop de menthe (un perroquet)*. A martini in France is not the dry thing with the olive; it's a brand of vermouth ordered by itself as an *apéritif.* Ice is provided only with certain cocktails, whiskey, Pernod, Pastis, or Ricard, that glorious Mediterranean anise *apéritif* that pours out rich and yellow and goes cloudy when mixed with water. Great on a hot afternoon on a café terrace with Lawrence Durrell's *Justine* in hand. If you prefer bottled water there's Perrier or Badoit on the sparkling side *(eau gazeuse)*, and Vittel and Vichy on the flat side *(plate)*. The only mixed drink served correctly in most cafés seems to be a gin-tonic.

---

**Other drinks include**

*un grog,* hot rum with lemon, water and sugar

*un cognac,* brandy from Cognac

*un armagnac,* brandy from Armagnac

*un calvados (un calva),* apple brandy from Normandy

*une poire Williams,* pear brandy

---

A word on café-restaurants: if the tables are set with cloths, they are reserved for those wishing to dine and should not be taken if you only plan to have a drink, snack or even a small salad. If you mistakenly sit down, you'll be chased off.

## Café Services

Toilets and telephones are always found in cafés—usually downstairs in the *sous-sol,* S/S, or somewhere at the back. If you want to use the rest room of a café without consuming anything, you have the law on your side. But getting away with it can sometimes be another matter. Be somewhat discreet. In chic cafés there might be a toilet attendant that has a plate out for a franc tip. Some toilets require a franc coin, but most don't. Although they are becoming rarer, the old Turkish toilets (hole in the porcelain floor with spots for your feet) are still common. They are a bit hard to get used to but a highly Parisian experience. Just get ready to jump out of the way before you pull the flusher if you want to avoid flooding your feet. Toilet paper is usually available, but not always, and very often a stiff, crinkly kind that is not very comfortable or practical. The telephones in cafés usually take one franc coins for local calls, but some cafés, mostly the smaller or older ones, still have booths with regular phones and the barman has to activate the line for you. You have to ask for a line out for each call *(Est-ce que je peux avoir la ligne, s'il vous plaît?)*. You pay afterwards at the bar, where there is a counter, usually one or two FF per unit. Occasionally, you'll still find the old phones that require a token *(un jeton)* from the bar. These have become almost extinct and are a bit quirky to use. A lot of cafés and restaurants now use a new telephone service, *téléphone bleu*, which costs 1,50 FF or 2 FF per local call.

## Shops/Markets/Foods

Upon arrival, one may be struck by the charming inconveniences of the Parisian shopping system. Although large supermarkets and mall-style complexes have cropped up all over—especially the suburbs—one who has spent time in North America might find French supermarkets both fascinating and annoying. These places tend to be an enigma of grandeur and chaos. Contradictions galore—lots of space with spotty selections, bright aisles and poorly maintained shelves, great slogans and surly or ill-trained service. First and foremost, remember to bring along your own shopping bags, basket or backpack. Only thin and tiny baggies are given away for free. They are practically useless for any major shopping. Stronger ones are available in supermarkets but will cost you at least 2 FF. One must also consider the flow of time, as most businesses close between noon and 14h or between 13h-15h and most small shops and grocery stores are closed on Mondays. One of Paris' greatest resources though is its proliferation of wonderful little shops and street markets. The lack of many large supermarkets *(grandes surfaces)* in convenient Paris locations often means having to frequent these small neighborhood shops, which necessitates organization and a deeper understanding of Paris fare and habits as well as waiting to be served in line after line. Though these circumstances may discourage one at first, taking part in the markets and different shops is a valuable way of enjoying a very basic and material aspect of the culture. The subtle varieties one finds in these shops prove to be intriguing as you'll discover that the merchant *(commerçant)* is an expert in his or her field and can give you all sorts of interesting tips. Going frequently to the same baker or butcher can also be helpful, as merchants are very quick to remember a face. This is one direct way of participating fully in daily Parisian life.

The larger supermarkets tend to feel like open air markets that have been roofed in and stocked with army sized quantities. The largest chains are Codec, Monoprix, Prisunic, Franprix, Inno, Continent, Carrefour, Casino, Mammouth, Uniprix, and Felix Potin. And Ed, the cut-rate bargain brand chain. Everybody has his or her favorite and least favorite, but many shoppers agree that the Monoprix seems to have a more progressive attitude towards service, quality, and variety. During their annual, two-week American special you can stock up on salsa and chips, Paul Newman salad dressing, and Budweiser in cans and bottles. The French prefer the cans because it ties into the myth of the macho truck driver on the open road. Back to supermarkets, often the food section is upstairs or in the basement of a department store. In French supermarkets don't expect much service. There are no baggers and your tender goods can get smashed as you scramble to bag them yourself as they pile up at the end of the mat and the check out person rushes you to pay up so he or she can move on to the next person. Don't try to make a special request in the meat section; there is no meat manager, nor will the produce manager mark down the bunch of bruised bananas that you've located. A typical response to your question "Where can I find spaghetti sauce? might be "I don't know" or "We don't carry it." Don't be surprised if a store clerk doesn't try to find what you're looking for or that no one is mopping up the splattered jar of pickles. No one ushers you to your car, and the shopping carts are rigged up to a system whereby you feed a ten franc coin into a locking mechanism to release it. You get the coin back when you return it and re-lock it onto the others. The internal organization of food and products may be disorienting to you at first. The grocery sections often flow directly into housewear, hardware, clothing, and garden centers in the really large stores. If your image of Parisian grocery shopping has been riveted to the quaint cheese shop followed by the beautiful bounty of the *pâtisserie*, you should treat yourself to a hectic visit to a massive supermarket in the *banlieue* (suburbs) to fully appreciate the daily or weekly habits of the *Français moyens* (middle class), where industrial *croissants* are purchased in cellophane packs of 15. Recently, Haägen Daz has carved out a place for itself in these stores.

### Les commerçants
(little shopkeepers)

There is, obviously, a wide range of shops in each Parisian neighborhood and the differences are sometimes very subtle, especially when food is concerned. This explains the chain of names one often sees on the awnings of shops. For example, a *boulangerie-pâtisserie-confiserie* will have bread, pastries, and fine candies.

### BOULANGERIES

Most *boulangeries* sell prepared sandwiches, mini pizzas, quiches, onion tarts and *croque-monsieurs* (the classic French common food available at all hours in all cafés, consisting of two slices of buttered toast, a slice of ham with grilled cheese on top—the *croque-madame* is the same thing topped with a sunny-side up egg) on the streets for about 15 to 20 FF. They'll microwave food for you upon request.

Note: you will often hear customers asking for their bread *"bien cuit"* (well done and crusty), *"pas trop cuit"* or *"bien tendre"* (less baked and doughier). You can also ask for *"une baguette coupée en deux"* (a *baguette* cut in half). This facilitates transportation and prevents the bread from breaking en route. All of your requests, whether they be at the bakery, the cheese shop or the hardware store, should of course be accompanied by a smile and followed by *"s'il vous plaît"* two things that will go a long way towards making any transaction simpler and easier. Also, get accustomed to carrying your bread in your hand, bag, or under your arm. Bread is seldom wrapped or bagged. Sometimes, in the more bourgeois boulangeries, your *baguette* will come with a square

of tissue paper wrapped around the center where you are to grasp the bread. If you ask for a second square of paper you'll probably get a strange look if not an outright *non*. Don't worry, though, in four centuries there are no documented cases of anyone getting sick from unprotected bread.

It's annoying, but that's the way it is—if you ask for your bread sliced on the slicing machine, expect to pay an additional franc or two. Don't even bother complaining.

It'll take some time before you become agile with all the nuances in the French *boulangerie*. The bread alone will stun you in its variety. The *baguette* is probably the best deal in France. The following are a few main items:

*Baguette*: (flour, water, yeast and salt), weight (250 grams) and price (3,80 FF) are all government regulated and nationally uniform in weight and price, although you'll get to know the good ones from the great ones.

*Demi-baguette*: half a *baguette*, around 1,90 FF.

*Bâtard*: same weight as a *baguette*, but shorter and less elegant, made from the squatty end of the rolled out dough.

*Pain*: a big *baguette* (400 grams).

*Pain au levain*: sour dough bread. Usually found in health food or specialty stores and relatively expensive. Sold by weight. Delicious with fresh butter and wonderful with *pâté* or *rillettes*.

**Boule**: round loaf, either small or large.

**Chapeau**: small round loaf topped with a *chapeau* (hat).

**Couronne**: ring-shaped *baguette*.

**Fer à cheval**: horseshoe-shaped *baguette*.

**Ficelle**: thin, crusty *baguette* of about 125 grams.

**Fougasse**: a flat, rectangular-shaped bread made of *baguette* dough filled with onions, herbs, spices or anchovies.

**Miche**: large, round country-style loaf.

**Pain de campagne**: a white bread dusted with flour, giving it a rustic look (and a higher price) or a hearty loaf that may be a blend of white, whole wheat and rye flour with added bran. Also called *baguette à l'ancienne* or *baguette paysanne*. It comes in every shape, from a small, round individual roll to a large family loaf.

**Pain complet**: bread made partially or entirely from whole wheat flour.

**Pain fantaisie**: "fantasy bread"—any imaginatively shaped bread.

**Pain de mie**: a rectangular, white, eggy and crusty sandwich loaf used for toast.

**Pain aux noix** and **pain aux noisettes**: unsweetened rye or wheat bread filled with walnuts or hazelnuts.

**Pain aux raisins**: rye or wheat bread filled with raisins, not to be confused with the sweet bun version.

**Pain de seigle**: closest thing to pumpernickel bread in a *boulangerie*. Two-thirds rye and one third wheat flour.

**Pain au son**: a dietetic bread that is "quality-controlled," containing bran flour.

**Pain viennois**: milk and sugar are added to the *baguette* dough for a finer texture.

**Pain brioché**: a rich dough made with milk, eggs and sugar. *Brioche* comes in all sizes and a variety of shapes. Proportionately expensive, but a real delight for those lazy mornings. Great to dunk in *café au lait*.

After bread, the most common items in the *boulangerie* include the following:

**Croissant ordinaire**: these are the crescent shaped puff pastry rolls now found all over the world. When the points are curled towards the center, this is the legal indication that the *croissant* has been made with margarine and has not been glazed with butter before baking. Price is always about 50 centimes less than the *croissant au beurre*. An interesting historical aside—*croissants* were first made by French chefs in transit for the rulers of the Ottoman Empire; the shape is after the Turkish crescent in the Ottoman flag.

**Croissant au beurre**: These *croissants* have their tips pointing straight out, signifying their pure butter content. Richer and definitely worth the extra half a franc.

**Pain au chocolat**: a rectangular flaky pastry filled with a strip of chocolate.

If you are lucky enough to catch a batch coming out of the oven, the chocolate will still be warm and soft—a favorite after-school snack for youngsters.

*Pain aux raisins*: a round, spiral-shaped croissant cooked with raisins and a light, egg cream.

*Croissant aux amandes*: topped with slivered almonds and filled with a rich almond butter paste.

*Chausson aux pommes:* a turnover with applesauce inside.

As for individual *gâteaux*, most *boulangeries* that are also *pâtisseries* offer:

*Millefeuilles* (Napoleon): puffed pastry with pastry cream.

*Eclair*: *chou* pastry filled with chocolate or coffee cream.

*Religieuse*: same as *éclair* but shaped like a nun's hat.

*Tartelette aux fruits*: small fruit tarts.

*Croissants* are usually purchased in the morning, cakes in the afternoon or evenings. *Boulangeries* also sell *bonbons*(candy) by the piece to kids, as well as soft drinks and bottled water that are cool but never really cold. It's nearly impossible to get a napkin. Not all *boulangeries* are open on Mondays so expect lines for bread on that day. Also, if you wait too long on Sundays by midday it might get a bit tough to find bread. Most *boulangeries* sell out their bread every day. Some *boulangeries* freeze unsold *baguettes* and re-bake them later at a slight compromise of taste and texture. You can detect this by the pattern of cracks on the sides of the *baguette* crust. Don't make a scene, just change *boulangerie*.

BOUCHERIES

The Parisian butcher shop has a fine array of its own idiosyncrasies. First of all, most butcher shops sell pork, beef, mutton, lamb, veal, liver and some sausages, pâtés, poultry, rabbit and game. Specialized poultry like turkeys, pheasant, pigeons and cornish hen should be bought in a *marchand de volaille*, your neighborhood poultry shop. If you see a butcher's shop with nice photos of thoroughbreds on its walls, get the message. Here is where horse meat is sold. Horse is reputed to be the finest meat on the market. Try some. You can buy steaks, roasts, hamburger meat, etc. at your local *Chevaline* shop. They're usually decked out with a gold horse's head over the shop door.

The cuts of meat are particular to France. Steaks are not pre-cut, nor is chopped meat previously packaged. If you're used to thick steaks you have to ask for one *très épais*. French meat is very tasty but on the whole not as tender as US beef. Less hormones though! The superior cuts of beef—*côte de bœuf, entrecôte, filet mignon*—are expensive. Pork, though, is excellent and relatively cheap. As are certain cuts of lamb and mutton. Don't be alarmed by scrawny slabs of lean red meat hanging above bellowed cutting boards on nasty aluminum hooks. The blood-stained butchers cut steaks out of these hanging slabs as they go. Fresher. Chopped steak for *tartare* should be purchased just before eating. Supermarkets have meat departments but there is no bell to ring to call for the butcher. You can't make special requests. If you want your steak thicker go to a butcher shop.

## A Word on Chicken

The French have a complex under-standing of chicken and its nuances. First, the understanding of the species in French culture is far more specific than in the Anglo-Saxon world. One French traveler who recently flew on the New York-Paris TWA flight was rather amused when the meal arrived. The stewardess asked him "Meat or fish?" "What kind of fish?" he replied, upon which she looked at him like he was a Martian. "Fish fish." Didn't they know in America that salmon is not sole! he wondered. Well, with chicken the distinctions are even finer; a *poulet*, exclusively male, is a grown-up *coquelet* that becomes either a *chapon* or a *coq*, depending if he is spared his male-ness. A *poularde*, on the other hand, the female, is an adult *poulette* that has never met up with a *coq*. Had she, though, she'd not be a *poularde* but a *poule!*
On the whole, French chicken is superior to US and UK chicken. You can tell by the color, the smell, the skin ("*chair de poule*"), and the taste. In France, there is a big distinction made between *poulet fermier* and normal *poulet* or *poulet industriel*. *Poulet fermier*, though, can mean two things: either the bird is a *poulet plein air*, which means he has spent his life in a two square meter coupe and has been fed grain and milk, or he is a *poulet liberté*, the highest quality chicken, and was able to freely run, although fed the same grain and milk. Yellower chickens are corn fed, while whiter chickens are wheat fed. It's doubtful if you'll ever need to know this, but in France the law sti-pulates that a chicken must be at least 81 days old before being killed. The label of *poulet fermier* will indi-cate the age.
(See lexicon on the following page).

## EPICERIES

Literally "spice shops," these are simply grocery stores that sell a little bit of everything. In most quartiers there are independent grocers as well as one or several chains, the old standby being Felix Potin, an institu-tion in Parisian grocery shopping. In recent years, Codec, which has numerous large supermarkets, has taken over many *épiceries*. The ones owned and operated by North Afric-ans usually stay open late—often until midnight in some of the out-lying neighborhoods. This is conve-nient (but quite expensive) for fin-ding munchies and beverages late at night.

## Lexicon

*bœuf* ............................beef
*bavette* ....................tender steak
*bifteck* .................ordinary thin steak
*bourguignon* .............cubed beef stew
*châteaubriand*........porterhouse steak
*faux-filet* ...............................sirloin
*entrecôte*...............................rib steak
*steak haché* .....................ground beef
*rosbif*...............................roast beef
*tartare*............................ground beef
   with zero percent fat
*tournedos*..............filet wrapped in fat

*mouton/agneau*............**mutton/lamb**
*brochette* ...........................skewered
*carré* ....................................roast rack
*côte* ..............................................chops
*épaule*...............................shoulder
*gigot*...............................leg of lamb
*noisette*...............................choice loin
*selle*..............................................saddle

*porc*....................................**pork**
*andouillette* .........(pork) belly sausage
*boudin noir* .................blood sausage
*jambon* .........................................ham
*épaule*................less-expensive ham,
   comes from shoulder
*jarret*...........................pork knuckle
*pied*...............................................foot
*rôti*............................................roast
*travers* ...................................spare ribs

*veau* ....................................**veal**
*blanquette* ....................stewing meat
*escalope* ....................................cutlet
*paupiette*.................rolled and stuffed
*ris de veau* .....................sweetbreads

*triperie*..............................tripe
*cervelle*...............................brain
*coeur*..............................................heart
*foie de génisse*.........young cow's liver
*gésier*...............................gizzard
*langue*...............................tongue
*rognons* ...............................kidneys
   (note: not to be confused
   with *reins*—human kidneys)

*gibier* ..............................**wild game**
*lapin* ...............................rabbit
*lièvre* ...............................wild hare
*marcassin*...............................baby boar
*sanglier* ...............................adult boar

*volailles*..............................**poultry**
*poulet* ...............................chicken
*coq*...............................................rooster
*coquelet* .....................young rooster
*poule*..............................................hen
*cuisse* ...............................thigh
*suprême* ...............................breast
*dinde* ...............................turkey
*dindonneau*...............young turkey
*caille* ...............................quail
*canard*...............................duck
*magret de canard*.........breast of duck
*oie*...............................................goose
*pintade* ...........................guinea hen
*pigeon* ...............................pigeon

## CHARCUTERIES

These are France's delis. The assortment of sliced meats, fish, sea-food in aspic, *saumon fumé*, avocados with crabmeat, *pâtés*, salads, fancy vegetables and prepared dishes like *brandade de morue, hachis parmentier, choucroute* and more are always a savory delight. These stores tend to be expensive but highly pleasurable. They offer a whole gamut of dishes guaranteeing instant culinary success when entertaining or when you want to treat yourself to something tasty and beautiful. When buying cold cuts, order by the number of slices, indicating if you want them *fine* (thin). When buying *pâtés* and *terrines*, you indicate the quantity by where the clerk places the knife. To avoid buying more than you want, state, *"un peu moins que ça, s'il vous plaît"*. Cold cuts are often pre-cut and servers don't like cutting additional, fresher and thinner slices. Insist.

## POISSONNERIES

The variety of fish available in Paris is remarkable. The French eat a lot more fish per capita than North Americans or Brits. After a number of visits to your local *poissonnerie* you'll learn the names of the fish and decide which ones you like best and which are the best buys. Whole fish are cleaned and scaled by the fishmonger at your request for no extra charge; crab and shrimp often come precooked. Sprigs of fresh parsley are given away too if the customer requests such, especially with the purchase of mussels, which are a particularly French and extremely reasonable meal. Purchase one liter per person. You can scrub the shells quickly and dump the shiny black mussels into a big pot of chopped shallots and garlic with a tad of cayenne pepper; dump in a half a bottle of cheap white wine and steam the mussels until they open. Toss in some chopped parsley at the end and serve. Don't eat the ones that don't open. Drink white wine with the dish and mop up the briny wine and shallot broth with hunks of *baguette*. Two people can have a great time for about 30 FF. Lobster is prohibitively expensive, especially the *langouste* sort which comes in from the *Antilles*. Small, frozen Canadian lobsters are available in good supermarkets at very reasonable prices. Smoked salmon is abundant and excellent. To avoid the very high prices, you can opt for the less expensive sea trout, which resembles salmon in color, texture, and taste. *Saumon fumé*, smoked salmon, is very popular, eaten on blinis and with *crème fraîche*. Avoid buying fish in supermarkets on Mondays. (See Lexicon.)

## Lexicon

| | |
|---|---|
| *fruits de mer* | seafood |
| *coquilles St. Jacques* | scallops |
| *crabe* | crab |
| *tourteau* | rock crab |
| *crustacé* | shellfish |
| *crevette* | shrimp |
| *langoustine* | sea crayfish |
| *homard* | lobster |
| *huîtres* | oysters |
| *langouste* | spiny lobster |
| *moules* | mussels |
| *praires* | venus clams |
| *oursin* | sea urchin |
| *bigorneaux* | periwinkle |
| *bulots* | whelk |
| *coques* | cockle |
| *poisson* | fish |
| *anchois* | anchovy |
| *bar* | bass |
| *barbue* | brill |
| *cabillaud* | cod |
| *morue* | dried salt cod |
| *congre* | eel |
| *calamar* | squid |
| *haddock* | smoked haddock |
| *éperlan* | smelt |
| *hareng* | herring |
| *lotte* | monkfish |
| *merlan* | whiting |
| *raie* | skate |
| *rouget* | mullet |
| *sole* | sole |
| *saumon* | salmon |
| *thon* | tuna |
| *truite* | trout |

## CREMERIES/FROMAGERIES

Winston Churchill is reported to have once said: "How can anyone govern a country with so many different cheeses?" Some people put the current cheese count at more than 400. The pungent cheese shops offer a wonderful sampling that you should take advantage of. A few things you should learn to appreciate during your *séjour* in France include *chèvre* (goat cheese), especially the fresh (*frais*) ones that are covered in *cendres* (ash). *Fromageries* also sell fresh butter, cut off of huge mountains in chunks, *fromage blanc* (white cheese that falls between sour cream and smooth cottage cheese), *crème fraîche* (a wonderfully rich, slightly sour cream that is used generously in sauces and on deserts), and fresh milk. In France, you'll find whole and skim milk also in vacuum packed cartons that need not be refrigerated and can last for many months unopened. This milk is labelled *longue conservation* or *stérilisé* and permits you to stock up all at once. Eggs, only brown ones, too are bought in the *crèmerie* in packages of six or by the unit. French "Swiss" cheese is *emmenthal*. Swiss cheese from Switzerland is *gruyère*.

| | |
|---|---|
| *fromage* | cheese |
| *mimolette* | cheddar |
| *fromage frais* | cream cheese |
| *chèvre* | goat cheese |
| *râpé* | grated |

*Gruyère, Emmenthal,* ..Swiss cheese
*lait* ...............................milk
*lait fermenté léger*...........buttermilk
*lait frais*...........................fresh milk
*homogénisé*................homogenized
*demi-écrémé*................low-fat milk
*lait écrémé*.......................skim milk
*lait stérilisé longue conservation* .......
                          sterilized milk
*lait entier*......................whole milk
*yaourt* ...............................yogurt
*maigre*..............................no fat
*nature* .................................plain
*nature sucré*.........plain but sugared
*aux fruits*........................with fruit

### A NOTE ON QUALITY CHOCOLATE

A friend from California related a story which says a lot about the differing concepts of quality in her country and in France. She set out to make a simple chocolate sauce for a dessert after returning home from a period of time spent in France. It was then that she discovered that Hershey Bars don't melt, they bubble and crack like plastic. The cocoa content is less than three percent. The cheapest supermarket brand chocolate in France has at least 20% cocoa and often contains between 40 and 50%. And the chocolate bought in specialty shops can contain as much as 80%! The more cocoa, the higher quality the chocolate—unlike ice cream, where more fat content equals higher quality. So, quality, on the whole, is higher and, with it,

importantly, come a new set of expectations that will change you for life. Your taste buds just might re-awaken. After a year or so in Europe it's doubtful, for example, that you'll be able to chomp on North American chocolate, guzzle the formerly favorite Milwaukee beer, or savor bagged and doughy sandwich bread. Some particularly good *chocolateries*:

### La Maison du Chocolat
225, rue du Faubourg St Honoré, 75008 Paris Tel: 42.27.39.44
56, rue Pierre Charron, 75008 Paris Tel: 47.23.38.25

### Lenôtre
44, rue du Bac, 75007 Paris
Tel: 42.22.39.39
49, av Victor Hugo, 75016 Paris
Tel: 45.01.71.71

### A la Marquise de Sévigné
32, place de la Madeleine, 75008 Paris
Tel: 42 65 19 47

For the *crème de la crème* of fine sweets and specialty items, a tour of the famous and pricey Fauchon at Place de la Madeleine is a must although the effect has been spoiled a bit by the introduction of banal American products that seem exotic in France. This has been a trend over the last few years, the marketing of North American groceries in France, ranging from nacho chips and salsa to supermarket salad dressing. Even

Oceanspray fresh cranberries are now available in Paris in November. More and more shops specializing in the importation of American and Tex-Mex food items have glutted the Parisian scene. And the outcrops of corresponding restaurants has continued to flourish since the late 80s.

## Food markets

Paris offers three kinds of food markets: the permanent street markets, the moving open air markets and the indoor markets. In all of these markets, unless you are encouraged to do so, you should not touch the produce which is carefully displayed for everyone's enjoyment. You should, however, feel free to specify exactly what you want and to banter freely with the often flamboyant merchants. It's not a bad idea to count your change.

The street markets are open Tuesday through Saturday from 9h00 to 12h30 or 13h00 and normally close for the rest of the day. On Sundays they are open from 9h00-13h00.

•Rue des Belles Feuilles: Begins av Victor Hugo, 16e. *Métro*: Victor Hugo.
•Rue Cler: Begins av de la Motte-Picquet, 7e. *Métro*: Ecole Militaire.
•Rue Lévis: Begins bd des Batignoles, 17e. *Métro*: Villiers.
•Rue Montorgueil: Begins rue Rambuteau, 1e. *Métro*: Les Halles. Les Halles was formally Paris' central marketplace.

•Rue Mouffetard: Begins rue de l'Epée-de-Bois, 5e. *Métro*: Monge. One of the oldest and most animated markets in Paris.
•Rue Poncelet: Begins av des Ternes, 17e. *Métro*: Ternes. Exceptional fruit.
•Rue du Poteau: Begins place Jules Joffrin, 18e. *Métro*: Jules-Joffrin.
•Rue de Seine/rue de Buci: Begins bd St. Germain, 6e. *Métro*: Odéon.

The moving markets move from neighborhood to neighborhood, making their appearance on fixed days. They often include clothing and other articles as well as food. These are open from 7h00 to 13h30.
•Alésia: Rue d'Alésia, 14e. *Métro*: Alésia. Wednesday and Saturday.
•Alibert: Rue Alibert and rue Claude-Vellefaux, 10e. *Métro*: Goncourt. Thursday and Sunday.
•Amiral-Bruix: bd Bruix, between rue Weber and rue Marbeau, 16e. *Métro*: Porte Maillot. Wednesday and Saturday.
•Auteuil: Between rue d'Auteuil, rue Donizetti, and rue La Fontaine, 16e. *Métro*: Michel-Ange-Auteuil. Wednesday and Saturday.
•Avenue de Versailles: Rue Gros and rue La Fontaine, 16e. *Métro*: Jasmin. Tuesday and Friday. av du Président Wilson, between rue Debrousee and place d'Iéna, 16e. *Métro*: Alma-Marceau. Wednesday and Saturday.
•Belgrand: Rue Belgrand, rue de la Chine and place de la Puy, 20e. *Métro*: Gambetta. Wednesday and Saturday.

•Belleville: On the island of bd de Belleville, 11e. *Métro*: Belleville. Tuesday and Friday.

•Bercy: bd de Reuilly, between rue de Charenton and place Félix-Eboué, 12e. *Métro*: Daumesnil. Tuesday and Friday.

•Berthier: Angle of av de la Porte d'Asnière and bd Berthier, 17e. *Métro*: Porte de Clichy. Wednesday and Saturday.

•Bobillot: Rue Bobillot, between place Rungis and rue de la Colonie, 13e. *Métro*: Maison Blanche. Tuesday and Friday.

•Breteuil: av de Saxe and av de Ségur, toward place Bréteuil, 7e. *Métro*: Ségur. Thursday and Saturday.

•Boulevard Brune: Between passage des Suisses and 49, bd Brune, 14e. *Métro*: Porte de Vanves. Thursday and Sunday.

•Boulevard de Charonne: Between rue de Charonne and rue Alexandre-Dumas, 11e. *Métro*: Alexandre-Dumas. Wednesday and Saturday.

•Carmes: Place Maubert, 5e. *Métro*: Maubert-Mutualité. Tuesday, Thursday and Saturday.

•Cervantes: Rue Bargue, 15e. *Métro*: Volontaires. Wednesday and Saturday.

•Cité Berryer: Begins rue Royale in the passage of the Cité Berryer, 8e. *Métro*: Madeleine. Tuesday and Friday.

•Clignancourt: bd d'Ornano, between rue du Mont-Cenis and rue Ordener, 18e. *Métro*: Ordener. Tuesday, Friday, and Sunday.

•Convention: Rue de la Convention, between rue Alain-Chartier and rue de l'Abbé-Groult, 15e. *Métro*: Convention. Tuesday, Thursday, Saturday.

•Cours de Vincennes: Between bd de Picpus and av du Dr. Arnorld Netter, 12e. *Métro*: Porte de Vincennes. Wednesday and Saturday.

•Crimée: 430, bd Ney, 18e. *Métro*: Porte de Clignancourt. Wednesday and Saturday.

•Davout: bd Davout, between av de la Porte de Montreuil and 94, bd Davout, 20e. *Métro*: Porte de Montreuil. Tuesday and Friday.

•Duplex: bd de Grenelle, between rue Lourmel and rue du Commerce, 15e. *Métro*: Duplex. Wednesday and Sunday.

•Edgar-Quinet: On the island of bd Edgar-Quinet, 14th. *Métro*: Raspail. Wednesday and Saturday.

•Exelmans: Along place de la Porte-Molitor, beginning av du Général-Sarrail toward bd Exelmans, 16e. *Métro*: Michel-Ange-Auteuil. Tuesday and Friday.

•Gobelins: bd August-Blanqui, between place d'Italie and rue Barrault, 13e. *Métro*: Corvisart. Tuesday, Friday, and Sunday.

•Javel: Rue St. Charles, between rue Javel and Rond-Point-St.-Charles, 15e. *Métro*: Charles-Michel. Tuesday and Friday.

•Jean-Jaurès: 145-185, avenue Jean-Jaurès, 19e. *Métro*: Pantin. Tuesday, Thursday and Sunday.

•Joinville: At the angle of rue de

Joinville and rue Jomard, 19e. *Métro*: Crimée. Tuesday, Thursday, Sunday.

•Lariboisière: bd de la Chapelle, across from Lariboisière hospital, 18e. *Métro*: Barbès-Rochechouart. Wednesday and Saturday.

•Lecourbe: rue Lecourbe, between rue Vasco-de-Gama and rue Leblanc, 15e. *Métro*: Place Balard. Wednesday and Saturday.

•Ledru-Rollin: Avenue Ledru-Rollin, between rue de Lyon and rue de Bercy, 12e. *Métro*: Gare de Lyon. Thursday and Saturday.

•Lefèbvre: bd Lefèbvre, between rue Olivier-de-Serres and rue de Dantzig, 15e. *Métro*: Porte de Versailles. Wednesday and Saturday.

•Maison Blanche: Avenue d'Italie and rue Bourgon, 13e. *Métro*: Porte d'Italie. Thursday and Sunday.

•Monge: Place Monge, 5e. *Métro*: Monge. Wednesday, Friday and Sunday.

•Montrouge: Along ruc Brézin, rue Saillard, rue Mouton-Duvernet and rue Boulard, 14e. *Métro*: Mouton-Duvernet. Tuesday and Friday.

•Mortier: bd Mortier, at av de la porte de Ménilmontant, 20e. *Métro*: St.-Fargeau. Wednesday and Saturday.

•Navier: Among rue Navier, rue Lantier and rue des Epinettes, 17e. *Métro*: Guy-Moquet. Tuesday and Friday.

•Ney: bd Ney, between rue Jean-Varenne and rue Camille-Flammarion, 18e. *Métro*: Porte de Clignancourt. Thursday and Sunday.

•Ordener: Between rue Montcalm and rue Championnet, 18e. *Métro*: Guy-Moquet. Wednesday, Sunday.

•Père-Lachaise: bd de Ménilmontant, between rue des Panoyaux and rue de Tlemcen, 11e. *Métro*: Père-Lachaise. Tuesday and Friday.

•Place des Fêtes: Place des Fêtes, alongside rue Pré-St.-Gervais, rue Petitot and rue des Fêtes, 19e. *Métro*: Place des Fêtes. Tuesday, Friday and Sunday.

•Popincourt: bd Richard-Lenoir, between rue Oberkampf and rue de Crussol, 11e. *Métro*: Oberkampf. Tuesday and Friday.

•Poniatowski: bd Poniatowski, between av Daumesnil and rue de Picpus, 12e. *Métro*: Porte Dorée. Thursday and Sunday.

•Point du Jour: av de Versailles, between rue Le Marois and rue Gudin, 16e. *Métro*: Porte-de-St.-Cloud. Tuesday, Thursday and Sunday.

•Porte Brunet: av de la porte Brunet, between bd Sérurier and bd d'Algérie, 19e. *Métro*: Danube. Wednesday and Saturday.

•Port-Royal: bd Port-Royal, alongside Hôpital du Val-de-Grâce, 5e. *Métro*: Port-Royal. Tuesday, Thursday and Saturday.

•Pyrénées: Rue des Pyrénées, between rue de l'Ermitage and rue de Ménilmontant, 20e. *Métro*: Ménilmontant. Thursday and Sunday.

•Raspail: bd Raspail, between rue du Cherche-Midi and rue de Rennes, 6e. *Métro*: St.-Placide. Tuesday and Friday.

•Réunion: Place de la Réunion, between the place and rue Vitruve, 20e. *Métro*: Alexandre-Dumas. Thursday and Sunday.
•Richard-Lenoir: bd Richard-Lenoir and rue Amelot, 11e. *Métro*: Bastille. Thursday and Sunday.
•Saint-Eloi: 36-38, rue de Reuilly, 12e. *Métro*: Reuilly-Diderot. Thursday and Sunday.
•Salpétrière: Place de la Salpétrière, alongside bd de l'Hôpital, 13e. *Métro*: St.-Marcel. Tuesday, Friday.
•Télégraphe: Rue du Télégraphe, to the right of Belleville cemetery, 20e. *Métro*: Télégraphe. Wednesday and Saturday.
•Tolbiac: Place Jeanne-d'Arc, 13e. *Métro*: Nationale. Thursday and Sunday.
•Villemain: av Villemain, on the island between av Villemain and rue d'Alésia, 15e. *Métro*: Plaisance. Wednesday and Sunday.
•Villette: 27-41, bd de la Villette, 19e. *Métro*: Belleville. Wednesday and Saturday.

The covered markets are generally open Tuesday through Saturday, from 8h00-13h00 and 16h00-18h30, and on Sunday from 9h00-13h00. Little has changed since the turn of the century in many of these markets.
•Batignolles: 96, rue Lemercier, 17e. *Métro*: Brochant.
•Beauvau-Saint-Antoine: Between rue d'Aligre and rue Cotte, 12e. *Métro*: Ledru-Rollin.

•Chapelle: Rue de l'Olive, 18e. *Métro*: Max-Dormoy. Open until midnight on Friday and Saturday.
•Enfants Rouges: 39, rue de Bretagne, 3e. *Métro*: Filles-du-Calvaire.
•Europe: Rue Corvetto, between rue Maleville and rue Treihard, 8e. *Métro*: Villiers.
•Passy: Angle of rue Bois-le-Vent and rue Duban, 16e. *Métro*: La Muette.
•Porte Saint-Martin: 31 and 33, rue du Château-d'Eau, 10e. *Métro*: St.-Martin.
•Riquet: 36-46, rue Riquet, 18e. *Métro*: Riquet. Open until 8:00 p.m. on Friday and Saturday.
•Saint-Didier: Angle of rue Mesnil and rue St.-Didier, 16e. *Métro*: Victor-Hugo.
•Saint Germain: Among rue Lobineau, rue Clément and rue Mabillon, 6e. *Métro*: Mabillon.
•Saint-Honoré: Place du Marché-St.-Honoré, 1e. *Métro*: Tuileries.
•Saint-Quentin: 85 bis, bd de Magenta, 10e. *Métro*: Gare-de-l'Est.
•Secrétan: 46, rue Bouret, and 33, av Secrétan, 19e. *Métro*: Bolivar.
•Ternes: Rue Lebon, rue Faraday and rue Torricelli, 17e. *Métro*: Ternes.

### Les marchés biologiques (Organic Markets)
These are the equivalent of old-fashioned country farmer's markets. From thirty to fifty independent organic farmers set up stalls on the weekends in Boulogne and Joinville (Parisian suburbs easily reachable by RER). They sell organically grown

fruits and vegetables; homemade breads; dried fruits and nuts; *charcuterie*; farm-raised chicken, ducks and geese; and natural wine. There are stands selling things like freshly made pizzas, whole-wheat breads, apple or pear cider, a huge variety of artisanal goat cheeses, sausages, beer, and dried flowers. Go early in the day for a good selection.

•Marché Boulogne: 140, Route de la Reine, 92 Boulogne-sur-Seine. *Métro*: Boulogne-Pont de Saint-Cloud, or via the No. 72 bus. Open 8h00-16h00 the first and third Saturdays of each month.

•Marché Joinville-le-Pont: Place Mozart, 94 Joinville. *Métro*: RER Line B to Joinville, then via the suburban No. 106 and 108N buses. Open 8h30-13h00 the second and fourth Saturdays of each month.

•Marché Sceaux-Robinson, rue des Mouille-Boeuf. *Métro*: RER Line B to Robinson. Every Sunday, 8h30-13h00.

## Restaurants

There is no reason for not eating well in Paris. However, learning how to eat very well, with good value, maximum *ambiance* (atmosphere) and exciting variety is an art. It has become increasingly easy to pay a lot for *pas grand-chose*. And in Paris it's not certain that you'll be impressed by the service offered in inexpensive or moderately priced eateries. The better news is that, to meet the recession, top Michelin Star chefs are opening less expensive bistros which make high quality food and service avaible to more people, for example, Jacques Cagna's *Rôtisserie d'en face*, 2, rue Christine, 75006 Paris, Tel: 43.26.40.98; and Guy Savoy's *La Butte Chaillot*, 112 av Kléber, 75016 Paris, Tel: 47.27.88.88. The trend in three-star restaurants these days is towards homestyle bistro classics (*pot-au-feu,* etc.). And remember that it's gauche to order a double Chivas before a great dinner—it numbs the tastebuds. Order a *coupe de Champagne*, currently the fashionable cocktail. The fact that in 1993, 21 top champagne producers signed a protocol to lower prices to *restaurateurs* explains it all.

Restaurants are run by a *patron* or *patronne* who on the whole regards his/her position more as one of host than business person. As in all human interactions in France, a smile and a polite *bonsoir monsieur/madame*, lots of *s'il vous plaît* and *merci bien* during service as well as an *au revoir monsieur/madame, merci* upon leaving will serve you well in getting friendly service and recognition when you return. The quick meal is not really understood so don't get too impatient if service is too slow for you to catch your 21h30 movie. Next time, eat earlier or see a late film. It's hard to rush service in Parisian restaurants. And waitresses and waiters don't work for tips. 15%

is always included. *Service compris* means that 15% is built into the prices. *Service non compris* means the 15% will be automatically added to the bill. Don't tip on top of the tip, other than a few coins you leave in the dish as a token of your pleasure.

First, a word about the strictness of eating hours. As of about 11h30 or noon most restaurants have their tables set for the onrush of lunchers. In Paris, 13h is the start of the lunch rush hour. Generally, you must be seated for lunch no later than 14h p.m. if you want to eat anything greater than a sandwich or a *salade composée* (mixed salad), 14h30 p.m. at the extreme if you're lucky. In the provinces, lunch is served between 12h30-13h. At 14h you could beg and plead and offer your first born child and still be refused a hot meal. Between 15h-18h it's pretty much impossible to have a sit-down meal. An early dinner would be at 19h; a normal time to dine would be between 20h-21h. But later than 21h30 is getting dangerous again (21h in the provinces). At 23h it's too late, except in pizzerias, couscousseries, some brasseries and bistros, and some American style restaurants in Paris. There are exceptions of course as noted in Patricia Well's book. And as the New Yorkization of Paris deepens in the Nineties several 24-hour establishments have cropped up.

The typical French meal—from simple to elaborate—is graceful and balanced: an opening course, a main dish, cheese, a dessert and coffee. And of course, wine. Most people ask for a pitcher of tap water *(une carafe d'eau, s'il vous plaît)* with their meal. This is highly expected. No real need to order a bottle of mineral water unless you prefer it; Paris city water is perfectly fine. Don't expect ice cubes though—very little ice is consumed in France. It's hard, if not impossible, to purchase cubes by the bag. The French are not in the habit of drinking their beverages at extreme temperatures. When something is very cold or very hot, the French will tell you, the flavor is less prominent. And flavor is more important, *n'est-ce pas?* They're right. Flavor and quality come before superficial exterior appearances. French people are often disappointed by American-style supermarket fruits and vegetables; the huge, colorful, waxed objects are visually pleasing but the intensity of flavor is often *fade* (bland). So, to get back to the point, don't expect ice with your water. Paris' culinary diversity and the keen attention Parisians give to food should contribute to the richness of your experience. There are about 30 guidebooks on Paris in which eating establishments are featured. Here are a few operating principles when selecting a restaurant, followed by a few of *Paris Inside Out's* favorites.

• In general, don't plan on eating in a large café on a major boulevard. You'll pay a lot of money for quickly prepared, average food and rapid, not particularly careful service. Here, slapped together salads at high prices is standard fare. If you're caught between hours and you're famished, use the café for a quick *croque-monsieur* (an open ham sandwich with grilled cheese on top) or an *oeuf dur* (hard-boiled egg with salt) for less than 5 FF at the counter. Otherwise, cafés are for coffee, drinks, passing time, meeting people, etc.

• Distinguish yourself from the unknowing tourist. Running shoes, guide books, cameras, and loud voices are give-aways. Attempting to recompose a fixed menu is not only revealing, it's taboo. As for ketchup, learn to settle for mustard.

• Read the menu posted outside before entering. It's uncool in Paris to be seated and then change your mind.

• Be prepared in advance to be squeezed into tight tables and booths. Paris restaurants can be densely packed, but privacy is respected. Don't get too annoyed if in a half-empty restaurant your expressed preference for a larger table is refused. If you're a party of two you will not be given a table for four. Non-smoking sections, despite a law passed in 1993, are often nonexistent although more and more Parisians are beginning to realize that some people don't like smoke.

• *Steack tartare* is raw, but delicious. *Carpaccio*, thinly sliced, cured beef, is also raw. It's very uncool to order these unknowingly, be repulsed, and

then try to send it back. Sending something back signifies that there is something very wrong with the dish.

• If the food (or service) is absolutely horrible, don't eat—and leave. Have an iron stomach or head for the door. If you eat half, forget it; there will be no recourse, no refund, no apologies, no free meal your next time back.

• Avoid the Champs-Elysées area unless someone else is paying. And even then suggest somewhere else.

## Le Menu

The lunch or dinner composed daily by the owner or chef of a restaurant is called *le menu* (don't get confused between the words *menu* and *carte*; the French *carte* is the English menu, and menu is a complete and prescribed meal, often the best bargain and the most promptly served). In simple restaurants there is often just one *menu*; otherwise there are often two or three packages to choose from, each a bit more complex or complete and expensive than the former. You can still find little restaurants with *menus* under 50 FF but these are getting rare. Some couscous restaurants or Chinese or Vietnamese restaurants have menus at 40 FF. These are generally in the less *chi-chi* neighborhoods, but a number still linger in the Latin Quarter.

The hot dish of the day is called *le plat du jour* and may very well consist of roast veal and a heap of braised Brussels sprouts, or a thin steak and some French fries, or salted pork with lentils.

In a restaurant, if you try to order something *à la carte* that breaks the rhythm or balance of the meal, you may find that the agreeableness of the service is reduced. This will be true if you try to order two appetizers (called *entrées*, because they are your entry into the meal)—or want to share a dessert or compose anything else that is original, personal or outside of the way that things are usually done. So beware.

When ordering red meat, remember that the French *cuisson* (cooking degrees)—*saignant* (rare), *à point*, (medium rare), and *bien cuit* (medium well)—tend to run rarer than you're used to. The French medium is the North American medium-rare on the rare side. So either compensate accordingly or let the chips fly and you may find that you've been really eating meat overcooked for years. In some restaurants frequented by tourists, waiters, exasperated at sent-back steaks, automatically compensate for Anglo-Saxon preferences. If there truly is a problem with your food, don't eat it. If you eat some of it, it may be difficult to get the waiter not to charge you. The art of public relations has not really made it yet into the average French eatery. A waiter or *maître d'hôtel* may end up arguing with you that your *magret de canard* is fine when you contend that it's inedible.

Stay cool and polite, but hold your ground and don't eat half before complaining. Many small restaurants do have ketchup, but they're certainly not obliged to provide it. The French use mustard in a rather expansive way. And the French mustard is so flavorful you should try a dab or two if you're not in the habit. Note: the cheaper Dijon mustard (that comes in jars that can be used as glasses when the mustard has been finished) tends to be wickedly strong.

## French Regional Restaurants

*Alsace*
**Chez Jenny**
39 bd du Temple
75003 Paris
Tel: 42.74.75.75
Open daily until 1:00 a.m.
Sauerkraut, sausage and beer.

*Auvergne*
**Ambassade d'Auvergne**
22, rue du Grenier St. Lazare
75003 Paris
Tel: 42.72.31.22
Open daily for lunch and dinner.
Hearty specialties from central France.

*Pays Basque*
**Auberge Etchegorry**
41 rue Croulebarbe
75013 Paris
Tel: 44.08.83.51
Closed Sunday. Dinner only. Basque

paëlla and savory *piperade* omelettes topped with Bayonne ham.

*Normandie*
**Chez Fernand/Les Fernandises**
17-19, rue de la Fontaine-au-Roi
75011 Paris
Tel: 43.57.46.25 / 48.06.16.96
Closed Sunday and Monday. Lots of cream and butter; don't miss the home-cured camemberts.

*Provence*
**Campagne et Provence**
25 quai de la Tournelle
75005 Paris
Tel: 43.54.05.17
Closed Sunday and for lunch on Monday and Saturday. Reasonably-priced southern bistro food from Chef Gilles Epié who runs the fancier Miraville restaurant across the river.

---

## Good Value

**Chartier**
7, rue du Faubourg Montmartre
75009 Paris
Tel: 47.70.86.29
This is a late 19th century gem that, despite its abundant tourist crowd, has preserved its authenticity. Extremely casual, inexpensive and lively. You're often seated with strangers, share baskets of bread and conversation. A large menu of typical, everyday French home-style dishes. Notice the little wooden drawers in the

walls, these were for the linen napkins of the "regular" customers. Waiters, often feisty and entertaining, tally up the bill from memory on the paper tablecloths. Get there before 21h. Crowded but worth doing from time to time.

**Le Drouot**
103, rue Richelieu
75002 Paris
Tel: 42.96.68.23
Owned by same people as Chartier. Same concept although a bit less picturesque—but also less tourists. Good idea for lunch.

**Café du Commerce**
51, rue du Commerce
75015 Paris
Tel: 45.75.03.27
Another restaurant in the Chartier style. Open every day. Newly renovated and highly promoted. When in the 15th, an excellent choice.

**Polidor**
41, rue Monsieur le Prince
75006 Paris
Tel: 43.26.95.34
Very reasonable prices, *cuisine traditionnelle*, "*vieux Paris*" ambiance.

**Le Petit Saint Benoît**
4, rue St. Benoît
75006 Paris
Tel: 42.60.27.92
Also very *vieux Paris. Cuisine traditionnelle* (*hachis parmentier, cassoulet,* etc.). Sartre and Simone de Beauvoir

were customers; Marguerite Duras dines here occasionally.

**Chez Julien**
16, rue du Faubourg St. Denis
75010 Paris
Tel: 47.70.12.06
Pleasantly fashionable, an in-spot in a tacky part of town. Plan on spending a bit more. Ornate decor. Don't miss the *profiterolles* for dessert.

**Roger la Grenouille**
26, rue des Grands Augustins
75006 Paris
Tel: 43.26.10.55
Great spot for fun-loving bawdiness with style, excellent French provincial cooking, served up with popular casualness. *Coq au vin* and *canard à l'orange* stand out. So do the not-so-timid waitresses. Good house wine. Order the designed-to-be-embarrassing *dessert spécial* for those highly puritanical friends.

**Le Gamin de Paris**
51, rue Vieille du Temple
75004 Paris
Tel: 42.78.97.24
This Marais restaurant has captured fine food, soulful atmosphere, and a sinful chocolate mud pie. Ask for Sammie, the manager; he knows how to lay on that special extra touch. Closed Fridays.

**Le Trumilou**
84, quai de l'Hôtel de Ville
75004 Paris

Tel: 42.77.63.98
Situated on the quay near Hôtel de Ville, this unassuming *resto* serves highly reliable and tasty traditional dishes at fair prices. The duck with prunes is always wonderful.

**Le Procope**
13, rue de l'Ancienne Comédie
75006 Paris
Tel: 43.26.99.20
Believed to be the oldest restaurant in Paris. A popular meeting place for both politicians and intellectuals during the French Revolution. Le Procope was remodeled on the occasion of the Bicentennial.

**Chez Papa**
3, rue St. Benoît
75006 Paris
Tel: 42.86.99.63
Traditional French cuisine served in a cosy, chatty atmosphere.

## A Note on Weight

At first you may think you've come to a country where being overweight is against the law, where fatness is a mortal sin. You may wonder how it is that in a country with such a passion for food, everyone seems underfed. You may find yourself perplexed to see so many vices being committed with impunity. You may ask yourself how, with so much sugar being consumed, the population can be so uniformly *mince* (thin). It is true that much of what one associates with classical French food is the rich sauce, the buttery and sweet bakery delights. But these do not constitute the average diet—they are special treats. Quality is important, and as in every aspect of French life, so is moderation.

A second reason for the relatively petite waistlines of the French comes from the fact that Parisians are obliged to be rather active in their daily routines. There is less reliance on cars, more steps to climb, more stops on the shopping circuit, and fewer hours spent mindlessly glued to televisions. The emphasis on form also contributes; meal times are adhered to rather strictly, compared to the haphazard snack times, missed meals and dinners in front of the TV or over work. One must remember also that in France, personal style and the public self is taken seriously. The French don't like going out if they don't look great. One's physical appearance is thus very important. Lastly, over the past few years a whole new generation of lower calorie prepared dishes with "light" or *allégé* on the packaging has appeared in Parisian supermarkets.

---

## American Food

One obviously doesn't come to Paris to eat burgers, pizza, and Tex-Mex. Well, Paris is getting more and more of this, some good, and some highly derivative and worthless. However, for those nostalgic moments when you're *croque-monsieur*ed to death, and tripe doesn't fit the bill, you'll be reassured to know that there are over 50 Anglo/American/Tex-Mex/etc. style restaurants now in Paris. The number keeps growing as North American entrepreneurs and their local clones keep opening up new ones. Pizza Hut is here in a big way, having invested heavily in promoting the name and conditioning the public. They sort of absorbed the smaller French version, Spizza 30. Dominos is battling for a larger part of the Paris market share and is about to open up scores of new locations. You see, Parisians eat record amounts of pizza. (See Pizza below). Häagen Daz has revolutionized the ice cream scene, becoming ubiquitous, imposing itself on the French and larger European market by investing huge amounts to reeducate the public that ice cream can be eaten year round, and that American ice cream is superior to the commercial French brands. The local, Bertillon ice cream on the Ile Saint Louis, though, is by far the best tasting ice cream in the city, but the portions are microscopic and there are no calorie-packed toppings. Without much difficulty you can find ribs to root beer, chile to cookies, although a few cultural culinary icons such as bagels, and the bottomless cup of coffee are still rare. A few stand-by American joints include: Joe Allen,

Cactus Charly, Café Pacifico, Chicago Pizza Pie Factory, Harry's New York Bar, Marshall's, Rio Grande, Sam Kearny's, Hollywood Canteen, and The Studio. Check the local give-aways for even more. Although the cuisine here is pretty much authentic, these places tend to fill up with a certain type of trend-seeking French clientele that emulates the look of "the American way of life." They also tend to be on the expensive side and haven't all quite captured the spirit of the huge American portion.

For commercial peanut butter, crumpets, corn meal, or brownie mix, try the General Store and The Real McCoy, both in the 7th, and Marks & Spencer, 6-8 rue des Mathurins, 75009 Paris, just across from Galeries Lafayette. Also, the American specialty shop Thanksgiving sells great pecan pie. Here are a few reliable culinary leads with dishes reminiscent of home, maybe.

**Susan's Place**
51, rue des Ecoles
75005 Paris
Tel: 43.54.23.22
Tex-Mex cuisine, excellent carrot cake.

**Chez Marianne**
2, rue des Hospitalières St. Gervais
75004 Paris
Tel: 42.72.18.86
Great pickles, corn beef, cheese cake, etc. Friendly atmosphere in the midst of the Jewish sector on rue des Rosiers in the Marais.

**Hard Rock Café**
14, bd Montmartre
75009 Paris
Tel: 42.46.10.00

**Hayne's**
3, rue Clauzel
75009 Paris
Tel: 48.78.40.63
Original soul food-since the 50s.

**Le Studio**
41, rue du Temple
75004 Paris
Tel: 42.74.10.38
Tex-Mex restaurant. Brunch Saturdays and Sundays. Service until 12:00 a.m.

**Le Texan**
3, rue St Philippe du Roule
75008 Paris
Tel: 42.25.09.88

**Slice Pizza**
62, rue Monsieur Le Prince
75006 Paris
Tel: 43.54.18.18
New York style pizza by the slice. Home delivery.

**Randy's Rib Joint**
14, rue Thouin
75005 Paris
Tel: 43.26.37.09
Barbecued ribs and chicken. As good as you find in Paris.

**Spizza 30'**
Tel: 43.44.91.11
Free delivery of American style pizza.
Based on the Domino theory.

**Natural's**
15, rue du Grenier-Saint-Lazare
75003 Paris
Tel: 48.87.09.49
Macrobiotic take-away.

**Cactus Charly**
68, rue Ponthieu
75008 Paris
Tel: 45.62.01.77

**Pizza Hut**
Toll Free Info Number
Home delivery in 30 minutes
05.30.30.30

**Domino's Pizza**
*Numéro unique* automatically routes
calls to nearest store: 36.67.21.21.

---

## International Cuisine

Paris is an international crossroads for
cuisines from all corners of the world.
Kurdish to Korean. One could
almost trace the colonial history of
France in the restaurants of its capital, from North Africa to Vietnam to
the Caribbean (*Les Antilles*) to black
Africa to the Middle East. For the
purchase of exotic and esoteric foods
and goods from the Third World and
politically correct collectives, try one
of Bertrand Tellier's: *Artisans du*

*Monde*, 20 rue du Rochechouart,
75009 Paris, Tel: 48.78.55.54

*Lebanese*
Currently one of the best international cuisines in Paris comes from Lebanon. With the political upheaval and
economic instability in Lebanon,
there has been a veritable exodus of
Lebanese wealth from Beirut and
subsequent investment in Paris.
Lebanese business people have preferred to invest substantially in Paris
knowing at least that their capital is
protected against run-away inflation
and the risk of violence and terror.
Lebanese restaurants in Paris tend to
be both elegant and casual at the
same time and the quality, quantity
and prices are all rather favorable.

Marrouche
32, bd Saint Michel
75006 Paris
Tel: 46.33.28.33

*Chinese*
Paris has hundreds of Chinese restaurants, a number of which can be a
good deal for days when your wallet
is thin. Many, especially in the Latin
Quarter, can be extremely reasonable
if you order the menu. On the
whole, the best and most authentic
Chinese food in Paris is concentrated
in Paris' two Chinatowns: the 13th
*arrondissement* between the Place
d'Italie and Porte de Choisy, and
Belleville in the northeast part of the
city, formerly dominated by North

Africans or *Maghrebins*. Many Chinese restaurants in the city, ironically, are run by Vietnamese. The result is a mixed bag of Vietnamese, Chinese and Thai influences, overpowered by the tastes and demands of the French palate. Go to the 13th or Belleville for the real thing. There are too many to list.

### Japanese
The Japanese have recently been investing heavily in France, from 18th century *châteaux* to Paris real estate, especially in the area around Opéra (rue Ste. Anne), which has become a kind of "Japanese quarter" with many Japanese restaurants and luxury boutiques. Lots of new restaurants around the Opéra as well as in the St. Germain area.

**Higuma**
32, rue Ste. Anne
75001 Paris
Tel: 47.03.38.59
Very authentic kitchen-style restaurant with excellent *gyoza*.

### Spanish
If you're looking for Spanish food here are a few suggestions:
**L'Auberge Espagnole**
1, rue Mouffetard
75005 Paris
Tel: 43.25.31.96
Closed Monday noon. Service until 12:00 a.m.
**Don Quixote**
10, rue Rochambeau

75009 Paris
Tel: 48.78.01.80. Closed Sunday. Service until 11:30 p.m.
**Roberto**
8, rue des Tournelles
75004 Paris
Tel: 42.77.48.37
Closed Sunday noon.

### Greek
The Latin Quarter is noted for its Greek restaurants complete with extravagant window displays of brochettes of seafood, stuffed eggplant and suckling pig. Also complete with aggressively affable male hosts beckoning the tourists. Most of these places serve reasonably priced, sometimes good food. Fun to do once in a while.

### North African
There are hundreds of North African restaurants specializing in couscous. The Berber chain is good but a bit more expensive than others.
**Oum El Banine**
16bis, rue Dufrénoy
75016 Paris
Tel: 45.04.91.22
Closed Saturday lunch and Sunday. Subtle and sophisticated north-african haute cuisine.

### Belgian
**Léon de Bruxelles**
82 bis, bd. du Montparnatsse
75014 Paris
Tel: 43.21.66.62.
Fun and reasonable meal of mussels and *frites*. Check for other locations.

*Russian*

Russian cuisine, which is often vodka-assisted, makes for a very satisfying change from the humdrum of daily food. Paris hosts a number of excellent, although a bit pricey, Russian eateries in the great tradition of Russian intellectual presence in Paris. Tolstoi lived on the rue de Rivoli for awhile. Parisians have come to love blinis with smoked salmon and *crème fraîche.*

**Le Komarov**
10, rue Saint-Lazare
75009 Paris
Tel: 48.78.51.09
Serves superb vodkas. Organizes memorable musical evenings in its cave; the owner is friends with the famed *Tzigane* pop group, Bratsch.

**Karlov**
197, rue de Grenelle
75007 Paris
Tel: 45.51.29.21
Dinner only. Blinis, bortsch, *shashlik,* romantic decor, and live gypsy music.

*Central European/Ashkenaze Jewish*

**Jo Goldenberg**
7, rue des Rosiers
75004 Paris
Tel: 48.87.20.16
Open until midnight. Noisy and boisterous; great chopped liver and pastrami. They have a second location on the avenue de Wagram in the 17th, but rue des Rosiers is the real thing.

**Chez Marianne**
2, rue des Hospitalières St. Gervais
75004 Paris
Tel: 42.72.18.86
Excellent falafels, and assortment of meats, smoked fish, salads, and pickles (Marianne's Tunisian mother-in-law's recipe).

*Italian*

**La Castafiore**
51, rue Saint-Louis-en-l'Ile
75004 Paris
Tel: 43.54.78.62
Open daily. Great pasta and veal in candlelit restaurant created by a British/US team of ex-ad agency execs.

*Mexican*

**Ay Caramba**
59, rue de la Mouzzaïa
75019 Paris
Tel: 42.41.23.80
Delightfully out of the way in the 19th, this cantina-style resto is sprawling and lively with a regulars and real Mexican music.

*Scandinavian*

**Flor Danica**
142, av des Champs-Elysées
75008 Paris
Tel: 44.13.86.26
Open daily for lunch and dinner.

*Brazilian*

**Guy**
6, rue Mabillon
75006 Paris
Tel: 43.54.87.61

Closed Sunday. Saturday lunch special: *feijoada* (black beans) with all the trimmings.

*Vegetarian*
The choice for vegetarians in Paris is limited, but new restaurants seem to appear every week as health consciousness becomes more *à la mode*.
**Banani (Indian Restaurant)**
148, rue de la Croix Nivert
75015 Paris
Tel: 48.28.73.92
Closed Sunday. Service until 11:00 p.m. Indian food, wide variety of curries.
**Bol en Bois**
35, rue Pascal
75013 Paris
Tel: 47.07.27.24
Closed Sunday. Service until 10:00 p.m. Natural and macrobiotic specialities, with bookstore and *épicerie*.
**Naturesto**
66, av des Champs-Elysées
Galerie Point Show
75008 Paris
Tel: 45.56.49.01
Closed Sunday. Service until 5:00 p.m. Specialty: fresh fruit and vegetable juices.
**Rayons de Santé**
8, place Charles Dublin
75018 Paris
Tel: 42.59.64.81
Closed Friday evening and Saturday.
**Country Life**
6, rue Daunou
75002 Paris
Tel: 42.97.48.51

## Resto-U

Students can eat at student restaurants called Resto-U, managed by the CROUS *(Centre régional des œuvres universitaires scolaires de Paris)*. Tel: 40.51.37.13. Food plentiful and cheap. Tickets available in each establishment.

*Assas*, 92 rue d'Assas, 75006.
M° Notre Dame des Champs.
*C.H.U. Bichat*, 16 rue Henri Huchard, 75018.
M° Porte de Saint Ouen.
*Bullier*, 39 av Georges Bernanos, 75005. M° Port Royal
*Censier*, 31 rue Geoffroy Saint Hilaire, 75005. M° Censier Daubenton.
*Châtelet*, 10 rue Jean Calvin, 75005.
M° Censier Daubenton.
*Citeaux*, 45 bd Diderot, 75012.
M° Gare de Lyon.
*Clignancourt*, rue Francis de Croisset, 75018. M° Porte de Clignancourt.
*Cuvier-Jussieu*, 8bis rue Cuvier, 75005. M° Jussieu
*Dareau*, 13-17 rue Dareau, 75014.
M° Saint Jacques.
*Dauphine*, av de Pologne, 75016.
M° Porte Dauphine.
*Grand Palais*, cours de la Reine, 75008. M° Champs-Elysées
*I.U.T.*, 143 av de Versailles, 75016.
M° Chardon Lagache.
*Mabillon*, 3 rue Mabillon, 75006.
M° Mabillon.
*Mazet*, 5 rue Mazet, 75006. M° Odéon
*CHU Pitié*, 105 bd de l'Hôpital.

## Fast Food

Fast food, which is anything but truly fast, has unfortunately overrun the Paris cityscape in the last five years, especially McDonalds but also Burger King, along with their French competition. Quick, which has recently bought out Free Time, has impressive franchises along the high-rent Champs-Elysées. French business people, office workers, student and kids flock to these meccas of American hamburger prestige, and at lunchtime it's often nearly impossible to get into one of these places, especially on Wednesdays, when there is no school, and school children line up for their "Happy Meal." The golden arches decor often suffers a transatlantic water change. Two great examples of marketing kitsch: McDonalds-Sorbonne (with fake bookshelves filled with fake editions of classic literature); and McDonalds-Versailles (glossy beige marble walls). McDonalds has flourished wildly in Paris and even has cornered a share of real prestige, after a rocky period in the Seventies when the king of burgers pulled out of France due to the shoddy standards of local franchises.

*Les sandwiches* are commonplace in Paris as more and more Parisians give up the Latin tradition for long meals in favor of the pursuit of more healthful and individual pleasures or simply to save time. Sandwiches usually consist of a third of a *baguette* with either butter and ham, *pâté, gruyère* (really French emmenthal; the real *gruyère*, which has less holes, comes from Switzerland and is twice the price), *camembert*, or *rillettes*, a flavorful but fatty paste made from duck, pork or goose-delicious with those crispy and vinegary *cornichons* (pickles). In a café, a sandwich will cost you between 15 FF and 20 FF, depending on where you are. Again, careful about asking for variations. One student once asked for a piece of lettuce on a ham sandwich and was charged double. "*Mais Monsieur, vous avez commandé un sandwich fantaisie,*" he was told. When you see signs for *Poilâne* bread, take advantage of the occasion. This coarse sour dough bread is both a tradition and delicacy in French culinary life.

When the weather is fine, or at least not too gray and sad (*triste)* as Paris can often be, you can always buy some bread, cheese, *charcuterie* (deli goods), etc. and sit in one of the parks (see Parks)—but not on the grass as the grass is off-limits (*"pelouse interdite"*). Or you may want to sit down by the Seine. In the fifth *arrondissement*, it's very pleasant to duck into the Arènes de Lutèce, an uncovered Roman amphitheater that is hidden behind a row of apartment houses on the rue Monge just below the Place Monge. In the seventh *arrondissement*, the Champ de Mars, the open space below the Eiffel Tower, is lovely. Other options-the Luxembourg Gardens, the Bois de

Vincennes, the Bois de Boulogne, the elegant Parc Monceau, or wherever there is a likely-looking bench.

You will see people in restaurants, cafés, and even McDonalds, paying for their food with coupons called *tickets-restaurants* or *chèques-déjeuner*. These are like money—usually between 35 FF and 50 FF each—that employers offer their personnel at half price as an additional benefit. They're cumulative. Establishments that accept them have stickers on their windows.

### A Word on pizza *à la française*

Parisians eat pizza often for lunch and dinner in Italian-style restaurants. Pizzas in France have been designed for one, meaning you never share a pizza in pizza restaurants. Additionally, Parisians don't eat pizza, or anything else for that matter, with their hands. Pizzas do not come sliced in eight wedges as Americans are accustomed to. Instead of adding hot peppers, you'll be presented with an oily bottle of olive oil with hot peppers swimming at the bottom. Yes, you sprinkle on this oil to spice up your pizza, most of the time making the pizza more oily than hot. Your choice of toppings in Paris pizzerias are almost always the same and they have been pre-selected for you and named. The basic pizza is called a *Marguerite*, which consists of cheese and tomato, and maybe a few black olives. Other stand-by varieties standardly found include:

*Quatre saisons*, which has four toppings, ham, mushrooms, cheese, anchovy; *Reine* has ham and mushroom. Others include capers, four-cheeses, merguez sausage, and even an egg. Asking for substitutions will confuse most waiters, but try if you like, and always ask for extra cheese. Pizza, until the arrival of Pizza Hut, has not had the social, junk-eating quality to it that surrounds American campus life. Although now there has been an explosion of home delivery services, Parisians still are not accustomed to eating slices out of a box with their fingers. After a pizza in a restaurant you're pretty much expected to have a dessert and coffee. No one just eats a pizza and splits.

## Typical Dishes and Special Foods

The following is a sampling of specialties commonly found in France.

*Bouillabaisse*: a Mediterranean-style fish stew with tomatoes, saffron, mussels, shellfish and the catch of the day. Each version is different than the last one, depending on the whim of the creator. Good ones are becoming hard to find. Two other regional variations of seafood soup: *Bourrida* and *Chaudrée*.

*Cassoulet*: A casserole of white navy beans, shallots and a variety of meats such as pork, lamb, sausage, and goose or duck, originating in the southwest region of France. Beans and meat are alternated in a casserole—sometimes topped with bread crumbs—then baked until crusty. Perfect for the winter.

*Couscous:* Specialty of North Africa originally brought to France by colonialists. A hearty blend of mutton, chicken and a spicy beef sausage (*merguez*) in a light stock with boiled zucchini, carrots, onions, turnips and chick peas. It is spooned over a fine semolina-like base, called couscous, from which the dish gets its name. A hot, red paste called *harissa* can be stirred into the broth.

*Fondue:* A Swiss Alps specialty popular in France, especially in the ski regions. There are two types: *bourguignon* beef-small chunks of beef cooked on long forks in pots of hot oil and accompanied by a variety of sauces; and *Savoyard* cheese-melted and flavored with kirsch or white wine, lapped up with chunks of stale French bread on long forks.

*Raclette:* Also a mountain cheese dish consisting of raking melted cheese onto baked potatoes, pickles, and ham. Cheese is melted at the table and served on tiny plates.

*Farce:* Spiced ground meat, usually pork, used for stuffing cabbage (*chou farci*), green pepper (*poivron vert farci*), or tomatoes (*tomates farcies*).

*Hachis Parmentier:* Mashed potatoes and ground meat topped with a *bechamel,* or white sauce, served in a casserole.

*Moussaka:* A Greek casserole dish combining slices of eggplant, tomatoes, and ground lamb, baked with a bechamel topping.

*Paëlla:* A Portuguese and Spanish dish with a rice base, saffron, pimento, chicken, pork and shellfish, cooked in a special two handled metal pan.

*Choucroute:* Of Alsatian origin, this dish is often served in brasseries as it is a good accompaniment to a strong draft beer. It consists of sauerkraut topped with a variety of sausages, cuts of pork, ham and boiled potatoes.

*Pot-au-feu:* Boiled meat and marrow bone with vegetables in a broth.

### Cooking Schools

One of the great clichés of Paris is *Le Cordon Bleu.* In fact, the school continues to be a leader in the culinary arts, offering four *diplômes,* the most ambitious being *Le grand diplôme Cordon Bleu.* With La Varenne no longer in business in Paris, *Le Cordon Bleu* is at center stage. 8 rue Léon Delhomme 75015 Paris. Tel: 48.56.06.06. Also check the Ritz's Escoffier School, 15, pl. Vendôme, 75001 Paris. Tel: 42.60.38.30.

## Wine

*No insider's guide to French life would be complete without some special commentary on wine and its place in daily life. The following section was prepared by long time residents of Paris and wine lovers and collectors, Petie and Don Kladstrup.*

Nearly the first act of King Louis XI, upon subduing the obstreperous Duchy of Burgundy and dragging it back into France, was to confiscate the entire 1477 vintage of Volnay wine. It must have been a good year. Since then, wine in France has become even more important, and no one can hope to understand or participate in the life and culture of France without knowing something about it. Happily, it is not necessary to be an expert to be an *amateur* (lover) of wine because everybody in France seems to drink wine, from the toddler at Grandma's for Sunday lunch to the Grandmas and Grandpas themselves. Almost all dinners include a glass or two, and even many lunches are accompanied by wine. However, as the pace of French life quickens to keep pace with the rest of the world, fewer and fewer working people have either the time or the desire for a two-hour lunch with all the trimmings. Those who do include a glass of wine frequently "baptise the wine" (literally, *baptiser le vin*) by adding some water to it. Heresy, of course, for serious wine-lovers and a mortal sin if the wine is anything but a *vin de table* (table wine).

It is probably the prevalence of wine that made the idea of a weekend bash of drinking parties almost non-existent in France. The difference between young people's attitudes toward drinking in the US and in France was summed up by one US college student who had been raised in France. "In France," he said, "my friends and I used to go out on Saturday night to have a good time and occasionally somebody got drunk. Here in the US, everybody seems to go out to get drunk, and occasionally somebody has a good time.

With a legal drinking age of 16, but with enforcement so rare as to be non-existent, it is almost never an issue. Small children run down to the neighborhood grocery store for the dinner wine, bars have no I.D. checks. Of course, the driving age in France is 18, and in the Paris area with public transport of some sort available around the clock, many of the real concerns about drinking and driving are eliminated.

So, like nearly everything else in France, wine has become an art form and an economic force. France produces nearly half of the wine made in Europe, and because of the high quality—and higher prices—French wine accounts for approximately three-quarters of the money generated by European wine sales.

The French, of course, drink almost exclusively French wine, but the wine makers do worry about the impact of lowered trade barriers in the European Union. Those with the most cause for worry are the makers of the medium-range of quality, because in that area, Italy, Spain and Portugal can put up a mighty competition with lower prices. The makers of the famous wines from Bordeaux and Burgundy and Champagne need only worry about having bank accounts that accept all currencies!

Figuring out French wines can seem intimidating, but in reality, it is much easier that trying to decipher the wines of most other countries. That is because the French wines are regionals, that is, named for the region in which they are produced. Almost every other country uses varietal names, so that you have to master the names of grape varieties before you can order. Horrible when you discover that the Pinot Noir (black pinot grape) can make a white wine, and that there is a Cabernet Sauvignon, a Sauvignon Blanc and a Cabernet franc grape, and they all make different kinds of wine. Isn't it nice to know that Champagne is just Champagne no matter what grape they make it with? And while Burgundy wines can be either red or white, they stay Burgundy. The same is true for all the wine regions of France-Bordeaux, Alsace, the Loire, Provence, the Rhone Valley. If you know those names, you are already on your way and can make the big connection of brain to palate with tasting and trying the different regions' selections.

Now, while wine does not have to be expensive to be good, it is unfortunately true that most good wines are priced more highly than poor ones. Unfortunately true, as well, is the fact that France makes a lot of bad wine, and if a bottle costs under 20 FF, you are almost assured that it won't be very good. That doesn't mean that it may not be enjoyable in certain circumstances, like an impromptu picnic or for washing down a pizza, just don't serve it at a dinner party or bring it as a gift to one.

Wine seems to absorb and enhance its setting, so get some advice from your local wine merchant or a knowledgeable friend before presenting a host or hostess with an accidental bottle of "plonk." In fact, don't take wine at all if you don't know your host or hostess very well. Instead, send flowers with a nice note of thanks the morning after the party. If you are the host, don't be afraid to consult wine merchants before buying your dinner party wine, and as wine is the only acceptable dinner party drink aside from water in France, be ready to serve some to your guests.

Decide what food you are serving before you select the wine and be prepared to tell your wine merchant the details. Don't be surprised to have him or her ask you how you are preparing the chicken you said you were going to serve. And don't be timid about your budget. If you can only spend 20-30 FF, say so, and if you have a merchant who grumbles or complains, take your business elsewhere. There are *Nicolas* wine stores all over France, and they have a very good, solid selection of wines at all price ranges. In the past, the *Nicolas* chain was almost as famous for its artistic ads as for its wine, which was considered the best buy in France. That was especially true at Christmas time, when it had a huge "Saint" Nicolas promotion, bringing out of its massive *caves* (cellars) special old wines and offering them for sale in limited quantities for very reasonable prices. Alas, those days have gone the way of the wooden *métro* cars, and the mighty chain has been sold and resold, with those famous *caves* going to one buyer and the stores to another. Still, the individual stores have good wines, decent prices and extremely knowledgeable owners/salespeople. And some of the ads are still rather nice. To get a feel for the old ones, stop in at the *Nicolas* store on the Place de la Madeleine, which is decorated with copies of the classic ads. (Lest you think we exaggerate, those ads were so good there was a museum exhibit of them a few years ago.)

A wonderful place to buy wine is the *Cave du Château*, 17, rue Raymond du Temple, Vincennes. Tel: 43.28.17.50. The owners are an enthusiastic couple who can go into great detail about any wine in their store, and they have lots of good, inexpensive ones. There is nothing fancy about the shop, and they deliver if you are ordering more than a couple of bottles. In fact, most wine stores do the same.

At the other end of the scale is *Vins Rares*, a gorgeous boutique of gorgeous wines. It is run by a charming, English-speaking Swede named Peter Thustrup. His stock of wines includes vintages from the last century as well as more recent classics; it is the place to go if you want a wine from a specific year or a vineyard for a special event. Peter's wines are reasonably priced for what they are, but no 1929 wine comes cheap! *Vins Rares* can be reached by calling 46.33.83.53.

A word about vintages. Vintage just means the year it was harvested. Some years are better than others, but any wine with a year attached to its label (and most French wines have that) is a vintage wine. It has nothing to do with quality. Most wine stores hand out vintage charts which rate the years and tell which vintages are ready to drink. The exception to the vintage rule is Champagne. Champagne is dated only in the years the makers consider to be extremely good. Oher than that, Champagne can be made from a blend of grapes from more than one year. Vintage Champagne is, of course, more expensive and should be better than others, but because of the blending, the big Champagne houses (Moët-pronounce the "t", Bollinger, Mumms, Roederer, Taittinger, Mercier, Lanson) never make bad Champagne. Of course, you may not like all of it, but each house has its own style, so it's just a matter of finding the style you like. And the finding is fun.

Champagne, like all the wine regions, has strict controls on the wine bearing its *appellation* (area name). The wine is made only from grapes grown in that region. They are labeled *Appellation d'origine contrôlée* (AOC) or *Appellation contrôlée* (AC). If a French wine does not have one phrase or the other, it probably does not have much to recommend it. It may be a blend of any old grapes, including very cheap ones imported from North Africa.

Then there is the system of *crus classés* (classed levels of quality). These are a fairly good guideline to quality, but they haven't been redone in years, so many are out of date. However, theoretically at the bottom of the heap is the *vin de pays* (country wines) and the *vin de table* (table wines). At the top are the *premier grand cru classé* (great first growths). There are lots of nice exceptions at the bottom levels as vineyards change hands and ideas, and there are some at the top which need to have their pedigrees examined, a cry you will hear from wine lovers, and even some growers, on a regular basis.

Most resistant to change are the big vineyards of Bordeaux. These wines in their square-shouldered bottles are some of the big economic powers in France, with large amounts of hectares per vineyard, and major distribution organizations behind them. While many of those unclassed or labeled "fifth growths" when the classifications were done in the 19th century would like to have the whole system reopened, those at the top are happy. To be fair, most of the *premier crus* have stayed that way, or become even better, but some have slipped disastrously and only nostalgia and hope keeps them in the running.

Wine is subject to fads, which can work in the favor of the discerning and financially cautious drinker. Currently out of fashion are the wines of the Loire Valley, which is very good news for people who like good wines that are inexpensive, because many of the Loire wines are of outstanding quality. For whites from bone-dry to very rich and sweet, look to the wines from Vouvray. Two very good makers are Gaston Huet and Prince Poniatowski. They both also make good sparkling wines at very low prices, generally about 50 FF a bottle. If you can't afford a good Champagne, these are marvelous substitutes, a little more full-bodied and richer, but still light and bubbly to make any event special. Huet and Poniatowski also make sweet wines that can last until your grandchildren are senior citizens. These cost more, but can be a wonderful souvenir of France, especially when accompanied by some *foie gras*. For a lovely cheap red try the Touraine, made by the Château du Petit-Thouars. This seems to be better made each vintage.

Myths surround wine, and some of them provide good guidelines, others can be shunted aside. For instance, red wine with red meat, white wine with white meat. That is a good starting point, but lots of chicken dishes are better with red wine, and even some fish is better that way. Just keep trying combinations to see which you like better. Another myth: wine doesn't travel. That is definitely true for badly made wines, but good wine doesn't mind a trip, they just like to have some time afterward to recover. Of course, no wine likes to sit on a dock in the sun for several hours, so if you want to ship wine, make sure you are dealing with good people who know what they are doing. Don't hesitate to take a bottle or so with you, though, as long as you carry it with you. But remember that the wine that tasted wonderful on a hot summer day on the Côte d'Azur may give little pleasure on a cold, blustery day in a *chambre de bonne* in Paris. Don't blame the wine for that! When serving wine, get clear glasses, the bigger the better. Don't fill them up; leave plenty of room for the aromas to swirl around. Avoid the flat-shaped Champagne *coupe* modeled after either the breast of Helen of Troy or of Madame de Pompadour, depending upon the myth you're listening to), and look for the long graceful flute that shows off the bubbles and avoids creating the big head of foam that attacks your nose in the flat glass. You can keep the foam down even more by pouring against the side of the glass instead of directly into the bottom of it. Don't worry too much; sparkling wine makes everything sparkle. If you want to pursue wine further, look into the courses taught in English at the Cordon Bleu School by James Lawther. Most of all, taste and enjoy. That is the only true way to learn about wine.

## A Selection of Cafés, Bars, Bistros, Brasseries

The following establishments have been listed here for their original style and glorious tradition. Be prepared to pay a premium, though, for the reputation. These places should become part of your working knowledge of Paris, but they probably won't become daily hang-outs. Otherwise, you end up watching tourists watch other tourists. But it is undeniably pleasant just to sit on the terrace and enjoy the moment. Bring out of town visitors or your parents for a look at the grand style they associate with Paris. Some of the best known, celebrated cafés, bistros and brasseries in the great Parisian tradition include the following. For a more complete list of cafés with illustrious literary lore, see Noel Riley Fitch's little book: *Literary Cafés of Paris.*

**La Coupole**
102 bd Montparnasse
75014 Paris
Tél: 43.20.14.20

**Le Select Montparnasse**
99 bd Montparnasse
75006 Paris
Tel: 45.48.38.24

**La Closerie des Lilas**
168 bd Montparnasse
75006 Paris
Tel: 43.26.70.50

**Café Les Deux Magots**
6 pl St Germain des Prés
75006 Paris
Tel: 45.48.55.25

**Café de Flore**
172 bd St Germain
75006 Paris
Tel: 45.48.55.26

**Le Balzar**
49 rue des Ecoles
75005 Paris
Tel: 43.54.13.67

**Les Noces de Jeannette**
14, rue Favart/9, rue d'Amboise
75002 Paris
Tel: 42.96.36.89

**IRISH PUBS IN PARIS**
The presence of the Irish in Paris, although not new, (Beckett, Joyce) has increased over the last five years, primarily due to the ease of movement between the two EU countries. As a result an outcrop of Irish pubs has joined the cityscape. Here are the key players:

**Edward & Sons Old Irish Pub**
10 bd de Clichy
75018 Paris
Tel: 44.92.90.91

**The Hideout**
1 rue de Pot de Fer
75005 Paris
Tel: 45.35.13.17

**Molly Malone's**
21 rue de Godot de Maure
75009 Paris
Tel: 47.42.07.77

**Oscar Wilde**
21 rue des Halles
75001 PARIS
Tel: 42.21.03.63

**Tigh Johnny**
55 rue Montmartre
75002 PARIS
Tel: 42.33.91.33

**Finnegans Wake**
9 rue des Boulangères
75005 Paris
Tel: 46.34.23.65

**The Sweeney**
18 rue Laplace
75005 Paris
Tel: 46.33.28.12

**James Ulysses**
5 rue du Jour
75001 Paris
Tel: 45.08.17.04

**Connolly's Corner**
12 rue de Mirbel
75005 Paris
Tel: 43.31.94.22

**Mulligan's**
16 rue de la Verrerie
75004 Paris
Tel: 40.29.03.89

**The Cruiskeen Lawn**
18 rue des Halles
75001 Paris
Tel 45.08.99.15

**Tony's**
11 rue du Cygne
75001 Paris
Tel: 42.33.29.82

**Flann O'Brien's**
6 rue Bailleul
75001 Paris
Tel: 42.60.13.58

**Kitty O'Shea's**
10 rue des Capucines
75002 Paris
Tel: 40.15.00.30

**The Quiet Man**
5 rue des Haudriettes
75003 Paris
Tel: 48.04.02.77

**IRISH RESTAURANTS**
**Bistrot Irlandais**
15 rue de la Santé
75013 Paris
Tel: 47.07.07.45

**Carr's Restaurant**
1 rue du Mont-Thabor
75001 Paris
Tel: 42.60.60.26

ENGLISH PUBS
**The Frog & Rosbif**
116, rue St. Denis
75002 Paris
Tel: 42.36.34.73
One of the newer and more fun anglo watering holes in Paris. Friendly atmosphere and friskly crowds. Flavourful English bitters, actually brewed on the premises. You can even tour the brewery. Ask for Paul.

# The Only English Pub in Paris!

Try Our Three Real Ales, Brewed On The Premises
Hot and Cold Home-Cooked Lunches Available Every Day
Live Music, Darts Matches, Quizzes, Pub Games
Visit Our Brewery And Learn The Ancient Craft Of Beer-Making
The Most Cordial Entente In Paris!!

Bring this page to "The Frog & Rosbif" and we'll be happy to offer you
your first pint of "Inseine", "Parislytic" or "An Ale of Two Cities"
ABSOLUTELY FREE!!!

**"The Frog & Rosbif"**
**116, rue Saint-Denis, 75002 Paris**
**Métros : Etienne-Marcel, Les Halles, Réaumur-Sébastopol**
**Open every day, 11am to 2am**

# THE PARIS REAL ALE BREWERY

## Wine Bars
## & Late Night Places

Here is a list of great little finds that can make daily life in Paris truly delightful, although the act of finding your own place will be a matter of personal taste.

### Au Petit Fer à Cheval
30 rue Vieille du Temple
75004 Paris
A tiny bar with a horse shoe *(fer à cheval)* shaped bar-there are very few of these remaining.

### La Tartine
24 rue de Rivoli
75004 Paris
One of the oldest, most reasonably priced, and best wine bars in Paris. Also serves great *Pain Poilâne* sandwiches. The decoration is Deco 20s and seventy years of cigarette smoke has mellowed the interior.

### La Palette
43 rue de Seine
(corner of rue Jacques Callot)
75006 Paris
The room behind the bar has some delightful caricatures of Parisians in the Twenties. *The* meeting place for artists and gallery people.

### Café de l'Industrie
16 rue Saint Sabin
75011 Paris
Tel: 47.00.13.53
Eccentric decor, good food.

### Le Cochon à l'Oreille
15 rue Montmartre
75001 Paris
The walls of this café are covered with painted tiles showing the old "Les Halles" market halls. Early in the morning you can share breakfast (or a last drink if you've been out all night) with the butchers from rue Montmartre.

### Le Clown Bar
114 rue Amelot
75011 Paris
Next to the Cirque d'Hiver, this tiny café has its painted ceiling depicting clowns and circus entertainers.

### Brasserie Lipp
151 bd St Germain
75006 Paris
Reservations must be made in person. Favorite Friday night spot of literary media star Bernard Pivot and a host of well known entertainers and politicians. A few tables inside to the left where you can order a drink without eating (the enclosed terrace is stuffy and boring). *Fin de siècle* decoration. The length of the waiters' aprons denotes superiority.

### Brasserie de l'Ile St. Louis
55 Quai Bourbon
75004 Paris
Stand at the bar and try one of the white Alsation wines whilst listening to the street musicians on the Pont St. Louis. There is a beautiful old coffee machine at the bar.

**Le Petit Gavroche**
Rue Sainte-Croix-de-la-Bretonnerie
75004 Paris
On the corner of the bar of this café/restaurant is one of of the few remaining examples of the water-holders used in the ritual of absinthe drinking (its sale was prohibited in 1915). Water was dripped onto a sugar cube and into the absinthe.

**Le Train Bleu**
Gare de Lyon
20 bd Diderot
75012 Paris
Sweep up the curved staircase from the inside of the station and through the revolving door into one of the most astonishing *fin-de-siècle* interiors in Paris. To the left is the bar with its soft leather sofas and an atmosphere of luxury and calm. Whilst most of the travelers below sit in orange plastic chairs drinking over-priced *demis*, you can be sipping a Pimms, wearing a linen suit and sporting a panama hat, dreaming of taking the Blue Train to the Mediterranean. The restaurant, a national historic site, has maintained its elegance amidst sprawling frescos, but the prices are high and the cuisine has slipped.

**Le Gutenberg**
29 rue Coquillière
75001 Paris
One of the prettiest cafés in Paris dating from 1913-original lights and mirrors. Try a *café-calva* (coffee and calvados) here on a winter morning.

**Twickingham**
70 rue des Saints-Pères
75007 Paris
The young French intellectual *(intello)* watering hole.

**Le Balto**
Rue Mazarine
75006 Paris
A local *bar-tabac* near the Académie des Beaux-Arts. Once a week the "Fanfare des Beaux-Arts" (brass band of the Beaux-Arts) practices here.

**Au Général Lafayette**
52 rue de La Fayette
75009 Paris
Popular French beer bar trying to look like an English pub. Great selection of beers—greater selection of beer mats, mugs, memorabilia and old Guinness posters.

## Good & Sleazy

Here is a short list of some of Paris' down and out drinking holes. They tend to come and go, so check for yourself.

**Académie du Billard**
84 rue de Clichy
75009 Paris
An enormous 19th century billiard hall with a small bar open late where you can watch the intensity of Frenchmen at play.

**Polly Magoo**
rue St. Jacques
75005 Paris
Revoltingly sleazy but can you leave Paris without saying you've been there?

**Chez George**
rue des Canettes
75006 Paris
Has to be experienced at least once. The only bar in the Latin Quarter with a licence to sell wine to take away (*vente à emporter*).

**Le Baragouin**
17 rue Tiquetonne
75002 Paris
An enormous late night bar packed with French "rockers." If you can push your way to the back you'll find some serious dart playing going on.

**Le Taxi Jaune**
13 rue Chapon
75003 Paris
Tel: 42.78.92.24
Serves light meals such as salads and Mexican dishes.

**Le Mazet**
61 rue St André des Arts
75006 Paris
Tel: 46.34.68.81
This rough, rowdy café is the favorite haunt of buskers and late night musicians.

**Le Café de la Plage**
59 rue de Charonne
75011 Paris. Tel: 47.00.91.60

## Special Markets

**Flea Markets** (*Marchés aux puces*)
• *Marché de Montreuil*: av de la Porte de Montreuil, 12e. *Métro*: Porte de Montreuil. Saturday, Sunday and Monday. This is probably the least touristy of the flea markets. Located on the eastern edge of Paris at the newly revamped Porte de Montreuil, this market is noted for its huge, cluttered tables of used clothes. Here, if you're not overly bothered by the idea of rummaging through old clothes and are filled with patience, you may find high quality and other wrinkled sweaters, skirts, dress shirts, ties, etc. of fine materials for tiny prices. Ten francs for a shirt, for instance. Otherwise, there are loads of old junk, some fine antiques, and piles of useless *bric-à-brac*. You may not be able to bargain quite as much as you imagined, but you usually can get things for 20-30% less than the asking price. It's not incorrect to try in any case. There is talk of closing down the *Marché de Montreuil* in the near future.
• *Marché de la Place d'Aligre*: Place d'Aligre, 12e. *Métro*: Ledru-Rollin. Daily from 9h to noon. One of Paris' best and least expensive open air markets.
• *Marché de la Porte de Clignancourt* (St. Ouen): rue des Entrepots, 75018 Paris. *Métro*: Porte de Clignancourt. This is the largest and most overwhelming of all Paris flea markets. Careful of pickpockets.

• *Marché de la Porte des Lilas:* 75019 Paris. *Métro:* Porte des Lilas. Sunday and holidays.
• *Marché de la Porte de Vanves:* av Georges-Lafenestre, 75004 Paris. *Métro:* Porte de Vanves. Saturday and Sunday. Particularly strong in antiques, old jewelry, and furniture.
• *Marché aux Oiseaux:* Same location as the *Marché aux Fleurs.* Sunday mornings. Bird amateurs from all over bring their birds to sell, trade and exhibit.
• *Marché aux Timbres:* *Métro:* Rond Point Clemenceau, 75008 Paris. Sunday mornings. Stamp collectors unite to trade and sell.
• *Marché aux Fleurs:* Ile de la Cité, 75001 Paris. *Métro:* Cité. Daily assortment of fresh flowers and exotic plants.

## Marjolaine

Every Fall (late October) Nature et Progrès sponsors the Marjolaine, the first European ecological fair, which is held in the Parc Floral de Paris in the Bois de Vincennes. The Marjolaine promotes an agriculture, alimentation, and lifestyle that respects the environment and health. These are the most "green" conscious folks you'll ever meet in the Paris area. Greenpeace included, which never regained the popularity it held in the mid 80s following the sinking of the Greenpeace Rainbow Warrior in New Zealand by French intelligence agents. As for the Marjolaine, it's a lot of "alternative" fun, and a healthy escape from the hedonism of café smoke, heavy meals, and the "*moi, je*", "*je m'en fous*" mentality of Parisian dailiness.

## Fashions and Shopping

In that "shopping" has been poled as the second or third most popular activity of foreign visitors, a word on the sport is needed. There are plenty of books and mags offering their favorite tips on the most "in" of the latest boutiques. Consult them if that's your passion. Hermés and Lancôme and a few other of the most exclusive couturiers open their doors each spring for a few hours for bargain basement sales. Here, the most dignified and cultivated ladies from Paris, New York, and especially Tokyo are transformed into ape women, scraping, pushing, and biting their way to the tables of marked-down silk scarves. *Cities of Fashion: An Insider's Guide to Shopping in Ten Cities* is one book that identifies the latest trends in the best seven shopping areas of Paris.

**Paris' Seven Major Shopping Districts:**
Victoires/Etienne Marcel
Les Halles
Le Marais
Saint Germain
Haussmann/St Honoré/Madeleine
Champs-Elysées
La Bastille

The American Maribeth Ricour de Bourgies, author of *The Chic Shopper's Guide to Paris,* offers personalized and expensive shopping tours called *Chic promenade* and apparently can lead you to great deals on crystal, smocked party dresses, porcelain-faced marionettes, kid gloves, and more. Tel: 43.80.35.35. Otherwise, just walk around. "Even French punks seem more stylishly packaged than their British counterparts," states *Cities of Fashion* author. "Parisians definitely subscribe to the maxim that fashion transcends fads, trends transcend fashion, and style transcends trends," she writes. You'll have time to sort this out for yourselves.

### Department & Chain Stores

*FNAC*—leading up-beat cooperative for books, records, photo, video, audio and electronics equipment with *après-vente* and photo service all over the city. An institution in France. Vast variety and prices marked 5% lower than suggested retail prices. Also a major outlet for concert tickets. Major locations at Montparnasse, Les Halles, Etoile, Wagram, the Bastille (music), and bd St. Germain (computers and electronics). Check Minitel 3615 FNAC.

*Darty*—large appliance chain, wide variety of brands at reasonably good prices. Noted for service, home delivery, guarantee, and repair services.

*La Samaritaine*—largest and oldest department store in Paris. The roof-top on Building 2 has a great view of the city.

*Galeries Lafayette*—major department store with principal location at Auber/Opéra. All major fashion houses are represented here.

*Printemps*—major department store with principal location at Auber/Opéra. All major fashion houses are represented here. A view of the Opéra and roofs of Paris can be enjoyed from the rooftop terrace. Also known for its reverse glass-domed restaurant.

*Au Bon Marché*—large department store chain that distinguishes itself as being the only Left Bank store of its kind. A bit less visible than Galeries Lafayette and Printemps.

*Bazar de l'Hôtel de Ville (BHV)*—a stand-by for all your needs. The chaotic basement is particularly well-equipped for hardware and houseware. Good for adapters and transformers for foreign appliances.

*Tati*—working-class department store for inexpensive clothes. Montparnasse and Barbès locations.

## Duty-free/*Détaxe*/TVA (value added tax)

Sales tax on goods and services, better known as (TVA) in France is steep—18.6% for most consumer goods and services and 33% for luxury items including certain food specialties.(The exorbitant price of gasoline is a result of hidden taxes totaling 74%!) Books, on the other hand, are taxed at only 5.5%. Bills marked TTC means *toute taxe comprise* or all taxes included. HT signifies *hors taxe* or tax not included. The TVA authorities are serious and severe. If you are working in France and sell any goods or services you must invoice the TVA and pay it to the TVA administration. Although illegal, sometimes goods or services will be offered to you for *espèces* (cash) which means that the sale will not be declared, an invoice not given, and TVA not collected.

For purchases that are being taken out of the country, a part of the TVA can be recovered *(récupéré)*. Anyone over 15 years old who is a foreign resident when spending less than six months in France can benefit from duty-free shopping. If you have a *carte de séjour* you don't comply with the law, but you can always simply show only your passport when *detaxing* your purchases. Your purchases, including tax, and from any single store, must amount to at least 2000 FF for foreign nationals or 2800 FF for EU citizens. The purchases can be cumulative. Be careful in that stores apply the law differently. The Musée de Paris gift shop at Les Halles insists that cumulative purchases must be made on the same day. Items which cannot be detaxed are the following: tobacco, medicines, firearms, unset gems, works of art, collectors items and antiques, private means of transport (cars, boats, planes and their equipment), and large commercial purchases. To benefit from the duty-free allowance, ask the vendor at the point of purchase to give you a three-slip form called a *bordereau* (export sales invoice) and an addressed, stamped envelope. Non-EU nationals must present the detaxed purchases, the three slips (two pink, one green) and the stamped envelope provided by the shop to the French Customs agents at the airport, border crossings or train crossings. At the airport there is a window marked *DETAXE* where you may be asked to show your purchases. Make sure not to pack your duty free items in your checked baggage before presenting them to customs in that you risk being denied the tax refund. If you leave the country by train, have your three slips validated by the customs agent on board. French customs will keep the pink copies and send them in the envelope directly to the point of purchase, who will then reimburse you the amount indicated on space B3 of the form via check or credit card credit (it is best to do this with your credit card to avoid astronomical fees for changing your refund into local currency); keep the green copy for your files. Sometimes you will be reimbursed at the time of purchase, however, you still must undergo the above process. If you are an EU resident, you will get a yellow invoice consisting of three copies, two yellow and one green. Upon reaching customs in your country, have all three slips validated by the Customs agent. Send the two yellow slips to the *Bureau des Douanes de Paris*-La-Chapelle, 61, rue de la Chapelle, 75018 Paris. Keep the green slip for your files.

## Le Café-Tabac (tobacco shop)

*Le tabac* plays a curious but dynamic role in daily French life. *Le tabac*, clearly marked with a red elongated diamond shaped sign hanging in the street, has a monopoly from the State to sell cigarettes, cigars and tobacco. You cannot buy cigarettes anywhere else in France. In exchange for this privilege, the *tabac*, which is usually also a café, performs certain services at face value, such as selling postage stamps. If you need some stamps for letters or cards, you can easily buy them from the cashier in a *tabac*. Don't expect total cooperation, however, if you want postal rates for the Ivory Coast. That's not their job. You will find a nearby mail box outside every *tabac* (always yellow and usually divided into two parts—Paris and its suburban codes 75, 77, 78, 91, 92, 93, 94 and the rest of the world). A *carnet* of stamps is a unit of ten basic letter stamps (2,80 FF) for France (often sold in little booklets or on convenient, self sticking—*auto-collant*—pages).

Single envelopes and writing paper can also be purchased in a *tabac*. This is handy when you have to mail something off in a hurry. You have envelope, stamp, and mailbox at hand—but you have to know the postal rates yourself.

*Le tabac* also handles, in many cases, off-track betting called PMU.

*Le tabac* sells Lottery tickets (LOTO), which has grown and developed rampantly in the last few years, inspired by the American instant "scratch and lose" series of game cards. Some of the games are Poker, Black Jack, Millionnaire, Banco, and all cost 10 FF a card.

*Le tabac* sells *timbres fiscaux* as well. This is important in that if you happen to get a parking ticket, you pay for it by purchasing a *timbre fiscal* (State Stamp Tax) and paste one portion to the return portion of the ticket and keep the other half as your proof of payment. Similarly, you often need a *timbre fiscal* when you renew your *carte de séjour* and process other official documents. *Le tabac* sells this, although they are frequently out of precisely the denomination you need and you have to walk until you find a better-stocked *tabac*.

If you own a car, you'll soon find out that your annual car registration tax is paid in December at any *tabac* in the *département* in which you live upon presentation of your *carte grise* and ID. You'll receive a *vignette* sticker for your windshield. Failure to do this in the prescribed time results in a 10% increase and a stiff fine.

# RESOURCES

Ambulance: 43.78.26.26

Bus Info. (in English): 40.46.42.12

Central Post Office (24 hours): 40.28.20.00

Charles de Gaulle airport: 48.62.22.80

Chronopost: Minitel: 3614 EMS

Customs Information Center: 42.60.35.90

Drug Crisis Center: 45.05.88.88 (free)

*Enfance et Partage* (Hotline for Kids in Trouble): 05.05.12.34 (free)

Fire: 18

Fax Office: Service Internationale: 40.28.20.00

Highway Information Center: 48.94.33.33

Directory Information
Ile de France (Paris region): 12
provinces: 16.11.12
international: 19.33

Le Bourget Airport: 48.62.12.12

Locksmith (24 hours): 47.07.99.99

Lost American Express Card: 47.77.77.77

Lost and Found/*Objets Trouvés:*
36 rue des Morrillons, 75015, Paris
45.31.14.80

Lost Animals: 47.98.57.40

Lost Diner's Club Card: 47.62.75.00

Lost Eurocard/Mastercard: 45.67.84.84

Lost Property: 45.31.14.80

Lost Visa Card: 42.77.11.90

Marine Radio Information: 05.19.20.21

Minitel Directory: 11

National Railroad Information: 47.23.54.02

Orly Airport: 49.75.52.52

Paris Culture Listing: 49.52.53.54

Parigramme (To order this book): 44.54.24.24

Police: 17

R.A.T.P. (public transport) Info: 43.46.14.14

Rape Crisis Hotline: 05.05.95.95 (free)

Restaurant Information: 43.59.12.12

Search For Hospitalized Persons: 40.27.30.81

SOS HELP English Crisis Hotline: 47.23.80.80

SOS Lawyer: 43.29.33.00

SOS Nurses: 48.87.77.77

SOS Oeil (eye care): 40.92.93.94

SOS Pediatre: 42.93.19.99

SOS Tailor: 40.15.03.14

Stock Market News: 42.60.00.18

Taxis Bleus: 49.36.10.10

Taxis Radio Etoile: 47.39.47.39

Telephone Complaints, Repairs: 13

Telex Office: 44.76.30.80

Tenant's Information: 48.06.82.75

Theater Information: 49.52.53.54

Time: 36.99

Tourist Office: 49.52.53.54

Train Info: 45.82.50.50

Wake-up Calls (electronically programmed): * 55 * plus the time in 4 digits (i.e., 7.30 am=0730) then your number. Electronically programmed.

Weather Info: 36.65.00.00 (Paris)
tel: 36.69.0101 (provinces)
45.56.71.71 (foreign)

Here is a random list of French colloquial expressions and some *argot* (slang), selected on the the basis of what you might hear in daily conversation or in the street. Although these and others are useful to know, be absolutely sure you understand the context and appropriate usage before throwing them around.

*à table* ...................................................................the meal is served (be seated)
*aie!* ......................................................................................................ouch!
*argot* .....................................................................................................slang
*berk* ....................................................................................................yucky
*bêtise* ...............................................................stupidity, foolishness, nonsense
*bof!* ......................................................(a noise used to say "I don't know")
*bonne chance,* ...............................................................................good luck
*bonne continuation* ...........................................................keep up the good work
*bonne courage* ......................................................................................chin up!
*branché* ..............................................................................................hip/in
*c'est absurde* .............................................................................that's absurd
*c'est chouette* ......................................................it's really great, fab
*c'est comme ça* .......................................................that's just the way it is
*c'est dingue* ........................................................................that's crazy
*c'est drôle* ...............................................................that's funny, strange
*c'est foutu* ............it's over, it doesn't work, it's broken (for events/people/objects)
*c'est génial* ..............................................................that's great, brilliant
*c'est impec* ......................................................that's impeccable, that's perfect
*c'est intéressant (in business)* ...............that's a good deal, opportunity, investment
*c'est marrant* ...................................................................that's funny
*c'est pas la peine* .......................................................it's not worth it
*c'est pas mal* .......................it's not bad, rather good (used as a compliment)
*c'est pourri* ...................................................................that's rotten
*c'est ridicule* ......................................................it's/that's ridiculous
*c'est super* ........................................................................that's super
*ça boum* .................................................it's hopping (as in a party)
*ça cocotte* ...............................................it smells strongly (perfume)
*ça gaze, ça baigne* ...............................................everything's going great
*ça m'énerve* ....................................................that unnerves me, annoys me
*ça m'est égal* .......................................I don't mind one way or the other
*ça marche* ...............................................................it works, it's okay
*ça me gêne* ........................................................that bothers me
*ça me gonfle* .......................that bothers me (literally, that makes my head swell)
*ça ne me dit rien* ...............................................................I'm not in the mood/
that doesn't ring any bells
*ça peut aller* ...............I'm okay (a positive but unenthusiastic response to *ça va?*)

*ça chlingue* ...................................................................................that stinks
*ça suffit*.......................................................................................enough!
*chacun son tour* ...........................................................................each his turn
*con, connard*................................................................................idiot, clot
*connasse* .......................................................................tart, stupid bitch
*connerie*.........................................................................rank stupidity
*coucou*.........................................................................................hi
*coup de foudre* .....................................................to have a crush on
*couper la poire en deux* .....cut the pear in half (split something in half, compromise)
*d'acc (d'accord)*..........................................................all right, okay
*dégage* ...............................................................get the hell out of here!
*dégoûtant*..................................................disgusting *(polite form)*
*dégueulasse* .............................................disgusting *(slang version)*
*elle me fait craquer*.............................she drives me crazy *(as in love)*
*engagé* .........................................................................committed
*ferme ta gueule* ................................................shut your face/trap
*flipper*..............................................................to flip out, to freak out
*fous le camp, barre-toi, casse-toi !*..................piss off, beat it, get lost *(very vulgar)*!
*fous moi la paix*..................................leave me alone, leave me in peace
*franchement*...............................................................................frankly
*grosses bises* .....................................................................hug and kisses
*il a perdu les pédales*.........................................he's lost control, nuts
*il a un grain*..................................................he has a screw loose
*il est culotté* .............................................................he's nervy, cheeky
*il est gonflé, il exagère* ...................................he's got a hell of a nerve
*il faut profiter*...........................................to take advantage of something
*j'ai d'autres chats à fouetter*.............................I have better things to do
*j'en ai assez* ...........................................................I've had enough!
*j'en ai marre* ...........................I'm fed up with *(this, it, him/her, everything)*
*j'en peux plus*.......................................................I can't go on like this
*je craque*...............................I'm giving in to temptation, I can't resist any longer
*je m'en fiche, je m'en fous*.................................................I don't care a hoot
*je n'ai pas envie*..............................I don't want to, I don't feel like it
*je suis crevé, KO* ...............................................I'm dead tired, beat
*je suis raide* ..........................................................I'm stoned, high
*je suis saoûl(e), je suis bourré(e)*.............................................I'm drunk
*je t'embrasse*...........*I kiss/hug you (for ending friendly phone conversations or letters)*
*la bagnole, la caisse* ...............................................................the car
*la nana, la gonzesse , la meuf*.................................the chick, girl, "babe"
*le boulot* ....................................................................job, work

*le fric, le pognon,* .................................................................bread, money
*le gars, le mec, le type* ...........................................................................guy
*les fringues, les sapes, nippes*.............................................duds, clothing
*ma frangine, mon frangin* ....................my sis, sister; my bro, brother
*merde* ..........................................................................................shit
*mince* (replacement for *merde*)...............................................darn
*mon cul*.......................................................................................my ass
*mon pote* .............................................................my buddy, pal
*ne quittez pas* ........................................hang on, don't hang up
*ne t'inquiète pas* ..........................................................don't worry
*on laisse tomber* ..........................................................let's forget it
*on s'apelle/on se téléphone* ...................we'll call each other (call me/I'll call you)
*p cul (PQ)*.................................................................toilet paper *(TP)*
*plouc* .................................................................................country hick
*putain*.................................................................whore *(holy shit)*
*punaise* (replacement for *putain*) ...............................thumb tack *(oh, damn)*
*quel bordel*.........................................................................what a mess!
*salaud, salope* ...........................dirty bastard; son of a bitch; slut, bitch
*saloperie*.............................................................................filthiness
*si tu veux*..................................................................it's okay with me
*sois pas vache*............................................................don't be nasty
*ta gueule*.............................shut up *(literally, your snout/face-vulgar)*
*tais-toi, taisez-vous*.......................................................shut up
*tant mieux*.........................................................so much the better
*tant pis* .....................................too bad, that's the way it is
*truc/machin*...........................thingamajig, whatchamacallit
*tu parles !*...............................no kidding *(sarcastic)*
*un clope* .........................................................a butt, cigarette
*un flic, les flics , les poulets*.................a cop, the cops, the fuzz, the pigs
*une toile* ....................................................................a film
*va te faire cuire un oeuf*.................................go jump in a lake!
*vachement* .........................................tremendously, very, extremely

## Selected Bibliography of Books, Guides, & Sources on Paris and France

• Ardagh, John, *France Today*, Penguin Books, London.
An indepth study of French society, seen through the eyes of a journalist and sociologist. Very enlightening, but not practical as a guide.

• Brame, Geneviève, *Chez vous en France*, Paris, Dunod, 1993.
The most complete and well researched single title on France for the foreign resident. Conceived for French-speakers.

• Dansel, Michel, *Les Cimetières de Paris*, Denoël.
Specialized guide to Paris' cemeteries. In French.

• Delorme, Jean-Claude, *Les Villas d'Artistes à Paris*, Les Editions de Paris, 1987.
Specialized guide in French on the city's villas and artists' ateliers.

• Dinh, Catherine, *Restaurants Etrangers à Paris*, MA Editions.
Guide to 1000 foreign restaurants in Paris.

• Dournon, Jean-Yves, *La correspondance pratique*, Livre de Poche, Paris.
Pocket guide to writing forms.

• Gault Millau, *Guide Paris*.
4500 restaurants.

• Hillairet, Jacques, *Dictionnaire historique des rues de Paris*, Paris: Minuit, 1972.

• Juvin, Herve, *Paris*, London: Times Books.

• Kjellberg, Pierre, *Nouveau guide du Marais*, Paris: La Bibliothèque des Arts, 1986.

• Lazareff, *Paris Rendez-Vous*, Guide Hachette.
400 dependable addresses for going out.

• Lebey, Claude, *Bistrots Parisiens*, Paris: Editions Robert Laffont.

• Lemoine, Bertrand, *Les Halles de Paris, Histoire d'un lieu*, Paris: L'Equette, 1980.

• Leprette, Veronique, *Paris Pressé*, Hermé.
A guide to Paris for people in a hurry.

• Léri, Jean-Marc, *Montmartre*, Paris, Veyrier, 1983.

• Martin, Hervé, *Guide de l'Architecture Moderne à Paris*, Syros.
Architecture guide to modern Paris.

• Martin, Michèle, *Week-ends plaisir aux environs de Paris*, Editions de Vecchi.

• McClure, Bert, *Architectural Walks in Paris,* La Découverte/Le Monde.

• Morton, Brian, *Americans in Paris,* Ann Arbor: Olivia and Hill, 1984.

• Raveneau, Alain & Courtat, Emilie, *Guide de la Campagne à Paris et en Ile-de-France,* Parigramme, Paris, 1994.
The best source for addresses and information on how to find natural settings and ecologically sound excursions in the Paris area.

• Simon, François, *Paris Vin,* Paris: Editions de Main.
Wine guide in French.

• Stéphane, Bernard, *Dictionnaire des Noms de Rues,* Editions Mengès, 1986.
5000 streets described historically. Fascinating and well-written.

• Turner, Miles, *Paupers' Paris,* Pan Books, Ltd., London.

• Wurman, Richard Saul, *Paris Access,* New York: Access Press.

• *Bloom Where You're Planted,* The Women of the Church, The American Church in Paris.
Welcome booklet for new residents, written and printed to correspond with this group's orientation program each October.

• *Dictionnaire de Paris,* Paris, Larousse, 1964.

• *L'Etat de la France 94-95,* La Découverte, Crédoc, 1994.

• *Fodor's 94 France,* Fodor's, New York, 1994.

• *Guide Bleu, Paris,* Hachette, Paris. Standby guide to Paris sites and addresses. In French.

• *Guide Consommateur Vert* Consumer guide to France.

• *Guide de Paris Mystérieux,* Tchou, Paris.

• *Guide des Etudes Supérieures 1990,* L'Etudiant, Paris.

• *Guide des Hôtels de Charme de Paris,* Paris: Rivage, 1993.

• *Guide du Routard Paris,* Paris, Hachette.

• *Histoire Secrète du Paris Souterrain,* Hachette.
Guide to Paris sewers, caves, etc.

• *Insight Cityguide's Paris,* Singapore: APA Publications.
Luxuriously illustrated and well-written and researched general guide to Paris in English, now published in the US by Houghton-Mifflin.

• *Média Sid:* L'Aide-Mémoire de la Presse, Service d'Information et de Diffusion du Premier Ministre, Paris, 1994.

The best single source of press addresses in France.

• *Paris Anglophone*, David Applefield, Editor, (formerly Frank Books), Montreuil, 1993.
The most complete single listing of English-language commercial, cultural, and professional activities in Paris, with addresses and phone numbers.
• *Paris-Combines*, MA Editions, Paris 3500 inexpensive restaurant addresses.

• *Paris en Bouteille*, Flammarion.

• *Paris Eyewitness Travel Guide*, New York: Doring Kindersley, 1993. By far, the most beautifully designed, well researched, practical, and aesthetically-pleasing single guide on Paris for visitors and intelligent tourists.

Distributed in the US by Houghton Mifflin, Hachette in France.

• *Paris mondial*, Paris: Editions du Seuil and Actuel, Paris: 1992.
The best guide available on the ethnic communities of Paris, restaurants, organizations, events, etc.

• *Paris pas Cher*, Paris: Flammarion, 1994.
The bible of Paris bargains and good value guide.

• *Paris Trafic*, éditions du May, Paris.

• *The Economist Business Traveller's Guide to France*, New York: Prentice Hall Press.

• *Time Out Guide to Paris.* London: Time Out Publications, 1993.